# Professional Java™ Native Interfaces with SWT/JFace

Jackwind Li Guojie

D0872668

WILEY

Wiley Publishing, Inc.

# Professional Java™ Native Interfaces with SWT/JFace

# About the Author

**Jack Li Guojie** is an independent Java developer who has been building various types of Java applications since 1998. His areas of interest and experience include artificial intelligence, user interfacing, Web applications, and enterprise system architecture. He has contributed articles to many leading software journals.

*I thank John Wiley & Sons, the publisher, for its trust in me and investment in this book. In particular, many thanks to Gaynor Redvers-Mutton, my acquisitions editor, who encouraged me to write this book. The book could never have been completed without my development editors, Emilie Herman and Kenyon Brown, who corrected my English and reshaped the manuscript into a readable form. I also thank Roy Miller, the technical reviewer, for his invaluable comments.*

# Credits

**Acquisitions Editor**
Gaynor Redvers-Mutton

**Development Editor**
Emilie Herman

**Technical Editor**
Roy Miller

**Copy Editor**
Nancy Rapoport

**Editorial Manager**
Kathryn A. Malm

**Vice President & Executive Group Publisher**
Richard Swadley

**Vice President and Publisher**
Joseph B. Wikert

**Project Coordinator**
Bill Ramsey

**Graphics and Production Specialists**
Beth Brooks
Kelly Emkow
Carrie Foster
Lauren Goddard
Jennifer Heleine

**Quality Control Technicians**
Susan Moritz
Brian H. Walls

**Proofreader**
Susan Sims

**Indexer**
Joan Griffitts

# Contents

# Contents

# Contents

# Contents

# Contents

# Contents

# Contents

# Contents

# Introduction

Eclipse is an open source universal tool platform, dedicated to providing a robust, full-featured industry platform for the development of highly integrated tools. With millions of downloads, Eclipse becomes more and more popular. One of the most important common facilities provided by the Eclipse framework is the portable native widget user interface called the Standard Widget Toolkit (SWT), which provides a set of OS-independent APIs for widgets and graphics. SWT is analogous to AWT and Swing except SWT uses a rich set of native widgets. Built on SWT, JFace is a user interface toolkit handling many common UI programming tasks. JFace is designed to work with SWT without hiding it. Some of the advantages SWT/JFace offers over Swing include support for native features, fast execution speed, and flexible programming models.

This book teaches you how to build practical user interfaces with SWT/JFace. After introducing each widget, I present a great deal of Java source code to show you how to use the widget effectively. You can use the sample code as the basis to develop real-world applications quickly. Additionally, many techniques and tips are presented to help you save time. Finally, the last chapter shows you how to build an FTP client by combining everything covered in the book.

The comprehensive coverage of the SWT/JFace framework also makes this book an ideal reference.

## Who Should Read This Book

This book is targeted primarily at Java user interface developers, Eclipse enthusiasts, and technical managers. The first few chapters help nontechnical people gain insight into the SWT/JFace framework. The later chapters contain a lot of technical details and practical examples that Java developers should find of great use.

In order to understand the code samples in this book, you need to have a good knowledge of the Java programming language. Background on user interface development is an advantage but not a necessity.

Those who have some experience with SWT/JFace programming can skip the first three chapters and jump right to Chapter 4. Others should read from start to finish.

## What This Book Covers

This book covers the latest SWT/JFace version 3.0, which was released in June 2004.

# How This Book Is Organized

This book is organized into 24 chapters. The first few chapters introduce the SWT/JFace framework and cover some SWT/JFace fundamentals such as event handling, layout, and the like. The next few chapters discuss each SWT widget individually and give practical advice on the usage of each one. After the introduction of all the SWT widgets, topics such as JFace dialogs and wizards are covered. Finally, the book covers special topics such as OLE support and Draw2D and concludes with the development of an FTP client application.

Note that while introducing some SWT widgets, I bring in some related JFace model-view-controller (MVC)–based components. For example, when discussing the SWT table widget, I cover the JFace table viewer. In this way, you learn two different approaches to achieve the same result—you can either use the traditional approach by manipulating the table widget directly, or you can take the MVC approach with the table viewer. You can compare the two approaches in order to choose the best one for you.

## Part I: Fundamentals

Part I introduces you to the fundamentals of SWT/JFace.

Chapter 1 offers you a tour of Java GUI frameworks. Toolkits such as AWT, Swing, and SWT/JFace are discussed and compared. The chapter covers the features of SWT/JFace and compares them with those from other toolkits.

Chapter 2 explains some of the mechanisms used by SWT/JFace. First, the chapter introduces the implementation of SWT. The rest of the chapter is about resource management in SWT; here you can find useful resource management techniques and practical tips. The last part explains how the model-view-controller (MVC) design fits in JFace.

Chapter 3 covers setting up your IDEs to develop applications with SWT/JFace, writing your first SWT programs, using JFace to simplify UI programming, and deploying your applications to multiple platforms using Java Web Start.

Chapter 4 introduces SWT event handling and the threading mechanism. The `Display` class, which plays the most important role in SWT event handling, is introduced, too.

Chapter 5 first provides a tour of the hierarchy of the SWT widgets. Several typical widget types are discussed. After that, you learn about three kinds of basic SWT widgets—Shells, Buttons, and Labels. Additionally, this chapter covers focus traversal.

Chapter 6 shows you how to use layouts to manage the position and size of children in composites. The chapter introduces you to four standard layouts and one custom layout provided in SWT: `FillLayout`, `RowLayout`, `GridLayout`, `FormLayout`, and `StackLayout`. At the end of this chapter, you learn how to create your own layouts.

## Part II: Design Basics

Part II introduces you to the basics of designing layouts in SWT/JFace.

Chapter 7 introduces two kinds of SWT controls: `Combos` and `Lists`. Both combos and lists allow the user to choose items from a list of items. Additionally, `ListViewer`, an MVC viewer based on the `List` control, is introduced.

Chapter 8 introduces two kinds of SWT text controls: `Text` and `StyledText`.

Chapter 9 teaches you how to use menus, toolbars, and cool bars in SWT. Additionally, you learn how to use the JFace action framework to simplify the task of creating menus and toolbars.

Chapter 10 shows you how to use the SWT `Table` control to display, navigate, and edit data. Additionally, the JFace `TableViewer` is introduced to help you simplify these tasks by taking advantage of MVC programming.

Chapter 11 shows you how to use the SWT `Tree` control to display and edit a hierarchy of items. Event handling of trees is also introduced. Additionally, you see how to use `TreeViewers` and the MVC approach to program with trees.

Chapter 12 covers UI objects that can be used to acquire particular types of data input from the user. In this chapter, you learn how to use each of the SWT dialogs: `ColorDialog`, `DirectoryDialog`, `FileDialog`, `FontDialog`, and `MessageBox`. Additionally, this chapter guides you to create your own dialogs.

# Part III: Dynamic Controls

Part III introduces you to adding dynamic controls in SWT/JFace.

Chapter 13 teaches you how to use controls that can be used to present numerical values. The controls include `Scale`, `Slider`, and `ProgressBar`.

Chapter 14 introduces several miscellaneous SWT components: `Group`, `Sash`, `SashForm`, `TabFolder`, and `Browser`.

Chapter 15 discusses topics concerning graphics and image handling. The first part of this chapter teaches you how to perform various drawing operations with graphics context—drawing lines, arcs, shapes, images, and text and filling shapes, and so forth. SWT image handling is introduced in the second part. You learn how an image is represented in SWT. Additionally, the chapter introduces practical image manipulation techniques.

Chapter 16 introduces various ways to transfer data within an application and between applications easily. I show you how to enable your applications to supply data and to accept data in the drag-and-drop process. Finally, you learn how to use the clipboard to exchange data within an application or between different applications.

Chapter 17 shows you how to add the printing functionality to your existing programs. This chapter first introduces you to the basic printing mechanism. A real-world example is then used to guide you step by step to code for printing and print preview. Finally, you learn about multiple page printing and pagination.

Chapter 18 shows you how to use the JFace windows framework (`org.eclipse.jface.window`) to simplify windows creation and management tasks. Additionally, this chapter covers JFace dialogs.

## *Part IV: Application Development*

Part IV takes you through the steps to create a sample application in SWT/JFace.

Chapter 19 introduces you to the JFace wizard framework with a sample application.

Chapter 20 gives you a brief overview of the JFace text framework. Then it shows you how to create a basic custom text editor with JFace text. The custom text editor is then improved by adding the following add-ons: content assist and syntax highlighting.

Chapter 21 provides a framework for creating flat, web-like user interfaces. This chapter shows you how to use the Eclipse Forms frame. You learn how to use a toolkit to create basic forms or scrollable forms. Eclipse Form custom widgets are then introduced, such as hyperlinks, form texts, sections, and so on.

Chapter 22 teaches you how to embed OLE documents and ActiveX controls in SWT widgets on Windows platforms. As an example, a Microsoft Word document is embedded in an SWT application. The chapter walks you through the steps to embed the OLE document: creating the OLE container, creating an OLE site for the OLE document, activating the OLE object, and deactivating the OLE object.

Chapter 23 introduces you to a lightweight rendering framework—Draw2D. With Draw2D, you can create complex figures easily. This chapter shows you how to create simple UML diagrams with Draw2D. The sample application displays the selected class in a UML diagram. By combining small figures, you can create manageable complex figures without tedious code.

Chapter 24 guides you through the development of a simple FTP client application using SWT/JFace. By combining knowledge acquired in previous chapters, you can create complex practical applications. With the FTP client sample application, you learn how to use application windows, actions, menu bars, and toolbars. Furthermore, you learn how to make main UI components resizable by using sash forms properly. You can use drag and drop to improve the user interface and make it more accessible to the user.

# What You Need to Use This Book

In order to run the sample code, you need to download and install Eclipse version 3.0, which is available online at www.eclipse.org/.

## *Conventions*

To help you get the most from the book and keep track of what's happening, I've used a number of conventions throughout.

> **Boxes like this one hold important, not-to-be forgotten information that is directly relevant to the surrounding text.**

*Tips, hints, tricks, and asides to the current discussion are offset and placed in italics like this.*

As for styles in the text:

- ❏ I *highlight* important words when I introduce them.
- ❏ I show keyboard strokes like this: *Ctrl+A*.
- ❏ I show file names, URLs, and code within the text like so: `persistence.properties`.
- ❏ I present code in two different ways:

```
In code examples I highlight new and important code with a gray background.
```

```
The gray highlighting is not used for code that's less important in the present
context, or has been shown before.
```

## Source Code

As you work through the examples in this book, you may choose either to type in all the code manually or to use the source code files that accompany the book. All of the source code used in this book is available for download at www.wrox.com. Once at the site, simply locate the book's title (either by using the Search box or by using one of the title lists) and click the Download Code link on the book's detail page to obtain all the source code for the book.

When you download the code, just decompress it with your favorite compression tool. Alternately, you can go to the main Wrox code download page at www.wrox.com/dynamic/books/download.aspx to see the code available for this book and all other Wrox books.

## Updates (Errata)

I've made every effort to ensure that there are no errors in the text or in the code. However, no one is perfect, and mistakes do occur. If you find an error, such as a spelling mistake or faulty piece of code, I would be very grateful for your feedback. By sending in errata you may save another reader hours of frustration and at the same time you will be helping to provide even higher quality information.

To find the errata page for this book, go to www.wrox.com and locate the title using the Search box or one of the title lists. Then, on the book details page, click the Book Errata link. On this page you can view all errata that has been submitted for this book and posted by Wrox editors. A complete book list including links to each book's errata is also available at www.wrox.com/misc-pages/booklist.shtml.

If you don't spot "your" error on the Book Errata page, go to www.wrox.com/contact/techsupport.shtml and complete the form there to send the error you have found. I'll check the information and, if appropriate, post a message to the book's errata page and fix the problem in subsequent editions of the book.

# p2p.wrox.com

For author and peer discussion, join the P2P forums at p2p.wrox.com. The forums are a Web-based system for you to post messages relating to Wrox books and related technologies and interact with other readers and technology users. The forums offer a subscription feature to e-mail you topics of your choosing when new posts are made to the forums. Wrox authors, editors, other industry experts, and your fellow readers are present on these forums.

At http://p2p.wrox.com you will find a number of different forums that will help you not only as you read this book, but also as you develop your own applications. To join the forums, just follow these steps:

1. Go to p2p.wrox.com and click the Register link.

2. Read the terms of use and click Agree.

3. Complete the required information to join as well as any optional information you wish to provide and click Submit.

4. You will receive an e-mail with information describing how to verify your account and complete the joining process.

*You can read messages in the forums without joining P2P but in order to post your own messages, you must join.*

When you join, you can post new messages and respond to messages other users post. You can read messages at any time on the Web. If you would like to have new messages from a particular forum e-mailed to you, click the Subscribe to this Forum icon by the forum name in the forum listing.

For more information about how to use the Wrox P2P forum, be sure to read the P2P FAQs for answers to questions about how the forum software works as well as many common questions specific to P2P and Wrox books. To read the FAQs, click the FAQ link on any P2P page.

# Part I: Fundamentals

**Chapter 1:** Overview of Java UI Toolkits and SWT/JFace

**Chapter 2:** SWT/JFace Mechanisms

**Chapter 3:** Jump Start with SWT/JFace

**Chapter 4:** SWT Event Handling, Threading, and Displays

**Chapter 5:** Basic SWT Widgets

**Chapter 6:** Layouts

# Overview of Java UI Toolkits and SWT/JFace

This chapter outlines the three main Java user interface (UI) toolkits: AWT, Swing, and JFace. First I provide a brief introduction to all three, and then I compare them, highlighting some of the advantages SWT/JFace offers. SWT/JFace allows you to access native features easily, and programs based on SWT/JFace are considerably faster than those based on Swing in terms of execution speed. SWT/JFace is designed to be very flexible, so you can program using either the traditional approach or the model-view-controller approach. After reading this chapter, you should have a general overview of SWT/JFace. The chapters that follow introduce various aspects of SWT/JFace in detail.

## Evolution of Java GUI Frameworks

This section covers the following Java graphical user interface (GUI) frameworks:

❑ **Abstract Window Toolkit (AWT):** The first and the simplest windowing framework.

❑ **Swing:** Built on AWT, Swing offers peerless components.

❑ **Standard Widget Toolkit (SWT) and JFace:** SWT is a native widget UI toolkit that provides a set of OS-independent APIs for widgets and graphics. JFace is a UI toolkit implementation using SWT to handle many common UI programming tasks.

This section outlines the evolution of the Java GUI framework and highlights the key features we'll compare and contrast in the next section.

# *Abstract Window Toolkit*

The first version of Java, released by Sun Microsystems in 1995, enabled you to create programs on one platform and deliver the products to other Java-supported systems without worrying about the local environment—"Write Once, Run Anywhere." Most early Java programs were fancy animation applets running in Web browsers. The underlying windowing system supporting those applets was the Abstract Window Toolkit (AWT).

AWT has a very simple architecture. Components, graphics primitives, and events are simply perched on top of similar elements from the underlying native toolkit. A layer of *impedance matching* sits between the AWT and various underlying native toolkits (such as X11, Macintosh, and Microsoft Windows) to ensure the portability of AWT.

AWT 1.0 uses a callback delegation event model. Events are propagated or delegated from an event "source" to an event "listener." The interested objects may deal with the event, and the super-event handler is not required. The event model in AWT 1.1 was reimplemented from the callback delegation event model to an event subscription model. In AWT 1.1, the interested objects must register themselves with the components to receive notification on certain events. When the events are fired, event object are passed to registered event listeners.

AWT was slightly enhanced in later releases of Java. However, even the latest version of AWT fails to delivery a rich set of GUI components. Following is a list of components provided by AWT:

- ❑ Button
- ❑ Canvas
- ❑ Checkbox
- ❑ Choice
- ❑ Container
    - ❑ Panel
    - ❑ ScrollPane
    - ❑ Window
- ❑ Label
- ❑ List
- ❑ Scrollbar
- ❑ TextComponent
    - ❑ TextArea
    - ❑ TextField

To give you a more complete overview of the AWT user interface, I've created a simple GUI program. This tiny program allows the user to upload a photo to a server, or anywhere else. Figure 1-1 shows the user interface of the photo uploader implemented using Abstract Window Toolkit.

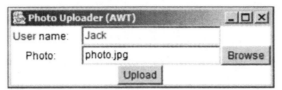

**Figure 1-1**

Click the Browse button to bring up the file selection dialog (see Figure 1-2). The name of the selected file is inserted into the text after the Photo label. The upload process starts when the user clicks the Upload button. The program exits when uploading is complete.

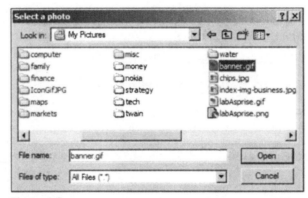

**Figure 1-2**

If you are familiar with Microsoft Windows systems, you may notice that the file selection dialog in Figure 1-2 is exactly the same as those used by native Windows programs. The Abstract Window Toolkit passes the call for file selection to the underlying native toolkit, i.e., Windows toolkit, and as a result, a native Windows file selection dialog pops up.

The Abstract Window Toolkit is sufficient for developing small user interfaces and decorations for Java applets, but it's not suitable for creating full-fledged user interfaces. Sun Microsystems recognized this as well and in 1997, JavaSoft announced Java Foundation Classes (JFC). JFCs consist of five major parts: AWT, Swing, Accessibility, Java 2D, and Drag and Drop. Swing helps developers to create full-scale Java user interfaces.

# Swing

Swing is a pure Java UI toolkit built on top of the core Abstract Window Toolkit (AWT) libraries. However, the components available in Swing are significantly different from those in AWT in terms of underlying implementation. The high-level components in Swing are lightweight and peerless, i.e. they do not depend on native peers to render themselves. Most AWT components have their counterparts in Swing with the prefix "J." Swing has twice the number of components of AWT. Advanced components such as trees and tables are included. The event-handling mechanism of Swing is almost the same as that of AWT 1.1, although Swing defines many more events. Swing has been included in every version of Java since Java 1.2.

The main Swing packages are as follows:

❑ **javax.swing:** Contains core Swing components.

❑ **javax.swing.border:** Provides a set of class and interfaces for drawing various borders for Swing components.

❑ **javax.swing.event:** Contains event classes and corresponding event listeners for events fired by Swing components, in addition to those events in the java.awt.event package.

❑ **javax.swing.plaf:** Provides Swing's pluggable look-and-feel support.

❑ **javax.swing.table:** Provides classes and interfaces for dealing with JTable, which is Swing's tabular view for constructing user interfaces for tabular data structures.

❑ **javax.swing.text:** Provides classes and interfaces that deal with editable and noneditable text components, such as text fields and text areas. Some of the features provided by this package include selection, highlighting, editing, style, and key mapping.

❑ **javax.swing.tree:** Provides classes for dealing with JTree.

❑ **javax.swing.undo:** Provides support for undo and redo features.

In addition to the lightweight high-level components, Swing introduced many other features over AWT. Pluggable look-and-feel is one of the most exciting of the bunch. Swing can emulate several look-and-feels, and you can switch the look-and-feels at runtime. If you do not like any of them , you can even create your own. Other features include tooltip support, keyboard event binding, and additional debugging support.

The photo uploader program can be rewritten using Swing. Figure 1-3 shows the user interface of the Swing photo uploader with Windows look-and-feel; Figure 1-4 shows the user interface with Java metal look-and-feel.

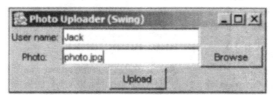

**Figure 1-3**

**Figure 1-4**

The Swing file selection dialog user interfaces for Windows look-and-feel and Metal look-and-feel are shown in Figures 1-5 and 1-6, respectively. The Swing file selection dialog with Windows look-and-feel looks similar to the AWT (i.e. the native dialog); however, they are quite different. Swing simply emulates

the Windows native file dialog. If you look carefully, you'll find that some features of Windows native file dialogs are missing in the Swing file dialog. In Windows native file dialogs, you can view the files using different modes: list, details, thumbnails, and so on. Additionally, more operations are available in the popup menu when you right-click. Both of these features are not available to Swing file selection dialogs.

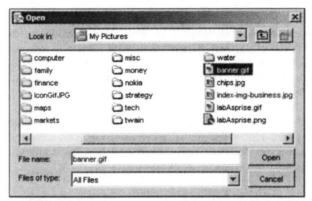

Figure 1-5

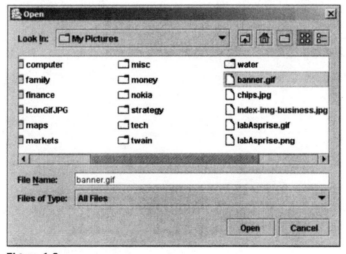

Figure 1-6

Swing fails to support native features of the underlying system. Another obstacle to widespread usage is that programming with Swing is very complex.

Swing is so powerful that you can use it to create full-scale enterprise Java user interface programs. So why do we see so few Swing-based GUI programs? James Gosling, creator of the Java language, said during a keynote presentation at a Mac OS X conference that there is a "perception that Java is dead on the desktop." Complexity of building Swing GUIs, lack of native features, and slow running speed are some of obstacles keeping Swing from succeeding on desktops.

Is any other Java GUI toolkit available that can create full-featured user interface programs? The answer is yes. Standard Widget Toolkit (SWT), along with JFace, provides a complete toolkit for developing portable native user interfaces easily.

# SWT and JFace

Eclipse is an open source universal tool platform dedicated to providing a robust, full-featured, industry platform for the development of highly integrated tools. IBM, Object Technology International (OTI), and several other companies launched the Eclipse project in 2001. Today, the Eclipse Board of Stewards includes companies such as Borland, Fujitsu, HP, Hitachi, IBM, Oracle, Red Hat, SAP, and Sybase. With more than 3 million downloads, Eclipse has attracted a huge number of developers in over 100 countries.

The Eclipse platform defines a set of frameworks and common services that are required by most tool builders as common facilities. One of the most important common facilities is the portable native widget user interface. The Standard Widget Toolkit (SWT) provides portable native user interface support, as well as a set of OS-independent APIs for widgets and graphics.

Built on SWT, JFace is a pure Java UI framework handling many common UI programming tasks. The following subsections introduce SWT and JFace in detail.

Figure 1-7 shows the Eclipse platform's native user interface — in this case, Windows. SWT is integrated tightly with the underlying native window system.

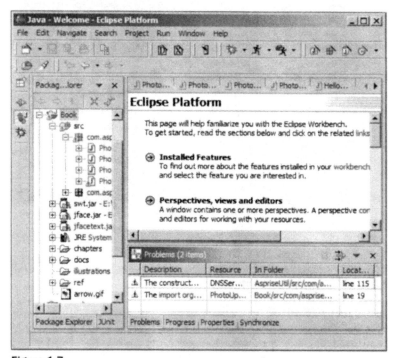

Figure 1-7

## Standard Widget Toolkit

SWT is analogous to AWT and Swing in Java except that SWT uses a rich set of native widgets. AWT widgets are implemented directly with native widgets, so to be portable it has to take the least common denominator of all kinds of window systems. For example, while Windows supports a tree widget, Motif does not. As a result, AWT cannot have the tree widget. Swing tackles this problem by emulating almost all kinds of widgets. However, this emulation strategy has some serious drawbacks. First, the emulated widgets lag behind the look and feel of the native widgets, and user interaction with the emulated widgets is quite different. Second, although Swing has been improved, Swing user interfaces are still sluggish.

SWT employs a slightly different strategy. It defines a set of common APIs available across supported window systems. For each native window system, the SWT implementation utilizes native widgets wherever possible. If no native widget is available, the SWT implementation emulates it. As mentioned previously, Windows has a tree widget so SWT simply uses the native tree widget on Windows systems. For Motif, because it does not have a tree widget, the SWT implementation provides a proper emulated tree widget. In this way, SWT maintains a consistent programming model on all platforms and takes full advantage of any underlying native window systems.

The user interface of the photo uploader, rewritten using SWT, and the file selection dialog are shown in Figures 1-8 and 1-9, respectively.

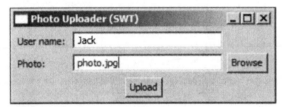

Figure 1-8

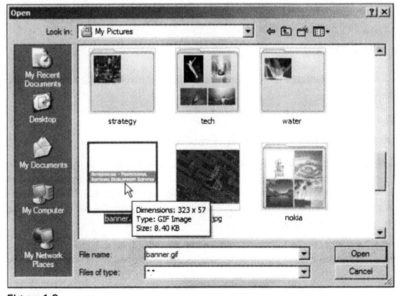

Figure 1-9

SWT is tightly integrated with the underlying native window system. Chapter 2 discusses the implementation of SWT and its advantages. Although SWT does not support pluggable look-and-feel (who needs Windows or Metal look-and-feels on a Mac, anyway?), it provides a number of other invaluable features: native UI interactions (such as drag and drop) and access to OS-specific components (such as Windows ActiveX controls like Microsoft Word, Acrobat Reader, and so on).

SWT enables developers to create native user interfaces with Java. However, most programmers with experience developing user interfaces on Windows, Linux, or any of the other platforms, know that developing a GUI is a very complicated and time-consuming process. Creating a native user interface with Java is no exception. Fortunately, Eclipse provides a UI toolkit named JFace to simplify the native user interface programming process.

## JFace

JFace is a UI toolkit implemented using SWT to handle many common user interface programming tasks. It is window system–independent in bots, its APIs, and implementation. JFace is designed to work with SWT without hiding it (see Figure 1-10).

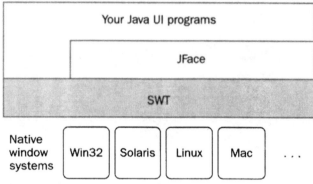

**Figure 1-10**

JFace offers the following components:

❏ **Image and font registries:** The image and font registries help the developer to manage OS resources.

❏ **Dialogs and wizards**

❏ **Progress reporting for long-running operations**

❏ **Action mechanism:** The action mechanism separates the user commands from their exact whereabouts in the user interface. An action represents a user command that can be executed by the user via buttons, menu items, or toolbar items. Each action defines its own essential UI properties, such as label, icon, tooltip, and so on, which can be used to construct appropriate widgets to present the action.

❏ **Viewers and editors:** Viewers and editors are model-based adapters for some SWT widgets. Common behaviors and high-level semantics are provided for those SWT widgets.

# SWT/JFace Advantages

Compared with AWT and Swing, SWT/JFace offers many advantages, as described in the subsections that follow.

## *Full Support for Native Features*

SWT/JFace is tightly integrated with the underlying native window system. For example, you can create Windows user interface programs with SWT on Windows, and they look and behave the same as those developed using Visual C++. Native features are available to SWT. This is a great advantage for the user.

Let's take the photo uploader as an example. When the user hits the Browse button, a file selection dialog pops up for the user to select the photo to be uploaded. In most of the cases, the user has quite a number of pictures. File names may help the user to identify the proper photo. However, file names are not intuitive enough to the user, especially if these photos are just exported from a digital camera. The best way to assist the user in choosing the proper photo is to provide a thumbnail preview.

The file chooser in Swing does not provide the picture preview function. Sun's Swing tutorial offers a way to do this: extending the file chooser with an accessory component to display a thumbnail of the selected file. Figure 1-11 shows a custom file chooser implemented using Swing.

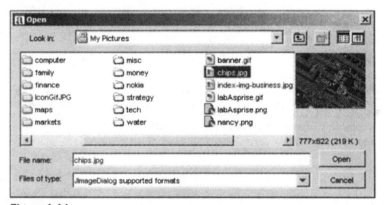

**Figure 1-11**

The Windows file chooser (refer to Figure 1-9) invoked from SWT offers more features than the custom Swing file chooser. In the custom Swing file chooser, the user has to click each file to view its corresponding thumbnail. However, the Windows file chooser displays all the thumbnails to the user (even photos in subfolders!) so he or she can easily find the proper file. Behind the scenes, Swing cannot display bitmap files (BMP) even though they're so popular on Windows and OS/2. On the other hand, SWT/JFace handles almost any kind of native image formats very well.

While the custom Swing file chooser may ultimately look even better than the Windows file chooser, it still looks strange to the user. The screen fonts in Figures 1-8 were smoothed with clear type method, except those from Swing. This means that the user selected clear type method to smooth the screen fonts' edges using the display panel of the native OS; however, Swing is unable to access this preference setting.

Such a small defect may not seem important to the developer, but to the user it is frustrating—especially when these small defects start to add up. Naturally, this leads to the loss of valuable customers. You can always hear such stories from the sales or marketing guys. This could be one of most important reasons why "Java is dead on the desktop."

Many components in Swing—including the file chooser—need improvement. You could fix them one by one and create a complete toolkit, but it is not necessary. With SWT/JFace, you do not have to create your own UI toolkit and you can still have total control of native features. If you are not satisfied with any aspect of SWT/JFace, you can always modify the source code provided.

## *Speed*

Most UI programs using SWT are more responsive than those using Swing. The following table provides an informal comparison of speeds of Swing and SWT.

|  | Swing | SWT |
|---|---|---|
| Time used from the click of the Browse button to the display of a file selection dialog | a. 2.39s  b. 2.53s  c. 2.46s<br>Avg. 2.46s | a. 0.63s  b. 0.58s  c. 0.68s<br>Avg. 0.63s |
| Time used from the display of the selection dialog to the dialog fully loaded | a. 1.48s  b. 1.40s  c. 1.44s<br>Avg. 1.44s | [Fully loaded immediately. Approximate 0 sec.] |
| Total time used | 3.90s | 0.63s |

Setup of the experiment: The photo uploader implemented with Swing was executed three times (a, b, c). For each run, the time was documented using a stopwatch from the click of the Browse button to the display of a file selection dialog and from the display of the selection dialog to the dialog fully loading. The average total time taken is computed. This process is repeated for photo uploader implemented with SWT.

Testing environment: Windows XP Professional; Sun Java 1.4.1 JRE; Mobile Intel Pentium 1.7 GHz CPU, 512MB memory.

The results from the experiment may not be entirely accurate, but we can make some generalizations. SWT runs significantly faster than Swing. It takes Swing up to six times as long to fully load the file selection dialog.

GUI design is an art as well as a science, so this comparison tells only part of the story. Trying out SWT and Swing applications reveals another part of the story: SWT is clearly superior to Swing in terms of visual perception.

SWT is designed to be very efficient. Unlike AWT (which uses a separate peer layer), SWT is a thin layer on top of the native window systems. To further reduce the overhead and potential incompatibilities, SWT attempts to avoid sugar-coating the limitations of the underlying window system. For example, SWT does not attempt to hide the existence of limitations on cross-threaded access to widgets.

A sluggish user interface has always been one of the top complaints about Swing. One of the primary problems was that Swing did not leverage much hardware acceleration. Over the past few years, this has improved, and a certain level of graphics acceleration was added with JDK 1.4. While it may be technically faster with this release, the perceived speed is still disappointing (especially to anyone not using high-end workstations).

Our experiment also shows that Swing is still slow compared with SWT. If a product has to satisfy the diverse execution environments (machines with different CUP power capabilities), SWT is the most suitable toolkit candidate.

## Portability

SWT provides a set of common programming APIs that developers can use to create portable applications on all of the SWT-supported operating systems. Following is a list of SWT (v2.1)–supported OSs:

- ❏ Windows 98/ME/2000/XP/CE
- ❏ Linux (x86/Motif; x86/GTK2)
- ❏ Solaris 8 (SPARC/Motif)
- ❏ QNX (x86/Photon)
- ❏ AIX (PPC/Motif)
- ❏ HP-UX (HP9000/Motif)
- ❏ Mac OS X (Mac/Carbon)

## Easy Programming

Some people bad-mouth SWT because the developer needs to take care of garbage collection on operating system resources, rather than the UI toolkit itself. It is true that SWT requires developers to track and dispose of these resources, but programming these kinds of tasks — and programming in SWT/JFace in general — is very straightforward. You could get started with SWT/JFace very quickly, although programming experience on a native user interface is an advantage.

The two simple rules developers should follow to develop UI programs with SWT are as follows:

- ❏ If you created it, you must dispose of it.
- ❏ Disposing of the parent disposes of the children (labels, text fields, and buttons).

Chapter 2 covers the resource management topic in detail. Here, I use code snippets to show you how to apply the preceding rules. These rules are very easy to adhere to, using the following steps:

**1.** In the photo uploader program, create a shell (window) first:

```
Display display = new Display();
Shell shell = new Shell(display);
```

2. Next, create labels, text fields, and buttons with the shell as their parent:

```
Label labelUser = new Label(shell, SWT.NULL);
Label labelPhoto = new Label(shell, SWT.NULL);
Text textUser = new Text(shell, SWT.SINGLE | SWT.BORDER);
Text textPhoto = new Text(shell, SWT.SINGLE | SWT.BORDER);
Button buttonBrowsePhoto = new Button(shell, SWT.PUSH);
Button buttonUpload = new Button(shell, SWT.PUSH);
```

3. Click the Upload button and execute the following code:

```
uploadPhoto(textUser.getText(), textPhoto.getText());
shell.dispose();
```

This disposes of the shell. As I said in the preceding text (the first rule), the shell is created and it must be disposed of. This rule does not apply to labels, text fields, and buttons; they are created, but they are never disposed of explicitly. However, when the shell is disposed of (the second rule in the preceding text) all of its children are disposed of, too.

Some may complain that the shell still has to be disposed of explicitly, but this process is necessary with almost all UI toolkits — including Swing. Chapter 2 covers programming in greater detail.

## Flexibility

SWT/JFace is designed to be very flexible. With SWT/JFace, you can use either of the following methods for programming:

❑ **The traditional approach:** The application model data must be transformed and copied from corresponding data structures to native UI components.

❑ **The model-view-controller (MVC) approach:** The MVC pattern is a classic design pattern. It separates the application object (model) from the way it is represented to the user (view) and from the way in which the user controls it (controller). Most MVC classes can be found in JFace.

Both approaches have advantages and disadvantages. The traditional approach is simple and easy to learn. The MVC approach requires much more time for developers to master, but it is more maintainable and extensible. In Swing, only the MVC approach is allowed.

Having both approaches available in SWT/JFace shortens the learning curve. Programming in the traditional approach is easy to learn, and the basic knowledge acquired from the traditional approach helps the developer understand the mechanisms behind the MVC approach.

Figure 1-12 shows a sample application displaying nesting of categories.

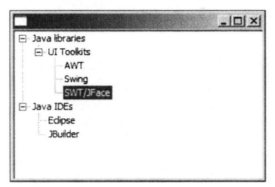

Figure 1-12

## Creating the Application Model Data

The application data can be modeled as following:

```java
/**
 * Represents a category of items.
 *
 */
class Category {
    private String name;
    private Vector subCategories;
    private Category parent;

    public Category(String name, Category parent) {
        this.name = name;
        this.parent = parent;
        if(parent != null)
            parent.addSubCategory(this);
    }

    public Vector getSubCategories() {
        return subCategories;
    }

    private void addSubCategory(Category subcategory) {
        if(subCategories == null)
            subCategories = new Vector();
        if(! subCategories.contains(subcategory))
            subCategories.add(subcategory);
    }

    public String getName() {
        return name;
    }

    public Category getParent() {
        return parent;
    }
}
```

The category represents a category of items. It may have subcategories. Category data can then be constructed as follows:

```
Vector categories = new Vector();

Category category = new Category("Java libraries", null);
categories.add(category);

category = new Category("UI Toolkits", category);
new Category("AWT", category);
new Category("Swing", category);
new Category("SWT/JFace", category);

category = new Category("Java IDEs", null);
categories.add(category);

new Category("Eclipse", category);
new Category("JBuilder", category);
```

A vector named "categories" contains a list of top-level categories (categories that have no parent category).

The application model data is ready. The category display function, using both the traditional and MVC approaches, is presented in the subsection that follows.

## Building the Tree Up with the Traditional Approach

The following code uses the traditional method:

```
final Tree tree = new Tree(shell, SWT.BORDER);

/**
 * Builds up the tree with traditional approach.
 *
 */
public void traditional() {
    for(int i=0; categories != null && i < categories.size(); i++) {
        Category category = (Category)categories.elementAt(i);
        addCategory(null, category);
    }
}

/**
 * Adds a category to the tree (recursively).
 * @param parentItem
 * @param category
 */
private void addCategory(TreeItem parentItem, Category category) {
    TreeItem item = null;
    if(parentItem == null)
        item = new TreeItem(tree, SWT.NONE);
    else
        item = new TreeItem(parentItem, SWT.NONE);
```

```
            item.setText(category.getName());

        Vector subs = category.getSubCategories();
        for(int i=0; subs != null && i < subs.size(); i++)
            addCategory(item, (Category)subs.elementAt(i));
}
```

The implementation of the traditional method is straightforward. For each of the top-level categories, a tree item is created directly under the root of the tree. For other categories, tree items are created under tree items representing their parent categories.

## Building the Tree Up with the MVC Approach

Following is the code for building the tree up using the MVC approach:

```
final Tree tree = new Tree(shell, SWT.BORDER);

/**
 * Builds up the tree with the MVC approach.
 *
 */
public void MVC() {

    TreeViewer treeViewer = new TreeViewer(tree);

    treeViewer.setContentProvider(new ITreeContentProvider() {
        public Object[] getChildren(Object parentElement) {
            Vector subcats = ((Category)parentElement).getSubCategories();
            return subcats == null ? new Object[0] : subcats.toArray();
        }

        public Object getParent(Object element) {
            return ((Category)element).getParent();
        }

        public boolean hasChildren(Object element) {
            return ((Category)element).getSubCategories() != null;
        }

        public Object[] getElements(Object inputElement) {
            if(inputElement != null && inputElement instanceof Vector) {
                return ((Vector)inputElement).toArray();
            }
            return new Object[0];
        }

        public void dispose() {
            //
        }

        public void inputChanged(Viewer viewer, Object oldInput,
                                                Object newInput) {
            //
```

```
        }
    });

    treeViewer.setLabelProvider(new LabelProvider() {
        public String getText(Object element) {
            return ((Category)element).getName();
        }
    });

    treeViewer.setInput(categories);

}
```

The MVC code is a little tedious, especially those two inner classes. Basically, the registered content provider ITreeContentProvider starts to provide content to the tree when the setInput method is called. Because the content provided comprises raw objects, the tree needs to consult the label provider LabelProvider about the text and image representation of those objects.

In this simple application, the traditional approach seems to be the preferred way. It is very straightforward. However, the MVC approach will shine if the application needs to be extended to support more features, such as category sorting.

If the requirement is not particularly complex and future changes are not likely to be big, then the traditional approach provides a fast path to your mission. On the other hand, if you are developing a large, complex system, the MVC approach could help you to create more scalable and maintainable software.

More on MVC is presented in Chapter 2.

## *Maturity*

Ever since the first version of SWT was released as part of the Eclipse platform in 2001, companies have built their commercial software with SWT/JFace as the UI toolkit. These companies include:

- ❑ C++/Fortran compilers, Intel
- ❑ WebSphere Application Studio, IBM
- ❑ XDE Professional, Rational Software (now under IBM)
- ❑ ColdFusion MX, Macromedia
- ❑ UML modeling tool, Embarcadero

# Summary

This chapter surveyed several major Java UI toolkits. Built on the Abstract Window Toolkit (AWT), Swing is a powerful UI toolkit with peerless components. Standard Widget Toolkit is a portable native UI toolkit, and the JFace framework simplifies programming with SWT by handling many common UI programming tasks. Compared to AWT and Swing, SWT/JFace offers many advantages such as full support of native features, fast execution speed, and flexibility of programming styles.

# 2

# SWT/JFace Mechanisms

This chapter explains some of the mechanisms used by SWT/JFace. First, you get an introduction to the implementation of SWT. You learn how SWT is implemented to maintain a rich set of consistent APIs on all platforms, which allows the underlying native window system's look-and-feel to shine. The chapter then covers resource management in SWT and offers useful resource management techniques and practical tips. The chapter then explains how the model-view-controller (MVC) design fits in JFace.

## The Implementation of SWT

SWT is a portable Java native UI toolkit. Using the consistent APIs provided by SWT, programs based on SWT can run on all of the SWT-supported platforms. As you have seen, SWT is implemented in Java. Java Native Interface (JNI) is used by SWT to invoke the native window systems from Java. JNI is a standard programming interface for writing Java native methods into native code.

Although both AWT and SWT are Java native UI toolkits, the implementations of them are quite different. AWT defines a common set of Java native methods, and these methods are then implemented on each system. The Java native methods in SWT are completely different, with each surfacing the methods specific to the native window system. All the logics are expressed in Java code for SWT.

The text that follows compares the implementations of AWT and SWT. It provides a good understanding of the implementation of SWT and why it is superior to that of AWT.

The `java.awt.Button` class of AWT has a `setLabel` method to set the text displayed on the button. The analogous class and method in SWT are `org.eclipse.swt.widgets.Button` and `setText`, respectively.

The code that follows provides details on how the `setLabel` method is implemented in AWT.

The code excerpt from the `java.awt.Button` is listed here:

```java
public class Button extends Component implements Accessible {

    String label;

    ...

    /**
     * Sets the button's label to be the specified string.
     */
    public void setLabel(String label) {
        boolean testvalid = false;

        synchronized (this) {
            if (label != this.label && (this.label == null ||
                    !this.label.equals(label))) {
                this.label = label;
                ButtonPeer peer = (ButtonPeer)this.peer;
                if (peer != null)
                        peer.setLabel(label);

                testvalid = true;
                }
        }

        // This could change the preferred size of the Component.
        if (testvalid && valid)
                invalidate();

    }

    ...
}
```

The `Button` class in AWT delegates the responsibility of `setLabel` to its peer widget `ButtonPeer`. `ButtonPeer` is an interface:

```java
package java.awt.peer;

import java.awt.*;

public interface ButtonPeer extends ComponentPeer {
    void setLabel(String label);
}
```

In order to be portable, ButtonPeer must be implemented on each supported window system. Button's peer widget on Windows is sun.awt.windows.WButtonPeer. WButtonPeer has a native method, setLabel:

```
class WButtonPeer extends WComponentPeer implements ButtonPeer {

  ...

  public native void setLabel(String label);


  ...
}
```

The implementation of this native method is as follows:

```
/*
 * Class:      sun_awt_windows_WButtonPeer
 * Method:     setLabel
 * Signature: (Ljava/lang/String;)V
 */
JNIEXPORT void JNICALL
Java_sun_awt_windows_WButtonPeer_setLabel(JNIEnv *env, jobject self,
                      jstring label)
{
    TRY;

    PDATA pData;

    JNI_CHECK_PEER_RETURN(self);
    AwtComponent* c = (AwtComponent*)pData;

    const char *labelStr = NULL;

    // By convention null label means empty string
    if (label == NULL) {
        labelStr = "";
    } else {
        labelStr = JNU_GetStringPlatformChars(env, label, JNI_FALSE);
    }

    if (labelStr == NULL) {
        throw std::bad_alloc();
    }

    c->SetText(labelStr);

    if (label != NULL)
        JNU_ReleaseStringPlatformChars(env, label, labelStr);

    CATCH_BAD_ALLOC;
}
```

`WButtonPeer`'s Motif implementation is as follows:

```
// sun.awt.motif.MButtonPeer

class MButtonPeer extends MComponentPeer implements ButtonPeer {
  ...

  public native void setLabel(String label);

  ...
}
```

The corresponding implementation of the native method is as follows:

```
/*
 * Class:      sun_awt_motif_MButtonPeer
 * Method:     setLabel
 * Signature: (Ljava/lang/String;)V
 */
JNIEXPORT void JNICALL Java_sun_awt_motif_MButtonPeer_setLabel
  (JNIEnv * env, jobject this, jstring label)
{
    struct ComponentData *wdata;
    char *clabel;
    XmString xim;

    AWT_LOCK ();

    wdata = (struct ComponentData *)
      JNU_GetLongFieldAsPtr(env, this, mComponentPeerIDs.pData);

    if (wdata == NULL) {
        JNU_ThrowNullPointerException (env, "NullPointerException");
        AWT_UNLOCK ();
        return;
    }
    if (JNU_IsNull (env, label) || ((*env)->GetStringLength (env, label) == 0)) {
        xim = XmStringCreateLocalized ("");
    } else {
        jobject font = awtJNI_GetFont (env, this);

        if (awtJNI_IsMultiFont (env, font)) {
            xim = awtJNI_MakeMultiFontString (env, label, font);
        } else {
            if (JNU_IsNull (env, label)) {
                clabel = emptyString;
            } else {
                clabel = (char *) JNU_GetStringPlatformChars (env, label, NULL);

                if (clabel == NULL) {        /* Exception? */
                    AWT_UNLOCK ();
                    return;
                }
            }
        }
```

```
            xim = XmStringCreate (clabel, "labelFont");

        if (clabel != emptyString) {
            JNU_ReleaseStringPlatformChars (env, label, (const char *)
clabel);;
        }
    }
}

    XtVaSetValues (wdata->widget, XmNlabelString, xim, NULL);
    XmStringFree (xim);
    AWT_FLUSH_UNLOCK ();
}
```

AWT defines a common set of APIs that must be implemented on every supported platform. If certain features are not available on one of the supported platforms, they must be sacrificed in order for the toolkit to maintain portability.

SWT takes a different approach. SWT provides a different set of widget classes for each platform; however, only the signatures of the public methods are the same, regardless of their host platforms.

The Windows-specific `org.eclipse.swt.widgets.Button` is listed here:

```
package org.eclipse.swt.widgets;


import org.eclipse.swt.internal.win32.*;
import org.eclipse.swt.*;
import org.eclipse.swt.graphics.*;
import org.eclipse.swt.events.*;

/**
 * Instances of this class represent a selectable user interface object that
 * issues notification when pressed and released.
 */

public class Button extends Control {
    Image image;
    static final int ButtonProc;
    static final TCHAR ButtonClass = new TCHAR (0,"BUTTON", true);
    static final int CheckWidth, CheckHeight;
    static {
        int hBitmap = OS.LoadBitmap (0, OS.OBM_CHECKBOXES);
        if (hBitmap == 0) {
            CheckWidth = OS.GetSystemMetrics (OS.IsWinCE ? OS.SM_CXSMICON :
OS.SM_CXVSCROLL);
            CheckHeight = OS.GetSystemMetrics (OS.IsWinCE ? OS.SM_CYSMICON :
OS.SM_CYVSCROLL);
        } else {
            BITMAP bitmap = new BITMAP ();
            OS.GetObject (hBitmap, BITMAP.sizeof, bitmap);
            OS.DeleteObject (hBitmap);
            CheckWidth = bitmap.bmWidth / 4;
```

```
            CheckHeight =  bitmap.bmHeight / 3;
        }
        WNDCLASS lpWndClass = new WNDCLASS ();
        OS.GetClassInfo (0, ButtonClass, lpWndClass);
        ButtonProc = lpWndClass.lpfnWndProc;
    }

/**
 * Constructs a new instance of this class given its parent
 * and a style value describing its behavior and appearance.
 */
public Button (Composite parent, int style) {
        super (parent, checkStyle (style));
}

int callWindowProc (int msg, int wParam, int lParam) {
    if (handle == 0) return 0;
    return OS.CallWindowProc (ButtonProc, handle, msg, wParam, lParam);
}

...

/**
 * Sets the receiver's text.
 */
public void setText (String string) {
    checkWidget ();
    if (string == null) error (SWT.ERROR_NULL_ARGUMENT);
    if ((style & SWT.ARROW) != 0) return;
    int newBits = OS.GetWindowLong (handle, OS.GWL_STYLE);
    int oldBits = newBits;
    newBits &= ~(OS.BS_BITMAP | OS.BS_ICON);
    if (newBits != oldBits) {
        OS.SetWindowLong (handle, OS.GWL_STYLE, newBits);
    }
    TCHAR buffer = new TCHAR (getCodePage (), string, true);
    OS.SetWindowText (handle, buffer);
}

    ...
}
package org.eclipse.swt.internal.win32;

import org.eclipse.swt.internal.*;

public class OS {
    ...

public static final boolean SetWindowText (int hWnd, TCHAR lpString) {
        if (IsUnicode) {
            char [] lpString1 = lpString == null ? null : lpString.chars;
            return SetWindowTextW (hWnd, lpString1);
        }
        byte [] lpString1 = lpString == null ? null : lpString.bytes;
```

```
        return SetWindowTextA (hWnd, lpString1);
}

public static final native boolean SetWindowTextW (int hWnd, char [] lpString);

    ...
}
```

The implementation of the native method SetWindowTextW is as follows:

```
JNIEXPORT jboolean JNICALL OS_NATIVE(SetWindowTextW)
    (JNIEnv *env, jclass that, jint arg0, jcharArray arg1)
{
    jchar *lparg1=NULL;
    jboolean rc;
    NATIVE_ENTER(env, that, "SetWindowTextW\n")
    if (arg1) lparg1 = (*env)->GetCharArrayElements(env, arg1, NULL);
    rc = (jboolean)SetWindowTextW((HWND)arg0, (LPWSTR)lparg1);
    if (arg1) (*env)->ReleaseCharArrayElements(env, arg1, lparg1, 0);
    NATIVE_EXIT(env, that, "SetWindowTextW\n")
    return rc;
}
```

Note that SetWindowTextW in bold font in the preceding code is a method provided by Windows.

The analogous class in Motif is as follows:

```
package org.eclipse.swt.widgets;

import org.eclipse.swt.internal.*;
import org.eclipse.swt.internal.motif.*;
import org.eclipse.swt.*;
import org.eclipse.swt.graphics.*;
import org.eclipse.swt.events.*;

/**
 * Instances of this class represent a selectable user interface object that
 * issues notification when pressed and released.
 */
public class Button extends Control {
    String text = "";
    Image image, bitmap, disabled;
    static final byte [] ARM_AND_ACTIVATE;
    static {
        String name = "ArmAndActivate";
        int length = name.length();
        char [] unicode = new char [length];
        name.getChars (0, length, unicode, 0);
        byte [] buffer = new byte [length + 1];
        for (int i = 0; i < length; i++) {
            buffer[i] = (byte) unicode[i];
        }
        ARM_AND_ACTIVATE = buffer;
```

```
    }
  /**
   * Constructs a new instance of this class given its parent
   * and a style value describing its behavior and appearance.
   */
  public Button (Composite parent, int style) {
       super (parent, checkStyle (style));
  }

...

  /**
   * Sets the receiver's text.
   */
  public void setText (String string) {
    checkWidget ();
    if (string == null) error (SWT.ERROR_NULL_ARGUMENT);
    if ((style & SWT.ARROW) != 0) return;
    text = string;
    char [] text = new char [string.length ()];
    string.getChars (0, text.length, text, 0);
    int mnemonic = fixMnemonic (text);
    byte [] buffer = Converter.wcsToMbcs (getCodePage (), text, true);
    int xmString = OS.XmStringParseText (
        buffer,
        0,
        OS.XmFONTLIST_DEFAULT_TAG,
        OS.XmCHARSET_TEXT,
        null,
        0,
        0);
    if (xmString == 0) error (SWT.ERROR_CANNOT_SET_TEXT);
    if (mnemonic == 0) mnemonic = OS.XK_VoidSymbol;
    int [] argList = {
        OS.XmNlabelType, OS.XmSTRING,
        OS.XmNlabelString, xmString,
        OS.XmNmnemonic, mnemonic,
    };
    OS.XtSetValues (handle, argList, argList.length / 2);
    if (xmString != 0) OS.XmStringFree (xmString);
  }

  int traversalCode (int key, XKeyEvent xEvent) {
    return super.traversalCode (key, xEvent) | SWT.TRAVERSE_MNEMONIC;
  }

  ...
}

package org.eclipse.swt.internal.motif;

import org.eclipse.swt.internal.*;
```

```
public class OS {
    ...
    public static final synchronized native void XtSetValues(int widget,
        int[] argList, int numArgs);
    ...
}
```

The corresponding JNI implementation of the native method is as follows:

```
// os.c

#include "swt.h"
#include "os_structs.h"

...

JNIEXPORT void JNICALL OS_NATIVE(XtSetValues)
    (JNIEnv *env, jclass that, jint arg0, jintArray arg1, jint arg2)
{
    jint *lparg1=NULL;
    NATIVE_ENTER(env, that, "XtSetValues\n")
    if (arg1) lparg1 = (*env)->GetIntArrayElements(env, arg1, NULL);
    XtSetValues((Widget)arg0, (ArgList)lparg1, arg2);
    if (arg1) (*env)->ReleaseIntArrayElements(env, arg1, lparg1, 0);
    NATIVE_EXIT(env, that, "XtSetValues\n")
}

...
```

XtSetValues is a method exposed in the Motif toolkit.

As illustrated in the preceding code, SWT provides different classes of Button on Windows, Motif, and other platforms, and the signature of each public method of every Button class is the same. Also, you may notice that SWT tries to put as much as possible the logic into Java code rather than the native code as AWT does. The main strategy here is one-to-one mapping between the Java natives and procedures offered by the native window system. In both implementations of OS.SetWindowText on Windows and OS.XtSetValues on Motif, only the absolutely necessary argument conversion code is included, and nothing extra happens there. The Java call is passed directly to the underlying native window systems. This implies that the equivalent C code is guaranteed to behave completely in the same way.

The implementation strategy of SWT offers a few advantages.

Debugging is made easy with SWT. The developer can find the cause of the bug easily. For example, if setLabel is malfunctioning, the native call made (SetWindowsText for Windows or XtSetValues for Modify) can be traced. The one-to-one mapping enables you to write simple C programs to isolate the bug and submit a bug report to the corresponding toolkit vendors.

For people who implement and maintain SWT, it is very maintainable and scalable, thanks to the one-to-one mapping. Because every native method in Java code has its analogous method in the native window system, native UI programmers can easily see how the Java native method works. Once they are in doubt, they can always refer to the documentation for the native window system because SWT natives are one-to-one mapped with those in the underlying native window system. Introducing new features to SWT is straightforward, too.

Most common low-level widgets are implemented natively everywhere. However, some native window systems lack certain high-level widgets, such as toolbars and trees. In this case, SWT emulates those widgets on the native window systems. For example, a tree widget is available natively on Windows; however, it is missing on Motif. SWT emulates the tree widget on Motif. This emulation technique is used universally by Swing. However, in SWT, only absolutely necessary emulation is employed.

> The implementation strategy of SWT enables it to maintain a rich set of consistent APIs on all platforms, allowing the underlying native window system's look-and-feel to shine.

# Resource Management with SWT/JFace

As you saw in the last section, SWT is an ultra-thin layer perching on the underlying native window system. For native user interface programming with C, programmers have to allocate and free operating system resources "manually." SWT programmers must do the same.

SWT is a Java native UI toolkit. One of the great features of Java is that it has a built-in garbage collection mechanism, which frees Java developers from allocating and freeing objects. When you program with SWT, you can still enjoy this feature, except that you have to manage operating system resources by yourself. Do not panic — the issue of resource management has been addressed very well in SWT/JFace.

## *Operating System Resources*

Operating system resources in SWT refer to native resources used by those (operating system) resource-based objects. Some of the resource-based objects are `Display`, `Color`, `Font`, `GC`, `Image`, `Printer`, `Region`, and `Widgets`.

Most of the classes in the following packages are resource-based:

- ❏ `org.eclipse.swt.custom`: Contains SWT custom widgets
- ❏ `org.eclipse.swt.graphics`: Provides the classes for primitive drawing, graphic handling, image loading/saving, and so on
- ❏ `org.eclipse.swt.widgets`: Contains basic SWT widgets

> If you are uncertain about whether an object/class is resource-based using operating system resources, check whether it has a dispose() method. If it does, then it is very likely resource-based. Otherwise, it isn't.

Are any operating system resources used in Swing?

Yes. As introduced in Chapter 1, Swing is built on the top of core AWT libraries and only "high-level" components in Swing are lightweight and peerless. Those "low-level" components are heavyweight, which make use of operating system resources. JFrame is one of the most notable examples. The JavaDoc document for the `dispose()` method says, "Releases all of the native screen resources used by this Window, its subcomponents, and all of its owned children."

# Rules of Operating System Resource Management

In Chapter 1, two simple rules were briefly introduced. We are going to discuss them in greater detail.

## Rule 1: If you create it, you must dispose of it

In SWT, all operating system resource classes allocate necessary native resources only in their constructors. No methods other than those constructors are responsible for allocating any operating system resources. This implies that only if you made a call to a constructor of a resource-based SWT class do you need to free the resources later by calling the `dispose` method of the object.

For example, the code listing that follows draws a rectangle onto a `shell`:

```
void draw(Shell shell) {
GC gc = new GC(shell);
gc.setLineWidth(3);

gc.drawRectangle(10, 10, 200, 100);
gc.dispose();
}
```

First, a GC (graphics context) object `gc` is created based on the specified shell. Then you can adjust settings of the `gc` object and call the `drawRectangle` method to draw the rectangle on the shell. After the drawing is done, the `dispose` method of `gc` is called to release the operating system resources associated with it.

Some may think that calling the `dispose` method is unnecessary because the `gc` object will be eligible for garbage collection when the method exits. It is very important to understand that those operating system resources wrapped by resource-based objects are unchanged when resource-based objects are garbage collected — i.e., if they have not been disposed of, they are still there even if the resource-based (Java) objects are gone. That's why the `dispose` method has to be called explicitly.

Why not call the `dispose` method in the finalizers of resource-based objects? In this way, when the resource-based objects are reclaimed by the garbage collector, the operating system resources are disposed of automatically. This strategy seems to be an elegant solution to managing operating system resources, but it causes many problems.

The timing for the `finalize` method of a garbage collected object is unknown. Additionally, the finalization process may fail if exceptions are thrown. According to the Java Language Specification (JLS), finalization invocations are not ordered. Even if you have unlimited memory, this could cause problems. For example, in the X Window system, a `Font` can be used by GC to provide text rendering. Due to the unordered nature of finalization, the Font object may be destroyed before the GC object, which leaves the operating system in an indeterminate state. JSL does not specify which thread will be used to perform finalization either. To dispose of operating system resources, the finalizers must be synchronized with the UI thread. This would cause a significant runtime overhead. The list of such problems goes on and on. The troubles caused by this approach may be even more difficult and complicated than the original problem itself.

Object finalization is nondeterministic and error prone. SWT does not rely on it to dispose of operating system resources. In SWT, those native resources must be disposed of explicitly.

## How to Dispose?

To dispose of a resource-based object, simply call its dispose() method. All resource-based classes share the same method signature for the dispose method:

```
public void dispose()
```

The dispose method can be called many times. All the operating system resources are released when the first call to this method is made, and subsequent calls have no actual effect. It is worth noting that when you dispose of a resource-based object, its children, if any, will be disposed of, too. Rule #2 discusses this in detail.

Once a widget or any other resource-based object is disposed of, calling most of its methods will result in the following exception:

```
SWTException(ERROR_WIDGET_DISPOSED)
```

Sometimes, you may need to check whether a resource-based object is disposed of or not by calling the isDisposed method:

```
public boolean isDispose()
```

Calling the dispose method is easy; however, the timing to do it must be opportune.

## When to Dispose?

Operating system resources should be disposed of as soon as they are not in use any more. As shown in the code snippet in the last section, *gc* is disposed of immediately after the drawing is done. Resources such as GCs and Printers are almost always created and disposed of within the scope of the same method. Code written in this way is easy to maintain and to debug.

Beware that you do not dispose of resources too early. For example, the following code draws a red rectangle onto the specified shell:

```
void draw(Shell shell) {
GC gc = new GC(shell);
gc.setLineWidth(3);

    Color color = new Color(display, 255, 0, 0);
gc.setForeground(color);
```

```
gc.drawRectangle(10, 10, 200, 100);
gc.dispose();

color.dispose();
}
```

In the preceding code, a `Color` object `color` is created. The `color` is set to the foreground of the `gc`. Because `color` is in use by `gc`, `color` is disposed of after `gc` is disposed of. What would happen if `color` was disposed of first? This may leave `gc`'s foreground as an invalid handle, and as a result, the program could crash.

If you use resource-based objects in a widget, you'd better to clean them up when the widget is disposed of. For example, the code list that follows sets the foreground of a label to red.

```
Label label = new Label(shell, SWT.NULL);

final Color color = new Color(display, 255, 0, 0);

label.setForeground(color);

label.addDisposeListener(new DisposeListener() {
    public void widgetDisposed(DisposeEvent e) {
        color.dispose();
    }
});

...
```

A disposed listener is used to listen for the `dispose` event. When the label is disposed of, the dispose listener will be notified and the method `WidgetDisposed` will be called. (More details on event handling are discussed in Chapter 4.)

## Do Not Dispose of It If You Did Not Create It

If you did not create a resource, do not dispose of it. This seems obvious, but sometimes it could be ignored in practice. In the last section, you saw how to set the foreground of a label to red. The following code is the alternative to the preceding procedure:

```
Label label = new Label(shell, SWT.NULL);

Color color = display.getSystemColor(SWT.COLOR_RED);

label.setForeground(color);
```

Should the `color` object here be disposed of with the label disposed? No. Do not dispose of a resource if you never created it. You "create" a resource only when you explicitly call its constructor. In the preceding code, the constructor of the `Color` class was not called explicitly; thus, you did not create the `color` object. Because you did not create it, it's not your responsibility to dispose of it. In this case, the SWT library manages the `color` object. You should not dispose of SWT-managed resource-based objects, or your programs may crash or throw exceptions.

The whole set of SWT APIs is designed with this in mind. For example, the method public void GC.getClipping(Region region) forces the developer to create a Region object in order to retrieve the clipping region data from a GC. Why does not this method simply return a Region object? If so, this rule will be broken and this inconsistence would be a nightmare for programmers. Whether you are developing SWT-based libraries or applications, this rule should always be enforced to make everyone's life easier.

## Rule 2: Disposing of the parent disposes of the children

This rule is very straightforward. When you dispose of a parent widget, all of the widget's children will be disposed of also:

- ❏ Disposing of a Composite disposes of all of the Composite's children.

- ❏ Disposing of a Menu disposes of all of its MenuItems.

- ❏ Disposing of a Tree or TreeItem disposes of all of its TreeItems.

- ❏ Disposing of a Table disposes of all of its TableColumn and TableItems.

For example, the following code builds up the component tree, as shown in Figure 2-1.

```
shell.setLayout(new GridLayout(2, true));
Label label = new Label(shell, SWT.NULL);
label.setText("Label");
Composite composite = new Composite(shell, SWT.NULL);
composite.setLayout(new GridLayout());
Button button1 = new Button(composite, SWT.PUSH);
button1.setText("Button 1");
Button button2 = new Button(composite, SWT.PUSH);
button2.setText("Button 2");

...

shell.dispose();
```

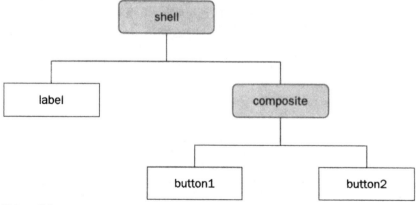

Figure 2-1

When the method `shell.dispose()` is called, the disposal process is performed in the depth-first order. This means that before the shell is fully disposed of, the shell has to dispose of its children (the label and the composite) first. To dispose of the composite, its children, `button1` and `button2` should be disposed of first. This process repeats recursively until all the components and their children are properly disposed of.

As you can see here, this rule saves you from having to dispose of each item one by one in a complex component tree. Disposing of a top-level widget will dispose of all of its descendant widgets. Also, this rule reflects the fact that a widget (except the top-level shell) existing without a parent is meaningless and useless.

What are the children of a parent widget? For a widget, its children are those widgets depending on it. Most of the child widgets are created in the following way or similarly:

```
XXX xxx = new XXX(parentWidget, style);
```

Typically, the first argument in the constructor of a child widget is the `parentWidget` object. In our example, the composite has two children: `button1` and `button2`.

The following code creates a red background composite with a button as its only child:

```
Composite composite = new Composite(shell, SWT.NULL);

GridLayout layout = new GridLayout();
composite.setLayout(layout);

Color color = new Color(display, 255, 0, 0);
composite.setForeground(color);

Button button = new Button(composite, SWT.PUSH);
button.setText("Button");

...

composite.dispose();
```

Will the color object be disposed of when the composite is being disposed of? No. The color object is not a child of the composite, and thus it will not be disposed of as the button will be.

> **The accessory resource-based objects that you created (e.g., *Colors*, *Fonts*, and *Images*) will not be disposed of when the parent widget is disposed of. Those resource-based objects created by SWT internally will be managed by themselves automatically. What about the *layout* object — who should dispose of it? Because the *layout* is not a resource-based object, like other normal Java objects, it will be garbage collected when it is not referenced by any other objects.**

Now you can easily apply this rule to `Menus` with `MenuItems` as their children, `Trees` with `TreeItems`, and `Tables` with `TableColumns` and `TableItems`.

## Shared Menus Side Effect

This rule is wonderful, but it does have a side effect related to Menus only. If the same Menu instance is shared by multiple controls or menu items, disposing of any one of the controls or menu items disposes of the Menu object.

The code that follows creates two composites sharing the same Menu instance:

```
shell.setLayout(new GridLayout(2, true));

final Composite composite1 = new Composite(shell, SWT.BORDER);
composite1.setBackground(display.getSystemColor(SWT.COLOR_BLACK));

final Composite composite2 = new Composite(shell, SWT.BORDER);
composite2.setBackground(display.getSystemColor(SWT.COLOR_BLUE));

Menu menu = new Menu(composite1);
MenuItem menuItem = new MenuItem(menu, SWT.PUSH);
menuItem.setText("Popup menu");

menuItem.addDisposeListener(new DisposeListener() {
    public void widgetDisposed(DisposeEvent e) {
        System.out.println("Menu item is disposed.");
    }
});

menuItem.addSelectionListener(new SelectionAdapter() {
    public void widgetSelected(SelectionEvent e) {
        System.out.println("Disposing ...");
        composite2.dispose();
    }
});

composite1.setMenu(menu);
composite2.setMenu(menu);
```

The component tree and the UI are shown in Figure 2-2 and Figure 2-3, respectively.

As shown in the component tree, composite1 and composite2 share the same popup menu menu. When the user right-clicks the button and selects the menu item, the widgetSelect method in the SelectionListener is called. As a result, composite2 is disposed of. The component tree clearly shows that menu is the direct child of composite2; thus menu will be disposed of when composite2 is disposed of. Similarly, menuItem will be disposed of when its parent menu is disposed of. The registered DisposeListener of menuItem is called upon the menuItem being disposed, so you will see the message "Menu item is disposed" printed in the console.

After composite2 is disposed of, only composite1 is shown on the shell. If you try to right-click composite1, no menu will show up because menu has already been disposed of.

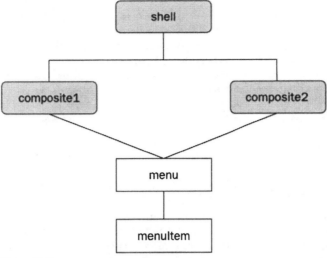

Figure 2-2

Figure 2-3

If your applications do not dispose of widgets with shared Menus in the middle of running, then you do not have to worry about this issue. If this side effect is undesired, you can work around it by doing one of two things:

❑ Remove the Menu instance, if any, from the control before calling the control's dispose method:

```
menuItem.addSelectionListener(new SelectionAdapter() {
    public void widgetSelected(SelectionEvent e) {
        System.out.println("Disposing ...");
        composite2.setMenu(null); // remove the menu.
        composite2.dispose();
    }
});
```

Just before composite2 is disposed, the menu is removed from it. So menu will be unchanged even if the composite2 is disposed.

❑ Create a new instance of Menu for each of the controls.

> The code *Menu menu = new Menu(composite1);* may give you the impression that the *menu* is a child of *composite1*. Actually, the constructor of *Menu* behaves quite differently from the constructors of other widgets. Internally, when the constructor is invoked, the parent of the *menu* is set to the first *org.eclipse.swt.widget.Decorations* parent of the *composite1* in the component tree. The first *Decorations* parent of a *composite* is the *composite's* nearest ancestor that is of type *Decorations*. In this case, the *shell* is the first *Decorations* parent of the *composite1*. So even if a *Menu* is not attached to any *Controls*, it will be disposed of when its parent (i.e., the first *Decorations* parent of the argument *Control*) is disposed of.

# Managing Fonts and Images with JFace

As a user interface programmer, you need to use fonts and images heavily. When you develop moderate to large native UI applications, you may soon realize that managing fonts and images becomes very challenging. For every font or image you create, you must explicitly dispose of it. Is there a better way to solve this problem? JFace provides a complete solution for you to manage fonts and images easily.

Managing shared resources is a classic programming problem. JFace adopts the classic solution: using central shared registries.

## Using the FontRegistry

The FontRegistry (org.eclipse.jface.resource.FontRegistry) is a registry of fonts. A FontRegistry maintains a mapping between symbolic font names and actual font objects. Before retrieving a font from a font registry, you first need to put the font into the font registry with a key. Then you can obtain the font with the corresponding key. You should not dispose of the font after use because the font registry takes care of this. The FontRegistry owns all the font objects registered with it and it will dispose of all the fonts when the Display is disposed of.

Here's an example:

```
Display display = new Display();
Shell shell = new Shell(display);

FontRegistry fontRegistry = new FontRegistry(display);

fontRegistry.put("button-text",
    new FontData[]{new FontData("Arial", 9, SWT.BOLD)} );
fontRegistry.put("code",
    new FontData[]{new FontData("Courier New", 10, SWT.NORMAL)});

Text text = new Text(shell, SWT.MULTI | SWT.BORDER | SWT.WRAP);
text.setFont(fontRegistry.get("code"));
text.setForeground(display.getSystemColor(SWT.COLOR_BLUE));
text.setText("public static void main() {\n\tSystem.out.println(\"Hello\");
\n}");
GridData gd = new GridData(GridData.FILL_BOTH);
gd.horizontalSpan = 2;
text.setLayoutData(gd);
```

```
Button executeButton = new Button(shell, SWT.PUSH);
executeButton.setText("Execute");
executeButton.setFont(fontRegistry.get("button-text"));

Button cancelButton = new Button(shell, SWT.PUSH);
cancelButton.setText("Cancel");
cancelButton.setFont(fontRegistry.get("button-text"));
shell.pack();
shell.show();
...
```

The preceding code creates the user interface shown in Figure 2-4.

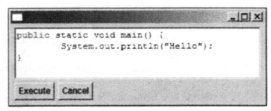

**Figure 2-4**

The FontData class is a lightweight class describing system fonts. A FontData to a Font is analogous to an ImageDescriptor to an Image. A FontData class describes the following properties of a Font:

❏   name: The face name of the font

❏   height: The height of the font in points

❏   style: Style bits, combination of SWT.NORMAL, SWT.ITALIC, and SWT.BOLD

You can treat the FontDatas as lightweight objects, which means they do not need to be disposed of to release operating system resources. The Font itself is resource-based, i.e., if you create it, you must dispose of it. However, as shown in the preceding text, you can employ a FontRegistry to manage allocation and disposal of the fonts.

The following are important methods of the FontRegistry class:

❏   public void put(String symbolicName, FontData[] fontData): Adds or replaces a font described by an array of FontDatas to this registry with the given symbolic name as the key. In Microsoft Windows platform, there is typically one element in the FontData array; however, you may need to supply several FontDatas in X Windows.

*Note that this method does not throw any exception as its **ImageRegistry** counterpart does. As you may remember, an exception will be thrown if you are trying to replace an existing image descriptor with the image loaded in an **ImageDescriptor**. Internally, a **FontRegistry** puts the replaced old **Font** if any into a stale font list and it will be disposed of, too, when the **Display** is disposed of.*

❏   public Font get(String symbolicName): Returns the font associated with the given symbolic font name or the default font if no special value is associated with the symbolic name.

❑     `public FontData getFontData(String symbolicName)`: Returns the font data associated with the specified symbolic name. The default font data will be returned if there is no special value associated with the given symbolic name.

❑     `public boolean hasValueFor(String symbolicName)`: Returns whether or not this registry has a value for the given symbolic name.

❑     `public FontData[] bestDataArray(FontData[] fonts, Display display)`: Returns the first (or first several for X Windows) valid `FontData` object from the given font data array. If none are valid, the first one in the array will be returned regardless.

You can use `FontData` to specify fonts programmatically; alternatively, you can let the user choose fonts through `FontDialog`, which is covered in later chapters.

## Using the ImageRegistry

`ImageRegistry`, as the name suggests, is a registry of images. `ImageRegistry` works much like a font registry. It maintains a mapping between symbolic image names and SWT image objects or lightweight image descriptor objects, which defer the creation of SWT image instances until they are needed. Before using an image, you must first put the image itself or its descriptor to the image registry with a key. Later, you can retrieve the image with the key. You must *not* dispose of the image after use because the `ImageRegistry` takes care of this. All the images in the `ImageRegistry` will be disposed of when the top-level `Display` object is disposed of.

The image descriptor `org.eclipse.jface.resource.ImageDescriptor` is a lightweight object that does not store the data of the image but can create the image on demand. The `ImageDescriptor` provides two ways to construct an image, from a file or from a URL. You could extend it to provide other methods to create images, such as retrieving image data using JDBC from a database.

To see how the `ImageRegisiter` simplifies image management, you will build a simple file browse, as shown in Figure 2-5.

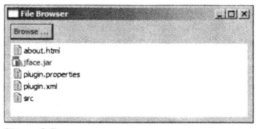

**Figure 2-5**

When the user clicks the Browse button, a directory dialog pops up. The user then selects a directory in which to list its file in the table below the button. If a file is a JAR file, the JAR icon is shown; otherwise, the default file icon is used. Of course, you can extend it to add more icons for other file types.

First, create the class and declare/define necessary variables:

```
public class SimpleFileBrowser {
    Display display = new Display();
    Shell shell = new Shell(display);
```

```
        ImageRegistry imageRegistry;

        Table table;
```

Then the Browse button and the table are created:

```
private void init() {
    shell.setText("File Browser");
    shell.setLayout(new GridLayout(1, true));

    Button button = new Button(shell, SWT.PUSH);
    button.setText("Browse ...");
    button.addSelectionListener(new SelectionAdapter() {
        public void widgetSelected(SelectionEvent e) {
            DirectoryDialog dialog = new DirectoryDialog(shell, SWT.NULL);
            String path = dialog.open();
            if (path != null) {
                File file = new File(path);
                displayFiles(file.list());
            }
        }
    });

    GridData gd = new GridData(GridData.FILL_BOTH);

    table = new Table(shell, SWT.MULTI);
    table.setLayoutData(gd);
```

Note that a SelectionListener has been registered to the Browse button to listen to the selection event. When the button is clicked, the widgetSelected method in the inner class is called. Thus the user can select a directory to list files. The method then invokes the displayFiles method to perform the actual file listing. The displayFiles method is covered shortly.

Then create an instance of ImageRegistry:

```
    imageRegistry = new ImageRegistry();
```

Remember that icons (the default icon and the JAR icon) are needed to list the files, so you need to put them into the image registry:

```
    ImageDescriptor defaultIcon =
        ImageDescriptor.createFromFile(null, "img/default.gif");
    imageRegistry.put("default", defaultIcon);

    ImageDescriptor jarIcon =
        ImageDescriptor.createFromFile(null, "img/jar.gif");
    imageRegistry.put("jar", jarIcon);
}
```

For the default icon, an ImageDescriptor (defaultIcon) is created. This ImageDescriptor provides information on how to retrieve the image — from a file named img/default.gif. Then, the ImageDescriptor instance along with the symbolic key is put into the ImageRegistry. The process is repeated for the JAR icon. Note that no images have been loaded at this stage. The ImageRegistry delays the creation of an image until it is needed.

The following code is the implementation of the method displayFiles:

```java
public void displayFiles(String[] files) {
    // Removes all existing table items.
    table.removeAll();

    for (int i = 0; files != null && i < files.length; i++) {
        TableItem item = new TableItem(table, SWT.NULL);
        Image image = null;

        if (files[i].endsWith(".jar")) {
            image = imageRegistry.get("jar");
        } else {
            image = imageRegistry.get("default");
        }

        item.setImage(image);
        item.setText(files[i]);
    }
}
```

This method first removes all items in the table. For each file, a TableItem is created with the table as its parent. The image icon for a file is set based on its extension. If it is a JAR file, the image is retrieved from the ImageRegistry with the key jar; otherwise, it is retrieved with the key default. Note that for all the non-JAR files, the exact same image (the default icon) is used. Regardless of the number of files and types of files, at most two images are used here. This is one of the advantages of using image registries. If you do not use an ImageRegistry, the displayFiles method needs to be rewritten as follows:

```java
public void displayFiles(String[] files) {

    // Disposes all of the images used by the table items first.
    TableItem[] items = table.getItems();
    for(int i=0; items != null && i < items.length; i++) {
        if(items[i].getImage() != null)
            items[i].getImage().dispose();
    }

    // Removes all existing table items.
    table.removeAll();

    for (int i = 0; files != null && i < files.length; i++) {
        TableItem item = new TableItem(table, SWT.NULL);
        Image image = null;

        if (files[i].endsWith(".jar")) {
            image = new Image(display, "img/jar.gif");
        } else {
            image = new Image(display, "img/default.gif");
        }
```

```
        item.setImage(image);
        item.setText(files[i]);
    }
}
```

The preceding code is not only tedious but also computationally expensive. For each file, an image is created and loaded. Suppose there are 1,000 files under a certain directory, the preceding code needs to create 1,000 images and load 1,000 times and the former version using an `ImageRegisitry` needs to create only two images and load only twice. In this case, using image registries is clearly the way to go.

The `ImageRegistry` class is very useful for managing small to moderate images such as icons and so on. However, for large images, you should use it with caution. All the images in an `ImageRegistry` are disposed of when the top-level `Display` object is disposed of. Suppose you are developing a graphic editing tool; clearly, you should not put the images being edited into an `ImageRegisitry`. If you do so, the memory is soon eaten up by the stale images residing in the `ImageRegistry`.

Another thing you must pay attention to is that, as mentioned in the beginning of this section, you must *not* dispose of any images in an `ImageRegistry`.

The four methods of the `ImageRegistry` class are as follows:

❑ `public void put(String key, ImageDescriptor descriptor)`: Adds an image descriptor to this `ImageRegistry`. The image specified in the descriptor will be computed and remembered the first time this entry is retrieved. This method replaces an existing image descriptor only if the corresponding image has not been computed yet; otherwise, an `IllegalArgumentException` is thrown.

❑ `public void put(String key, Image image)`: Adds an image to this `ImageRegistry`. Keep in mind that the image must not be disposed of by the clients after the image has been put into the registry. This seems to break Rule 1 discussed earlier in the chapter. Actually, by making this call, the caller transfers the responsibility of resource management to the `ImageRegistry`.

❑ `public Image get(String key)`: Returns the image associated with the specified key, or `null` if it does not exist.

❑ `public ImageDescriptor getDescriptor(String key)`: Returns the image descriptor associated with the specified key, or `null` if it does not exist.

# Model-View-Controller Pattern

Chapter 1 shows that you can program with SWT/JFace in either the traditional way or the MVC way. Here, you get a close look at how the MVC pattern fits in SWT/JFace.

The model-view-controller (MVC) pattern is a well-known user interface design pattern that separates the modeling of the domain, the presentation, and the actions based on the user input into three separate components.

# The MVC Architecture

The three main components in the MVC architecture are model, view, and controller.

## Model

The model manages the basic behavior and the data of the application domain. It responds to requests for information about its state (usually from the view) and it also responds to commands to change state (usually from the controller). The model may notify views when it changes.

For example, the model component of the List control shown in Figure 2-6 might contain information about the items of the list and the current selected index.

**Figure 2-6**

## View

The view is responsible for displaying information about the model. For the List control shown in Figure 2-6, the view presents all the items and highlights the currently selected item. There could be many different types of views for the same model. For example, you can use a Table instead of a List to display the model. Additionally, the view forwards user input to the controller.

## Controller

The controller acts as the intermediary between the view and the model. As a portion of the user interface, it dictates how the components interact with events such as mouse clicks, keyboard events, and so on. For example, when you click the second item in the List, the second item is highlighted. The controller interprets your mouse click and informs the view and model to change appropriately.

## MVC Interaction

The interaction of the three components in MVC is illustrated in Figure 2-7. The user takes some input actions and the controller notifies the model to change its state accordingly. The model then records the change as requested and broadcasts to the view (or multiple views) about the change. The view responds by querying the model for its state and updating the display if necessary.

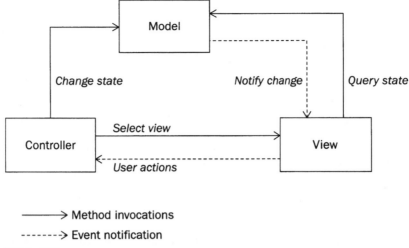

Figure 2-7

# Benefits of MVC

Architecting the user interface around the MVC pattern results in the following benefits:

❑ **Supports multiple views:** As you have seen, the model does not depend on the view; thus the user interface can display multiple views of the same data at the same time. For example, a visual HTML editor may have source view, visual UI view, and Web view using the same model data: the HTML file.

❑ **Accommodates changes:** Changes can be easily made for any component in the MVC. Changes to one aspect of the MVC are not coupled to other aspects, and this makes debugging easy. Also, adding new types of views does not affect the model.

# Costs of MVC

The benefits of MVC do not come free. Costs of the MVC include the following:

❑ **Complexity.** The new levels of indirection increase the complexity of the solution. The event-driven nature of MVC also increases the difficulty in debugging programs.

❑ **Limited reuse of the controller.** MVC decouples the model from the view, but the control is tied to both the model and the view. This reduces the potential that the controller logic will be reused in other parts of the application or other applications.

## *UI Delegation*

MVC is well defined; however, sometimes separating the viewer from the controller is difficult. Instead, people combine the viewer and the controller into one unit, calling it a representation. This modified version of MVC is often called "user interface delegation."

# JFace and MVC

SWT is designed to be efficient and easy to use, so it does not support MVC directly. However, on the top of SWT, JFace does provide excellent MVC support to meet diverse requirements. There are two notable MVC frameworks within JFace.

## *JFace Viewers*

A viewer in JFace is an MVC-based adapter on an SWT widget. A viewer plays the controller role in the MVC paradigm. A viewer's model is comprised of elements, represented by objects. By using a well-defined generic infrastructure, a viewer is capable of handling model input, updates, and selection in terms of elements. The view in the MVC is the SWT widget wrapped by a viewer. The model elements are not displayed directly, and they are mapped to labels containing text and/or an image using the viewer's label provider (ILabelProvider). Figure 2-8 shows how a ListViewer fits in the MVC model.

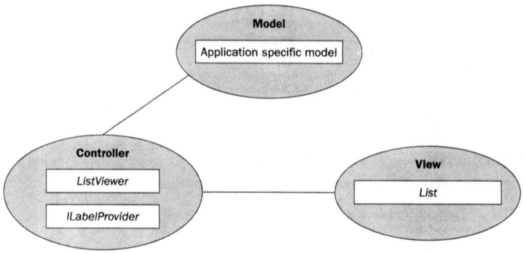

Figure 2-8

The package org.eclipse.jface.viewers contains the viewer framework, which contains the following abstract classes for viewers:

❑ Viewer: A viewer is an MVC-based adapter on a widget.

❑ StructuredViewer: Represents a structure-oriented viewer (such as a tree, a list, or a table) that supports custom sorting, filtering, and rendering.

❑ AbstractTreeViewer: Represents a tree structure–oriented viewer.

The package also contains the following concrete classes:

❑   ListViewer: A viewer based on the SWT List control

❑   TreeViewer: A viewer based on the SWT Tree control

❑   TableViewer: A viewer based on the SWT Table control

❑   TableTreeViewer: A viewer based on the SWT TableTree control

❑   CheckboxTreeViewer: A tree-structured viewer based on the SWT Tree control with Checkboxes on each node

❑   CheckboxTableViewer: A viewer based on the SWT Table control with Checkboxes on each node

Viewers are discussed further in later chapters.

## *JFace Text*

JFace Text is a full-featured MVC-based framework for creating, manipulating, and displaying text documents. JFace Text is implemented in the package org.eclipse.jface.text and its subpackages.

Details about the JFace Text framework are discussed in Chapter 21.

# Summary

The first part of this chapter introduced the implementation of SWT. The superior implementation strategy of SWT enables it to maintain a rich set of consistent APIs on all platforms, allowing the underlying native window system's look-and-feel to shine. The second part discussed resource management with SWT/JFace. The developer is responsible for allocating and freeing operating system resources. To do this, the developer can simply follow two rules: If you created it, you must dispose of it. And disposing of the parent disposes of the children. Fonts and images are operating system resources. SWT provides font and image registries for the developer. MVC and various JFace MVC frameworks are introduced in the last part. With knowledge of SWT implementation and resource management, you are now ready to move forward to the next chapter and develop your first SWT-based applications.

# 3

# Jump Start with SWT/JFace

In this chapter, you learn about:

❑ Downloading and installing SWT/JFace

❑ Setting up your IDEs to develop applications with SWT/JFace

❑ Writing your first SWT programs

❑ Using JFace to simplify UI programming

❑ Deploying your applications to multiple platforms using Java Web Start

After completing this chapter, you should able to write, run, and deploy SWT/JFace-based Java programs.

## Preparation

Before you start programming with SWT/JFace, you have to download SWT/JFace packages and configure your Java IDEs.

### Downloading and Installing SWT/JFace

Both SWT and JFace are included in the Eclipse distributions. From Eclipse version 2.1, SWT binary and source code can be downloaded separately from the Eclipse distribution. However, there are no separate JFace distributions.

If you plan to use SWT only, all you need to do is download the latest SWT binary and source code. If JFace is required, you can do one of the following:

❑   Retrieve the code for JFace from the CVS of the Eclipse project and build it yourself

❑   Download the complete Eclipse SDK

The latter method is much easier than the former one. You will use the latter method here.

1.   Download the latest release or stable build of Eclipse SDK from www.eclipse.org/downloads. There are different distributions for various platforms, and you need to choose the corresponding distribution file to the platform you are running.

2.   Decompress the release file. On Windows, you can use WinZip or Windows' built-in unzip utility to unzip the file; on Linux/Unix, try to run unzip eclipse-SDK-3.0xxx.zip. A folder named eclipse will be created. The complete Eclipse SDK is contained in this folder.

> **Later in this book, this folder is referred to as $ECLIPSE_HOME. When you meet $ECLIPSE_HOME, always replace it with your actual installation folder.**

3.   Check your Java runtime environment (JRE) version. On the download page of the Eclipse SDK, the minimum JRE is specified. Check your current JRE version by typing the following command: **java -version**. If there is no JRE installed in your system or you are using an unsupported version of JRE, you must download and install the latest JRE.

4.   Finally, test your installation by executing the file $ECLIPSE_HOME/eclipse[.exe]. On Windows, you can simply double-click the file. On Linux/Unix, type the file's complete file path to run it. You should see a flash window followed by the Eclipse IDE workbench.

*This book focuses on two major platforms: Windows and Linux. You can easily apply the knowledge to other platforms.*

# Configuring Your IDEs

SWT/JFace does not depend on the Eclipse workbench, so you do not have to use Eclipse as your Java IDE. Here, you learn how to configure your IDEs to develop SWT/JFace-based programs.

## Configure Eclipse

To configure Eclipse, follow these steps:

1.   Create a project if you do not have one yet. To create a project, open the Eclipse workbench and select File⇨New⇨Project from the menu. You can specify project settings in the new project wizard; be sure to create a Java Project.

**2.** Add SWT jars to your classpath. Right-click a Java Project, and select Properties. Select Java Build Path from the left panel of the Properties dialog. On the right panel, select the Libraries tab. Click Add External JARs to add SWT JAR files. To use SWT only, you need to add all the JAR files under the directory:

```
$ECLIPSE_HOME/
```

```
+-- plugins/
    +-- org.eclipse.swt.NATIVE_WINDOW_SYSTEM.x.x.x/
        +-- ws/
            +-- NATIVE_WINDOW_SYSTEM/
```

in which NATIVE_WINDOW_SYSTEM should be replaced by the name of the underlying native window system and x.x.x represents the version number.

For example, on Windows, there is only one JAR file, swt.jar, under the directory $ECLIPSE_HOME\ plugins\org.eclipse.swt.win32_3.0.0\ws\win32. However, on Linux, there are three files (Eclipse SDK, stable build 3.0M6) under directory $ECLIPSE_HOME/ plugins/org.eclipse.swt.gtk_3.0.0/ws/gtk: swt.jar, swt-mozilla.jar, and swt-pi.jar. As mentioned in previous chapters, SWT provides different sets of widget classes for each platform—thus the file swt.jar in the Windows distribution is completely different from its counterpart in other distributions. You should not use swt.jar in the Windows distribution on Linux because it will not work at all.

Now you have a clear understanding of which JAR files should be included. Adding those JAR files to the project's classpath is very straightforward. Click the Add External JARs button, and select the target JAR file. Then press OK; the JAR file appears in the build path as shown in Figure 3-1. Alternatively, you can use the Add Variable option.

To have more user-friendly content assist, you could attach the source code for the JAR files you added. The source files are located at the following directory:

```
$ECLIPSE_HOME/plugins/org.eclipse.platform.source.OPERATING_SYSTEM
.NATIVE_WINDOW_SYSTEM.ARCHITECTURE.x.x.x/src/org.eclipse.swt
.NATIVE_WINDOW_SYSTEM.x.x.x/ws/NATIVE_WINDOW_SYSTEM
```

On Windows, the SWT source directory is:

```
$ECLIPSE_HOME\plugins\org.eclipse.platform.source.win32.win32.x86_3.0.0\src\org.
eclipse.swt.win32_3.0.0\ws\win32
```

On Linux, it is:

```
$ECLIPSE_HOME\plugins\org.eclipse.platform.source.linux.gtk.x86_3.0.0\src\org.
eclipse.swt.gtk_3.0.0\ws\gtk
```

On the Libraries tab, click the plus sign to the right of a JAR file and select Source Attachment; then click Edit to locate its corresponding source file.

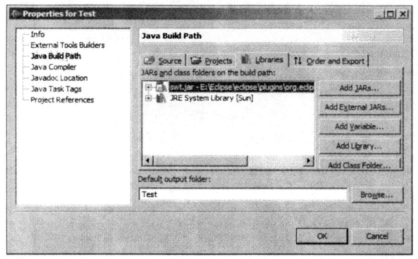

Figure 3-1

3.  Add JFace JAR files to your classpath if you need to use JFace besides SWT. The following are two main JAR files of JFace that you should add to your classpath:

```
$ECLIPSE_HOME/plugins/org.eclipse.jface_x.x.x/jface.jar
$ECLIPSE_HOME/plugins/org.eclipse.jface.text_x.x.x/jfacetext.jar
```

If you do not need to use any classes in the package org.eclipse.jface.text and its sub-packages, the second one can be omitted.

JFace is used heavily in Eclipse workbench UI. A few classes are required by jface.jar in the following JAR files:

```
$ECLIPSE_HOME/plugins/org.eclipse.text_x.x.x/text.jar
$ECLIPSE_HOME/plugins/org.eclipse.core.runtime_x.x.x/runtime.jar
$ECLIPSE_HOME/plugins/org.eclipse.core.boot_x.x.x/boot.jar
$ECLIPSE_HOME/plugins/org.apache.xerces_x.x.x/xercesImpl.jar
```

Let's call them "auxiliary JFace packages." You need to add them to your classpath also.

4.  Click OK to save your classpath setting and close the Properties dialog.

In addition to Eclipse, you can develop SWT/JFace-based programs on other IDEs.

## Configure JBuilder

Setting up the classpath in JBuilder is very similar to doing it in Eclipse:

1.  Create a project if you do not have one yet. To create a project, open the JBuilder IDE (JBuilder version: Enterprise 10.0) and select File⇨New Project from the menu. You can specify project settings in the new project wizard.

2.  Add SWT/JFace JAR files to the classpath of the project. The JAR files required are given in the last section. Right-click the project, and select Properties from the menu. On the tree in the left panel, select Paths. Select the Required Libraries tab at the bottom of the Paths panel. Click the Add button and a dialog pops up. Click New to create a new library set. In the new library wizard, specify the name for the library, such as SWT-JFace, and then click Add to add each of the JAR files required. Click OK to add the newly created library to the project, as shown in Figure 3-2.

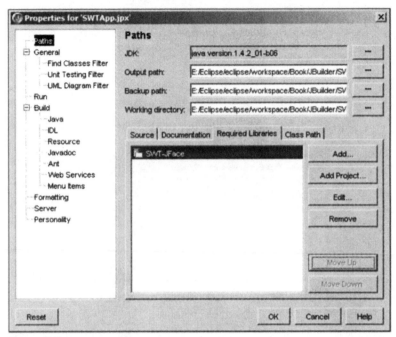

Figure 3-2

3.  Click OK in the Properties dialog to save your classpath setting and close the Properties dialog.

# Your First SWT Program

You have already set up your IDEs, and now you can develop your first SWT program.

## Coding Your First SWT Program: Hello World

The following code is probably the simplest SWT program. When it is executed, a window with the title "Hello, world!" pops up, as shown in Figure 3-3.

```
package com.asprise.swt.example.ch03;
import org.eclipse.swt.widgets.Display;
import org.eclipse.swt.widgets.Shell;
public class HelloWorld {
```

```
public static void main(String[] args) {
    Display display = new Display();
    Shell shell = new Shell(display);

    shell.setText("Hello, world!");

    shell.open();
    // Set up the event loop.
    while (!shell.isDisposed()) {
        if (!display.readAndDispatch()) {
            // If no more entries in the event queue
            display.sleep();
        }
    }
    display.dispose();
}
}
```

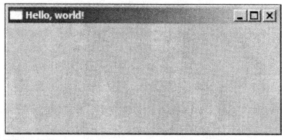

**Figure 3-3**

At the beginning of the main method, a Display object and a Shell object are created. The Display object is responsible for managing the connection between SWT and the underlying native window system. One of its primary functions is to implement the SWT event loop in terms of the platform event model. For almost all the SWT applications, only a single Display instance is required. The Shell object represents the window shown in Figure 3-3. The Shell object is linked to the Display object in the constructor. Once this linkage exists, you can get the Display from the Shell anytime with the getDisplay() method.

After the shell is created, set the window title by calling its setText method. Then open the shell by calling the open method, and a window appears immediately when this line is executed. Finally, set up an event loop to listen and react to events. When the user closes the window, the shell is disposed of and the event loop is broken. The program exits right after the disposal of the Display object.

*If you do not have any experience with native UI programming, you may be confused about the event loop. It simply reads and dispatches events. Details on the SWT event handling mechanism are covered thoroughly in Chapter 4.*

# Running Your First SWT Program

As you saw in previous chapters, SWT employs JNI mechanisms to communicate with the underlying native window systems. Before you run your SWT programs, make sure your JRE can find those native libraries that SWT depends on. Otherwise, you may encounter the following exception:

```
java.lang.UnsatisfiedLinkError: no swt-win32-3024 in java.library.path
    at java.lang.ClassLoader.loadLibrary(ClassLoader.java:1403)
    at java.lang.Runtime.loadLibrary0(Runtime.java:788)
    at java.lang.System.loadLibrary(System.java:832)
    at org.eclipse.swt.internal.Library.loadLibrary(Library.java:100)
    at org.eclipse.swt.internal.win32.OS.<clinit>(OS.java:46)
    at org.eclipse.swt.widgets.Display.internal_new_GC(Display.java:1411)
    at org.eclipse.swt.graphics.Device.init(Device.java:541)
    at org.eclipse.swt.widgets.Display.init(Display.java:1436)
    at org.eclipse.swt.graphics.Device.<init>(Device.java:96)
    at org.eclipse.swt.widgets.Display.<init>(Display.java:306)
    at org.eclipse.swt.widgets.Display.<init>(Display.java:302)
    at com.asprise.swt.example.ch03.HelloWorld.main(HelloWorld.java:21)
Exception in thread "main"
```

To avoid such exceptions, add the directory containing the required native libraries to your Java library path.

The native library required by SWT is located at the following directory (this directory will be referred to as $SWT_NATIVE_LIBRARY_PATH):

```
$ECLIPSE_HOME/
+-- plugins/
    +-- org.eclipse.swt.NATIVE_WINDOW_SYSTEM.x.x.x/
        +-- os/
            +-- OPERATING_SYSTEM/

                +-- ARCHITECTURE/
```

where NATIVE_WINDOW_SYSTEM, OPERATING_SYSTEM, and ARCHITECTURE represent the name of the underlying native window system, the name of the underlying operating system, and the name of the hardware architecture, respectively.

The native library directory for Windows (Windows on x86) is:

```
$ECLIPSE_HOME\plugins\org.eclipse.swt.win32_x.x.x\os\win32\x86
```

and its Linux counterpart (Linux on x86) is:

```
$ECLIPSE_HOME/plugins/org.eclipse.swt.gtk_x.x.x/os/linux/x86
```

You need to add the following virtual machine (VM) argument when you run SWT/JFace-based programs:

```
-Djava.library.path=$SWT_NATIVE_LIBRARY_PATH
```

If you need to run SWT programs from the Eclipse workbench, you can add the argument in the Run dialog, as shown in Figure 3-4.

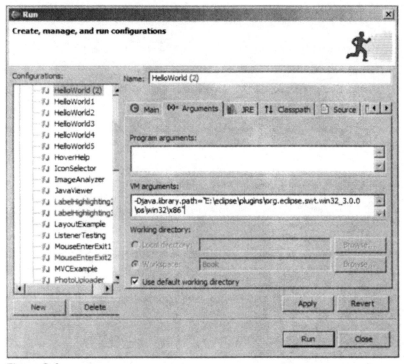

Figure 3-4

You can configure other IDEs in the same way.

*There are many other ways to add the SWT native library path to your Java library path. The most convenient approach is probably adding the SWT native library path to your platform-specific variables.*

**On Windows: Adding the SWT native library path to the PATH variable.** *Right-click the My Computer icon and select Properties from the menu, and the System Properties dialog appears. Select the Advanced tab and click the Environment Variables button to append the SWT native library path to the PATH variable.*

**On Linux: Adding the SWT native library path to the $LD_LIBRARY_PATH variable.** *Execute the following commands:*

*[Bash Shell] >* **export** *LD_LIBRARY_PATH=YOUR_SWT_NATIVE_LIB_PATH*

*[C Shell] >* **setenv** *LD_LIBRARY_PATH YOUR_SWT_NATIVE_LIB_PATH*

*You can append these commands to the startup files of the corresponding shells to set the variable automatically on each subsequent login. If you take this approach, you do not have to specify the SWT native library path whenever you run an SWT/JFace-based application.*

## *Creating a Bigger Application — Temperature Converter*

The Hello World program does nothing but print the window title. Let's create some practical application with SWT. Here, you are going to create a temperature converter that can convert temperature readings in Fahrenheit into their Celsius equivalents and vice versa. The GUI of this application is shown in Figure 3-5. When a user types a temperature reading in the Fahrenheit text field, its equivalent Celsius value will be displayed in the Celsius text field. The same mechanism applies to Celsius-to-Fahrenheit conversion.

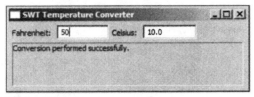

**Figure 3-5**

First, declare the class and all widget controls to be used:

```
...

import org.eclipse.swt.widgets.Button;
import org.eclipse.swt.widgets.Display;
import org.eclipse.swt.widgets.Label;
import org.eclipse.swt.widgets.Shell;
import org.eclipse.swt.widgets.Text;
/**
 *
 */
public class TemperatureConverter {
    Display display = new Display();
    Shell shell = new Shell(display);

    Label fahrenheitLabel;
    Label celsiusLabel;
Label messageLabel;

    Text fahrenheitValue;
    Text celsiusValue;
```

SWT classes such as Button and Label share the same names with their AWT counterparts. One of the common mistakes is using AWT components in SWT programs. So make sure you import widgets from SWT/JFace packages instead of AWT packages.

For this application, you put all the GUI construction code in the constructor:

```
    public TemperatureConverter() {
        shell.setText("Temperature Converter");
        shell.setLayout(new RowLayout());
        fahrenheitLabel = new Label(shell, SWT.NULL);
```

```
        fahrenheitLabel.setText("Fahrenheit: ");

        fahrenheitValue = new Text(shell, SWT.SINGLE | SWT.BORDER);

        celsiusLabel = new Label(shell, SWT.NULL);
        celsiusLabel.setText("Celsius: ");

        celsiusValue = new Text(shell, SWT.SINGLE | SWT.BORDER);

        messageLabel = new Label(shell, SWT.BORDER);
        GridData gridData = new GridData(GridData.FILL_BOTH);
        gridData.horizontalSpan = 4;
        messageLabel.setLayoutData(gridData);

        ModifyListener listener = new ModifyListener() {
            public void modifyText(ModifyEvent e) {
                valueChanged((Text)e.widget);
            }
        };

        fahrenheitValue.addModifyListener(listener);
        celsiusValue.addModifyListener(listener);
        shell.pack();
        shell.open();
        while (!shell.isDisposed()) {
            if (!display.readAndDispatch()) {
                display.sleep();
            }
        }
        display.dispose();
    }
```

At the beginning of the constructor, you set the title of the shell and its layout. A layout defines a positioning algorithm applying to the children of a composite whenever it's resized. Here, you set a RowLayout instance as the shell's layout. The RowLayout class is a layout placing all the child widgets either in horizontal rows or vertical columns with the composite. Chapter 6 is dedicated to SWT layouts.

After the layout of the shell has been set, you can add all the widgets that you need. To do that, you simply put the shell as the first argument in constructors of those widgets. The style of a widget can usually be specified in the second argument. A label is added to the shell to display status information.

To enable the application and react to the user's input, you need to use event listeners to listen to interested events and react accordingly. In this application, you need to listen to text modification events generated from both text fields. A ModifyListener is created and registered to both text fields to listen to modification events. When the user modifies the content of any of the text fields, the function modifyText in the listener will be called with a ModifyEvent object. Then the function makes a call to the custom function valueChanged.

Finally, you open the shell and set up the event loop.

The following code lists the method `valueChanged`:

```
/**
 * Performs conversion when one of the text fields changes.
 *
 * @param text
 *              the event source
 */
public void valueChanged(Text text) {
    if (!text.isFocusControl())
        return;
    if (text == fahrenheitValue) {
        try {
            double fValue = Double.parseDouble(text.getText());
            double cValue = (fValue - 32) / 1.8;
            celsiusValue.setText(Double.toString(cValue));
            messageLabel.setText("Conversion performed successfully.");
        } catch (NumberFormatException e) {
            celsiusValue.setText("");
            messageLabel.setText("Invalid number format: " +
                text.getText());
        }
    } else {
        try {
            double cValue = Double.parseDouble(text.getText());
            double fValue = cValue * 1.8 + 32;
            fahrenheitValue.setText(Double.toString(fValue));
            messageLabel.setText("Conversion performed successfully.");
        } catch (NumberFormatException e) {
            fahrenheitValue.setText("");
            messageLabel.setText("Invalid number format: " +
                text.getText());
        }
    }
}
```

The `valueChanged` method is quite easy to understand. It first detects which text field is the event source. If the event source is the Fahrenheit text field, it tries to perform Fahrenheit-to-Celsius conversion and the calculated value will be put into the Celsius text field; otherwise, it performs Celsius-to-Fahrenheit conversion and puts the calculated value into the Fahrenheit text field.

When a `Text`'s `setText` is called programmatically, the `Text` generates a `ModifyEvent`. The current focus control check at the beginning of the `valueChanged` method helps to prevent the event handling deadlock.

To launch the application, simply using the following `main` method:

```
public static void main(String[] args) {
    new TemperatureConverter();
}
```

# Rewriting the Temperature Converter with JFace

In the previous section, you created your first few SWT-based programs. Now rewrite the temperature converter application using JFace to see how JFace can make your life easier.

First, review the code (`TemperatureConverterJFace.java`):

```java
import org.eclipse.jface.action.StatusLineManager;
import org.eclipse.jface.window.ApplicationWindow;
...
public class TemperatureConverterJFace extends ApplicationWindow {
    Label fahrenheitLabel;
    Label celsiusLabel;
    Text fahrenheitValue;
    Text celsiusValue;

    public TemperatureConverterJFace() {
        super(null);

        addStatusLine();
    }
```

The first thing you may notice is that the `TemperatureConverterJFace` class is inherited from the `org.eclipse.jface.window.ApplicationWindow` class. An `ApplicationWindow` instance is a high-level "main window," which has built-in support for an optional menu bar, an optional toolbar, and an optional status line. It also wraps the event loop inside itself. In the constructor of the `TemperatureConverterJFace` class, a `null` parent is passed to the super class's constructor, indicating that this window is a top-level window. The `addStatusLines` method adds a status line to the window for the purpose of displaying messages.

In order to add temperature conversion widgets to the window, you need to override the `createContents` method:

```java
/* (non-Javadoc)
 * @see org.eclipse.jface.window.Window#createContents(Composite)
 */
protected Control createContents(Composite parent) {
    getShell().setText("JFace Temperature Converter");

    Composite converterComposite = new Composite(parent, SWT.NULL);

    converterComposite.setLayout(new GridLayout(4, false));
    fahrenheitLabel = new Label(converterComposite, SWT.NULL);
    fahrenheitLabel.setText("Fahrenheit: ");
    fahrenheitValue = new Text(converterComposite, SWT.SINGLE | SWT.BORDER);
    celsiusLabel = new Label(converterComposite, SWT.NULL);
    celsiusLabel.setText("Celsius: ");
    celsiusValue = new Text(converterComposite, SWT.SINGLE | SWT.BORDER);
    ModifyListener listener = new ModifyListener() {
        public void modifyText(ModifyEvent e) {
            valueChanged((Text) e.widget);
        }
```

```
        };
        fahrenheitValue.addModifyListener(listener);
        celsiusValue.addModifyListener(listener);

        return converterComposite;
    }
```

The preceding GUI-building code is very similar to that used in the SWT version of the temperature converter. The method createContents(Composite parent) will be called after all other widgets (optional menus, toolbars, status line, and so on) have been created and before the window is opened. The parent argument passed is the shell instance representing the window. The expected return type for this method is Control. If you need to add multiple widgets, you should create a top-level composite containing all the widgets and return the composite, as shown in the preceding code.

The event listener registration procedure is the same as that using SWT. There are some minor changes in the valueChanged method:

```
/**
 * Performs conversion when one of the text fields changes.
 *
 * @param text
 *            the event source
 */
public void valueChanged(Text text) {
    if (!text.isFocusControl())
        return;
    if (text == fahrenheitValue) {
        try {
            double fValue = Double.parseDouble(text.getText());
            double cValue = (fValue - 32) / 1.8;
            celsiusValue.setText(Double.toString(cValue));
            setStatus("Conversion performed successfully.");
        } catch (NumberFormatException e) {
            celsiusValue.setText("");
            setStatus("Invalid number format: " + text.getText());
        }
    } else {
        try {
            double cValue = Double.parseDouble(text.getText());
            double fValue = cValue * 1.8 + 32;
            fahrenheitValue.setText(Double.toString(fValue));
            setStatus("Conversion performed successfully.");
        } catch (NumberFormatException e) {
            fahrenheitValue.setText("");
            setStatus("Invalid number format: " + text.getText());
        }
    }
}
```

The setStatus method in ApplicationWindow is used to set the message to be displayed on the status line. In the SWT version, you create a Label object and use its setText method; here, the ApplicationWindow manages this for you.

The GUI of this JFace implementation (as shown in Figure 3-6) is more appealing than that of the SWT implementation, especially the status line part.

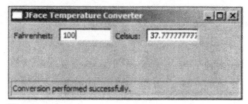

**Figure 3-6**

Besides the status line, ApplicationWindow can help you to simplify other common tasks such as menu creation and toolbar creation, which is covered in later chapters.

# SWT/JFace Software Deployment with Java Web Start

You have completed your SWT/JFace applications; now it's time for you to deploy those applications to the end users. Here, you learn how to use Java Web Start to deploy your applications to multiple platforms.

## Introduction to Java Web Start

The Java Web Start technology provides a robust and flexible deployment solution for Java applications. With Java Web Start, you can deploy your applications through the Web easily. When a user clicks a link to a special Java Network Launch Protocol (JNLP) file, this brings up the Java Web Start software, which then automatically detects the current running environment and downloads, caches, and runs the given Java application.

To download Java Web Start software and to find more details on the topic, please visit Sun's Java Web Start home page at http://java.sun.com/products/javawebstart.

To deploy your SWT/JFace-based applications with Java Web Start, simply follow four steps:

1. Identify files to be deployed.
2. Package and sign files.
3. Write the JNLP script.
4. Upload the files to your Web server and test.

Let's deploy the JFace implementation of the temperature converter to Windows (Windows 98, NT, ME, XP) and Linux step by step.

## Identifying Files to be Deployed

The files to be deployed include the `TemperatureConverterJFace` class file and the required SWT/JFace packages and SWT native libraries, as shown in the following table.

| File Type | Target Platforms | |
|---|---|---|
| | **Windows** | **Linux** |
| Application code | `TemperatureConverterJFace.class` | |
| Main JFace library | `$ECLIPSE_HOME/plugins/org.eclipse.jface_x.x.x/jface.jar` | |
| Auxiliary JFace libraries | `ECLIPSE_HOME/plugins/org.eclipse.core.runtime_x.x.x/runtime.jar`<br>`$ECLIPSE_HOME/plugins/org.eclipse.core.boot_x.x.x/boot.jar` | |
| SWT library | `$ECLIPSE_HOME\ plugins\`<br>`org.eclipse.swt.win32_`<br>`3.0.0\ws\win32\*.jar` | `$ECLIPSE_HOME/plugins/`<br>`org.eclipse.swt.gtk_`<br>`3.0.0/ws/gtk/*.jar` |
| SWT native library | `$ECLIPSE_HOME\plugins\`<br>`org.eclipse.swt.win32_`<br>`x.x.x\os\win32\x86\*.dll` | `$ECLIPSE_HOME/plugins/`<br>`org.eclipse.swt.gtk_`<br>`x.x.x/os/linux/x86/*.os` |

Note: *.jar, *.dll, and *.os represent all the JAR files, DLL files, and OS files, respectively, under the specified directory.

Note that in the preceding table, not all the auxiliary JFace packages are included. Some of the auxiliary packages are not required by this simple application; you can omit them to reduce the total size of the deployment files. If you are not sure whether an auxiliary package is required or not, you should include it to avoid possible `ClassNotFound` exceptions.

## Packaging and Signing Files

According to the Java Web Start Specification, applications with unsigned JAR files are restricted to run in a secure sandbox, which prevents them from calling native libraries. Because the temperature converter application depends on the SWT native libraries, you have to sign all the files to remove this restriction.

The Java Web Start Specification requires that all applications be delivered as a set of JAR files, so you have to package non-JAR files into a set of JAR files. Because the Java libraries of SWT/JFace are already in the JAR format, there are only two kinds of files you need to pack up into JAR files:

❑ **Your application code (Java classes, property files, and resource files):** Most IDEs export these into JAR files or you can use the `jar` command. For the temperature converter application, you need to pack the class file into a JAR file (`tc.jar`):

```
jar cf tc.jar CLASS_OUTPUT_DIRECTORY
```

❑ **Native libraries:** Similarly, you can put all the required native libraries into one or more JARs:

```
[Windows] jar cf swt-native-lib-win32.jar
$ECLIPSE_WIN32_HOME\plugins\org.eclipse.swt.win32_x.x.x\os\win32\x86\*.dll
[Linux] jar cf swt-native-lib-linux.jar
$ECLIPSE_LINUX_HOME/plugins/org.eclipse.swt.gtk_x.x.x/os/linux/x86/*.os
```

You need to download and unzip both Windows and Linux releases of Eclipse SDK regardless of the type of operating system you're running. In the preceding commands, `$ECLIPSE_WIN32_HOME` and `$ECLIPSE_LINUX_HOME` represent the home directories of the Eclipse SDK Windows release and the Linux release, respectively.

Now all the files to be deployed are packed, as shown in the following table.

| File Type | Target Platforms | |
|---|---|---|
| | **Windows** | **Linux** |
| Application code | `ct.jar` | |
| Main JFace library | `$ECLIPSE_HOME/plugins/org.eclipse.jface_x.x.x/jface.jar` | |
| Auxiliary JFace libraries | `$ECLIPSE_HOME/plugins/org.eclipse.core.runtime_x.x.x/` `runtime.jar` `$ECLIPSE_HOME/plugins/org.eclipse.core.boot_x.x.x/boot.jar` | |
| SWT library | `$ECLIPSE_HOME\plugins\` `org.eclipse.swt.win32_` `3.0.0\ws\win32\*.jar` | `$ECLIPSE_HOME/plugins/` `org.eclipse.swt.gtk_` `3.0.0/ws/gtk/*.jar` |
| SWT native library | `swt-native-lib-win32.jar` | `swt-native-lib-linux.jar` |

Now, you can digitally sign the JAR files. Signing files lets people know that you are the genuine distributor of the files. You need a public key, a private key, and a certificate to sign files. If you do not have them yet, you can use the following command to create a dummy set of public key, private key, and certificate using Sun's keytool:

```
keytool -genkey -alias dummy -validity 10000 -keypass dummypass -storepass
dummypass -keystore dummy.keystore -dname "CN=Dummy, OU=Dummy, O=D, L=CA, S=CA,
C=US"
```

The preceding command creates a public key, a private key, and a self-signed certificate in the file `dummy.keystore`. However, I recommend that you obtain a certificate from a certificate authority and that you use it in production.

Now, you can sign each JAR file using the `jarsigner` tool:

```
jarsigner -keystore dummy.keystore -storepass dummypass -keypass dummypass
$JAR_FILE dummy
```

# Writing the JNLP Script

Now, all the files are ready to be deployed. You can arrange the files into the following structure:

```
javaui [Dir]
+-- tc [Dir]
    +-- boot.jar
    +-- jface.jar
    +-- runtime.jar
    +-- tc.jar
    +-- linux [Dir]
        +-- swt.jar (Linux version of SWT library)
        +-- swt-pi.jar
        +-- swt-native-lib-win32.jar (SWT native libraries for Linux)
    +-- win32 [Dir]
        +-- swt.jar (Windows version of SWT library)

        +-- swt-native-lib-win32.jar (SWT native libraries for Windows)
```

Let's write a JNLP script that will be used to inform the Java Web Start software on the client machines about the temperature converter application. Such details such as the title and vendor of the application, required resources, and main class are included in the JNLP script as follows:

```xml
<?xml version="1.0" encoding="utf-8"?>
<!-- JNLP File for Temperature Converter Application --->
<jnlp
  spec="1.0+"
  codebase="http://www.asprise.com/javaui/tc"
  href="tc.jnlp">
  <information>
    <title>Temperature Converter</title>
    <vendor>Jack Li Guojie</vendor>
    <homepage href="index.html"/>
    <description>A simple temperature converter</description>
    <description kind="short">A simple temperature converter implemented in
JFace</description>
    <icon href="temperature.gif"/>
    <offline-allowed/>
  </information>
```

The top-level element in a JNLP file is `<jnlp>`. In the preceding code, specify the following attributes:

❑ spec: The JNLP specification version

❑ codebase: The base for all relative URLs specified in the href attribute

❑ href: The URL pointing to the JNLP file itself

The information element is used to provide information about the application, such as its title, description, and icon.

Next, request the Java Web Start software to grant the application all the permissions:

```
<security>
    <all-permissions/>
</security>
```

Then, tell the Java Web Start software which files are needed to run the application:

```
<resources>
  <j2se version="1.4.0"/>
  <jar href="tc.jar"/>
  <jar href="boot.jar"/>
  <jar href="runtime.jar"/>
  <jar href="jface.jar"/>
</resources>
<resources os="Windows">
  <jar href="win32/swt.jar"/>
  <nativelib href="win32/swt-native-lib-win32.jar"/>
</resources>
<resources os="Linux">
  <jar href="linux/swt.jar"/>
  <jar href="linux/swt-pi.jar"/>
  <nativelib href="linux/swt-native-lib-linux.jar"/>
</resources>
```

The first resources element, which has no attributes specified, specifies all the shared code across all kinds of platforms. The second resources element specifies extra files required on the Windows platform. Similarly, the last resources element indicates extra files required on the Linux platform. The Java Web Start software uses this information to determine the file set to be downloaded.

Finally, you need to tell the Java Web Start software your main class to start the application:

```
<application-desc
    main-class="com.asprise.book.javaui.ch03.TemperatureConverterJFace"/>
</jnlp>
```

Now, you are ready to upload all the files to your Web server.

## Uploading and Running

First, you need to configure your Web server to recognize JNLP files by adding the following MIME type to the Web server's configuration files:

```
application/x-java-jnlp-file JNLP
```

You can let the user point directly to the absolute path of the JNLP file or you can use a launch HTML file. The latter is more user-friendly. You can create a launch page that's as simple as the following:

```
<!DOCTYPE html PUBLIC "-//W3C//DTD HTML 4.01 Transitional//EN">
<html>
<head>
```

```
    <title></title>
  </head>
  <body>
  Click <a href="tc.jnlp">here</a> to launch Temperature
  Converter.
  </body>
  </html>
```

Save this HTML file as index.html and put it with the JNLP file tc.jnlp under the directory javaui/tc. Upload the whole javaui directory to your Web server.

Now you can visit the launch page at www.asprise.com/javaui/tc/index.html. Click the link to launch the JNLP file. The Java Web Start software downloads and parses the JNLP file for information and resources about the application. After all the information is obtained, it starts to download required files, as shown in Figure 3-7.

Figure 3-7

After all the required resources are downloaded, the Java Web Start software tries to start the application. First a warning message complaining that the certificate cannot be authenticated (because you used a dummy certificate) appears, as shown in Figure 3-8. Click Start to start the application.

Figure 3-8

65

The Windows application runs properly, as shown in Figure 3-8. Figure 3-9 shows the application deployed on Linux.

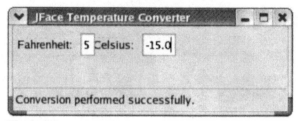

Figure 3-9

# Summary

This chapter helped you to jump start programming with SWT/JFace. First, you need to download and install the SWT/JFace library. After obtaining the library, you need to configure your favorite Java IDE (Eclipse, JBuilder, and so on) to add SWT/JFace library jars into Java path. Then you can start coding your SWT/JFace-based programs. Creating SWT-based programs is very straightforward; you can use a `Display` object to open a window (represented by the `Shell` class). Alternatively, you can develop JFace-based programs. Because JFace handles many common UI tasks, the code length is likely to be reduced. After you write and test your programs, you are ready to deploy them. The Java Web Start technology is becoming more and more popular. The last part of this chapter guides you to deploy your programs to multiple platforms using Java Web Start.

An event loop always exists in an SWT program. The next chapter demystifies the event loop and explains SWT event handling mechanisms.

# SWT Event Handling, Threading, and Displays

This chapter introduces SWT event handling, multiple threading, and the event model in SWT. The Display class, which plays the most important role in SWT event handling, is introduced as well.

SWT's event handling is quite different from that of Swing. Even the simplest SWT application requires a certain amount of code to manage event loop explicitly. The first few questions from developers with a Swing background are usually about the "mystery" event loop, which is why you should read this chapter before you move on to the more advanced material. After you are comfortable with SWT event handling, you can continue on your SWT journey. If you need to know more about event handling and threading, refer back to this chapter. Finally, you learn how to listen and react to various SWT events using either a typed or untyped model.

## SWT Event Handling Fundamentals

This section first introduces the native event handling mechanism, and then it shows how SWT handles events with Display objects.

### Native Event Handling Mechanism

For all kinds of GUI applications, regardless of programming languages and user interface toolkits, the underlying operating system is responsible for detecting GUI events and placing them into appropriate event queues. GUI events include events such as mouse movements, mouse clicks, keystrokes, window repaint, and so on. For example, when a user clicks a mouse button, the operating system generates an event representing this mouse click. It then determines which application should accept this event and places the event in the target application's event queue.

How does the GUI application handle events? Any GUI application utilizes an event loop to detect the GUI event from the event queue and react appropriately. This event loop plays a critical role in GUI applications. Without an event loop, a GUI application terminates immediately when the main function exits.

Most C programmers are very familiar with this event loop. However, Swing developers are rather new to this mechanism. The Swing toolkit shields the event loop from programmers. In Swing, a dedicated toolkit user interface (UI) thread is used to read and dispatch events from the event loop and redirect events to an internal maintained queue, which is serviced by the application running in separate threads.

## SWT Event Handling Basics

SWT follows the threading model supported directly by the platform. The application manages the event loop in its user interface thread and dispatches events from the same thread.

So why doesn't SWT use toolkit UI threads as Swing does to shield event loops from developers? There are two main reasons why SWT uses the threading model directly:

❑ First, from the performance perspective, the threading model is more efficient than the toolkit UI thread model. Most operating systems perform considerable optimizations with the event queue. For the toolkit UI thread model, the toolkit UI thread pulls the events off the queue so fast that event optimizations are almost impossible. This could be one of the reasons that SWT is faster than Swing.

❑ Second, because SWT is built on JNI, it would be very difficult to debug and to diagnose problems if GUI event processing depends on the Java threading implementation. (Note: On different platforms, the Java threading implementations vary.)

For these reasons, SWT uses the threading model instead of the toolkit UI thread model. Developers have to manage event loops explicitly in all SWT applications. The Display plays the most important role in event handling, and I will introduce it before discussing event handling further.

## Using Displays

Display instances act as the middleware, responsible for managing the connection between SWT and underlying native operating systems. The Display class is in the package org.eclipse.swt.widgets. For those who are familiar with the X Windows system, a Display instance is equivalent to an X Windows display. The primary functions of Display instances are as follows:

❑ Implementing the SWT event loop in terms of a platform event model

❑ Providing methods for accessing information about the operating system

❑ Managing operating system resources used by SWT

Only a single Display instance is required in most SWT-based applications. Furthermore, some platforms do not allow more than one active display — a display that has not been disposed of.

### Accessing Operating System Information

Besides event handling, the Display class provides several methods for you to access information about the underlying operating system. The functions of these methods are as follows:

- ❑  void beep(): Causes the system hardware to emit a short sound if it supports this capability.

- ❑  Rectangle getBounds(): Returns a rectangle describing the display's size and location. For instance, on a $1024 \times 768$ resolution Windows system, getBounds returns Rectangle {0, 0, 1024, 768}.

- ❑  Rectangle getClientArea(): Returns a rectangle describing the area of the display that is capable of displaying data. The client area can be the same size as the bounds area, although this is not always true.

- ❑  int getDismissalAlignment(): Returns the button dismissal alignment; can be either SWT.LEFT or SWT.RIGHT. The button dismissal alignment is the ordering that should be used when positioning the default dismissal button for a dialog. For instance, for a dialog containing OK and CANCEL buttons, on platforms where the button dismissal alignment is LEFT, the button order should be OK, CANCEL; on RIGHT-aligned button dismissal platforms, this order is reversed.

- ❑  int getDoubleClickTime(): Returns the longest duration in milliseconds between two mouse button clicks that will be deemed a double-click by the operating system.

- ❑  int getIconDepth(): Returns the maximum allowed depth of icons on the display.

- ❑  Monitor[] getMonitors(): Returns all the monitors attached to the device. To find the primary monitor, call getPrimaryMonitor.

- ❑  Color getSystemColor(int id): Returns the matching standard color for the given constant, which should be one of the color constants specified in class SWT. If it is not a constant defined in SWT, the returning color will be black. Notice that the returned color should not be freed because it was allocated and managed by the system.

- ❑  Font getSystemFont(): Returns a reasonable font for the application to use.

## SWT Event Handling with Displays

Earlier in this chapter, I discussed the basic SWT event-handling mechanism. Here, you get a detailed look at how it works with the following sample code extracted from the "Hello, World" example from the last chapter.

```
public static void main(String[] args) {
  Display display = new Display();
  Shell shell = new Shell(display);
  shell.setText("Hello, world!");
  shell.open();

  while(! shell.isDisposed()) { // Event loop.
      if(! display.readAndDispatch())
        display.sleep();
  }
  display.dispose();
}
```

When you run the "Hello, World" example, a thread is required to execute these instructions; I'll call this thread the user interface (UI) thread. (Strictly speaking, the UI thread is the thread that creates the `Display` instance.) The UI thread first creates the `Display` object, and then it creates and displays the shell. After the shell has been displayed, the UI thread reaches the event loop. It constantly checks whether the shell has been disposed of. If the shell has been disposed of, then it disposes of the display instance and releases all the associated operating system resources. Otherwise, the UI thread reads and dispatches GUI events by calling the method `display.readAndDispatch`.

The flow of the event loop is illustrated in Figure 4-1.

The `readAndDispatch` method of the `Display` class reads events from the operating system's event queue and then dispatches them appropriately. Besides events, this method also checks and dispatches inter-thread messages. I discuss the inter-thread messaging in subsequent sections. The `readAndDispatch` method returns `true` if there is potentially more work to do or `false` if the caller (the UI thread) can sleep upon return from it.

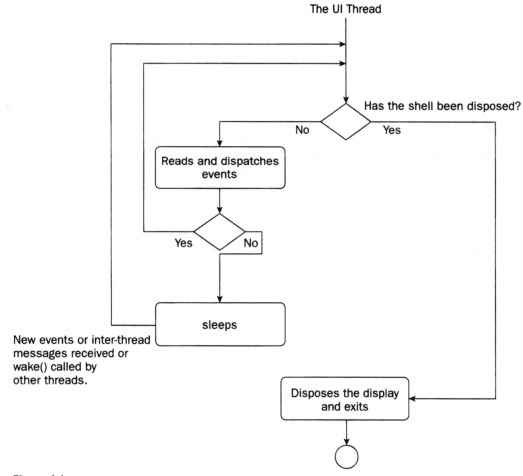

**Figure 4-1**

The UI thread can sleep (be placed in a state that it does not consume CPU cycles) if there are no more tasks to perform. The `Display.sleep` method causes the UI thread to sleep until an event is queued or it is awakened.

Suppose the shell has been displayed; the user can terminate this sample application by closing the shell. An event will be sent to the event queue when the user closes the shell. The UI thread will be awakened if it is sleeping, and it will read the event and dispatch the event. In this case, `shell.dispose()` will be called. The event loop breaks because the shell has been disposed—`shell.isDisposed()` returns `true`.

Finally, `display.dipose()` disposes of all the native operating system resources used and disconnects the display instance from the underlying native window system. Note that in all modern operating systems, exiting to the operating system releases all resources acquired by the process, so it is not necessary to dispose of the display object as long as the program exits. However, it is always good to remember disposal of resources that you acquired, so the line is kept to remind you of disposing of acquired resources.

# Multithreaded UI Programming

Multithreading helps to make UI responsive. In SWT, you can use various methods provided by the `Display` class to execute tasks in separate threads.

## Multithreading with the UI Thread and Non-UI threads

The last section illustrated the event handling mechanism. The UI thread is responsible for reading and dispatching events from the operating system event queue, and invoking listeners in response to these events. All the listener code is executed in this UI thread. A long operation executed by a listener will run in the UI thread and block it from reading and dispatching events—thus the application hangs.

A common solution to this problem is to fork another thread to perform the operation and update the user interface. However, SWT does not allow non-UI threads to access user interface components directly.

> **Only the UI thread (the thread that creates the display) is allowed to perform all of the UI-related calls. If a non-UI thread tries to make calls that must be made from the UI thread, an SWTException is thrown.**

Let's look at an example that calculates the value of π (PI, the ratio of a circle's circumference to its diameter). Figure 4-2 shows the user interface of the sample application.

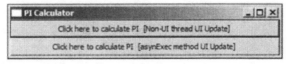

Figure 4-2

Because the calculation of PI's value may take considerable time, obviously, it should be put in a separate thread. Programmers familiar with Swing could rush to the following code:

```
Button buttonThread = new Button(shell, SWT.PUSH);

buttonThread.addSelectionListener(new SelectionListener() {
  public void widgetDefaultSelected(SelectionEvent e) { }
  public void widgetSelected(SelectionEvent e) {
    buttonThread.setText("Calculation in progress ...");
      getTask(buttonThread).start();
  }
});

public Thread getTask(Button button) {
  final Button theButton = button;
  return new Thread() {
      public void run() {
          double pi = calculatePI(9999999);
          theButton.setText("PI = " + pi); // Updates UI.
      }
  };
}
```

The first line creates a button, and the next few lines add a selection listener to the button. When the button is clicked, the widgetSelected method in the listener will be called. This method starts a new thread obtained from the getTask method. This non-UI thread calculates the value of PI, and updates the button's text with calculated PI value.

The above describes how the application works. Everything seems logical, but when you run it, the following exception is thrown:

```
org.eclipse.swt.SWTException: Invalid thread access
    at org.eclipse.swt.SWT.error(SWT.java:2369)
    at org.eclipse.swt.SWT.error(SWT.java:2299)
    at org.eclipse.swt.widgets.Widget.error(Widget.java:388)
    at org.eclipse.swt.widgets.Widget.checkWidget(Widget.java:318)
    at org.eclipse.swt.widgets.Button.setText(Button.java:607)
    at com.asprise.swt.example.PICalculator$3.run(PICalculator.java:92)
    at java.lang.Thread.run(Thread.java:536)
```

This exception is thrown because the newly created thread tries to update the UI, and this operation can be performed only by the UI thread. Non-UI threads can request the UI thread to perform UI calls only on behalf of themselves. The right way to perform this lengthy operation is as follows.

```
Button buttonAsyncExec = new Button(shell, SWT.PUSH);

buttonAsyncExec.addSelectionListener(new SelectionListener() {
    public void widgetDefaultSelected(SelectionEvent e) {
    }
```

```
        public void widgetSelected(SelectionEvent e) {
            buttonAsyncExec.setText("Calculation in progress ...");
            getTask2(buttonAsyncExec).start();
        }
});

public Thread getTask2(Button button) {
    final Button theButton = button;
    return new Thread() {
        public void run() {
            final double pi = calculatePI(9999999);

            display.asyncExec(new Runnable() {
                public void run() {
                theButton.setText("PI = " + pi);
                }
            });
        }
    };
}
```

Instead of directly making UI calls in the non-UI thread, you simply pass a Runnable instance to the asyncExec method of the display. The Runnable instance is put into the inter-thread message queue, and the UI thread checks this queue and executes the run method of the Runnable object. Now the code can be properly executed without any exceptions thrown. The asyncExec method is explained in detail shortly. For the complete list of code, please refer to the sample program PICalculator.java.

Some Swing developers may feel it is stupid that only one thread can access the UI calls. Actually, there is a good reason for this — most UI calls are not thread-safe. (Code is thread-safe if it works without any problem even if many threads execute it simultaneously.) When two threads try to access the same UI calls, this may result in a crash or a deadlock. It is true that Swing does allow any thread to access UI calls. However, this does not mean that Swing UI calls are all thread-safe — in fact, most of Swing UI calls are *not* thread-safe. We have encountered several problems arising from multithreads accessing UI calls in some of our Swing projects. Even in Swing, safe updates to components must be executed within the UI thread. In Swing, safe multithread UI programming must follow the same rule: only the UI thread should make most of the UI calls. Swing provides a help class javax.swing.SwingUtilities that allows Runnable instances to be put in a queue and the UI thread then executes them. The invokeLater method of SwingUtilities is the Swing counterpart of the method asyncExec used in the preceding code. To summarize then: Swing allows any thread to access UI calls at the risk of crashes and deadlocks; SWT allows only the UI thread to make most UI calls. In both frameworks, safe multithread UI programming requires that only the UI thread should make UI calls, and there are some methods by which non-UI threads can delegate their UI calls to the UI thread.

> *Putting the time-consuming operation and UI updating procedures altogether into the **run()** method of the **Runnable** instance passed to the **asyncExec(syncExec, timerExec)** method is actually no different than executing everything in the UI thread. Remember that the **Runnable** instance passed to asyncExec is not used to create a new thread. **asyncExec** simply calls its **run()** method. Many developers often make this mistake, so it is good to create a small pattern about it.*

## *SWT Time-Consuming Operation UI Pattern*

The follow pseudo-code illustrates how to run time-consuming operations in a separate thread and update the UI after finishing:

```
Thread operationThread = new Thread() {
    public void run() { // Override the method.
        // Your time-consuming operations go here
        ...

        // Update UI.
        display.asyncExec/syncExec(new Runnable() {
            public void run() {

                // UI Updating procedures go here ...

            }
        });
    }
};

operationThread.start();
```

# *Thread-Safe UI calls*

Most UI calls can be accessed only through the UI thread; however, a few UI calls are accessible for all kinds of threads. Methods `asyncExec`, `syncExec`, and `timerExec` are used for inter-thread messaging between non-UI threads and the UI thread. The `wake` method can be called from any thread to wake up the sleeping UI thread.

## *asyncExec*

Syntax:

```
public void asyncExec(Runnable runnable)
```

This method takes a `Runnable` object as the argument. It causes the `run` method of the `Runnable` instance to be executed by the UI thread at the next reasonable opportunity. This method returns immediately. The caller thread continues to run in parallel, and is not notified when the `run` method of the `Runnable` instance has completed. Note that by calling this method there is no guaranteed relationship between the timing of the background thread and the executing of the `Runnable` instance. If UI access must be finished before the non-UI thread continues its execution, `syncExec` should be used instead. The Swing counterpart of `asyncExec` is `SwingUtilities.invokeLater()`.

### When to Use It

Use `asyncExec` when you have a background thread to perform a lengthy operation and the GUI needs to be updated. For example, the following code sample shows a background thread downloading a file and continuously updating a progress indicator:

```
Thread downloadThread = new Thread() {
  Runnable runnable;
  double ratio;

  public void run() {
    int fileSize = 0;
    int currentDownloaded = 0;

    ... // Determine file size here
    while(currentDownloaded < fileSize) {
      // Download part of the file
      currentDownloaded += downloadFilePart();

      ratio = currentDownloaded * 1.0 / fileSize;

      // update the progress indicator.
      if(runnable == null)  // Lazy initialization
        runnable = new Runnable() {
          public void run() {
            progressBar.setSelection((int)(ratio*100));
          }

      display.asyncExec(runnable);
    }
  }
}

downloadThread.start();
```

*You do not have to create a new **Runnable** instance every time you need to call **asyncExec** or **syncExec**. Reusing **Runnable** instances can save a lot of object creation overheads.*

## syncExec

Syntax:

```
public void syncExec(Runnable runnable)
```

This method is very similar to asynExec, except that the calling thread will be blocked (suspended) until the UI thread has completed the execution of the Runnable instance. Its Swing counterpart is SwingUtilities.invokerAndWait().

### When to Use It

Use syncExec when the code in a non-UI thread depends on the return value from the UI code or it needs to ensure that the Runnable instance must be completed before returning to the thread.

The following code demonstrates how syncExec works:

```
final Runnable print = new Runnable() {
    public void run() {
        System.out.println("Print from thread: \t" +
            Thread.currentThread().getName());
```

```
        }
    };

    final Thread applicationThread = new Thread() {
        public void run() {
            System.out.println("Hello from thread: \t" +
            Thread.currentThread().getName());
            display.syncExec(print);
            System.out.println("Bye from thread: \t" +
                Thread.currentThread().getName());
        }
    };

    button.addSelectionListener(new SelectionListener() {
        public void widgetDefaultSelected(SelectionEvent e) { }
        public void widgetSelected(SelectionEvent e) {
            applicationThread.start();
        }
    });
    ...
```

In the preceding code, when the button is clicked, a new thread `applicationThread` starts. The `applicationThread` first prints a message with the name of the running thread (`applicationThread`). The `applicationThread` then calls `display.syncExec` with the `Runnable` object. `syncExec` blocks `applicationThread` until the `run()` method of the `Runnable` instance has been executed by the UI thread. The UI thread executes the `run()` method of the `Runnable` object and `syncExec` returns. The `applicationThread` continues to execute and prints another message with the name of the executing thread (`applicationThread`). The output is as follows.

```
Hello from thread:      applicationThread
Print from thread:      main
Bye from thread:        applicationThread
```

Note that "applicationThread" is the name of the `applicationThread` thread, and "main" is the name of the main thread of the program, (the UI thread).

For the complete program, please refer to `SyncExecExample.java`.

## timerExec

Syntax:

```
public void timerExec(int milliseconds, Runnable runnable)
```

The `timerExec` method behaves similarly to `asyncExec`, except that the `Runnable` instance is invoked by the UI thread after the specified number of milliseconds has elapsed. If the number of milliseconds is set to less than zero, the `Runnable` instance is never executed.

### When to Use It

Use `timerExec` when UI access should be delayed for a certain amount of time and the code in the non-UI thread does not depend on the return value from the UI code.

### wake

Syntax:

```
public void wake()
```

If the UI thread is sleeping, any other threads can call this method to wake it. However, in most cases, it is not necessary to call this method. When a Runnable instance is passed to asyncExec, syncExec, or timerExec, the UI thread will be automatically awakened if it is sleeping. Any event queued in the operating system event queue will wake the sleeping UI thread also. Except for the above thread-safe methods, you should not try to access UI calls from non-UI threads. Most other methods are not thread-safe, so they cannot be accessed directly from non-UI threads.

# The Event Model

This section introduces event model and event listeners in detail.

SWT uses the observer design pattern based event model, as other modern MVC frameworks such as SmallTalk and Swing do. The observer design pattern defines a one-to-many dependency between objects so that when one object changes state, all its dependents are notified and updated automatically, as shown in Figure 4-3.

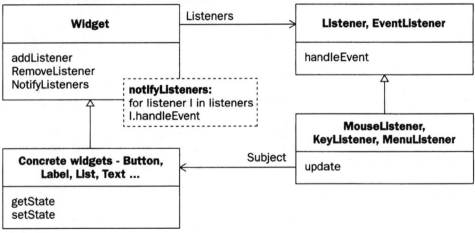

Figure 4-3

The observer pattern applied in the SWT event model is presented in Figure 4-3. An observer pattern–based event model has several components:

❑ **Event sources** (instances of Widget and Display): Widgets or displays that generate events

❑ **Event listeners** (objects implementing interface Listener and instances of EventListener): Listeners to particular types of events

❏ **Event listener registration process** (for example, `Display.addListener`, `Widget.addListener`, `Button.addSelectionListener`): The process that a listener registers as an interested party to a particular type of event that can occur in specific event sources

❏ **Event data:** A data representation of an event that occurs, allowing listeners to react based on the event context

❏ **Event delivery process:** The process by which events are delivered to interested listeners. SWT handles this internally.

## Events, Listeners, and the Listener Notification Process

When the user clicks a mouse button or presses a key on the keyboard, an event occurs. Any object can be notified of the event provided that the object implements the appropriate interface and registers as an event listener on the event source. Multiple listeners can be registered to be notified of events of a particular type from a particular source. In SWT, only `Widgets` and `Displays` can have event listeners.

The following code demonstrates usage of a listener:

```
Button button = new Button(shell, SWT.PUSH);

button.addSelectionListener(new SelectionListener() {
    public void widgetDefaultSelected(SelectionEvent e) {
    }
    public void widgetSelected(SelectionEvent e) {
        System.out.println("Button pushed.");
    }
});
```

In preceding code, a `Listener` object (instance of the anonymous inner class) is registered to the button for the selection event. This listener implements the `SelectionListener` interface. When the button is pushed, a selection event occurs and the event listener is invoked (the method `widgetSelected` of the listener instance is called).

You have seen how to create an event loop to read and dispatch events in the first section of this chapter. So how exactly does the `Display` instance read and dispatch events?

In the event loop, the method `readAndDispatch` plays the most important role. This method is constantly invoked in the event loop. When `readAndDispatch` is invoked, it first checks the thread event queue for a posted event. If no events are queued, this method is returned. Otherwise, an event is popped out and passed to various listeners. First, all the `Display` instance's filter listeners (the filter listeners will be notified when an event of a given type occurs anywhere in the display — any shell, widget, and controls based on the display) to this type of event will be notified. After that, listeners (of the event source) to this type of event will be called. After all interested listeners have been properly called, this method will return. Figure 4-4 is the flow chart of the method `readAndDispatch`.

In this process, only two sets of listeners are notified. One set includes the `Display` instance's filter listeners to the event type, and the other set comprises the event source's (the widget or display that generates the event) listeners to the event type. If you need to listen for an event and react accordingly, your listener must be put in one or both of the two sets of listeners. More details on `Display` filter listeners and `Widget` listeners are covered later in this section.

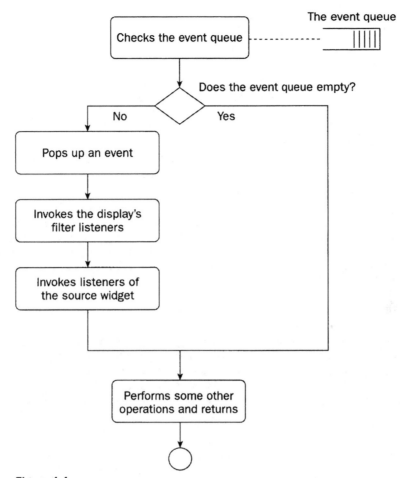

**Figure 4-4**

The following code sample illustrates the listener notification process:

```java
class SimpleListener implements Listener{
    String name;

    public SimpleListener(String name) {
        this.name = name;
    }

    public void handleEvent(Event e) {
        System.out.println("Event: [" + EventUtil.getEventName(e.type) + "] from "
            + name + ". \tCurrent Time (in ms):  " + System.currentTimeMillis());
    }
}
    ...
```

```
Display display = new Display();
Shell shell = new Shell(display);
shell.setText("Left click your mouse");
shell.setSize(200, 100);
shell.open();

shell.addListener(SWT.MouseDown, new SimpleListener("Shell mouse down listener"));

display.addFilter(SWT.MouseDown,
    new SimpleListener("Display mouse down Listener"));

display.addFilter(SWT.MouseUp,
    new SimpleListener("Display mouse up Listener"));
```

In the preceding code, the first few lines define the `SimpleListener` class, which implements the `org.eclipse.swt.widgets.Listener` interface. The only method, `handleEvent`, has been implemented. This method simply prints out the name of the event and the system current time. Next, the display and the shell are created. A `SimpleListener` is then added to the shell to listen for the mouse down event. A mouse down filter listener is registered with the display instance. A mouse up filter listener is added to the display.

After the user launches the program, the shell will be displayed. If the user clicks one of the mouse buttons on the shell, a mouse down event is generated followed by the mouse up event. (A click comprises two actions: mouse button down and mouse button up.) The `readAndDispatch` method first reads the mouse down event because the event queue is on a First-In First-Out (FIFO) basis. The mouse down filter listener of display will be called first, and then the mouse down listener of the shell will be invoked. The mouse up event is then dispatched in a similar way. This time, because no mouse up listeners have been registered to the shell, only the mouse up filter listener of display install will be invoked.

The output is as follows:

```
Event: [mouse down] from Display mouse down Listener.    Current Time (in ms):
1067275267676
Event: [mouse down] from Shell mouse down listener.    Current Time (in ms):
1067275267676
Event: [mouse up] from Display mouse up Listener.    Current Time (in ms):
1067275267746
```

Note that, for the same event, filter listeners registered to displays will always be invoked before any widgets' listeners get called. See `ListenerTest.java` for the complete program.

SWT provides two kinds of event listening mechanism: *typed* and *untyped*. A typed listener can be used to listen for only one particular typed event. For example, in the code at the beginning of this section, `SelectionListener` is a typed listener for event `SelectionEvent`. Untyped event listeners offer a generic, low-level mechanism to listen for events. You can use either or both of them to handle events effectively.

## *Untyped Events and Untyped Event Listeners*

An untyped event listener can be registered to listen for any type of event. SWT provides only two classes for untyped event listening: an interface `Listener` and an event class named `Event`. Both classes are in the `org.eclipse.swt.widgets` package. There is only one method that needs to be implemented for an untyped listener in the `Listener` interface:

```
public void handleEvent(Event event)
```

This method will be called by the UI thread when the untyped listener is notified. Note that an `Event` object will be passed to the `handleEvent` method. The event object provides a description of a particular event. Some properties (fields) of the event object include:

- ❑  `Button`: The button that was pressed or released

- ❑  `character`: The character represented by the key that was typed

- ❑  `detail`: The event specified field

- ❑  `display`: The display where the event occurred

- ❑  `gc`: The graphics context to use

- ❑  `height`: The height of the bounding rectangle of the region that requires painting

- ❑  `item`: The item that the event occurred in (possibly null)

- ❑  `keyCode`: The key code of the key that was typed

- ❑  `time`: The time that the event occurred. For example, `Event.time` returns the time in milliseconds that the event occurred. It is important to note that the time may not necessarily be expressed in the conventional way, i.e., the difference, measured in milliseconds, between the current time and midnight, January 1, 1970 UTC. On Microsoft Windows platforms, the time is an integer that specifies the elapsed time, in milliseconds, from the time the operating system was started to when the event occurred.

- ❑  `type`: The type of event

- ❑  `x`: The x offset of the bounds that requires repainting or the x coordinate of the pointer

- ❑  `y`: The y offset of the bounds that requires repainting or the y coordinate of the point

- ❑  `type`: All kinds of untyped events are represented by the same `Event` class, and the only way to tell the type of a particular event is through its `Event.type` (`public int type`) field. Class SWT defines all the event types as constant integers. For example, if a key is pressed down, the `Event.type` of the generated event will be `SWT.KeyDown`. Many other properties of `Event` are event type–dependent. For instance, for a `SWT.MouseDown` type of event, event properties such as x, y (coordinates of pointer) prove very useful; however, contents of properties such as `character` are undefined.

- ❑  `item`: Another very important property of `Event` is `Event.item` (`public Widget item`), which gives the widget that the event occur in. If you register an untyped event listener to multiple widgets for a particular type of event, you have to check this field for the event source to react accordingly.

An untyped listener must be registered to displays or widgets to listen for interested events. In the Display class and the Widget class, the methods used to add and remove an untyped event are:

```
public void addListener(int eventType, Listener listener)
public void removeListener(int eventType, Listener listener)
```

*All kinds of methods for adding or removing event listeners are accessible only from the UI thread. Non-UI thread can use only **Display.asyncExec**, **Display.syncExec**, or **Display.timerExec** methods to delegate the operation to the UI thread.*

You can specify the type of event listened to in the first argument eventType. The second argument listener is the untyped listener to be added or removed from the widget or display for the specified event type. The Display class provides the following additional methods to add and remove filter listeners:

```
public void addFilter(int eventType, Listener listener)
public void removeFilter(int eventType, Listener listener)
```

All filter listeners will be notified when an event of the specified type occurs anywhere in the display. In the last section, you saw an example using filter listeners. Filter listeners can be useful if you need to implement a special mechanism such as logging all events.

I will use a sample application to show how to implement an untyped listener and register it to a widget for a particular event.

Figure 4-5 shows the initial shell displayed. When the mouse pointer moves onto the text (a Label object) in the center, the label is highlighted, as you can see in Figure 4-6. When the cursor moves outside the label, its background is restored (see Figure 4-7).

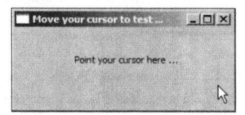

**Figure 4-5**

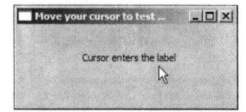

**Figure 4-6**

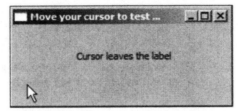

**Figure 4-7**

The code for the sample application is as follows:

```
public class MouseEnterExit1 {
    Display display = new Display();
    Shell shell = new Shell(display);
    Label label = new Label(shell, SWT.SHADOW_IN | SWT.CENTER);
    Listener listener = new MouseEnterExitListener();

    public MouseEnterExit1() {
        label.setText("Point your cursor here ...");
        label.setBounds(30, 30, 200, 30);

        label.addListener(SWT.MouseEnter, listener);
        label.addListener(SWT.MouseExit, listener);

        shell.setText("Move your cursor to test ...");
        shell.setSize(260, 120);
        shell.open();


        while(! shell.isDisposed()) {
            if(! display.readAndDispatch()) {
            display.sleep();
            }
        }

        display.dispose();
    }

    class MouseEnterExitListener implements Listener {
        public void handleEvent(Event e) {
            switch (e.type) {
            case SWT.MouseEnter :
                display.syncExec(new Runnable() {
                    public void run() {
                        label.setBackground(
                      display.getSystemColor(SWT.COLOR_YELLOW));
                        label.setText("Cursor enters the label");
                    }
                });

            break;
```

```
                case SWT.MouseExit :
                    display.syncExec(new Runnable() {
                        public void run() {
                            label.setBackground(
                    display.getSystemColor(SWT.COLOR_WIDGET_BACKGROUND));
                            label.setText("Cursor leaves the label");
                    }
                    });

            break;
        }
    }
}


public static void main(String[] args) {
        new MouseEnterExit1();
    }
}
```

An inner class named MouseEnterExitListener implementing the Listener interface is defined. This class monitors two types of events: SWT.MouseEnter and SWT.MouseExit. When the mouse pointer enters a widget, an event of type SWT.MouseEnter occurs. Similarly, when the mouse pointer leaves a widget, an event of type SWT.MouseExit occurs. If this type of listener is notified, its method handleEvent is called. This method will first check its event type. If the event is of type SWT.MouseEnter, the label's background will be changed using syncExec. In case of SWT.MouseExit, the label's background will be restored. If the event is not of type SWT.MouseEnter or SWT.MouseExit, nothing happens.

An instance of class MouseEnterExitListener is created at the beginning of the constructor. Remember that an event listener is never notified unless it has been registered to one or more event sources, so you register this untyped event listener to the label for both events of SWT.MouseEnter and SWT.MouseExit. Finally, the event loop is set up to read and dispatch events.

You can try the program yourself by running MouseEnterExit1 (source code: MouseEnterExit1.java).

The untyped event listener is very similar to the callback window procedure in native UI programming. Both use the message type as an argument in a big switch statement with individual messages handled by separate case statements. Those with native UI programming experience may easily adopt the untyped event handling mechanism; however, Swing developers may have some trouble because there are no such generic event listeners in Swing. The good news is that SWT also provides a rich set of typed event listeners, as Swing does.

## Typed Events and Typed Event Listeners

Typed event listeners are event-specific listeners. A typed event listener listens only for one particular typed event. Common typed listeners and typed events are located in the org.eclipse.swt.events package. Some special typed listeners and typed events scatter over packages org.eclipse.swt.dnd, org.eclipse.swt.custom, and org.eclipse.swt.graphics. A typed event represents a particular set of similar events. (The term "events" here refers to low-level events as discussed in untyped event listeners. To avoid confusion, when I say events without type, I mean low-level events, otherwise, typed events.) A typed listener listens for a particular typed event only. For instance, KeyEvent is a typed event comprising low-level key-pressed events and key-released events. Correspondingly, the typed listener for KeyEvent, KeyListener listens for the KeyEvent exclusively.

In the last section, you saw the Event class with a long list of fields describing all kinds of information for every type of low-level event. For a typed event, only a very small set of essential properties exclusive to that particular typed event are included as its fields. All typed events are a direct or indirect subclass of the TypedEvent class. TypeEvent, a subclass of java.util.EventObject, provides the following useful public fields:

- ❑  data [public Object data]: Field for application use

- ❑  display [public Display display]: The display where the event occurred

- ❑  time [public int time]: The time that the event occurred

- ❑  widget [public Widget widget]: The widget that generated the event. The same object will be returned when getSource() is called.

Each subclass of TypedEvent provides some extra fields describing itself. For example, KeyEvent has a character field representing the key that was typed.

All typed listeners are a subclass of java.util.EventListener. Examples of typed listeners are KeyListener, MenuListener, and FocusListener. If a widget is capable of generating a particular typed event, methods must exist to add or remove typed listeners for the typed event in its class definition. For example, a Button can generate SelectionEvent. It has addSelectionListener and removeSelectionListener methods to add and remove SelectionListener typed event listeners:

```
public void addSelectionListener(SelectionListener listener)
public void removeSelectionListener(SelectionListener listener)
```

Because a typed listener listens for a fixed set of low-level events, when adding a typed listener, the declaration of the event types to be listened for is not required.

In the preceding section, we used an untyped listener to listen for menu events. Now we will rewrite the label highlighting sample application using a typed listener:

```
class MouseEnterExitListener implements MouseTrackListener {
    public void mouseEnter(MouseEvent e) {
        display.syncExec(new Runnable() {
            public void run() {
                label.setBackground(
                    display.getSystemColor(SWT.COLOR_YELLOW));
                label.setText("Cursor enters the label");
            }
        });

    }

    public void mouseExit(MouseEvent arg0) {
        display.syncExec(new Runnable() {
            public void run() {
```

```
                    label.setBackground(
                  display.getSystemColor(SWT.COLOR_WIDGET_BACKGROUND));
                    label.setText("Cursor leaves the label");
            }
        });
    }


    public void mouseHover(MouseEvent arg0) {
        // do nothing
    }
}

    . . .

MouseTrackListener listener = new MouseEnterExitListener();

    . . .

label.addMouseTrackListener(listener);
    . . .
```

First, an inner class implementing the MouseTrackListener interface is defined. The MouseTrack Listener listens for mouse track events including low-level events: mouse pointer passing into the control area, mouse pointer passing out of the control area, and mouse pointer hovering over the control. There are three methods defined in the class corresponding to three types of low-level event. An instance of the MouseExterExitListener is created and then registered to the label.

The complete list of code is available in LabelHighlighting2.java. When you run the code, you will find that the application behaves exactly the same as the one using untyped listeners in the last section. The listener notification mechanism in LabelHighLighting2 is very similar to that of LabelHighlighting. When the mouse pointer moves into the control area, the listener is notified. There are three methods declared in the MouseTrackListener interface, so which method or which set of methods will be called? Because the low-level event is the mouse passing into the control area, as expected, only the method mouseEnter will be called, with the MouseEvent object as the only argument. More details about typed events and listeners for particular widgets appear in subsequent chapters.

*If you do not want to implement each method in a typed listener interface, you can simply extend its corresponding adapter class. For example, in **LabelHighlighting2.java**, you can rewrite the **MouseEnterExitListener**, extending the **MouseTrackAdapter** class and override only the **mouseEnter** and **mouseExit** methods. See **LabelHighlighting3.java** for the complete code.*

We've used both untyped and typed event listeners to accomplish the same task. Both models are very easy to understand and to code for. Which model should you choose, untyped or typed? Actually, either model will be okay because the performance of both models is almost the same. However, most of my colleagues who worked with Swing before prefer the typed model, and they also find that it is easy to read code with the typed model. However, if you plan to port your applications to embedded platforms such as Windows CE, you should use the untyped event model. On embedded platforms, a typed listener API may be removed from SWT due to the constraints of limited memory and storage. Whichever model you choose, keep in mind that it is not a good idea to mix them. It makes your code hard to maintain.

# Summary

This chapter discusses SWT event handling and the threading mechanism. SWT follows the threading model supported by the native platform. The application manages the event loop and dispatches events in the UI thread. You can easily use the `Display` class to create an event loop. Multithreading in SWT can be realized by using various methods provided by the `Display` class. Non-UI thread can access only UI objects through the `asyncExec` and `syncExec` methods. The chapter then covered the event model and event dispatching process. Typed and untyped listeners can be registered to widgets to listen for and react to corresponding events. An untyped event listener can be registered to listen for any type of events; however, a typed event listener can be registered to listen only for a certain type of event.

You should now have a general understanding of SWT/JFace. The next chapter introduces basic SWT widgets in detail.

# 5

# Basic SWT Widgets

The beginning of this chapter guides you through the hierarchy of SWT widgets. Several typical widget types are discussed. After that, you learn about three kinds of basic SWT widgets:

❑ Shells

❑ Buttons

❑ Labels

You learn how to use these widgets, register proper listeners, and complete many other operations such as setting text labels and image labels. In addition, this chapter covers focus traversal.

By the end of the chapter, you should have a good understanding of how widgets in SWT are structured, how to set styles for widgets, and how to perform event handling on them. In particular, you should be able to use shells, buttons, and labels in SWT-based applications.

## Overview of SWT/JFace Widgets

This section first gives an overview of the SWT UI component hierarchy. Then it covers three important classes: Widget, Control, and Composite.

### SWT/JFace UI Component Hierarchy

Many UI components are available in SWT/JFace. Main SWT components are organized in the following hierarchy:

```
Widget
+-- Caret
+-- Menu
+-- ScrollBar
```

```
+-- Tracker
+-- Control
|    +-- Button
|    +-- Label
|    +-- ProgressBar
|    +-- Sash
|    +-- Scale
|    +-- Slider
|    +-- Scrollable
|    |    +-- Composite
|    |    |    +-- Canvas
|    |    |    |    +-- Decorations
|    |    |    |         +-- Shell
|    |    |    +-- Combo
|    |    |    +-- CollBar
|    |    |    +-- Group
|    |    |    +-- TabFolder
|    |    |    +-- Table
|    |    |    +-- ToolBar
|    |    |    +-- Tree
|    |    +-- List
|    |    +-- Text
+-- Item
     +-- CoolItem
     +-- MenuItem
     +-- TabItem
     +-- TableColumn
     +-- TableItem
     +-- ToolItem
     +-- TreeItem
```

All classes in italic are abstract classes. All of the components in the preceding tree are in the org.eclipse.swt.widgets package. Package org.eclipse.swt.custom provides extra custom widgets. Few other components are in JFace packages. You learn most of the other components in later chapters. Now, let's focus on SWT main components.

# The Widget Class

The org.eclipse.widgets.Widget class is the top-level class of all the UI components in SWT/JFace. A Widget can be created and disposed of, and it is capable of issuing notifications to listeners when events occur.

You can create a Widget instance by calling the constructor with optional widget styles. After you finish using the widget, you must invoke the dispose method to release the system resources. Additionally, you can register event listeners to listen and react to widget-specific events.

## The Constructor: public Widget(Widget parent, int style)

This is the only constructor of the Widget class. Because the Widget class is declared abstract, you can't use it to create new instances directly. Almost all kinds of UI components in SWT/JFace have similar constructors as this one, so it is worth looking at it in detail.

The first argument is a `Widget` that will be the parent of the object. The parent argument passed must not be `null`; otherwise, an `IllegalArgumentException` will be thrown.

The second argument specifies the style of the component. The style value is either one of the constants defined in the `org.eclipse.swt.SWT` class that is applicable to this kind of widget, or must be built by bitwise OR'ing together (using the "`|`" operator) two or more of those style constants. The `Widget` class does not have any styles; however, most of its child classes do. For example,

```
Button button = new Button(shell, SWT.PUSH | SWT.LEFT);
```

creates a push `Button` with text left-aligned.

In this book, when the UI components are introduced, their associated styles are discussed. Alternatively, you may find the UI components' possible styles from the SWT/JFace Javadoc. Styles are inherited from superclasses. They are marked as HINT if they are available either only on some window systems, or for a differing set of widgets on each window system. If a window system does not support a style, that style is ignored. The good news is that there are very few such styles.

The following method can be used to check the styles of a widget:

```
public int getStyle()
```

Here's an example:

```
if( (button.getStyle() & SWT.PUSH) == 1) {
    System.out.println("The button is push button.");
}else{
    System.out.println("The button is push button.");
}
```

The value returned by `getStyle` may differ from the value that is provided to the constructor if:

❑   The underlying operating system does not support a particular combination of requested styles

or

❑   One or more of the styles specified is not applicable to this widget

## public Display getDisplay()

This method returns the `Display` that is associated with this `Widget`. A widget's display is either provided when created, for example:

```
Shell shell = new Shell(display);
```

or is the same as its parent's display. For example:

```
Button button = new Button(shell, SWT.PUSH);
// This button's display is the same as the display of its parent (the shell).
```

This method throws an SWTException (SWT.ERROR_WIDGET_DISPOSED) if the Widget has already been disposed of. To check whether a Widget has been disposed of or not, use the method:

```
public boolean isDisposed()
```

which returns true when the widget is disposed of and false if not.

## Dispose of the Widget: public void dispose()

As shown in Chapter 2, operating system resources associated with a widget and all of its descendants will be disposed of when this method is called. After this widget is disposed of, the method isDisposed returns true.

## Event Handling

The following lists important methods of the Widget class in terms of event handling.

### public void addListener(int eventType, Listener listener)

This method adds the given listener to the collection of listeners that will be notified when an event of the given type occurs. When an event of the specified type occurs in the widget, the listener is notified and the listener handleEvent method is called.

For example, the following code adds a listener to listen to the dispose event:

```
widget.addListener(SWT.Dispose, new Listener() {
    public void handleEvent(Event event) {
        System.out.println(event.widget + " disposed");
    }
});
```

### public void addDisposeListener(DisposeListener listener)

Because every widget has a dispose method generating dispose events, the Widget class provides a typed listener registration method:

```
public void addDisposeListener(DisposeListener listener)
```

The previous dispose listening code can be rewritten as:

```
shell.addDisposeListener(new DisposeListener() {
    public void widgetDisposed(DisposeEvent e) {
        System.out.println(e.widget + " disposed");
    }
});
```

For details about untyped listener and typed listeners, please refer to Chapter 4.

### public void removeListener(int eventType, Listener listener)

This method removes the given listener from the collection of listeners registered for events of the specified event type.

There is another `removeListener` method in the class:

```
protected void removeListener(int eventType,
org.eclipse.swt.internal.SWTEventListener listener)
```

This method is declared as *protected* and is not part of the SWT public API. To keep your code portable, you should never use such non-public API elements in your application code.

### public void removeDisposeListener(DisposeListener listener)

When this method is called, the given listener is removed from the collection of listeners registered for the dispose event.

## Getting and Setting Application Data

The `Widget` class provides four methods that allow you to associate application data to widgets and retrieve data later.

```
public void setData(Object data)
```

This method associates the application data object to the widget. If you need to "store" more than one data object to the widget, you can use the following method:

```
public void setData(String key, Object value)
```

To get the application data associated with the widget, you can use the following methods:

```
public Object getData()
public Object getData(String key)
```

If the data objects associated with the widget need to be notified when the widget is disposed of, you should handle this yourself in your application code by creating and registering listeners to hook the `Dispose` event on the widget.

# The Control Class

The `Control` class is the superclass of all windowed user interface components. As one of the child classes of the `Widget` class, it provides many more features than the `Widget` class.

## Styles

Styles supported by the `Control` class include:

❑ BORDER: This style bit causes a control to have bordered behavior.

❑ LEFT_TO_RIGHT, RIGHT_TO_LEFT: This style bit specifies the orientation of textual information. Only one may be specified. When the orientation of a control is not specified, orientation is inherited from its parent.

> **All widget styles are defined as constants in the `org.eclipse.swt.SWT` class.**

93

## Size and Location

There are several methods to get and set the size and location of a control. Figure 5-1 illustrates how the size and location of a control are measured in SWT.

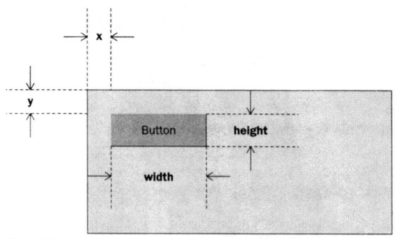

Figure 5-1

Based on the preceding information, you can easily calculate the following properties for the button in Figure 5-1:

❑   Size = new Point(width, height)

❑   Location = new Point(x, y)

❑   Bounds = new Rectangle(x, y, width, height)

The getting and setting methods for these properties are:

```
public Point getSize()
public void setSize(int width, int height)
public void setSize(Point size)

public Point getLocation()
public void setLocation(int x, int y)
public void setLocation(Point location)

public Rectangle getBounds()
public void setBounds(int x, int y, int width, int height)
public void setBounds(Rectangle rect)
```

Sometimes you may find that these setting methods do *not* work properly — when you resize the ancestral shell of a control, the control sticks back to its original bounds. The cause of this problem is the layout of the parent composite. When the composite is resized, its associated layout rearranges all of its children. During this process, the layout queries its children and changes the bounds of them; as a result, your bounds setting of the control is lost. Controls such as Button exhibit this kind of behavior. If this behavior is undesired, you may consider using one of the following methods:

- ❑ Not using any layout
- ❑ Using custom layout data
- ❑ Creating your own layouts

For more details about layouts, refer to Chapter 6.

Before displaying a control, you need to know the best size for displaying it. This size is normally referred to as *preferred size*. The following methods return the preferred size of a control:

```
public Point computeSize(int wHint, int hHint)
public Point computeSize(int wHint, int hHint, boolean changed)
```

The preceding methods compute the best size with the width hint and the height hint in mind. If you do not want to constrain a particular dimension, you can pass SWT.DEFAULT for the hint. For the second method, if the changed flag is set to true, it indicates that the control's contents have changed. The two computeSize methods are frequently used by layouts to query for preferred sizes.

## Fonts and Colors

To get and set the font that a control uses to paint textual information, call the following methods:

```
public Font getFont()
public void setFont(Font font)
```

If a null argument is passed to the setFont method, the default font for that kind of control will be used.

Fonts utilize operating system resources; thus, they need to be disposed of after use. The best way to manage fonts is to use one or more FontRegistrys. See Chapter 2 for details on FontRegistry.

A control can have foreground color and background color. To query these colors, you can use:

```
public Color getBackground()
public Color getForeground()
```

To change background color or foreground color of a control, use the following methods:

```
public void setBackground(Color color)
public void setForeground(Color color)
```

If a null argument is passed to any of the preceding methods, the default system color will be used.

## UI Updating

This method marks the entire bounds of a control that needs to be redrawn:

```
public void redraw()
```

The control will be completely painted the next time a paint request is processed.

If only part of the control needs to be redrawn, you can use this method:

```
public void redraw(int x, int y, int width, int height, boolean all)
```

The preceding method causes the marked rectangular area of the control as needing to be redrawn. If the all flag is set to true, all children of this control that intersect with the specified area will also paint their intersecting areas.

If the contents of a control have changed and redrawn areas have been marked, you can use the following method to force all outstanding paint requests for the control to be processed:

```
public void update()
```

If you need to resize a control to its preferred size, you can use the following:

```
public void pack()
public void pack(boolean changed)
```

If the control is a composite that can contain other controls as its children, the pack methods compute the preferred size from its layout if there is one. For the second pack method, if the changed flag is set to true, it indicates that the contents of the control have been changed.

To set a control's visibility, you can use the following:

```
public void setVisible(boolean visible)
```

If one of the control's ancestors is not visible, marking the control visible may not actually cause it to be displayed. The following method can be used to query the control's visibility:

```
public boolean isVisible()
```

Similarly, the following method can be used to enable and disable a control:

```
public void setEnabled(boolean enabled)
```

To query the status, call this method:

```
public boolean isEnabled()
```

If you want a control to gain focus, try this method:

```
public boolean setFocus()
```

This method causes the control to gain the keyboard focus, so that all keyboard events will be delivered to it. The method may fail if platform constraints disallow such focus reassignment under some situations. The return boolean value indicates whether the operation is successful or not.

## Event Handling

The `Widget` class handles only the `dispose` event. The `Control` class handles many more events than the `Widget` class, as listed in the following table.

| Event Type | Description | Methods in the Control Class |
|---|---|---|
| `Control` | Generated when a control is moved or resized | `public void addControl Listener(ControlListener listener)` `public void removeControl Listener(ControlListener listener)` |
| `Focus` | Generated when a control gains or loses focus | `public void addFocusListener (FocusListener listener)` `public void removeFocusListener (FocusListener listener)` |
| `Help` | Generated when the user requests help for a control | `public void addHelpListener(Help Listener listener)` `public void removeHelpListener (HelpListener listener)` |
| `Key` | Generated when the user presses or releases a key | `public void addKeyListener (KeyListener listener)` `public void removeKeyListener (KeyListener listener)` |
| `Mouse` | Generated when the user presses, releases, or double clicks the mouse | `public void addMouseListener (MouseListener listener)` `public void removeMouseListener (MouseListener listener)` |
| `MouseMove` | Generated when the user moves the mouse | `public void addMouseMoveListener (MouseMoveListener listener)` `public void removeMouseMoveListener (MouseMoveListener listener)` |
| `MouseTrack` | Generated when the mouse enters, exits, or hovers over the control | `public void addMouseTrackListener (MouseTrackListener listener)` `public void removeMouseTrackListener (MouseTrackListener listener)` |
| `Paint` | Generated when the control needs to be repainted | `public void addPaintListener (PaintListener listener)` `public void removePaintListener (PaintListener listener)` |
| `Traverse` | Generated when a control is traversed by the user's using keystrokes | `public void addTraverseListener (TraverseListener listener)` `public void removeTraverseListener (TraverseListener listener)` |

## Miscellaneous Methods

The following methods can be used to get and set a control's pop-up menu:

```
public Menu getMenu()
public void setMenu(Menu menu)
```

To set a control's cursor, use the setCursor method:

```
public void setCursor(Cursor cursor)
```

If the argument passed is null, the system default cursor is set. When the mouse pointer moves over the control, its shape is changed to match the control's cursor.

Use the following to query the parent of a control:

```
public Composite getParent()
```

and its nearest ancestor shell:

```
public Shell getShell()
```

If the control is of the type Shell, the shell will return itself.

To get and set the tooltip text for a control, use the following methods:

```
public String getToolTipText()
public void setToolTipText(String string)
```

To perform focus traversal programmatically, you can call this method:

```
public boolean traverse(int traversalType)
```

The argument specifies the type of traversal that the system performs. For example, to initiate a TAB forward traversal, you should pass SWT.TRAVERSE_TAB_NEXT as the traversal type. If the traversal succeeds, true is returned; otherwise, false is returned. The next section discusses focus traversal in detail.

# The Composite Class

A composite is a control that is capable of containing other controls.

## Styles

Styles supported by the Composite class in addition to those inherited include:

*The first four styles listed here are intended to be used with the **Composite**'s subclass **Canvas** only.*

❑   NO_BACKGROUND: Before a widget paints, the client area is filled with the current background color by default. If this style bit is set, the background is not filled and you need to take care of filling every pixel of the client area. Typically, setting this style helps to reduce canvas flickering.

❑ NO_FOCUS: This style bit indicates that the composite does not take focus behavior.

❑ NO_MERGE_PAINTS: This style bit prevents Paint event-merging behavior.

❑ NO_REDRAW_RESIZE: This style stops a canvas's entire client area from being invalidated when the size of the canvas changes:

    ❑ If the size of the canvas decreases, no Paint event is sent.

    ❑ If the size of the canvas increases, a Paint event is sent along with a GC clipped to the new areas to be painted.

    This style also helps to stop canvases from flickering.

❑ NO_RADIO_GROUP: This style bit disables child radio group behavior.

❑ H_SCROLL, V_SCROLL: Inherited from the Composite's superclass Scrollable, these two style bits control horizontal scrollbar behavior and vertical scrollbar behavior, respectively.

## Layout

Layouts are often used by composites to help arrange their children. The following method can be used to set the layout of a composite:

```
public void setLayout(Layout layout)
```

To query a composite for its layout, call this method:

```
public Layout getLayout()
```

If no layout is associated with the composite, null is returned.

The following methods can be used to request a composite to lay out all of its children:

```
public void layout()
public void layout(boolean changed)
```

If there is no layout associated with the composite, the preceding methods do nothing. For the second method, if the changed flag is set to true, the layout is requested to refresh cached information about the children. If it is set to false, the layout may simply use the cached information.

## Focus Traversal

Focus traversal support enables the user to change focus owner (current control receiving keyboard input) without moving the mouse cursor. Focus traversal can be either forward to the next control or backward to the previous component. Usually, the user can press the Tab key to forward the focus to the next control or press *Shift+Tab* to move the focus to the previous control. Additionally, applications can initiate traversal programmatically.

The following method of Composite defines the tabbing order for the specified children controls:

```
public void setTabList(Control[] tabList)
```

Every control in the tab list passed as the argument must be a direct child of the composite. Otherwise, `IllegalArgumentException` is thrown.

Suppose you are required to build a GUI, as shown in Figure 5-2. The canvas in the middle of the right composite is used to display the character corresponding to a keystroke when the canvas has the focus. All other controls are for illustration only.

**Figure 5-2**

The order of each control in a focus traversal cycle is specified in Figure 5-3.

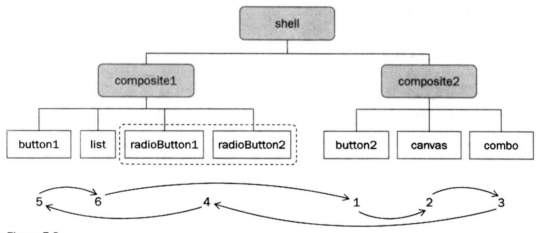

**Figure 5-3**

First, you need to build up the component tree:

```
Display display = new Display();
Shell shell = new Shell(display);

shell.setLayout(new RowLayout());

Composite composite1 = new Composite(shell, SWT.BORDER);
composite1.setLayout(new RowLayout());
composite1.setBackground(display.getSystemColor(SWT.COLOR_WHITE));

Button button1 = new Button(composite1, SWT.PUSH);
button1.setText("Button1");
```

```
List list = new List(composite1, SWT.MULTI | SWT.BORDER);
list.setItems(new String[]{"Item-1", "Item-2", "Item-3"});

Button radioButton1 = new Button(composite1, SWT.RADIO);
radioButton1.setText("radio-1");
Button radioButton2 = new Button(composite1, SWT.RADIO);
radioButton2.setText("radio-2");

Composite composite2 = new Composite(shell, SWT.BORDER);
composite2.setLayout(new RowLayout());
composite2.setBackground(display.getSystemColor(SWT.COLOR_GREEN));

Button button2 = new Button(composite2, SWT.PUSH);
button2.setText("Button2");

final Canvas canvas = new Canvas(composite2, SWT.NULL);
canvas.setSize(50, 50);
canvas.setBackground(display.getSystemColor(SWT.COLOR_YELLOW));

Combo combo = new Combo(composite2, SWT.DROP_DOWN);
combo.add("combo");
combo.select(0);
```

Now, you need to add a KeyListener to listen to the keystroke and display the corresponding character:

```
canvas.addKeyListener(new KeyListener() {
    public void keyPressed(KeyEvent e) {
        GC gc = new GC(canvas);
        // Erase background first.
        Rectangle rect = canvas.getClientArea();
        gc.fillRectangle(rect.x, rect.y, rect.width, rect.height);

        Font font = new Font(display, "Arial", 32, SWT.BOLD );
        gc.setFont(font);

        gc.drawString("" + e.character, 15, 10);
        gc.dispose();
        font.dispose();
    }

    public void keyReleased(KeyEvent e) {
    }
});
```

Finally, set the traversal policy:

```
composite1.setTabList(new Control[]{button1, list});
composite2.setTabList(new Control[]{button2, canvas, combo});

shell.setTabList(new Control[]{composite2, composite1});
```

First, the tab lists for `composite1` and `composite2` are set. Then the tab list for the top-level shell is set. You may notice that neither of the radios buttons appears in the tab list passed to `composite1`. This is because when a composite gains focus, it sets focus on its first radio control. If no radio control is contained in the composite, the first control (the first one added to the composite) will be set focus. Thus in the preceding code, radio buttons are omitted in the tab list.

When you run the preceding code, you encounter this problem: When the canvas has the focus, pressing the Tab key does not forward the focus to the next control because, by default, when the Tab key is pressed while a canvas is the focus, the system will not traverse and the Tab key will be delivered to key listeners of the canvas. To change this default behavior, you can add a `TraverseListener` to the canvas:

```
canvas.addTraverseListener(new TraverseListener() {
    public void keyTraversed(TraverseEvent e) {
        if(e.detail == SWT.TRAVERSE_TAB_NEXT ||
            e.detail == SWT.TRAVERSE_TAB_PREVIOUS)
            e.doit = true;
    }
});
```

When the canvas is traversed, the `keyTraversed` method in the `TraverseListener` will be called with a `TraverseEvent` object. There are two fields in `TraverseEvent`:

❑ `detail`: Indicates the type of traversal. You can modify the traversal type by changing this field. For example, you can set the details to `SWT.TRAVERSE_NONE` to disable traversal actions.

❑ `doit`: Indicates whether the traversal operation should be allowed. If this field is set to `false`, the traversal operation will be cancelled and the traversal keystroke will be delivered to the control. If it is set to `true`, the traversal operation will be performed.

In the `keyTraversed` method, if the traversal type is `SWT.TRAVERSE_TAB_NEXT` or `SWT.TRAVERSE_TAB_PREVIOUS` the `doit` field in the event object is set to `true` to have the traversal operation performed. Similarly, the following code prevents escape from closing a dialog:

```
...
Shell dialog = new Shell(shell, SWT.DIALOG_TRIM);
dialog.addListener(SWT.Traverse, new Listener() {
    public void handleEvent(Event e) {
        if (e.detail == SWT.TRAVERSE_ESCAPE) {
            e.doit = false;
        }
    }
});
...
```

As you have seen in the preceding sample application, you can use the `setTabList` method to set the focus traversal order of controls. Additionally, the traversal event provides fine control over focus traversal in a widget.

# Shells

Shells are the most fundamental controls in SWT. A shell is a window that the desktop or window manager (part of the underlying window system) is managing. The class org.eclipse.swt.widgets.Shell shares a significant amount of code with its parent class org.eclipse.swt.widgets.Decorations.

## *Styles*

You can apply the following styles to a shell:

❑ CLOSE, TITLE, MIN, MAX, RESIZE | NO_TRIM (inherited from the Decorations class): The CLOSE, MIN, MAX, and RESIZE style bits specify Close box trim, Title area trim, Minimize box trim, Maximize box trim, and Resize box trim, respectively. The NO_TRIM style causes no trimmings associated with the shell. (These styles are hints. The window manager has the ultimate control over the appearance and behavior of trimming and modality.) Two shells with different trimming styles are shown in Figure 5-4.

SWT provides two convenient constants for the frequently used trimming style combinations:

❑ SHELL_TRIM = (CLOSE | TITLE | MIN | MAX | RESIZE): This style constant can be used to produce top-level shells.

❑ DIALOG_TRIM = (CLOSE | TITLE | BORDER): The style constant can be used to produce dialog shells.

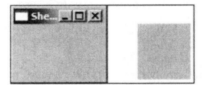

Figure 5-4

❑ APPLICATION_MODAL, MODELESS, PRIMARY_MODAL, SYSTEM_MODAL: These style bits can be used to specify the modal state of shells. (They are hints, too.) Only one of them may be specified.

❑ ON_TOP: This style bit causes the shell to always float on the top of the desktop.

❑ TOOL: This style bit indicates that the shell is a tool window. It is a hint. Shells with this style can be used as floating toolbars. Figure 5-5 shows a shell with (SHELL_TRIM | TOOL) styles.

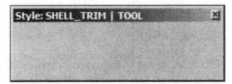

Figure 5-5

## Shell States

A shell is always displayed in one of the following states:

- ❑ **Normal:** In the normal state, the shell's appearance is controlled by the style bits specified in the constructor and the restrictions of the window manager.

- ❑ **Maximized:** To set the shell to the maximized state, the window manager typically resizes it to fill the entire area of the display.

- ❑ **Minimized:** If the shell is in the minimized state, its contents are usually invisible. The window manager may "iconify" the shell by replacing it with a small representation of it or hide it.

To minimize a shell, you can use the following method:

```
public void setMinimized(boolean minimized)
```

If the minimized flag is set to `true`, this method causes the shell to switch to the minimized state. If the minimized flag is set to `false` and the shell is currently in the minimized state, the shell will be switched back to either the maximized state or the normal state.

To check whether a shell is minimized or not, use:

```
public boolean getMinimized()
```

The counterparts methods for the maximized state are as follows:

```
public void setMaximized(boolean maximized)
public boolean getMaximized()
```

All of the preceding four methods are inherited from the `Decorations` class.

## Creating Shells

Shells can be separated into two categories: top-level shells and secondary/dialog shells. Shells that do not have a parent are top-level shells. All dialog shells have a parent. The `Shell` class provides many constructors for you to create both top-level shells and dialog shells.

Use the following constructors to create top-level shells:

```
Shell()
Shell(int style)
Shell(Display display)
Shell(Display display, int style)
```

For the first two constructors, no display object is required. In this case, if the current display exists, it will be set to the display of the shell. If there is no current display object, a default display object will be created and set to the display of the shell. You can specify the style constants in the `style` arguments.

Dialog shells can be created using the following constructors:

```
Shell(Shell parent)
Shell(Shell parent, int style)
```

Chapters 3 and 4 showed many example of creating top-level shells. Now, let's create a simple book rating application, as shown in Figure 5-6, to see how you can create dialog shells.

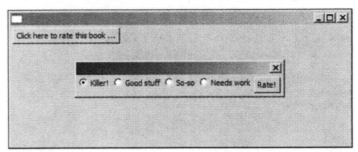

**Figure 5-6**

When the user clicks the button in the top-level shell, a dialog shell pops up. The user rates this book by selecting one of the radio buttons. After this, the user can press the "Rate!" button to save the rating status and close the dialog.

The following code creates the top-level dialog and the dialog invocation button:

```
Display display = new Display();
final Shell shell = new Shell(display);

shell.setLayout(new RowLayout());
shell.setSize(500, 200);

final Button openDialog = new Button(shell, SWT.PUSH);
openDialog.setText("Click here to rate this book ...");
```

You need to add a selection listener to the openDialog button to listen for button selection events:

```
openDialog.addSelectionListener(new SelectionListener() {
  public void widgetSelected(SelectionEvent e) {
      final Shell dialog =
          new Shell(shell, SWT.DIALOG_TRIM | SWT.APPLICATION_MODAL);
      dialog.setLayout(new RowLayout());

      final String[] ratings = new String[] { "Killer!", "Good stuff",
                      "So-so", "Needs work" };
      final Button[] radios = new Button[ratings.length];
      for (int i = 0; i < ratings.length; i++) {
          radios[i] = new Button(dialog, SWT.RADIO);
          radios[i].setText(ratings[i]);
      }
```

```
            Button rateButton = new Button(dialog, SWT.PUSH);
            rateButton.setText("Rate!");
            rateButton.addSelectionListener(new SelectionListener() {
                public void widgetSelected(SelectionEvent e) {
                    for (int i = 0; i < radios.length; i++)
                        if (radios[i].getSelection())
                            openDialog.setText("Rating: " + ratings[i]);
                    dialog.close();
                }

                public void widgetDefaultSelected(SelectionEvent e) {
                }
            });

            dialog.pack();
            dialog.open();

        }

    public void widgetDefaultSelected(SelectionEvent e) {
    }
});
```

In the widgetSelected method of the openDialog button's selection listener, first the dialog shell and its contents are created. Then another selection listener is added to the rateButton button in the dialog. Finally, the dialog is opened and centered. When the user clicks the rateButton, the only selection listener of rateButton puts the rating information and closes the dialog. The following method:

```
public void close()
```

sends a close request to the window manager in the same way as if the user clicks the Close box. As a result, the dialog is closed.

Finally, open the top-level shell and set up the event loop:

```
shell.open();

// Set up the event loop.
while (!shell.isDisposed()) {
 if (!display.readAndDispatch()) {
        // If no more entries in event queue
        display.sleep();
 }
}

display.dispose();
```

After a shell has been created, you need to call its open method to display it:

```
public void open()
```

This method makes the shell visible, sets the focus, and requests that the window manager make the shell active.

## Shell Events

Besides types of events shared by all kinds of controls, shells can generate a unique type of event: shell events (ShellEvent). A shell event is generated when a shell is minimized, maximized, activated, deactivated, or closed. You can register ShellListeners to shells to listen to shell events and react accordingly.

To add a shell listener to a shell, use this method:

```
public void addShellListener(ShellListener listener)
```

To remove a shell listener from a shell, use this method:

```
public void removeShellListener(ShellListener listener)
```

The preceding section showed you how to modify the default focus traversal using the doit field of passed TraverseEvent objects. You can apply the same technique to change the default behavior of shells. For example, a document editor usually needs to warn the user about losing unsaved data when the user tries to exit the application. You can register a ShellListener to warn the user before closing the top-level shell:

```
Display display = new Display ();
final Shell shell = new Shell (display);
shell.setSize(500, 300);
shell.addListener (SWT.Close, new Listener () {
    public void handleEvent (Event event) {
        MessageBox messageBox = new MessageBox (shell,
                    SWT.APPLICATION_MODAL | SWT.YES | SWT.NO);
        messageBox.setText ("Warning");
        messageBox.setMessage ("You have unsaved data. Close the shell anyway?");
        if(messageBox.open() == SWT.YES)
            event.doit = true;
        else
            event.doit = false;
    }
});

shell.open();
while (!shell.isDisposed ()) {
    if (!display.readAndDispatch ()) display.sleep ();
}
display.dispose ();
```

When the user clicks the Close box, a message box pops up, as shown in Figure 5-7.

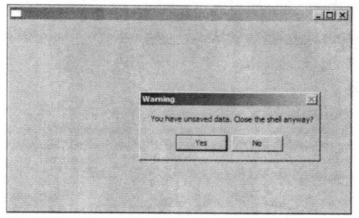

**Figure 5-7**

If the user clicks Yes, the shell is closed; otherwise, the shell remains open.

# Miscellaneous

In this section, you learn how to create irregular-shaped shells, set title and icon image for shells, and set the default button for shells.

## Creating Irregular-Shaped Shells

You can create an irregular-shaped shell with the `setRegion` method:

```
public void setRegion(Region region)
```

This shell must be created with the style NO_TRIM in order to specify a region. For example, the following code creates a ring shell, as shown in Figure 5-8.

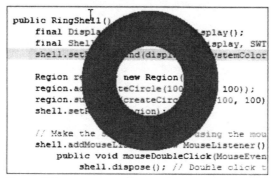

**Figure 5-8**

```
    Point originalPosition = null;

public RingShell() {
    final Display display = new Display();
    final Shell shell = new Shell(display, SWT.NO_TRIM | SWT.ON_TOP);
    shell.setBackground(display.getSystemColor(SWT.COLOR_DARK_MAGENTA));

    Region region = new Region();
    region.add(createCircle(100, 100, 100));
    region.subtract(createCircle(50, 100, 100));
    shell.setRegion(region);

    // Make the shell movable by using the mouse pointer.
    shell.addMouseListener(new MouseListener() {
        public void mouseDoubleClick(MouseEvent e) {
            shell.dispose(); // Double click to dispose the shell.
        }

        public void mouseDown(MouseEvent e) {
            originalPosition = new Point(e.x, e.y);
        }

        public void mouseUp(MouseEvent e) {
            originalPosition = null;
        }
    });

    shell.addMouseMoveListener(new MouseMoveListener() {
        public void mouseMove(MouseEvent e) {
            if(originalPosition == null)
                return;
            Point point = display.map(shell, null, e.x, e.y);
            shell.setLocation(point.x - originalPosition.x,
                    point.y - originalPosition.y);
        }
    });

    Rectangle regionBounds = region.getBounds();
    shell.setSize(regionBounds.width, regionBounds.height);
    shell.open();

    // Set up the event loop.
    while (!shell.isDisposed()) {
        if (!display.readAndDispatch()) {
            // If no more entries in event queue
            display.sleep();
        }
    }
    display.dispose();
    region.dispose();
}
```

Note that regions use operating system resources; thus they must be explicitly disposed of. The following is the function that creates an array of points representing a circle:

```
int[] createCircle(int radius, int centerX, int centerY) {
    int[] points = new int[360 * 2];
    for(int i=0; i<360; i++) {
        points[i*2] = centerX +
            (int)(radius * Math.cos(Math.toRadians(i)));
        points[i*2+1] = centerY +
                (int)(radius * Math.sin(Math.toRadians(i)));
    }
    return points;
}
```

## Setting Images

The setImage method, inherited from the Decorations class, can be used to set a shell's image.

```
public void setImage(Image image)
```

The image of a shell is typically displayed when the shell is iconified, and may also appear in the trim of the shell.

A shell's image is used as an icon in many places—for example, the trim of the shell, the *Alt+Tab* window (Windows). The trim icon usually is very small; however, the icon shown in the *Alt+Tab* window is much larger. The window system will scale up a small image if it needs a large one. In this case, it is desirable to specify an array of images and let the window manager choose the image with the "best" size. The setImages method is implemented for this purpose:

```
public void setImages(Image[] images)
```

You can use the following methods to get the image (images) of a shell:

```
public Image getImage()
public Image[] getImages()
```

## Setting the Title

The setText method can be used to set a shell's title:

```
public void setText(String text)
```

## The Default Button

The default button of a shell is the button that gains the focus and is pressed automatically when a SWT.TRAVERSE_RETURN type traversal happens. You can get and set the default button of a shell by using the following methods:

```
public Button getDefaultButton()
public void setDefaultButton(Button defaultButton)
```

The following sample code illustrates the use of default buttons.

```
...
shell.setLayout(new RowLayout());

final String[] ratings = new String[] {
                "Killer!", "Good stuff", "So-so", "Needs work" };
final Button[] radios = new Button[ratings.length];
for (int i = 0; i < ratings.length; i++) {
    radios[i] = new Button(shell, SWT.RADIO);
    radios[i].setText(ratings[i]);
}

Button cancelButton = new Button(shell, SWT.PUSH);
cancelButton.setText("Cancel");

Button rateButton = new Button(shell, SWT.PUSH);
rateButton.setText("Rate!");
rateButton.addSelectionListener(new SelectionListener() {
    public void widgetSelected(SelectionEvent e) {
        for (int i = 0; i < radios.length; i++)
            if (radios[i].getSelection())
                System.out.println("Rating: " + ratings[i]);
    }

    public void widgetDefaultSelected(SelectionEvent e) {
    }
});

shell.setDefaultButton(rateButton);
...
```

When the user selects one of the radio buttons using the mouse pointer, he or she can then simply press the Enter key to click the `rateButton` (as shown in Figure 5-9).

**Figure 5-9**

# Buttons and Labels

This section introduces two kinds of basic controls in SWT: buttons and labels. You learn how to create them, set their styles, capture events, and more.

111

# Buttons

A button is a selectable user interface component that issues notifications when pressed and released.

## Styles

Styles supported by the Button class include the following:

❑   ARROW, CHECK, PUSH, RADIO, TOGGLE: These five styles specify five different kinds of buttons: arrow buttons, checkbox buttons, push buttons, radio buttons, and toggle buttons. Only one of the five styles may be specified when constructing a button. Figure 5-10 shows buttons with various styles.

**Figure 5-10**

❑   FLAT: This is a hint. It makes the button look flat.

❑   UP, DOWN, LEFT, RIGHT: Each specifies a direction that the arrow on an arrow button points to. Only one of them may be specified. UP and DOWN styles are available for arrow buttons only. For buttons except arrow buttons, LEFT and RIGHT styles specify the alignments. (See the next bullet.) In Figure 5-10, the arrow is pointing UP.

❑   LEFT, RIGHT, CENTER: These three styles specify the text/image alignment in buttons.

## Button Basics

To get and set a button's text label, use the following method:

```
public String getText()
public void setText(String text)
```

If a button is an arrow button, the getText method returns an empty string and setText does not have any effect.

You can include the mnemonic character in the text label. Inserting an ampersand (&) before a character makes the character the mnemonic. When the user presses a key matching the mnemonic, the corresponding button is selected and a selection event is generated as a result. To escape the mnemonic character &, you can double it and a single "&" will be displayed.

To get and set a button's image label, use the following method:

```
public Image getImage()
public void setImage(Image image)
```

The setImage method causes a button's text label to be hidden; on the other hand, the setText method hides the button's image if it exists. To make a button's image visible, you must not call its setText method after executing the setImage method, and vice versa.

You can set the alignment of the text/image label of a button in the constructor of the Button class, or you can use the setAlignment method after it has been created:

```
public void setAlignment(int alignment)
```

To query a button for its label alignment, call the getAlignment method:

```
public int getAlignment()
```

## Selection Events

Selection events are generated when buttons get selected and pressed. You can register selection listeners to buttons. There are two methods defined in the SelectionListener interface you must implement in your selection listener:

```
public void widgetSelection(SelectionEvent e)
public void widgetDefaultSelection(SelectionEvent e)
```

The first method is called when a button is selected. Because default selection is not applicable to buttons, you can simply leave it blank.

If you need to select a button programmatically, use the following method:

```
public void setSelection(boolean selected)
```

This method is applicable for checkbox buttons, radio buttons, and toggle buttons only. It has no effect on push buttons and arrow buttons.

To check the selection status of a button, use the following method:

```
public boolean getSelection()
```

Similarly, the above method is only applicable for check buttons, radio buttons, and toggle buttons. It always returns false if the button is a push button or an arrow button.

## Radio Buttons

Radio buttons are normally used as a group to let the user select one option from all the available options.

By default all the radio buttons sharing the same parent belong to the same group. This may cause problems sometimes. For example, the following code creates a GUI to enable a user to select the gender and the title as shown in Figure 5-11.

```
...
Display display = new Display();
    Shell shell = new Shell(display);

    shell.setLayout(new RowLayout());

    Label label = new Label(shell, SWT.NULL);
    label.setText("Gender: ");
```

```
        label.setBackground(display.getSystemColor(SWT.COLOR_YELLOW));

        Button femaleButton = new Button(shell, SWT.RADIO);
        femaleButton.setText("F");

        Button maleButton = new Button(shell, SWT.RADIO);
        maleButton.setText("M");

        label = new Label(shell, SWT.NULL);
        label.setText("  Title: ");
        label.setBackground(display.getSystemColor(SWT.COLOR_YELLOW));

        Button mrButton = new Button(shell, SWT.RADIO);
        mrButton.setText("Mr.");
        Button mrsButton = new Button(shell, SWT.RADIO);
        mrsButton.setText("Mrs.");
        Button msButton = new Button(shell, SWT.RADIO);
        msButton.setText("Ms.");
        Button drButton = new Button(shell, SWT.RADIO);
        drButton.setText("Dr.");

    ...
```

**Figure 5-11**

Suppose the user is male. He selects the M option by clicking the radio button marked M. Then he tries to select "Mr." as his title. After the Mr. radio button is selected, the selection of the M radio button is gone! The cause of this problem is that all the radio buttons belong to the same group.

To fix this problem, you have to break the radio buttons into two groups. One viable approach is to put the four radio buttons about the title into a separate composite and leave anything else unchanged:

```
    ...
  Composite composite = new Composite(shell, SWT.NULL);
    composite.setLayout(new RowLayout());

    Button mrButton = new Button(composite, SWT.RADIO);
    mrButton.setText("Mr.");
    Button mrsButton = new Button(composite, SWT.RADIO);
    mrsButton.setText("Mrs.");
    Button msButton = new Button(composite, SWT.RADIO);
    msButton.setText("Ms.");
    Button drButton = new Button(composite, SWT.RADIO);
    drButton.setText("Dr.");
    ...
```

# Labels

Labels are non-selectable user interface components that display strings or images. The org.eclipse. swt.widgets.Label class provides basic label functions. If you need labels with advanced features, use the org.eclipse.swt.custom.CLabel class.

## Styles

Styles supported by the Label class are as follows:

❑   SEPARATOR, HORIZONTAL, VERTICAL: The SEPARATOR style causes a label to appear as a single line whose orientation can be either HORIZONTAL (default) or VERTICAL.

❑   SHADOW_IN, SHADOW_OUT, SHADOW_NONE: These three styles specify the shadow behavior of labels with the SEPARATOR style.

❑   LEFT, RIGHT, CENTER: These styles specify the text/image alignment in labels.

❑   WRAP: Labels with this style can automatically wrap long lines. The following code compares labels with and without WRAP styles as shown in Figure 5-12.

The code that follows creates two labels with different styles. The second label has the WRAP style set:

```
Display display = new Display();
Shell shell = new Shell(display);

String text = "Professional Java Interfaces With SWT/JFace, by Jack Li Guojie";

Label labelNoWrap = new Label(shell, SWT.BORDER);
labelNoWrap.setText(text);
labelNoWrap.setBounds(10, 10, 100, 100);

Label labelWrap = new Label(shell, SWT.WRAP | SWT.BORDER);
labelWrap.setText(text);
labelWrap.setBounds(120, 10, 100, 100);
...
```

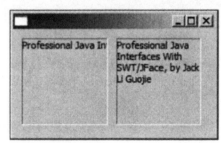

Figure 5-12

## Label Basics

The Label class is very similar to the Button class in terms of API functions.

The following methods can be used to get and set the text label for a label:

```
public String getText()
public void setText(String text)
```

To get and set the image label for a label, you can use the following:

```
public Image getImage()
public void setImage(Image image)
```

The same constraint on text and image as the Button class applies here.

## The CLabel Class

The CLabel class provides some advanced features over the Label class.

An instance of the CLabel class is capable of displaying its text label and image label at the same time. If there is enough space for both the text label and the image label, both of them will be displayed; otherwise, only the text label is displayed.

For the Label class, the style constants SHADOW_IN, SHADOW_OUT, SHADOW_NONE are applicable to label separators only. These three style constants can be used to specify the border behaviors for generic instances of CLabels, as shown in Figure 5-13.

Figure 5-13

Use the following method to set the background image of a CLabel object:

```
public void setBackground(Image image)
```

If the image and the bounds of the CLabel instance are of differing sizes, the image will be stretched or shrunk to fit the bounds of the CLabel instance.

The CLabel class enables you to create labels with gradient colors as background using this method:

```
public void setBackground(Color[] colors, int[] percents)
```

You specify the colors to appear in the gradient to display from left to right in the first argument. The percentages of the width of the label at which color should change are specified as an array in the second argument. For example, the following code creates a label with a background gradient that varies from green to white and then to red (see Figure 5-14):

```
CLabel labelGradientBg = new CLabel(shell, SWT.SHADOW_IN);
labelGradientBg.setText("CLabel with gradient colored background");
labelGradientBg.setImage(image);
labelGradientBg.setBounds(10, 10, 300, 100);
labelGradientBg.setBackground(
    new Color[] {
        display.getSystemColor(SWT.COLOR_GREEN),
        display.getSystemColor(SWT.COLOR_WHITE),
        display.getSystemColor(SWT.COLOR_RED)},
    new int[] { 50, 100 });
```

It's okay.

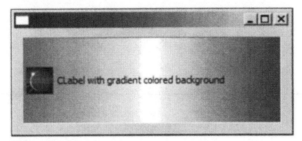

**Figure 5-14**

# Summary

You have learned about the hierarchy of the SWT widgets and several basic controls. The Widget class is the top class in the hierarchy. A widget can be created and disposed of and it is capable of issuing notifications to listeners when events occur. The Control class is the superclass of all windowed UI components. You learned how to set the font and colors for a control, update its UI, and throw the redraw and update methods. A composite is capable of containing other controls, and you learned how to configure the focus traversal over child controls on a composite. The Shell class represents a window in SWT. Buttons and labels are two fundamental controls. You learned how to create buttons and labels with different styles.

The next chapter shows you how to position and size the children of a composite using a layout manager.

# 6

# Layouts

Layouts can be used to manage the position and size of children in composites. This chapter provides a brief overview and definition of layouts. Then you learn about four standard layouts and one custom layout provided in SWT:

- ❑  FillLayout
- ❑  RowLayout
- ❑  GridLayout
- ❑  FormLayout
- ❑  StackLayout

The last section of this chapter explains how to create your own layouts.

## Introduction to Layouts

A layout can be used to control the position and size of children of a composite. For a composite without a layout, you, the developer, have to set the bounds of each of its children one by one. When the composite is resized, you have to update the position and size of its children. Layouts relieve you of the tedious task of controlling positioning and sizing. If you're used to layouts in Swing, SWT layouts should be refreshingly easy to use.

### General Terms

A layout defines an algorithm positioning children of a composite into its client area. In SWT, all layouts must extend the org.eclipse.swt.widgets.Layout class. SWT provides four standard layouts, which are covered later in this chapter. Before going into detail about layouts, you need to understand a few terms that are used frequently when discussing layouts:

❑ **Client area:** The client area of a composite is the area that is capable of displaying data. Usually, the size of the client area is the size of the composite's bounds minus its trim, as shown in Figure 6-1.

❑ **Margins:** A margin specifies the number of pixels that will be placed on a certain side between the edge of the layout and the border of the composite's client area. Some layouts such as the RowLayout allow you specify all of the four margins: the top margin, the bottom margin, the left margin, and the right margin. Other layouts allow you to specify only the horizontal margin and the vertical margin because the size of the top margin is equal to that of the bottom margin and the same rule applies to the left margin and the right margin.

❑ **Spacing:** Spacing specifies the number of pixels between the edges of children of a composite.

❑ **Preferred size:** The preferred size of a control is the size that it would best be displayed at. Usually, this preferred size is also the minimum size that is required to display the control. If a control is a composite, its preferred size is computed in this way: The layout is asked to compute the "best" size of a client area where its children will be displayed, and the preferred size is determined by adding the preferred client area and the trim.

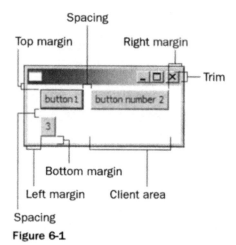

**Figure 6-1**

# Setting Layouts

You can use the following methods to get and set a composite's layout:

```
public Layout getLayout()
public void setLayout(Layout layout)
```

By default, a composite does not have any layout. To set a layout for a composite, you need to pick a proper layout and pass an instance of the selected layout class to the composite's setLayout method. To remove the layout of a composite, you can call the setLayout method with null as the argument.

## Layout Data Objects

Some layout classes have corresponding layout data classes to enable you to achieve fine UI layout control over children of composites. You can associate a layout's data to a specific child control. For example, the following code enables the text control to grab excess horizontal space:

```
Shell shell = new Shell();
shell.setLayout(new GridLayout()); // Only with GridLayout you can use GridData
Text text = new Text(shell, SWT.SINGLE);
Text.setLayoutData(new GridData(GridData.GRAB_HORIZONTAL));
```

The methods in the `Control` class to get and set layout data are:

```
public Object getLayoutData()
public void setLayoutData(Object layoutData)
```

The corresponding layout data, if any, for each standard layout will be introduced in the next few sections.

## Laying Out Children of a Composite

In most cases, you do not have to explicitly lay out children of a composite. For example, when a composite is resized, its layout is automatically called and lays out its children according to the new size.

Sometimes, you may need to explicitly force the layout to lay out the children — for example, if the contents of a composite change. The following method can be used to lay out the children of a composite:

```
public void layout(boolean changed)
```

Setting the `changed` flag to `true` forces the layout to refresh any cached information about its children. If the `changed` flag is `false`, the layout may rely on the cached information. On Windows, the information about the children is always updated regardless of the value of the `changed` flag. The following method of the `Composite` class is equivalent to `layout(true)`:

```
public void layout()
```

Figure 6-2 shows the sample application. When the user clicks the "Add new button" button, a new button is created and put into the composite on the left.

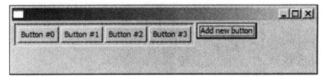

Figure 6-2

The code snippet for the sample application is as follows:

```
Display display = new Display();
Shell shell = new Shell(display);
shell.setLayout(new RowLayout());

final Composite composite = new Composite(shell, SWT.BORDER);
composite.setLayout(new RowLayout());
composite.setBackground(display.getSystemColor(SWT.COLOR_YELLOW));

Button buttonAdd = new Button(shell, SWT.PUSH);
buttonAdd.setText("Add new button");
buttonAdd.addSelectionListener(new SelectionAdapter() {
    public void widgetSelected(SelectionEvent e) {
        Button button = new Button(composite, SWT.PUSH);
        button.setText("Button #" + (count++));
        shell.layout(true);
    }
});
```

When the `buttonAdd` button is clicked, a new button is created with the composite as its parent. Then `shell.layout(true)` is called, which causes the shell to lay out its children, i.e., the composite and the `buttonAdd` button. The layout of the shell finds that the preferred size of the composite has changed. The layout then allocates new space for the composite. After the layout of the shell finishes setting size and location for the composite and the `buttonAdd` button, it then notifies the composite to resize itself. The layout of the composite then lays out all of its children in a similar way.

If you change the `shell.layout(true)` line to `composite.layout(true)`, the composite will not resize and thus you will not be able to see the newly created button because the layout of a composite has no effect on the composite's parent.

> Changing the **shell.layout(true)** to **shell.pack(true)** makes the shell resize itself to its preferred size before its children are laid out.

What about `composite.pack(true)`? If you use `composite.pack(true)`, the composite resizes itself as expected; however, it does not take care of the `buttonAdd` button. After one or two buttons are added, the `buttonAdd` button will be hidden behind the composite. This is not desired, so you should use `shell.layout(true)` or `shell.pack(true)` here.

As a general guideline, if the content of a control changes, you should perform the layout operation on its ancestors instead of the control itself.

# Using FillLayouts

`FillLayout` is a very simple layout. It lays out controls of a composite into a single row or column (without wrap) and forces all the children to be the same size. A `FillLayout` lays out the children into the whole client area of a composite.

In the beginning, all the controls will be set as tall as the tallest control and as wide as the widest. You can specify the margins and spacing properties. There are no corresponding layout data types for this kind of layout. The primary usage of `FillLayout`s is laying out controls in task bars and toolbars.

To use a `FillLayout`, you create it first:

```
FillLayout fillLayout = new FillLayout(SWT.HORIZONTAL);
```

The preceding line creates a `FillLayout` that lays out controls in a row. You can replace the `SWT.HORIZONTAL` style with `SWT.VERTICAL` to create a `FillLayout` that lays out controls in a column. You can also configure the layout orientation by using the type field of the `FillLayout` class:

```
fillLayout.type = SWT.HORIZONTAL // Laying out the children in a row

fillLayout.type = SWT.VERTICAL // Laying out the children in a column
```

Then, you can define the margins and spacing properties. Note that the default (initial) value of each property is 0.

```
// Width of horizontal margins placed along the left and right edges
fillLayout.marginWidth = 5;

// Height of vertical margins placed along the top and bottom edges
fillLayout.marginHeight = 5;

// Number of pixels between the edge of a cell and edges of its neighboring cells
fillLayout.spacing = 1;
```

Now, you can set the layout to a composite:

```
shell.setLayout(fillLayout)
```

After you associate a layout to a composite, you can still modify the layout's properties. Let's add some controls on the shell:

```
Button button1 = new Button(shell, SWT.PUSH);
button1.setText("button1");

Button button2 = new Button(shell, SWT.PUSH);
button2.setText("button number 2");

Button button3 = new Button(shell, SWT.PUSH);
button3.setText("3");

shell.pack();
shell.open();
...
```

Figures 6-3 and 6-4 show the shell with a horizontal `FillLayout` and a vertical `FillLayout`, respectively.

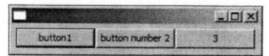

Figure 6-3

Figure 6-4

# Using RowLayout

RowLayout offers several more features over FillLayouts. A RowLayout is capable of wrapping controls, and it can also lay out controls into different sizes. You can customize a RowLayout by modifying the values of its properties (i.e., the fields of the RowLayout class).

## Properties of RowLayouts

The properties of RowLayout are as follows:

- ❑ fill: Specifies whether all the controls in a row should share the same height if the type of this layout is HORIZONTAL; otherwise, it indicates whether all the controls in a column should share the same width. The default value is false.

- ❑ justify: Specifies whether the controls in a row should be justified. The default value is false.

- ❑ marginLeft, marginRight, marginTop, marginBottom: Specify the size of the left margin, the right margin, the top margin, and the bottom margin in pixels. The default value for each of the margins is 3.

- ❑ pack: Specifies whether all controls should take their preferred size. If pack is set to true, all controls have the same size, which is the size required to accommodate the largest preferred height and the largest preferred width of all the controls. The default value is true.

- ❑ spacing: Specifies the space between controls in pixels.

- ❑ type: Specifies whether the layout places controls in rows or columns. The default value is HORIZONTAL. The other possible value is VERTICAL.

- ❑ wrap: Specifies whether controls will be wrapped to the next row or column if there is not enough space left on the current row or column. The default value is true.

The following table shows how the layout properties affect the display of controls.

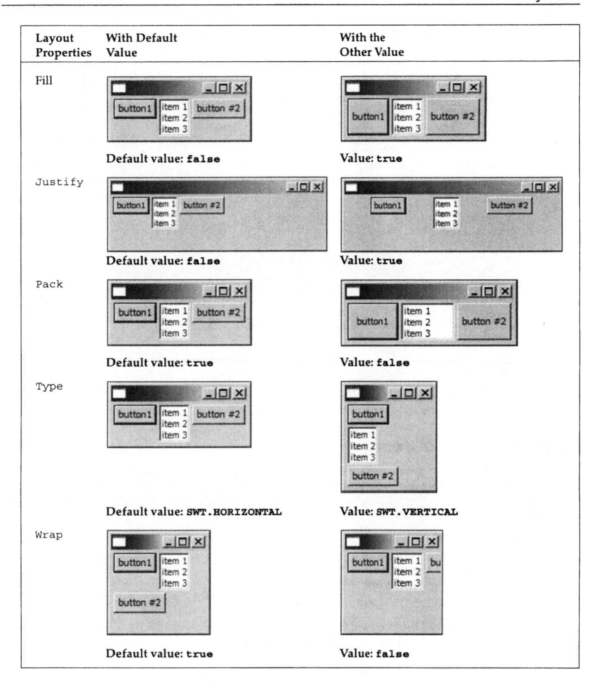

| Layout Properties | With Default Value | With the Other Value |
|---|---|---|
| Fill | Default value: **false** | Value: **true** |
| Justify | Default value: **false** | Value: **true** |
| Pack | Default value: **true** | Value: **false** |
| Type | Default value: **SWT.HORIZONTAL** | Value: **SWT.VERTICAL** |
| Wrap | Default value: **true** | Value: **false** |

The corresponding code to generate the preceding GUIs is as follows:

```
    . . .
Shell shell = new Shell(display);

    RowLayout rowLayout = new RowLayout();
    //rowLayout.fill = true; // Overriding default values.
    //rowLayout.justify = true;
    //rowLayout.pack = false;
    //rowLayout.type = SWT.VERTICAL;
    //rowLayout.wrap = false;

    shell.setLayout(rowLayout);

    Button button1 = new Button(shell, SWT.PUSH);
    button1.setText("button1");

    List list = new List(shell, SWT.BORDER);
    list.add("item 1");
    list.add("item 2");
    list.add("item 3");

    Button button2 = new Button(shell, SWT.PUSH);
    button2.setText("button #2");

    //shell.setSize(120, 120);
    shell.pack();
    shell.open();
    . . .
```

## Using RowData Objects

The corresponding layout data type for the RowLayout class is the RowData class. You can use a RowData object to specify the initial width and height of a control. The following code modifies the preceding code by associating a RowData object to change the initial size of the first button in the shell, as shown in Figure 6-5.

```
    . . .
    Button button1 = new Button(shell, SWT.PUSH);
    button1.setText("button1");
    button1.setLayoutData(new RowData(100, 35));
    . . .
```

Layout data objects should *not* be reused in SWT/JFace, unlike the usage in Swing. The implementations of layout data objects in SWT/JFace and Swing are simply different.

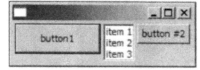

Figure 6-5

# Using GridLayouts

A GridLayout lays out the children of a composite in a grid. GridLayout is the most powerful standard layout and it is also the most complicated, but don't worry. It's actually quite intuitive once you understand the fundamentals of how it works. SWT GridLayouts give you lots of layout power without the same pain as a Swing GridBagLayout.

## *Properties of GridLayouts*

The properties of GridLayout are as follows:

- ❑ horizontalSpacing, verticalSpacing: Specify the horizontal spacing and vertical spacing between controls in a layout. The default value for each of them is 5.

- ❑ marginHeight, marginWidth: Specify the horizontal margin and vertical margin of the layout. The default value for each of them is 5.

- ❑ numColumns: Specifies the number of cell columns in the layout. The default value is 1.

- ❑ makeColumnsEqualWidth: Specifies whether all columns should be forced to have the same width as the widest cell. The default value is false.

The following table shows how the property configurations of a GridLayout affect the final layout of controls.

| Property Configuration | Display |
|---|---|
| `[Defaults]`<br>`numColumns = 1`<br>`makeColumnsEqualWidth = false` | |
| `numColumns = 3`<br>`makeColumnsEqualWidth = true` | |

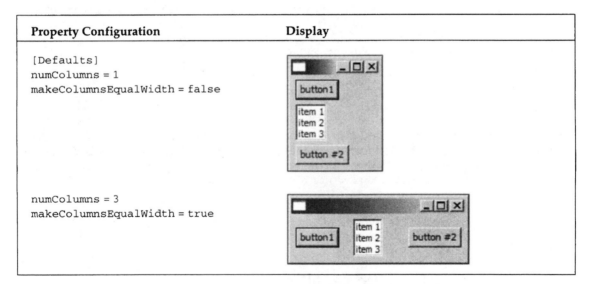

The code to generate a GUI is listed here:

```
    ...
Shell shell = new Shell(display);

    GridLayout gridLayout = new GridLayout();
```

```
//  gridLayout.numColumns = 3;
//  gridLayout.makeColumnsEqualWidth = true;

shell.setLayout(gridLayout);

Button button1 = new Button(shell, SWT.PUSH);
button1.setText("button1");

List list = new List(shell, SWT.BORDER);
list.add("item 1");
list.add("item 2");
list.add("item 3");

Button button2 = new Button(shell, SWT.PUSH);
button2.setText("button #2");

. . .
```

The properties of the GridLayout offer very limited customization. The power of the GridLayout lies in the flexible configurations of GridData objects.

# Using GridData Objects

The GridData class is the layout data type associated with the GridLayout class. As you have seen in previous sections, you can call a control's setLayoutData method to set a control's GridData object.

The GridData class enables you to configure its properties through the constructors or its fields. For example, the following code creates a GridData object:

```
GridData gridData = new GridData();
gridData.horizontalAlignment = GridData. END;
gridData.verticalAlignment = GridData.BEGINNING;
```

However, this code has a problem. All of the constants containing the text HORIZONTAL or VERTICAL are intended to be used in constructors only. If you assign such constants directly to the fields of GridData objects, you may get unexpected layout data configurations. So the only acceptable way to create a GridData instance with horizontal and vertical alignment characteristics is as follows:

```
GridData gridData = new GridData(
  GridData.HORIZONTAL_ALIGN_END
  | GridData.VERTICAL_ALIGN_BEGINNING
);
```

## Horizontal Alignment and Vertical Alignment

The horizontalAlignment and verticalAlignment fields of GridData specify how a control is positioned horizontally and vertically in a cell.

Several possible values for horizontalAlignment are as follows:

❑    BEGINNING: Left-aligned (the default value)

❑    CENTER: Center-aligned

❑  END: Right-aligned

❑  FILL: Filling all the available horizontal space

Figure 6-6 shows layout data objects of controls using different horizontal alignment configurations. The first button is left-aligned; the list is center-aligned; the second button is right-aligned; and the third button is stretched to fill the horizontal space.

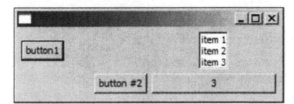

**Figure 6-6**

The code to generate a GUI is as follows:

```
GridLayout gridLayout = new GridLayout();
gridLayout.numColumns = 2;
gridLayout.makeColumnsEqualWidth = true;

shell.setLayout(gridLayout);

Button button1 = new Button(shell, SWT.PUSH);
button1.setText("button1"); // Default alignment

List list = new List(shell, SWT.BORDER);
list.add("item 1");
list.add("item 2");
list.add("item 3");
list.setLayoutData(new GridData(GridData.HORIZONTAL_ALIGN_CENTER));

Button button2 = new Button(shell, SWT.PUSH);
button2.setText("button #2");
button2.setLayoutData(new GridData(GridData.HORIZONTAL_ALIGN_END));

Button button3 = new Button(shell, SWT.PUSH);
button3.setText("3");
button3.setLayoutData(new GridData(GridData.HORIZONTAL_ALIGN_FILL));
...
```

The verticalAlignment functions in exactly the same way as the horizontalAlignment does, except it is used to specify the vertical positioning.

Possible values for verticalAlignment include the following:

❑  BEGINNING: Top-aligned

❑  CENTER: Center-aligned (the default value)

❑   END: Bottom-aligned

❑   FILL: Filling all the available vertical space

Figure 6-7 shows the four controls (from left to right) with the following vertical alignment configurations: BEGINNING, CENTER, END, and FILL.

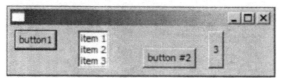

Figure 6-7

## Horizontal Indentation

The horizontalIndent field specifies the number of pixels of indentation that is placed along the left side of the cell. The default value is 0.

In Figure 6-8, the second button has a 5-pixel horizontal indentation.

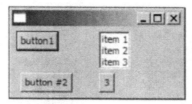

Figure 6-8

The corresponding code is:

```
GridData gridData = new GridData(GridData.VERTICAL_ALIGN_END);
gridData.horizontalIndent = 5;
button2.setLayoutData(gridData);
```

## Horizontal Span and Vertical Span

The horizontalSpan and verticalSpan fields can be used to specify the number of column cells and the number of row cells that a control takes up. The default value for each of them is 1.

For example, in Figure 6-9, the second button spans two columns horizontally.

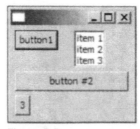

Figure 6-9

The corresponding code is:

```
Button button2 = new Button(shell, SWT.PUSH);
button2.setText("button #2");
GridData gridData = new GridData(GridData.VERTICAL_ALIGN_END);
gridData.horizontalSpan = 2;
gridData.horizontalAlignment = GridData.FILL;
button2.setLayoutData(gridData);
```

## Grabbing Excess Space

The grabExcessHorizontalSpace and grabExcessVerticalSpace properties allow controls to grow if their parent composite grows. Of course, when the parent composite gets smaller, the controls with grab space properties set shrinks. Because cells in the same column share the same width and cells in the same row share the same height, when a control grabs excess space, the entire column or row grows, too. Usually, you enable these properties with controls such as Text, List, Tree, Table, or Canvas.

The default value of each of the two properties is false.

For example, the following code causes the text field to grab excess horizontal space, as shown in Figure 6-10.

```
Display display = new Display();
Shell shell = new Shell(display);

GridLayout gridLayout = new GridLayout();
gridLayout.numColumns = 3;
shell.setLayout(gridLayout);

Label label = new Label(shell, SWT.BORDER);
label.setText("label");

Text text = new Text(shell, SWT.SINGLE | SWT.BORDER);
text.setText("text");

GridData gridData = new GridData();
gridData.grabExcessHorizontalSpace = true;
gridData.horizontalAlignment = GridData.FILL;
text.setLayoutData(gridData);

Button button = new Button(shell, SWT.PUSH);
button.setText("button");

shell.setSize(300, 80);
shell.open();
```

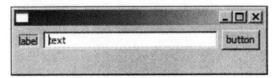

Figure 6-10

Here's the preceding code modified to enable both the text field and the button to grab excess vertical space, as shown in Figure 6-11:

```
    . . .
Text text = new Text(shell, SWT.SINGLE | SWT.BORDER);
    text.setText("text");

    GridData gridData = new GridData();
    gridData.grabExcessHorizontalSpace = true;
    gridData.grabExcessVerticalSpace = true;
    gridData.horizontalAlignment = GridData.FILL;
    gridData.verticalAlignment = GridData.FILL;
    text.setLayoutData(gridData);

    Button button = new Button(shell, SWT.PUSH);
    button.setText("button");

    GridData gridData2 = new GridData();
    gridData2.grabExcessVerticalSpace = true;
    gridData2.verticalAlignment = GridData.FILL;
    button.setLayoutData(gridData2);
    . . .
```

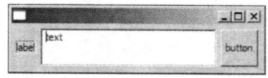

**Figure 6-11**

If more than one control are grabbing excess space, the excess space is distributed to them evenly. For example, the following code makes both the text and the button grab excess horizontal space, as shown in Figure 6-12.

```
Text text = new Text(shell, SWT.SINGLE | SWT.BORDER);
text.setText("text");

GridData gridData = new GridData();
gridData.grabExcessHorizontalSpace = true;
gridData.grabExcessVerticalSpace = true;
gridData.horizontalAlignment = GridData.FILL;
gridData.verticalAlignment = GridData.FILL;

text.setLayoutData(gridData);

Button button = new Button(shell, SWT.PUSH);
button.setText("button");

GridData gridData2 = new GridData();
gridData2.grabExcessVerticalSpace = true;
```

```
gridData2.grabExcessHorizontalSpace = true;
gridData2.verticalAlignment = GridData.FILL;
gridData2.horizontalAlignment = GridData.FILL;

button.setLayoutData(gridData2);
...
```

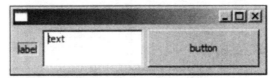

Figure 6-12

### Size Hints

You can use widthHint and heightHint to specify the minimum width and height of a control. The default value for them is SWT.DEFAULT, indicating that no minimum width or height is specified.

Now modify the code used previously to set the size hints for the label:

```
Label label = new Label(shell, SWT.BORDER);
label.setText("label");

GridData gridData3 = new GridData();
gridData3.widthHint = 60;
gridData3.heightHint = 20;

label.setLayoutData(gridData3);
...
```

The display is shown in Figure 6-13.

Figure 6-13

## A Sample GUI Using GridLayouts

To get you familiar with GridLayout and GridData objects, you can build a book entry program. Figure 6-14 shows a sketch of the GUI. First, determine the total number of columns for the grid and the position of each of the controls.

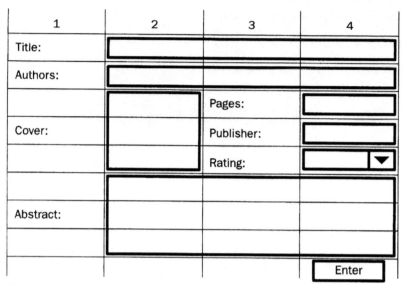

**Figure 6-14**

Now, you can start coding the program:

```
Display display = new Display();
Shell shell = new Shell(display);

shell.setText("Book Entry Demo");

GridLayout gridLayout = new GridLayout(4, false);
gridLayout.verticalSpacing = 8;

shell.setLayout(gridLayout);

// Title
Label label = new Label(shell, SWT.NULL);
label.setText("Title: ");

Text title = new Text(shell, SWT.SINGLE | SWT.BORDER);
GridData gridData =
    new GridData(GridData.HORIZONTAL_ALIGN_FILL);
gridData.horizontalSpan = 3;
title.setLayoutData(gridData);

// Author(s)
label = new Label(shell, SWT.NULL);
label.setText("Author(s): ");

Text authors = new Text(shell, SWT.SINGLE | SWT.BORDER);
gridData =
    new GridData(GridData.HORIZONTAL_ALIGN_FILL);
```

```java
gridData.horizontalSpan = 3;
authors.setLayoutData(gridData);

// Cover
label = new Label(shell, SWT.NULL);
label.setText("Cover: ");

gridData = new GridData();
gridData.verticalSpan = 3;
label.setLayoutData(gridData);

CLabel cover = new CLabel(shell, SWT.NULL);

gridData =
    new GridData(GridData.FILL_HORIZONTAL);
gridData.horizontalSpan = 1;
gridData.verticalSpan = 3;
gridData.heightHint = 100;
gridData.widthHint = 100;

cover.setLayoutData(gridData);

// Details.
label = new Label(shell, SWT.NULL);
label.setText("Pages");

Text pages = new Text(shell, SWT.SINGLE | SWT.BORDER);
pages.setLayoutData(new GridData(GridData.HORIZONTAL_ALIGN_FILL));

label = new Label(shell, SWT.NULL);
label.setText("Publisher");

Text publisher = new Text(shell, SWT.SINGLE | SWT.BORDER);
publisher.setLayoutData(new GridData(GridData.HORIZONTAL_ALIGN_FILL));

label = new Label(shell, SWT.NULL);
label.setText("Rating");

Combo rating = new Combo(shell, SWT.READ_ONLY);
rating.setLayoutData(new GridData(GridData.HORIZONTAL_ALIGN_FILL));
rating.add("5");
rating.add("4");
rating.add("3");
rating.add("2");
rating.add("1");

// Abstract.

label = new Label(shell, SWT.NULL);
label.setText("Abstract:");

Text bookAbstract =
    new Text(
```

```
              shell,
              SWT.WRAP
                    | SWT.MULTI
                    | SWT.BORDER
                    | SWT.H_SCROLL
                    | SWT.V_SCROLL);
    gridData =
        new GridData(
            GridData.HORIZONTAL_ALIGN_FILL | GridData.VERTICAL_ALIGN_FILL);
    gridData.horizontalSpan = 3;
    gridData.grabExcessVerticalSpace = true;

    bookAbstract.setLayoutData(gridData);

// Button.
    Button enter = new Button(shell, SWT.PUSH);
    enter.setText("Enter");

    gridData = new GridData();
    gridData.horizontalSpan = 4;
    gridData.horizontalAlignment = GridData.END;
    enter.setLayoutData(gridData);

// Fill up information.
    title.setText("Professional Java Interfaces with SWT/JFace");
    authors.setText("Jack Li Guojie");
    pages.setText("500pp");
    publisher.setText("John Wiley & Sons");
    cover.setBackground(new Image(display, "X:\\web\\img\\photo.jpg"));
    bookAbstract.setText("This book provides a comprehensive guide for \n" +
            "you to create Java user interfaces with SWT/JFace. ");
    shell.pack();
    shell.open();
```

The initial display and the display after resizing are shown in Figure 6-15 and Figure 6-16, respectively.

Figure 6-15

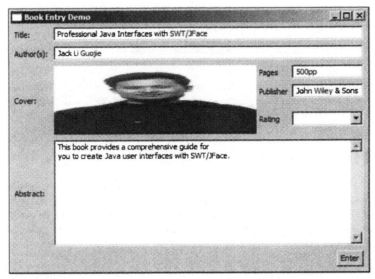

**Figure 6-16**

You should be very careful when you use grabExcessHorizontalSpace and grabExcessVertical Space options. In the demo program, only two controls have such properties set:

❑    The CLabel used to display the book cover: grabExcessHorizontalSpace = true

❑    The Text control used to display the abstract: grabExcessVerticalSpace = true

Obviously, the text fields used to display the title and authors should grab excess horizontal space. However, you should *not* explicitly set these properties for them. Because the title text spans three columns, including the column in which the CLabel belongs, if that column grabs excess horizontal space, the title text grabs excess horizontal space as a result. If you explicitly set the grabExcessHorizontalSpace of the title text's layout object to true, you will find that the CLabel as well as the text fields and the combo resize when the shell is resized.

A final note: You should fully understand the meaning and impact of a constant before using it in the constructors:

❑    HORIZONTAL_ALIGN_BEGINNING, HORIZONTAL_ALIGN_CENTER, HORIZONTAL_ALIGN_END, HORIZONTAL_ALIGN_FILL: Set the horizontalAlignment field to value BEGINNING, CENTER, END, and FILL, respectively.

❑    VERTICAL _ALIGN_BEGINNING, VERTICAL _ALIGN_CENTER, VERTICAL _ALIGN_END, VERTICAL _ALIGN_FILL: Set the verticalAlignment field to value BEGINNING, CENTER, END, and FILL, respectively.

❑    GRAB_HORIZONTAL: Sets the grabExcessHorizontalSpace field to true.

❑    GRAB_VERTICAL: Sets the grabExcessVerticalSpace field to true.

❑   FILL_HORIZONTAL: Sets the horizontalAlignment field to FILL and grabExcessHorizontalSpace to true.

❑   FILL_VERTICAL: Sets the verticalAlignment field to FILL and grabExcessVerticalSpace to true.

❑   FILL_BOTH: Sets the horizontalAlignment field and the verticalAlignment field to FILL and the grabExcessHorizontalSpace field and the grabExcessVerticalSpace field to true.

# Using FormLayouts

The FormLayout is another sophisticated layout. A FormLayout controls the position and size of the children of a composite by using FormAttachment objects to configure the left, right, top, and bottom edge of each child. A FormAttachment attaches a side of the control either to a position in the parent composite or to one of its sibling controls within the layout. Without FormAttachment objects, FormLayouts are useless.

The FormLayout allows you to configure the following properties:

❑   marginHeight: Specifies the size of the vertical margin in pixels. The default value is 0.

❑   marginWidth: Specifies the size of the horizontal margin in pixels. The default value is 0.

❑   spacing: Specifies the number of pixels between the edge of one control and the edge of its neighboring control. The default value is 0.

## FormData Objects and FormAttachment Objects

FormData objects specify how controls should be laid out. A FormData object can be used to define the preferred size and the attachments for four sides of the control. The FormAttachment objects are used to control the position and size of the control.

You can set the preferred width and height of the control by setting the following properties of the FormData object:

❑   width

❑   height

To configure the attachment of each side, you need to set the following properties with proper FormAttachment objects:

❑   top: Specifies the attachment of the top of the control.

❑   bottom: Specifies the attachment of the bottom of the control.

❑   left: Specifies the attachment of the left of the control.

❑   right: Specifies the attachment of the right of the control.

A `FormAttachment` object specifies the attachment of a specific side of a control. You can attach a side to a position in the parent composite, to the adjacent side of another control, to the opposite side of another control, or centered on another control. I discuss these approaches in detail in the material that follows.

## Attaching a Control to a Position in the Parent Composite

To attach the control to a position in the parent composite, you need to define the position of a side of the control using a percentage value.

For example, the following code creates a `FormAttachment` object with the percentage value of 50 (with the default dominator 100):

```
FormData formData = new FormData();
formData.left = new FormAttachment(50);
```

Now you can set the `FormData` to a control:

```
Button button1 = new Button(shell, SWT.PUSH);
button1.setText("button1");
button1.setLayoutData(formData);
```

The left side of the button is centered horizontally on the shell, as shown in Figure 6-17.

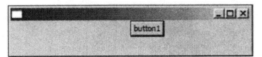

**Figure 6-17**

You can also specify the offset of the control side from the attachment position. If the value of the offset is positive, the control side is offset to the right of or below the attachment position. If the value is negative, then the control side is offset to the left of or above the attachment position.

Now center the button on the shell (i.e., the left side of the button needs to be shifted left by half of the width of the button).

```
Button button1 = new Button(shell, SWT.PUSH);
button1.setText("button1");

Point size = button1.computeSize(SWT.DEFAULT, SWT.DEFAULT);
int offset = size.x / 2;

FormData formData = new FormData();
formData.left = new FormAttachment(50, -1 * offset);

button1.setLayoutData(formData);
```

The preceding code centers the button on the shell, as shown in Figure 6-18.

Figure 6-18

If you do not define FormAttachment objects for a control, the control will be attached to the top-left edges of the parent composite by default.

For example, place two buttons in a shell without specifying their FormData and FormAttachment objects:

```
shell.setLayout(new FormLayout());
Button button1 = new Button(shell, SWT.PUSH);
button1.setText("button1");

Button button2 = new Button(shell, SWT.PUSH);
button2.setText("button number 2");
```

Because both of the buttons will be attached to the top-left corner of the shell, one button will stack on top of the other, as shown in Figure 6-19.

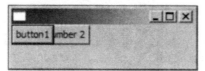

Figure 6-19

You can specify attachments for all four sides of a control. For example, the following code attaches a button to the bottom quarter of a shell, as shown in Figure 6-20.

```
shell.setLayout(new FormLayout());
Button button1 = new Button(shell, SWT.PUSH);
button1.setText("button1");

FormData formData = new FormData();
formData.left = new FormAttachment(50);
formData.right = new FormAttachment(100);
formData.top = new FormAttachment(50);
formData.bottom = new FormAttachment(100);

button1.setLayoutData(formData);
```

If you need more accurate layout control, you can specify the value of the denominator for a FormAttachment object. For example, the code that follows creates a FormAttachment object with the percentage value of $\frac{499}{1000}$ (equivalent to 49.9 percent):

```
FormAttachment formAttachment = new FormAttachment(499, 1000, 0);
```

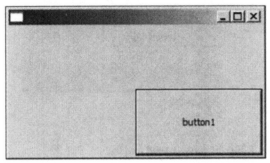

Figure 6-20

## Attaching a Control to Another Control

In addition to attaching a control to a position in the parent composite, you can attach the side of the control to another control within the layout. The side of the control can be attached to the adjacent side of the other control (default alignment), to the opposite side of the other control, or centered on the other control. Additionally, you can specify offsets.

### Attaching to the Adjacent Side of Another Control

By default, the control is attached to the adjacent side of the other control.

In the following code, the left side of button2 is attached to the right side of button1, and the top side of button3 is attached to the bottom side of button2 with an offset value of 10:

```
shell.setLayout(new FormLayout());
Button button1 = new Button(shell, SWT.PUSH);
button1.setText("button1");

Button button2 = new Button(shell, SWT.PUSH);
button2.setText("button number 2");

FormData formData = new FormData();
formData.left = new FormAttachment(button1);
button2.setLayoutData(formData);

Button button3 = new Button(shell, SWT.PUSH);
button3.setText("3");

formData = new FormData();
formData.top = new FormAttachment(button2, 10);
button3.setLayoutData(formData);
```

The GUI is shown in Figure 6-21.

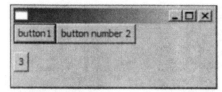

**Figure 6-21**

## Attaching to the Specified Side of Another Control

The default behavior of attachments is attaching the side a control to the adjacent side of another control. You can change this behavior by setting the alignment property of a FormAttachment object. The following constants are possible values for the alignment property:

- ❑ TOP: Attaches the side of the control (the control to which the FormData object will be associated) to the top side of the specified control, "another control" (for top and bottom alignments only).

- ❑ BOTTOM: Attaches the side of the control to the bottom side of the specified control (for top and bottom alignments only).

- ❑ LEFT: Attaches the side of the control to the left side of the specified control (for left and right alignments only).

- ❑ RIGHT: Attaches the side of the control to the right side of the specified control (for left and right alignments only).

- ❑ CENTER: Attaches the side of the control at a position that will center the control on the specified control. This style is covered in the following subsection.

- ❑ DEFAULT: Attaches the side of the control to the adjacent side of the specified control.

All the constants are defined in the org.eclipse.swt.SWT class.

For example, to horizontally align button2 and button3 of the GUI in the preceding subsection, you can use the following code:

```
    ...
Button button3 = new Button(shell, SWT.PUSH);
    button3.setText("3");

    formData = new FormData();
    formData.top = new FormAttachment(button2, 10);
    formData.left = new FormAttachment(button2, 0, SWT.LEFT);
    button3.setLayoutData(formData);
```

The line of code in boldface is the only line inserted. The new layout is shown in Figure 6-22.

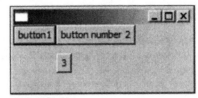

Figure 6-22

## Centering a Control on Another Control

If you need to center a control on another control, you can use the CENTER alignment. For example, the following code

```
formData.top = new FormAttachment(button1, 0, SWT.CENTER);
button2.setLayoutData(formData);
```

centers button2 on button1 — the top of button2 is put in a position allowing the control to be centered on button1.

Next, the following code centers button2 on button1 both horizontally and vertically, as shown in Figure 6-23.

```
Button button1 = new Button(shell, SWT.PUSH);
button1.setText("button1");

FormData formData = new FormData();
formData.left = new FormAttachment(20);
formData.top = new FormAttachment(20);
button1.setLayoutData(formData);

Button button2 = new Button(shell, SWT.PUSH);
button2.setText("button number 2");

formData = new FormData();
formData.left = new FormAttachment(button1, 0, SWT.CENTER);
formData.top = new FormAttachment(button1, 0, SWT.CENTER);
button2.setLayoutData(formData);
```

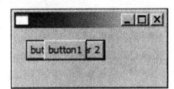

Figure 6-23

If you need to center a control horizontally on another one, you need to set its FormAttachment object for the left side or the right side with CENTER alignment. Similarly, to center a control vertically on another one, you can set its FormAttachment object for the top side or the bottom side. FormLayout is a very powerful layout. As an exercise, try to rewrite the book entry program using FormLayout.

# Using StackLayouts

The StackLayout class is in the package org.eclipse.swt.custom. A StackLayout stacks all the controls one on top of the other and resizes all controls to share the same size and location.

To set a particular control on the top, you should first set the topControl field of the StackLayout with that control and then call the layout method of the parent composite.

For example, the following code creates a stack of buttons on a shell, as shown in Figure 6-24.

```
. . .
final StackLayout stackLayout = new StackLayout();
shell.setLayout(stackLayout);

final Button[] buttons = new Button[3];

for(int i=0; i<buttons.length; i++) {
    buttons[i] = new Button(shell, SWT.NULL);
    buttons[i].setText("Button #" + i);

    buttons[i].addSelectionListener(new SelectionListener() {
        public void widgetSelected(SelectionEvent e) {
            // Flip to next button.
            Button nextButton = null;
            for(int i=0; i<buttons.length; i++) {
                if(buttons[i] == e.widget) {
                    if(i == buttons.length - 1)
                        nextButton = buttons[0];
                    else
                        nextButton = buttons[i+1];
                }
            }
            stackLayout.topControl = nextButton;
            shell.layout();
        }

        public void widgetDefaultSelected(SelectionEvent e) {
        }
    });
}

// Initial
stackLayout.topControl = buttons[0];

shell.setSize(200, 100);
shell.open();
. . .
```

When a button is clicked, the next button will be flipped as the top control.

Additionally, you can configure the marginHeight and marginWidth fields of the StackLayout to control margins.

Figure 6-24

# Creating Your Own Layouts

Sometimes, none of the layouts discussed can satisfy your requirements; in such a case, you can create your own layouts.

A layout must extend the `org.eclipse.swt.widgets.Layout` class, which has only two abstract methods:

```
protected abstract Point computeSize(
    Composite composite,
    int wHint,
    int hHint,
    boolean flushCache)
```

The `computeSize` method computes and returns the minimum size of the specified composite's client area according to this layout.

The other method is:

```
protected abstract void layout(Composite composite, boolean flushCache)
```

which lays out the children of the composite.

The following code implements a layout that is very similar to the `BorderLayout` in Swing.

```java
/**
 * Lays out a composite, arranging and resizing its components to fit in five
 * regions: north, south, east, west, and center.
 */
public class BorderLayout extends Layout {
    // Region constants.
    public static final int NORTH = 0;
    public static final int SOUTH = 1;
    public static final int CENTER = 2;
    public static final int EAST = 3;
    public static final int WEST = 4;

    /**
     * Indicates the region that a control belongs to.
     *
```

**145**

```
      */
    public static class BorderData {
        public int region = CENTER; // default.

        public BorderData() {
        }

        public BorderData(int region) {
            this.region = region;
        }
    }

    // Controls in all the regions.
    public Control[] controls = new Control[5];

    // Cached sizes.
    Point[] sizes;

    // Preferred width and height
    int width;
    int height;

    /*
     * (non-Javadoc)
     *
     * @see Layout#computeSize(org.eclipse.swt.widgets.Composite, int, int,
boolean)
     */
    protected Point computeSize(
        Composite composite,
        int wHint,
        int hHint,
        boolean flushCache) {

        if (sizes == null || flushCache == true)
            refreshSizes(composite.getChildren());
        int w = wHint;
        int h = hHint;
        if (w == SWT.DEFAULT)
            w = width;
        if (h == SWT.DEFAULT)
            h = height;

        return new Point(w, h);
    }

    /*
     * (non-Javadoc)
     *
     * @see
org.eclipse.swt.widgets.Layout#layout(org.eclipse.swt.widgets.Composite,
     *          boolean)
     */
    protected void layout(Composite composite, boolean flushCache) {
```

```
        if (flushCache || sizes == null)
            refreshSizes(composite.getChildren());

    Rectangle clientArea = composite.getClientArea();

    // Enough space for all.
    if (controls[NORTH] != null) {
        controls[NORTH].setBounds(
            clientArea.x,
            clientArea.y,
            clientArea.width,
            sizes[NORTH].y);
    }
    if (controls[SOUTH] != null) {
        controls[SOUTH].setBounds(
            clientArea.x,
            clientArea.y + clientArea.height - sizes[SOUTH].y,
            clientArea.width,
            sizes[SOUTH].y);
    }
    if (controls[WEST] != null) {
        controls[WEST].setBounds(
            clientArea.x,
            clientArea.y + sizes[NORTH].y,
            sizes[WEST].x,
            clientArea.height - sizes[NORTH].y - sizes[SOUTH].y);
    }
    if (controls[EAST] != null) {
        controls[EAST].setBounds(
            clientArea.x + clientArea.width - sizes[EAST].x,
            clientArea.y + sizes[NORTH].y,
            sizes[EAST].x,
            clientArea.height - sizes[NORTH].y - sizes[SOUTH].y);
    }
    if (controls[CENTER] != null) {
        controls[CENTER].setBounds(
            clientArea.x + sizes[WEST].x,
            clientArea.y + sizes[NORTH].y,
            clientArea.width - sizes[WEST].x - sizes[EAST].x,
            clientArea.height - sizes[NORTH].y - sizes[SOUTH].y);
    }

}


private void refreshSizes(Control[] children) {
    for (int i = 0; i < children.length; i++) {
        Object layoutData = children[i].getLayoutData();
        if (layoutData == null || (!(layoutData instanceof BorderData)))
            continue;
        BorderData borderData = (BorderData) layoutData;
        if (borderData.region < 0 || borderData.region > 4) // Invalid.
            continue;
        controls[borderData.region] = children[i];
    }
```

```
        width = 0;
        height = 0;

        if (sizes == null)
            sizes = new Point[5];

        for (int i = 0; i < controls.length; i++) {
            Control control = controls[i];
            if (control == null) {
              sizes[i] = new Point(0, 0);
            } else {
              sizes[i] = control.computeSize(SWT.DEFAULT, SWT.DEFAULT, true);
            }
        }

        width = Math.max(width, sizes[NORTH].x);
        width =
            Math.max(width, sizes[WEST].x + sizes[CENTER].x + sizes[EAST].x);
        width = Math.max(width, sizes[SOUTH].x);

        height =
            Math.max(Math.max(sizes[WEST].y, sizes[EAST].y), sizes[CENTER].y)
                + sizes[NORTH].y
                + sizes[SOUTH].y;

    }
}
```

Let's use the BorderLayout in a sample application:

```
public class BorderLayoutSample {
    Display display = new Display();
    Shell shell = new Shell(display);

    public BorderLayoutSample() {
        shell.setLayout(new BorderLayout());

        Button buttonWest = new Button(shell, SWT.PUSH);
        buttonWest.setText("West");
        buttonWest.setLayoutData(new BorderLayout.BorderData(BorderLayout.WEST));

        Button buttonEast = new Button(shell, SWT.PUSH);
        buttonEast.setText("East");
        buttonEast.setLayoutData(new BorderLayout.BorderData(BorderLayout.EAST));

        Button buttonNorth = new Button(shell, SWT.PUSH);
        buttonNorth.setText("North");
        buttonNorth.setLayoutData(new BorderLayout.BorderData(BorderLayout.NORTH));

        Button buttonSouth = new Button(shell, SWT.PUSH);
        buttonSouth.setText("West");
        buttonSouth.setLayoutData(new BorderLayout.BorderData(BorderLayout.SOUTH));
```

```
        Text text = new Text(shell,
             SWT.MULTI | SWT.BORDER | SWT.V_SCROLL | SWT.H_SCROLL);
        text.setText("Center");
        text.setLayoutData(new BorderLayout.BorderData(BorderLayout.CENTER));

        shell.pack();
        shell.open();

        // Set up the event loop.
        while (!shell.isDisposed()) {
            if (!display.readAndDispatch()) {
                // If no more entries in event queue
                display.sleep();
            }
        }

        display.dispose();
    }

    public static void main(String[] args) {
        new BorderLayoutSample();
    }
}
```

The initial display and the display after resizing are shown in Figure 6-25 and Figure 6-26, respectively.

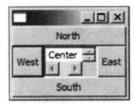

Figure 6-25

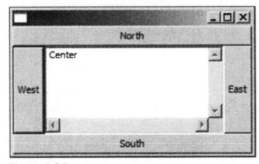

Figure 6-26

The BorderLayout class offers only the basic functions. You may add more features to the BorderLayout, such as margins, spacing, and so on.

# Summary

This chapter introduced SWT layout support. Layouts can be used to position and size child controls on composites. Five typical layouts were discussed. A FillLayout lays out controls into a single row or column and forces all the children to be the same size. A RowLayout offers more flexibility than a FillLayout. You use a RowLayout to lay out controls into rows; it is capable of wrapping controls. A GridLayout is one of the most sophisticated layouts. It lays out controls in a grid. You can use a GridData object to customize the position and size of a particular control. A sample application showed you how to apply GridLayout in practical applications. A FormLayout positions and sizes controls using their associated FormAttachment objects. A FormAttachment object attaches a side of the control either to a position in the composite or to one of its sibling controls. Last, a StackLayout stacks all the controls one on top of the other and resizes all controls to share the same size and location. Finally, you learned how to create your own controls to satisfy your own needs.

# Part II: Design Basics

# 7

# Combos and Lists

In this chapter, you learn about two kinds of SWT controls: Combo and List. Both combos and lists allow the user to choose items from a list of items. The primary difference between them is that a Combo (also know as a "drop-down") allows only one selected item while a List may have multiple items selected at a time. Additionally, the chapter introduces ListViewer, an MVC viewer based on the List control.

## Using Combos

Combos are controls that enable the user to choose an item from a list of items, or optionally enter a new value by typing it into a text field. In SWT, the org.eclipse.swt.widgets.Combo class represents a combo. Although the Combo class is a subclass of Composite, it does not make sense to add children to it.

### Styles

There are two Combo styles:

❑    READ_ONLY: By default, a combo allows the user to enter new values that are not in the list. To disable this feature, you can set READ_ONLY.

❑    DROP_DOWN, SIMPLE: Combos with DROP_DOWN and SIMPLE styles are shown in Figure 7-1. The left combo has the DROP_DOWN style set, while the right one has the SIMPLE style set. Combos with the SIMPLE style occupy more space than those with the DROP_DOWN style.

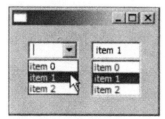

Figure 7-1

## Building Combos and Capturing Item Selections

The following code creates a simple programming language survey form that's shown in Figure 7-2.

```
Display display = new Display();
Shell shell = new Shell(display);

shell.setLayout(new GridLayout(2, false));

(new Label(shell, SWT.NULL)).
 setText("Select your favorite programming language: ");

final Combo combo = new Combo(shell, SWT.NULL);

String[] languages = new String[]{"Java", "C", "C++", "SmallTalk"};

for(int i=0; i<languages.length; i++)
    combo.add(languages[i]);
```

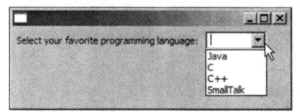

Figure 7-2

A combo is created with default styles (editable; DROP_DOWN). Then you add string items to it by calling the add method.

To track the user's selection, you can register a selection listener:

```
combo.addSelectionListener(new SelectionListener() {
    public void widgetSelected(SelectionEvent e) {
        System.out.println("Selected index: " + combo.getSelectionIndex() +
            ", selected item: " + combo.getItem(combo.getSelectionIndex()) +
            ", text content in the text field: " + combo.getText());
    }
```

```
    public void widgetDefaultSelected(SelectionEvent e) {
        System.out.println("Default selected index: " + combo.getSelectionIndex() +
            ", selected item: " +
            (combo.getSelectionIndex() == -1 ?
                "<null>" : combo.getItem(combo.getSelectionIndex())) +
            ", text content in the text field: " + combo.getText());
    }
});
```

The widgetSelected method of the selection listener is called when the combo's list selection changes; the widgetDefaultSelected method is typically called when the user presses the Enter key in the combo's text field. The preceding code calls the following method to retrieve the selection information:

```
public int getSelectionIndex()
```

The getSelectionIndex method returns the index of items currently selected or -1 if no item is selected. To get the item text, you can call:

```
public String getItem(String index)
```

This method throws IllegalArgumentException if the argument is not in the range ([0, combo.getItemCount()-1]) of the current list of the combo. To retrieve the content text of the text field of a combo, you can use the following:

```
public String getText()
```

For example, when the user selects "Java" from the list, the following line prints out:

```
Selected index: 0, selected item: Java, text content in the text field: Java
```

Suppose the user's favorite programming language is Perl. Because Perl is not in the list, the user needs to type the word. During the typing process, no selection events are generated. When the user presses the carriage return key after he or she finishes typing, a default selection event is generated and the widgetDefaultSelected method is called. As a result, the following line prints out:

```
Default selected index: -1, selected item: <null>, text content in the text field:
Perl
```

Because the user does not select an item from the list, the selected index is -1.

To programmatically select an item from the list, use this method:

```
public void select(int index)
```

If the index is out of range of the list, the request is ignored. To deselect an item, use the following:

```
public void deselect(int index)
```

If the item is not currently selected, this method does nothing. Otherwise, the selection is cleared and a call of the `getSelectionIndex` method returns -1. To deselect all selected items in the list, use the following:

```
public void deselectAll()
```

# Accessing Items in Combos

The `Combo` class provides many methods that you can use to get, set, find, add, and remove items in the list.

## Getting Items

The `getItem` method returns the item at the specified index:

```
public String getItem(int index)
```

An `IllegalArgumentException` is thrown if the index is not in the range of the list. Remember that the range of the list is `[0, getItemCount()-1]`. The `getItemCount` method gives the total number of items in the list:

```
public int getItemCount()
```

To get all the items in the list, you can use the `getItems` method.

```
public String[] getItems()
```

This method returns an array of strings. Note that modifying the returned array of `getItems` does not affect the combo.

## Setting Items

The preceding section introduced how to get methods for items in the list. The corresponding setting methods are:

```
public void setItem(int index, String text)
public void setItems(String[] items)
```

The `setItem` method sets the text of the item at a specified index. If the index specified is out of range of the list, an `IllegalArgumentException` is thrown.

The `setItems` method sets the list to be the specified array of items.

## Finding Items

The `Combo` class provides two `indexOf` methods. These two methods function in a very similar way as the `indexOf` methods in the `java.lang.String` class.

The following method searches a combo's list from the given index until an item is found that is equal to the argument and returns the index of the found item. If no such item is found, -1 is returned.

```
public int indexOf(String text, int startIndex)
```

The other `indexOf` method starts the search from 0:

```
public int indexOf(String text)
```

which is equivalent to

```
indexOf(text, 0);
```

## Adding Items

To add an item to the specified position in the list, use the following:

```
public void add(String text, int index)
```

If the specified index is less than zero (0) or greater than the total number of items currently in the list, an `IllegalArgumentException` is thrown. If the specified index is in the middle of the range, all the items with an index equal to or larger than the specified index will move downward by one position. The convenient `add` method appends an item to the end of the list:

```
public void add(String text)
```

This is equivalent to the following:

```
public void add(String text, getItemCount());
```

## Removing Items

To remove a single item from the list, use the following:

```
public void remove(int index)
```

Naturally, if the index is out of range of the list, an `IllegalArgumentExeption` is thrown.

To remove multiple items, use the following:

```
public void remove(int startIndex, int endIndex)
```

The preceding method removes all the items between the specified start index and the end index (inclusive).

The following method removes the first found item with given text:

```
public void remove(String text)
```

To remove all the items, use the following:

```
public void removeAll()
```

## Creating a Combo with Sorted List

Using alphabetically sorted lists with combos makes the user interface more accessible and user friendly. In this section, we are going to improve the sample application by implementing alpha-beta list sorting and automatic item adding functions. The automatic item adding function enables the user to put the newly added value into the list by pressing the carriage return. The new features are demonstrated in Figure 7-3.

Figure 7-3

The following code provides a sample implementation of these features:

```
    final Combo combo = new Combo(shell, SWT.NULL);

    String[] languages = new String[]{"Java", "C", "C++", "SmallTalk"};

    Arrays.sort(languages);

    for(int i=0; i<languages.length; i++)
        combo.add(languages[i]);

    combo.addSelectionListener(new SelectionListener() {
        public void widgetSelected(SelectionEvent e) {
            System.out.println("Selected index: " + combo.getSelectionIndex() +
            ", selected item: " + combo.getItem(combo.getSelectionIndex()) +
            ", text content in the text field: " + combo.getText());
        }

        public void widgetDefaultSelected(SelectionEvent e) {
            System.out.println("Default selected index: " +
                combo.getSelectionIndex() + ", selected item: " +
            (combo.getSelectionIndex() == -1 ?
                "<null>" :
                combo.getItem(combo.getSelectionIndex())) +
            ", text content in the text field: " + combo.getText());
            String text = combo.getText();
            if(combo.indexOf(text) < 0) { // Not in the list yet.
                combo.add(text);
```

```
            // Re-sort
            String[] items = combo.getItems();
            Arrays.sort(items);
            combo.setItems(items);
        }
    }
});
```

New code added appears in boldface. The sort method of the java.util.Arrays class is used to sort arrays of strings into ascending order. When a default selection event is detected, the application first checks whether the content of the text field is in the list or not. If it is not in the list, the new text will be added to the list. After adding the new item, the program resorts the items in the list.

## About the CCombo Class

In previous sections, we use the org.eclipse.swt.widgets.Combo class to implement combo boxes. The org.eclipse.swt.custom.CCombo class can also be used to create combo boxes. CCombo is very similar to Combo, except that it supports the FLAT style without supporting the SIMPLE style. CCombos are usually used inside table cells.

# Using Lists

A list is very similar to a combo, except a list allows the user to select more than one item. In SWT, lists are represented by the org.eclipse.swt.widgets.List class.

## Single and Multi Selection

While creating a list, you can specify its selection mode using one of the following styles:

❑ SINGLE: If SINGLE is set, the list allows, at most, one item to be selected at any time. This is the default selection mode for lists.

❑ MULTI: Lists with MULTI style allow multiple items to be selected. To select multiple items, the user may need to hold the Ctrl key while clicking an item.

Figure 7-4 shows two lists with different selection modes. The list on the left side allows, at most, one item to be selected at any time, while the other one allows multiple items to be selected.

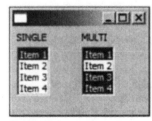

Figure 7-4

159

# Building Lists and Capturing Item Selections

In previous sections, you learned how to use combos through the survey form sample application. Here, let's use a list to create another survey form (as shown in Figure 7-5) to see how a list works. In this survey, the user can select one or more programming languages in which he or she is proficient.

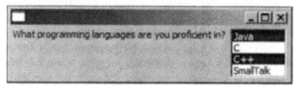

**Figure 7-5**

First, you need to create a shell and add a label and a list:

```
Display display = new Display();
Shell shell = new Shell(display);

RowLayout rowLayout = new RowLayout();
shell.setLayout(rowLayout);

(new Label(shell, SWT.NULL)).
    setText("What programming languages are you proficient in? ");

final List list = new List(shell, SWT.MULTI | SWT.BORDER | SWT.V_SCROLL);

String[] languages = new String[]{"Java", "C", "C++", "SmallTalk"};

for(int i=0; i<languages.length; i++)
    list.add(languages[i]);
```

The list is created with multiple selection enabled. The V_SCROLL style enables the user to scroll the list if there is not enough vertical space to display all the items. The H_SCROLL style also enables horizontal scrolling. After that, you can add items to the list by using its add method.

For the purposes of this example, a RowLayout is fine, so you can establish that with the following code:

```
RowLayout rowLayout = new RowLayout();
shell.setLayout(rowLayout);
```

Next, set the label for the combo, and create the list:

```
(new Label(shell, SWT.NULL)).setText("blah blah blah");
final List list = new List(shell, SWT.MULTI | SWT.BORDER | SWT.V_SCROLL);
```

When you create a list, you have to add it to its shell (or other composite). You also have to specify the format of the list. In this case, you're saying you'd like a multiselection list, with a basic border and vertical scroll capability. That last parameter enables the user to scroll the list if there isn't enough vertical space to display all of the items. (You can add H_SCROLL to enable horizontal scrolling for wide lists.) Now that the list is set up, populate it with this code:

```
String[] languages = new String[]{"Java", "C", "C++", "SmallTalk"};
for(int i=0 . . .
```

To capture the user's selections, you have to add a selection listener:

```
list.addSelectionListener(new SelectionListener() {
    public void widgetSelected(SelectionEvent e) {
        int[] indices = list.getSelectionIndices();
        String[] items = list.getSelection();
        StringBuffer sb = new StringBuffer("Selected indices: ");
        for(int i=0; i < indices.length; i++) {
            sb.append(indices[i]);
            sb.append("(");
            sb.append(items[i]);
            sb.append(")");
            if(i == indices.length-1)
                sb.append('.');
            else
                sb.append(", ");
        }
        System.out.println(sb.toString());
    }

    public void widgetDefaultSelected(SelectionEvent e) {
        int[] indices = list.getSelectionIndices();
        String[] items = list.getSelection();
        StringBuffer sb = new StringBuffer("Default selected indices: ");
        for(int i=0; i < indices.length; i++) {
            sb.append(indices[i]);
            sb.append("(");
            sb.append(items[i]);
            sb.append(")");
            if(i == indices.length-1)
                sb.append('.');
            else
                sb.append(", ");
        }
        System.out.println(sb.toString());
    }
});
```

The selection listener listens for selection and default selection events and prints out the selected items as strings. The getSelectedIndices method returns indices of the items that are currently selected:

```
public int[] getSelectionIndices()
```

To retrieve all the selected items as a string array, you can use the getSelection method:

```
public String[] getSelection()
```

When the user single-clicks the first item, "Java," a selection event is generated. The `widgetSelected` method of the listener is called, and the following line prints out:

```
Selected indices: 0(Java).
```

Suppose this user is proficient in both Java and C++. The user then single-clicks the third item, "C++", while holding the Ctrl key. Another selection event is generated, and as a result, the following prints out:

```
Selected indices: 0(Java), 2(C++).
```

A selection event is generated when the user single-clicks an item. If the user makes another click in such a short period that the two clicks are deemed to be a double-click, a default selection event is generated. The following lines print out if the user double-clicks the last item, "SmallTalk":

```
Selected indices: 3(SmallTalk).
Default selected indices: 3(SmallTalk).
```

You have seen `getSelection` and `getSelectionIndices` in action. Here, I show you some other selection-related methods.

The `getSelectionCount` method returns the index of the currently selected item. If there is no item selected, this method returns -1. If more than one item are selected, the index of the latest selected item is returned.

```
public int getSelectionCount()
```

To programmatically make selections, you can use the following methods:

❑ `public void select(int index)`: This method selects the item at the given index. If the item is already selected, it does nothing. If the index is out of range, the request is ignored with no exceptions being thrown.

❑ `public void select(int[] indices)`: This method selects all the items in the specified index array. Indices that are out of range or duplicated are ignored. If the list allows at most one item to be selected, the item at the first index (if the array is not empty) will be selected.

❑ `public void select(int start, int end)`: This one selects items with indices falling in the specified range. The bounds of the range are included in the selection. Indices that are out of range will be ignored. If the end argument is less than the `start` argument, this method does nothing. If the list is of the `SINGLE` style, the last item in the range will be selected.

❑ `public void selectAll()`: This method selects all of the items. If the list is of the `SINGLE` style, this method has no effect on the selection status of the list.

Corresponding to the select methods listed previously, there are a few deselect methods:

❑ `public void deselect(int index)`: This method deselects the item at the index specified. If the index is out of range, the request is ignored. If the item is already deselected, it remains deselected.

❑ `public void deselect(int[] indices)`: This method can be used to deselect multiple items in one call. Indices that are out of range or duplicated are ignored.

❑ public void deselect(int start, int end): You can use this method to deselect a series of items. The bounds of the indices are inclusive. Any index that is out of range is ignored.

❑ public void deselectAll(): This method deselects all the items in the list.

If the newly selected items are not visible, you can use the following method to scroll down the list until the selection is visible.

```
public void showSelection()
```

To check whether a particular item is selected or not, you can use the isSelected method:

```
public boolean isSelected(int index)
```

## Accessing Items in Lists

Item-handling methods in the List class are very similar to those in the Combo class described in the previous section.

### Getting Items

The getItem method returns the item at the specified index:

```
public String getItem(int index)
```

An IllegalArgumentException is thrown if the index is not in the range of the list. Remember that the range of the list is [0, getItemCount()-1]. The getItemCount method gives the total number of items in the list:

```
public int getItemCount()
```

To get all the items in the list, you can use the getItems method:

```
public String[] getItems()
```

This method returns an array of strings. Note that modifying the returned array of getItems does not affect the list.

### Setting Items

The preceding section introduced how to get methods for items in the list; the corresponding setting methods are:

```
public void setItem(int index, String text)
public void setItems(String[] items)
```

The setItem method sets the text of the item at a specified index. If the specified index is out of range of the list, an IllegalArgumentException is thrown.

The setItems method sets the list to be the specified array of items.

## Finding Items

The `List` class provides two `indexOf` methods. The way these two methods function is very similar to `indexOf` methods in the `java.lang.String` class.

The following method searches a combo's list from the given index until an item is found that is equal to the argument, and returns the index of the found item. If no such item is found, `-1` is returned.

```
public int indexOf(String text, int startIndex)
```

The other `indexOf` methods start the search from 0:

```
public int indexOf(String text)
```

which is equivalent to:

```
indexOf(text, 0);
```

## Adding Items

To add an item to the specified position in the list, use the following:

```
public void add(String text, int index)
```

If the specified index is less than zero (0) or greater than the total number of items currently in the list, an `IllegalArgumentException` is thrown. If the specified index is in the middle of the range, all the items with an index equal to or larger than the specified index will be moved downward by one position. The convenient `add` method appends an item to the end of the list:

```
public void add(String text)
```

which is equivalent to:

```
public void add(String text, getItemCount());
```

## Removing Items

To remove a single item from the list, use the following:

```
public void remove(int index)
```

Naturally, if the index is out of range of the list, an `IllegalArgumentException` is thrown.

To remove multiple items, use the following:

```
public void remove(int[] indices)
public void remove(int startIndex, int endIndex)
```

The first method removes all the items with specified indices, and the second one removes all the items between the specified `start` index and `end` index (inclusive).

The following method removes the first found item with the given text:

```
public void remove(String text)
```

To remove all the items, use the following:

```
public void removeAll()
```

# Using ListViewers

Chapter 2 introduced the model-view-controller architecture. JFace viewers are one of the MVC frameworks available in JFace. In the preceding section, you learned how to program with Lists in a traditional way. In this section, you look at how to use ListViewers to accomplish the same tasks using the MVC approach.

JFace viewers (org.eclipse.jface.viewers.Viewer) are model-based adapters on widgets. Structured viewers (org.eclipse.jface.viewers.StructuredViewer) are structure-oriented viewers that support custom sorting, filtering, and rendering. A ListViewer is a StructuredViewer based on an SWT List control.

The steps to program with StructuredViewers are as follows:

1.  Create domain-specific model objects.
2.  Create StructuredViewers.
3.  Set content providers and content.
4.  Set label providers (optional).
5.  Add selection listeners (optional).
6.  Add filters (optional).
7.  Set sorters (optional).
8.  Handle events (optional).

Let's rewrite the proficient languages survey application using a ListViewer.

## Creating Domain-Specific Model Objects

Domain-specific model objects are queried by the list viewer to create a corresponding label. A programming language has a name and it can be object-oriented or not. The following code models programming languages with the Language subclass:

```
public class SampleListViewer {
    Display display = new Display();
    Shell shell = new Shell(display);

    ListViewer listViewer;
```

```
/**
 * Represents programming languages.
 *
 */
public static class Language {
    public String genre;
    public boolean isObjectOriented;

    public Language() { }
    public Language(String genre, boolean isObjectOriented) {
        this.genre = genre;
        this.isObjectOriented = isObjectOriented;
    }

    public String toString() {
        return "Lang: " + genre + " [" +
            (isObjectOriented ? "Object-oriented" : "Procedural") + "]";
    }
} // End of the Language subclass.
...
```

The Language class has two properties: genre and isObjectOriented. For the sake of simplicity, these properties can be accessed directly (declared public) instead of using getters and setters. Here, you create a Language object for each programming language and add each language to the list:

```
Vector languages = new Vector();

languages.add(new Language("Java", true));
languages.add(new Language("C", false));
languages.add(new Language("C++", true));
languages.add(new Language("SmallTalk", true));
```

You put all of the Language instances in a Vector in order to configure the ListViewer more easily.

## Creating a ListViewer

The ListViewer class provides two constructors that enable you to create a ListViewer in much the same way that you create a List control:

```
public ListViewer(Composite parent)
public ListViewer(Composite parent, int style)
```

The first constructor creates a List control with MULTI | H_SCROLL | V_SCROLL | BORDER styles, and "hooks" the List control with the new ListViewer instance. You can create a custom styled ListViewer with the second constructor. Additionally, you can create a ListViewer based on an existing List control:

```
public ListViewer(List list)
```

In the sample application, the following line creates the `ListViewer` instance:

```
listViewer = new ListViewer(shell);
```

# Setting the Content Provider and the Content

Before you can feed the domain-specific model into the `ListViewer`, you have to set a content provider for the `ListViewer`. A content provider mediates between the viewer's model and the viewer itself. Because `ListViewer` is a structure-oriented viewer, you have to set a structure-oriented content provider:

```
listViewer.setContentProvider(new IStructuredContentProvider() {
    public Object[] getElements(Object inputElement) {
        Vector v = (Vector)inputElement;
        return v.toArray();
    }

    public void dispose() {
        System.out.println("Disposing ...");
    }

    public void inputChanged(Viewer viewer, Object oldInput, Object newInput) {
        System.out.println("Input changed: old=" +
            oldInput + ", new=" + newInput);
    }
});
```

The `getElements` method is called by the `ListViewer` to get an array of elements from the input object. In the sample application, we are going to use the `languages` vector as the input, so the `getElements` method simply returns an array with all the elements in the vector as the content. When input is changed, the `inputChanged` method will be called. While the list viewer is being disposed of, the `dispose` method is called. The content provider has been set. Now, you can set the model as the input to the `ListViewer`:

```
listViewer.setInput(languages);
```

At runtime, the previous line triggers the following output:

```
Input changed: old=null, new=[Lang: Java [Object-oriented], Lang: C [Procedural],
Lang: C++ [Object-oriented], Lang: SmallTalk [Object-oriented]]
```

The preceding content provider takes a `Vector` as the input element. In many cases, the input element is a `Collection` or an array. JFace provides a convenient class, the `org.eclipse.jface.viewers .ArrayContentProvider` class, to handle such cases. The input element for `ArrayContentProviders` must be `Collection` or `Object[]`. You can replace the `setContentProvider` code with this line:

```
listViewer.setContentProvider(new ArrayContentProvider());
```

If there is an input element set for a `ListViewer` while no content provider is being set, an exception is thrown.

## Setting the Label Provider

All the elements (instances of `Language`) returned by the `getElements` method of the content provider are displayed on the list. The text representation for each element is determined using a label provider. If you do not set a label provider for a `ListViewer`, a default label provider is used. The default label provider simply takes the return value of the `toString()` method of each element as its text representation, as shown in Figure 7-6.

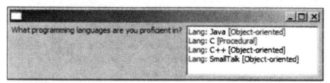

**Figure 7-6**

The item texts seem quite tedious. To display only the genre of a programming language, you need to supply a custom label provider:

```
listViewer.setLabelProvider(new LabelProvider() {
    public Image getImage(Object element) {
        return null;
    }

    public String getText(Object element) {
        return ((Language)element).genre;
    }
});
```

In the preceding code, an inner class subclassing `LabelProvider` is created. Alternatively, you can implement the `ILabelProvider` interface. The `getText` method returns a text label for the given element object. The `ListViewer` shows this text label in its associated `List` control. Because `ListViewer` does not support images, the `getImage` method simply returns a `null` object. If you need to display images, you should consider a `TableViewer`, which is covered in Chapter 10.

The `ListViewer` with custom label provider is shown in Figure 7-7.

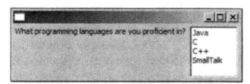

**Figure 7-7**

## Capturing Events and Getting Selections

In the preceding section, we use a `SelectionListener` to capture selection events. `Viewers` support `ISelectionChangedListeners` instead of `SelectionListeners`. The following code registers a listener listening for a selection changed event and printing out the selected items:

```
listViewer.addSelectionChangedListener(new ISelectionChangedListener() {
    public void selectionChanged(SelectionChangedEvent event) {

        IStructuredSelection selection =
            (IStructuredSelection)event.getSelection();

        StringBuffer sb = new StringBuffer("Selection - ");
        sb.append("total " + selection.size() + " items selected: ");
        for(Iterator iter = selection.iterator(); iter.hasNext(); ) {
                sb.append(iter.next() + ", ");
        }
        System.out.println(sb);
    }
});
```

When a selection changes, the selectionChanged method is called with an event object of type SelectionChangedEvent as the argument. To retrieve the selection from a SelectionChangedEvent object, you can call its getSelection method. For structure-oriented viewers, selection objects are of the IStructuredSelection type, so you need to cast the return object of getSelection into an IStructuredSelection object. Important methods of the IStructuredSelection interface are as follows:

❑ public int size(): This method returns the total number of elements selected.

❑ public Iterator iterator(): This method returns an iterator over elements of this selection.

❑ public Object[] toArray(): This method returns the selected elements as an array.

❑ public Object getFirstElement(): This convenient method returns the first selected element if it exists.

When you program with the raw List control, you get selections as indices or text labels. For the ListViewer viewer, you get selections as domain-specific element objects. This property of MVC-based viewers enables you to focus on a business model and logic without spending too much time on the implementation details of the UI controls.

When you click the first item in the list, the following line appears:

```
Selection - total 1 items selected: Lang: Java [Object-oriented],
```

Now, press and hold the Shift key and click the third item to select the first three items. The selection now changes to:

```
Selection - total 3 items selected: Lang: Java [Object-oriented], Lang: C
[Procedural], Lang: C++ [Object-oriented],
```

At any time, you can always use the following method to track the selection status:

```
public ISelection getSelection()
```

Again, you need to cast the return object into an `IStructuredSelection` object. To set selection programmatically, you can use the `setSelection` method:

```
public void setSelection(ISelection selection, boolean reveal)
```

The `selection` argument is the selection to be made, and the `reveal` argument indicates whether the selection should be made visible. One convenient method available in the `Viewer` class is `setSelection(ISelection selection)`, which is equivalent to `setSelection(selection, false)`.

For example, the following code sets the last two elements selected:

```
Object[] toBeSelectedItems = new Object[2];
toBeSelectedItems[0] = languages.elementAt(languages.size()-1);
toBeSelectedItems[1] = languages.elementAt(languages.size()-2);
IStructuredSelection selection = new StructuredSelection(toBeSelectedItems);

listViewer.setSelection(selection, true);
```

In addition to selection changed events, you can also register listeners to listen to post selection changed events using the `addPostSelectionChangedListener` method. A post selection changed event is equivalent to a selection changed event, except it has a delay when the selection change is triggered by keyboard navigation.

The following table shows all the events that `StructuredViewers` support.

| Event (Event Object Class) | Remarks | Declared in Class | Methods |
| --- | --- | --- | --- |
| Double-clicks (DoubleClickEvent) | Generated when double-clicks occur | StructuredViewer | addDoubleClickListener removeDoubleClick-Listener |
| Help (HelpEvent) | | Viewer | addHelpListener removeHelpListener |
| Open (OpenEvent) | Selection-open for trees | StructuredViewer | addOpenListener removeOpenListener |
| Post Selection Changed (SelectionChanged-Event) | | StructuredViewer | addPostSelection-ChangedListener removePostSelection-ChangedListener |
| Selection Changed (SelectionChanged-Event) | | Viewer | addSelection-ChangedListener removeSelection-ChangedListener |

In rare cases, you may need to listen for other low-level events, such as mouse movement. In such cases, you can first obtain the wrapped control of a viewer and then register corresponding listeners to the control. The following method returns the wrapped control:

```
public Control getControl()
```

After obtaining the control, you can then cast the object into its appropriate type. `ListViewer` provides a convenient method to get the wrapper `List` control:

```
public List getList()
```

which is equivalent to `(List)getControl()`.

## Adding Filters

Filters can be used to filter out unwanted elements. You can add one or more filters to a `StructuredViewer`. An element is not displayed unless it passes through every one of the filters.

For example, to display object-oriented languages only, you can apply a filter to the list viewer.

```
listViewer.addFilter(new ViewerFilter() {
    public boolean select(Viewer viewer, Object parentElement, Object element){
        if(((Language)element).isObjectOriented)
            return true;
        else
            return false;
    }
});
```

In the preceding code, we create an inner class subclassing the `ViewFilter` class. The `select` method is the only method that has to be implemented. It returns whether the given element makes it through the filter. The `ListViewer` queries this method with three arguments. The first argument passed is the viewer itself. The second one, `parentElement`, is the input object. The last argument is the element to be checked.

The `addFilter` method not only adds a `ViewerFilter` to the viewer, it also triggers refiltering and resorting of the elements.

When you run the program, only the object-oriented languages are shown (see Figure 7-8).

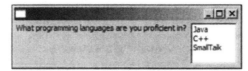

**Figure 7-8**

# Setting a Sorter

Sorters can be used to reorder the elements provided by content providers. A viewer can have no more than one sorter. In JFace, a sorter is represented by the `ViewerSorter` class.

The following sorter sorts the elements by their genres alphabetically, and the result is shown in Figure 7-9.

```
listViewer.setSorter(new ViewerSorter(){
    public int compare(Viewer viewer, Object e1, Object e2) {
        return ((Language)e1).genre.compareTo(((Language)e2).genre);
    }
});
```

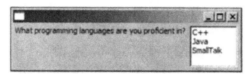

**Figure 7-9**

Behind the scenes, the list viewer calls the following method of the sorter:

```
public void sort(Viewer viewer, Object[] elements)
```

The default implementation of this `sort` method uses the `Arrays.sort` algorithm on the given array, calling the `compare` method to compare elements. So you can also override the `sort` method to implement the sorting logic.

The `setSorter` method of the `StructuredViewer` class also triggers viewers to refresh elements displayed.

# Updating/Refreshing the Viewer

When you make some changes on the model, you need to notify the viewer to update itself. The following method can be used to update the presentation of a particular element:

```
public void update(Object element, String[] properties)
```

The `element` argument is the element object whose representation is to be updated. The second argument, `properties`, can be used by the viewer to optimize the update. For example, if a label provider is not affected by changes of specified properties, an update is not required. Setting the `properties` argument to `null` forces a full update of the element. If the viewer has a sorter, the element position is updated to maintain the order. Filters of the viewer are also applied to the element.

If you need to update multiple elements at the same time, you can use the following method:

```
public void update(Object[] elements, String[] properties)
```

Neither of preceding `update` methods handles structural changes—for example, addition or removal of elements. To handle structural changes, you can use the `refresh` methods. The following method refreshes the viewer with information freshly obtained from the model (the input object).

```
public void refresh(boolean updateLabels)
```

If `updateLabels` is set to `true`, all labels of the existing elements are updated, too. The method:

```
public void refresh()
```

is equivalent to `refresh(true)`.

Finally, the following method refreshes the viewer, starting with the given element:

```
public void refresh(Object element)
```

This method is useful for table and tree viewers only. When you add or remove children from a particular element, you can call this method.

To illustrate how to use such update and refresh methods, let's extend the sample application to allow addition, removal, and modification of programming languages (see Figure 7-10).

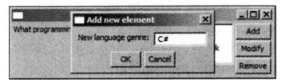

**Figure 7-10**

The corresponding code is listed here:

```
Button buttonAdd;
Button buttonRemove;
Button buttonModify;

buttonAdd = new Button(composite, SWT.PUSH);
buttonAdd.setText("Add");

buttonModify = new Button(composite, SWT.PUSH);
buttonModify.setText("Modify");

buttonRemove = new Button(composite, SWT.PUSH);
buttonRemove.setText("Remove");

buttonAdd.addSelectionListener(new SelectionAdapter() {
    public void widgetSelected(SelectionEvent e) {
        InputDialog dialog = new InputDialog(shell,
            "Add new element", "New language genre: ", "", null);
```

```
            dialog.open();
            String newGenre = dialog.getValue();
            if (newGenre != null) {
                languages.add(new Language(newGenre, true));
            }

            listViewer.refresh(false);
        }
    });

    buttonModify.addSelectionListener(new SelectionAdapter() {
        public void widgetSelected(SelectionEvent e) {
            IStructuredSelection selection =
                    (IStructuredSelection) listViewer.getSelection();
            Language language = (Language) selection.getFirstElement();
            if (language == null) {
            System.out.println("Please select a language first.");
                return;
            }

            InputDialog dialog = new InputDialog(shell,
                    "Modify genre", "Rename: ", language.genre, null);
            dialog.open();
            String newName = dialog.getValue();
            if (newName != null) {
                language.genre = newName;
            }

            listViewer.update(language, null);
        }
    });

    buttonRemove.addSelectionListener(new SelectionAdapter() {
        public void widgetSelected(SelectionEvent e) {
            IStructuredSelection selection =
                (IStructuredSelection)listViewer.getSelection();
            Language language = (Language)selection.getFirstElement();
            if(language == null) {
                System.out.println("Please select a language first.");
                return;
            }

            languages.remove(language);
            System.out.println("Removed: " + language);

            listViewer.refresh(false);
        }
    });
```

The three buttons are put into a composite located at the right part of the shell. When the Add or Modify buttons are pressed, dialogs appear. Those dialogs are used to get user input. For more details on the SWT dialog, please refer to Chapter 12.

When an element is added or removed, `refresh(false)` is called to refresh the viewer. If an element has been modified, then the `update` method is capable of performing viewer updating. You can always use `refresh` methods to replace `update` methods; however, `refresh` methods are more computationally expensive that `update` ones.

# Summary

This chapter covers two kinds of SWT widgets: `Combos` and `Lists`. You learned how to create combos and capture item selections. Items in a combo can be gotten, set, found, added, and removed easily with methods provided by the `Combo` class. Similarly, you can create lists and capture single or multiple selections.

The `ListViewer` class is an MVC-based JFace viewer based on the `List` control. To develop a `ListViewer`-based program, you need to create domain-specific model objects first. Then you need to create an instance of the `ListViewer` and set the content provider and the content for it. Optionally, you can set a label provider, filters, and sorters for it. Because structured viewers hide UI implementation details, you can program with other structured viewers in a very similar way. Table viewers and tree viewers are introduced in Chapter 10 and Chapter 11, respectively.

# 8

# Text Controls

In this chapter, two kinds of SWT text controls are introduced:

- ❑   Text
- ❑   StyledText

You learn basic text operations, selections with the Text control, and the StyledText control. In addition, this chapter introduces features of the StyledText control, such as text styles and line background customization.

## Using Texts

The Text control represents a selectable user interface object that allows the user to input and modify text.

### Styles

The following styles are used:

- ❑   CENTER, LEFT, RIGHT: You can use CENTER, LEFT, and RIGHT to specify the alignment of the text within the control. Only one of them may be specified. The default alignment is left-aligned.

- ❑   MULTI, SINGLE: MULTI indicates the text control supports multiple lines. If SINGLE is set, the text control supports one line only. Only one style, MULTI or SINGLE, may be specified. If neither style is specified and none of the WRAP, V_SCROLL, and H_SCROLL styles is set, the text control supports a single line only.

❏ READ_ONLY: A text control with this style does not allow the user to modify the text. However, you can still modify the text programmatically. By default, this style is not set.

❏ WRAP: This style applies only to text controls supporting multiple lines. If the WRAP style is set, the text control automatically wraps long lines. Figure 8-1 shows two text controls with the same series of characters as their text content. The text control on the left side does not have a WRAP style, but the one on the right does.

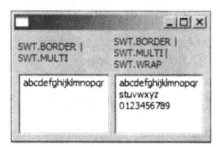

**Figure 8-1**

The Text class is a subclass of the Scrollable class; thus the H_SCROLL and V_SCROLL styles are inherited. Usually, you need to set H_SCROLL and V_SCROLL styles for text controls supporting multiple lines to enable the user to navigate the whole text content easily.

# Text Basics

Creating text controls is not difficult. This subsection shows you how to create single-line and multiple-line text controls. In addition, you can use methods provided by the Text class to access text information.

## Creating Single-Line Text Controls

There is only one constructor in the Text class:

```
public Text(Composite parent, int style)
```

The following code creates two Text controls, as shown in Figure 8-2.

```
(new Label(shell, SWT.NULL)).setText("User name: ");

textUser = new Text(shell, SWT.SINGLE | SWT.BORDER);
textUser.setText("default_user");
textUser.setTextLimit(16);

(new Label(shell, SWT.NULL)).setText("Password: ");

textPassword = new Text(shell, SWT.SINGLE | SWT.BORDER);
textPassword.setEchoChar('*');
```

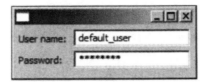

Figure 8-2

Both of the two text controls have the SINGLE and BORDER styles. For the first one, the setText method of the Text class is used to set the default user name. The other text control is used to accept a password; thus you need to set an echo character to make the text control display echo characters instead of plain password text. The setEchoChar method is used to set the echo character for a text control. The corresponding method to query the echo character is getEchoChar. The setTextLimit method of the Text class can be used to specify the maximum number of characters that a text control is capable of holding. To reset the text limit to the default value, you can use setTextLimit(Text.LIMIT).

## Creating Multiple-Line Text Controls

The following code creates a text control supporting multiple lines, as shown in Figure 8-3.

```
(new Label(shell, SWT.NULL)).setText("Remarks:");

text = new Text(shell, SWT.MULTI | SWT.BORDER | SWT.V_SCROLL | SWT.H_SCROLL);
text.setText("1234\r\n56789");
```

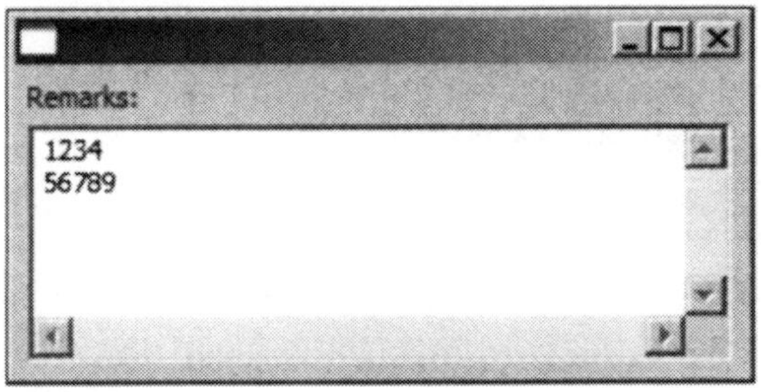

Figure 8-3

The text control is created with MULTI | BORDER | V_SCROLL | H_SCROLL styles. The setText method is used to put initial text into the text control. Two characters, \r and \n in the argument of the setText method, indicate a line break. A \r followed by \n forms a line delimiter. When the user presses an Enter key on an editable text control, a line delimiter is inserted at the caret position. As a result, two characters, \r and \n, are inserted. Line delimiters on different operating systems may vary. To check the line delimiter for the host operating system, you can call the getLineDelimiter method:

```
public String getLineDelimiter()
```

> It is important to notice that characters used as line delimiters are always included when calculating total number of chars, caret offset, and so on.

For example, the following code

```
System.out.println("Number of chars: " + text.getCharCount());
```

prints the total number of characters in the text control:

```
Number of chars: 11
```

The nine visible characters plus two characters used for the line delimiter results in a total of eleven characters.

## Accessing Text Information

The Text class provides several methods for you to access text information easily.

In the preceding section, the getCharCount method was introduced. The getLineCount method can be used to get the total number of lines in a text control:

```
public int getLineCount()
```

To check whether a text control is editable, you can use the getEditable method:

```
public boolean getEditable()
```

The getText method returns all the characters in the text control as a string:

```
public String getText()
```

To get a range of the text, you can use this method:

```
public String getText(int start, int end)
```

The start argument and the end argument specify the position of the first character and the position of the last character in the range. An empty string is returned if the end of the range is less than the start.

The following methods can be used to get and set the number of tabs:

```
public int getTabs()
public void setTabs(int tabs)
```

The width of a tab stop is equal to the total width of the specified number of the space ( ) characters.

To get the position of the caret, you can use the following:

```
public int getCaretPosition()
```

The line number that the caret is at can be determined using the getCaretLineNumber method.

```
public int getCaretLineNumber()
```

# Text Operations

Text controls enable the user to append, insert, delete, or replace the text. Alternatively, the Text class provides methods for text operations such as inserting, cutting, and so on.

## Appending, Pasting, and Inserting Text

To append a string to the text of a text control, you can use the append method:

```
public void append(String string)
```

The insert method can be used to insert a string at the current caret position:

```
public void insert(String string)
```

If there is a text selection called upon the insert method, the selected portion of the text is replaced with the given string. To insert a string at a particular position, you may first set the caret position using the setSelection method before inserting the string. More details on the setSelection method are introduced in the next section.

If you have used any text processing software, you must be very familiar with the copy, cut, and paste commands. To equip your applications with those operations, you can consider using the following methods of the Text class:

```
public void copy()
public void cut()
public void paste()
```

The copy method copies the selected text to the system clipboard. The cut method not only copies the selected text to the clipboard, it also deletes the selected text. The paste method acts like the insert method, except it inserts text from the clipboard.

## Verifying the Input

The text control allows you to verify the text when the text is about to be modified. A verify event is sent when a text change is about to occur. Verify events are sent prior to actual modification of the text. The Text class allows you to register verify listeners using the addVerifyListener method:

```
public void addVerifyListener(VerifyListener listener)
```

The corresponding method to remove a verify listener is removeVerifyListener. The sole method in the VerifyListener interface you need to implement is the verifyText method.

```
public void verifyText(VerifyEvent e)
```

When the text is about to be modified, the verifyText method is called with a VerifyEvent object as the argument. The text modification information is stored in fields of the VerifyEvent object:

- ❑ public int start, public int end: These two fields indicates the start and the end of the range of the text being modified.

- ❑ public String text: This field contains the new text to be inserted.

Because VerifyEvent is a subclass of the KeyEvent class, you may also access fields provided by the KeyEvent class:

❑ public char character: The character represented by the key that was typed.

❑ public int keyCode: This field represents the key code of the key that was typed. The key code constants are defined in the SWT class.

❑ public int stateMask: This field records the state of the keyboard modifier keys (including Alt, Shift, and Ctrl) at the time the event was generated.

❑ public boolean doit: This flag indicates whether the operation should be allowed or not. To cancel the operation, you can set the doit flag to false.

You can use verify listener to alter the behavior of text modification. For example, the following code converts all the input to a text control to uppercase.

```
text.addVerifyListener(new VerifyListener() {
    public void verifyText(VerifyEvent e) {
        e.text = e.text.toUpperCase();
    }
});
```

Verify listeners can also be used to implement an auto-completion mechanism. The code that follows automatically completes the word "VerifyListener" when you press *Ctrl+spacebar* after an uppercase *V*.

```
text.addVerifyListener(new VerifyListener() {
    public void verifyText(VerifyEvent e) {
        if(e.end == e.start) { // Insert.
            if( e.character == ' ' && (e.stateMask & SWT.CTRL) != 0 ) {
                if(text.getText(e.end-1, e.end-1).equals("V")) {
                    e.text = "verifyListener";
                }else{
                    e.doit = false;
                }
            }
        }
    }
});
```

First, you need to make sure the text modification to be performed is an insertion. This can be done by checking the start and the end of the range of selected text (if the start point is the same as the end point, which means that no text is selected, it's an insertion operation). Next, you need to check whether Ctrl and space keys are pressed. If the character immediately prior to the caret position is an uppercase *V*, you can modify the text field of the VerifyEvent object to append the remaining letters of the word. Otherwise, the action should be cancelled by setting the doit field of the event object to false. To implement a powerful auto-completion function, you can use a dictionary to perform word lookups.

## Capturing Modification Events

After the text in a text control is modified, a modify event is generated and dispatched. You can register one or more modify listeners for modify events of a text control using the addModifyListener method of the Text class:

```
public void addModifyListener(ModifyListener listener)
```

The method to remove a registered modify listener is removeModifyListener. The modifyText method is only a single method to be implemented in the ModifyListener interface.

```
public void modifyText(ModifyEvent e)
```

During the modify event dispatching process, the modifyText method is called with a ModifyEvent object as the argument. However, this event object does not contain any information about the text change. You have to directly query the text control for text change.

For example, the following code registers a modify listener listening to the modify events and printing the current character count.

```
text.addModifyListener(new ModifyListener() {
        public void modifyText(ModifyEvent e) {
          System.out.println("New character count: " + text.getCharCount());
        }
});
```

# Text Selections

A text control allows the user to select a part or whole of the text content. You can also manipulate text selections programmatically.

To select a range of text, you can use the setSelection method.

```
public void setSelection(int start, int end)
```

You specify the start and the end of a range of the text to be selected in terms of caret positions. The text between the two caret positions is selected. For example, if the text content is 123456789 and setSelection(1, 4) is called, text 234 is selected. If end is set equal to start, no character is selected and the caret is moved to the position of start. Alternatively, you can use the following method to set the caret position.

```
public void setSelection(int start)
```

After a text selection has been made, you can use the showSelection method to scroll the text selection into view. To select all the text in a text control, you can use the selectAll method.

```
public void selectAll()
```

The `clearSelection` method clears the current selection.

```
public void clearSelection()
```

To get information about the current selection, you can use the following methods:

```
public Point getSelection()
public int getSelectionCount()
public String getSelectionText()
```

Again, assuming the text content is 123456789 and `setSelection(1, 4)` is called, the results of calling each of the three methods are:

```
getSelection:        Point (1, 4)
getSelectionCount:     3
getSelectionText:    234
```

Although you can register `SelectionListeners` to a text control, they listen to selection events of the text control rather than the text content so that they are not notified for text selections. Typically, the `widgetDefaultSelected` is called when the Enter key is pressed in a single-line text control.

# Using StyledTexts

The `StyledText` control is a very customizable text control. It provides all of the features provided by the `Text` control. Additionally, it enables you to:

❑ Use various text foreground and background colors within the text

❑ Use different font styles

❑ Set line background colors

Most of the APIs introduced in the preceding section apply to the `StyledText` class, too. In this section, we will focus on the additional features provided by the `StyledText` class.

## Setting Text Styles with StyleRanges

For styled text controls, you need to use `StyleRanges` to set text styles. Fields of the `StyleRange` class are:

❑ `public int start, public int length`: These two fields are used to define the range of the text to which the text style should be applied. The target text is the text starting from the `start` offset with `length` characters. You must make sure offsets `start` and `start+length-1` are in the range of text content. Otherwise, an `IllegalArgumentException` is thrown when you try to set styles. The default value for both is 0.

❑ `public Color foreground, public Color background`: These fields represent the foreground color and the background color of the text. If they are not set (i.e., having `null` values), the styled text control will use the default control colors. You can make use of this feature to remove styles from a styled text control.

❑     `public int fontStyle`: The `StyledText` control does not support mixing multiple fonts or italic fonts. You can use the `setFont` method of the `StyledText` class to set the font of the whole text content within the control. The `fontStyle` field can be used to specify the style of the font to be used, either `SWT.NORMAL` or `SWT.BOLD`.

To add a style to a styled text control, you can use the `setStyleRange` method of the `StyledText` class:

```
public void setStyleRange(StyleRange range)
```

For example, the following code highlights part of the text, as shown in Figure 8-4.

**Figure 8-4**

```
styledText = new StyledText(shell,
    SWT.MULTI | SWT.WRAP | SWT.BORDER | SWT.H_SCROLL | SWT.V_SCROLL);

styledText.setLayoutData(new GridData(GridData.FILL_BOTH));

Font font = new Font(shell.getDisplay(), "Courier New", 12, SWT.NORMAL);
styledText.setFont(font);

styledText.setText("123456789\r\nABCDEFGHI");

StyleRange styleRange1 = new StyleRange();
styleRange1.start = 2;
styleRange1.length = 16;
styleRange1.foreground = shell.getDisplay().getSystemColor(SWT.COLOR_BLUE);
styleRange1.background = shell.getDisplay().getSystemColor(SWT.COLOR_YELLOW);
styleRange1.fontStyle = SWT.BOLD;

styledText.setStyleRange(styleRange1);
```

After the text for the styled text control is set, a `StyleRange` is created and set to the control. The target text to be set style starts at offset `2` with length `16`. The foreground color and background color are set to blue and yellow, respectively. The font style is set to bold. After the `StyleRange` instance has been properly configured, the `setStyleRange` method is called to apply the style.

You can add as many styles as you like to a styled text control. Let's apply a new style for the text DEF in the styled text control (see Figure 8-5).

**Figure 8-5**

```
StyleRange styleRange2 = new StyleRange();
styleRange2.start = 14;
styleRange2.length = 3;
styleRange2.fontStyle = SWT.NORMAL;
styleRange2.foreground = shell.getDisplay().getSystemColor(SWT.COLOR_YELLOW);
styleRange2.background = shell.getDisplay().getSystemColor(SWT.COLOR_BLUE);

styledText.setStyleRange(styleRange2);
```

You may notice that only the range of text specified in this StyleRange has been applied to the new style. The text outside the new style range keeps its existing style information.

When new text is inserted, all the existing text keeps its style information and the new text is not styled. For example, the following code inserts new text into the styled text control and the newly added text is not styled, as shown in Figure 8-6.

```
styledText.setSelection(4);
styledText.insert("000");
```

**Figure 8-6**

Two other methods enable you to add new styles to a styled text control:

```
public void replaceStyleRanges(int start, int length, StyleRange[] ranges)
public void setStyleRanges(StyleRange[] ranges)
```

The replaceStyleRanges deletes the existing styles in the specified range and adds the new styles. The StyleRange instance in the array should not overlap and should be within the specified start and length. Otherwise, exceptions could be thrown.

The setStyleRanges method replaces all the existing styles with the new StyleRange instances, which is equivalent to the following:

```
replaceStyleRanges(0, getCharCount(), ranges)
```

## Setting Line Backgrounds

You can also customize the line background using the setLineBackground method:

```
public void setLineBackground(int startLine, int lineCount, Color background)
```

The lines specified must be in the range; otherwise an IllegalArgumentException is thrown.

The following code sets the line background of a styled text control, as shown in Figure 8-7.

```
shell.setLayout(new GridLayout());

styledText = new StyledText(shell,
        SWT.BORDER | SWT.MULTI | SWT.WRAP | SWT.H_SCROLL | SWT.V_SCROLL);

styledText.setLayoutData(new GridData(GridData.FILL_BOTH));


Font font = new Font(shell.getDisplay(), "Courier New", 12, SWT.NORMAL);
styledText.setFont(font);

styledText.setText("abcdefg\r\nhijklmn");

StyleRange styleRange1 = new StyleRange();
styleRange1.start = 2;
styleRange1.length = 3;
styleRange1.foreground = shell.getDisplay().getSystemColor(SWT.COLOR_BLUE);
styleRange1.background = shell.getDisplay().getSystemColor(SWT.COLOR_YELLOW);
styleRange1.fontStyle = SWT.BOLD;

styledText.setStyleRange(styleRange1);


styledText.setLineBackground(0, 1,
        shell.getDisplay().getSystemColor(SWT.COLOR_GREEN));
styledText.setLineBackground(1, 1,
        shell.getDisplay().getSystemColor(SWT.COLOR_YELLOW));
```

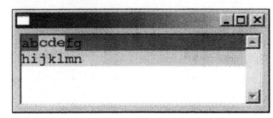

Figure 8-7

The background of the first line is set to green, and the background of the second one is set to yellow. You may notice that the styles applied are not affected by the line background setting method. If line background color and styles with custom background colors are used in conjunction with each other, the style background colors are displayed after the line background color is displayed.

# Using LineStyleListeners and LineBackgroundListeners

In fact, there are two ways to specify text style information. You can use the methods provided by the `StyleText` class (as shown in preceding sections) or you may define your own `LineStyleListeners`. Similarly, you can either use the methods provided by the `StyleText` class to define line backgrounds (as shown in preceding sections) or define your own `LineBackgroundListener`.

You cannot use `LineStyleListeners` when you use the text style API methods provided by the `StyleText` class, and vice versa. Similarly, you cannot use `LineBackgroundListeners` when you use the line background API methods, and vice versa.

## Using LineStyleListeners

To use a `LineStyleListener`, you must first create it and then register it to the styled text control with the method `addLineStyleListener` of the `StyledText` class.

The only method you need to implement a `LineStyleListener` is the `lineGetStyle` method:

```
public void lineGetStyle(LineStyleEvent event)
```

This method is called in order to get the line's style information when a line is about to be drawn. The fields of the `LineStyleEvent` class are as follows:

❑   `public int lineOffset`: This field contains the start offset of the line.

❑   `public String lineText`: This field contains the text content of the line.

❑   `public StyleRange[] styles`: You need to set this field to specify the text styles.

For example, the following code creates a styled text control with search keyword highlighting function as shown in Figure 8-8.

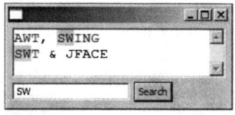

**Figure 8-8**

```
public class SearchStyleText {
    Display display = new Display();
    Shell shell = new Shell(display);
```

```
StyledText styledText;
Text keywordText;
Button button;

String keyword;

public SearchStyleText() {
    shell.setLayout(new GridLayout(2, false));

    styledText = new StyledText(shell,
        SWT.MULTI | SWT.WRAP | SWT.BORDER | SWT.H_SCROLL | SWT.V_SCROLL);
    GridData gridData = new GridData(GridData.FILL_BOTH);
    gridData.horizontalSpan = 2;
    styledText.setLayoutData(gridData);

    keywordText = new Text(shell, SWT.SINGLE | SWT.BORDER);
    keywordText.setLayoutData(new GridData(GridData.FILL_HORIZONTAL));
    Font font = new Font(shell.getDisplay(), "Courier New", 12, SWT.NORMAL);
    styledText.setFont(font);

    button = new Button(shell, SWT.PUSH);
    button.setText("Search");
    button.addSelectionListener(new SelectionAdapter() {
        public void widgetSelected(SelectionEvent e) {
            keyword = keywordText.getText();
            styledText.redraw();
        }
    });

    styledText.addLineStyleListener(new LineStyleListener() {
        public void lineGetStyle(LineStyleEvent event) {
            if(keyword == null || keyword.length() == 0) {
                event.styles = new StyleRange[0];
                return;
            }

            String line = event.lineText;
            int cursor = -1;

            LinkedList list = new LinkedList();
            while( (cursor = line.indexOf(keyword, cursor+1)) >= 0) {
                list.add(getHighlightStyle(
                    event.lineOffset+cursor, keyword.length()));
            }

            event.styles = (StyleRange[])
                list.toArray(new StyleRange[list.size()]);
        }
    });

    styledText.setText("AWT, SWING \r\nSWT & JFACE");

    shell.pack();
    shell.open();
```

```
        while (!shell.isDisposed()) {
            if (!display.readAndDispatch()) {
                // If no more entries in event queue
                display.sleep();
            }
        }

        display.dispose();
    }

    private StyleRange getHighlightStyle(int startOffset, int length) {
        StyleRange styleRange = new StyleRange();
        styleRange.start = startOffset;
        styleRange.length = length;
        styleRange.background =
            shell.getDisplay().getSystemColor(SWT.COLOR_YELLOW);
        return styleRange;
    }


    public static void main(String[] args) {
        new SearchStyleText();
    }
}
```

When the user keys in a keyword in the text field and then clicks the search button, all the occurrences of the keyword in the text are highlighted.

## Using LineBackgroundListeners

The method in the StyledText class to register a LineBackgroundListener is addLineBackgroundListener:

```
public void addLineBackgroundListener(LineBackgroundListener listener)
```

Only one method is declared in the LineBackgroundListener interface:

```
public void lineGetBackground(LineBackgroundEvent event)
```

This method is called when a line is about to be drawn in order to get its background color.

The following code highlights the lines with odd indices, as shown in Figure 8-9.

```
styledText = new StyledText(shell,
    SWT.MULTI | SWT.WRAP | SWT.BORDER | SWT.H_SCROLL | SWT.V_SCROLL);
styledText.setLayoutData(new GridData(GridData.FILL_BOTH));

styledText.addLineBackgroundListener(new LineBackgroundListener() {
    public void lineGetBackground(LineBackgroundEvent event) {
        if(styledText.getLineAtOffset(event.lineOffset) % 2 == 1)
            event.lineBackground =
                    shell.getDisplay().getSystemColor(SWT.COLOR_YELLOW);
```

```
        }
    });

    styledText.setText(
        "Line 0\r\nLine 1\r\nLine 2\r\nLine 3\r\nLine 4\r\nLine 5\r\nLine 6");
```

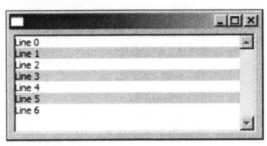

Figure 8-9

The content implementation for the StyleText class can also be user-defined. This can be achieved by implementing the StyledTextContent interface and using the setContent method to initialize a styled text control. However, developing a customized StyledTextContent implementation is very time consuming and error prone. We are not going to cover this topic here. In most of cases, you can easily utilize the text framework (see Chapter 20) to bypass this complicated task. If you still insist on implementing StyleTextContent, you can take a look at its default implementation in SWT — org.eclipse.swt.custom.DefaultContent.

# Summary

This chapter introduced SWT text controls: Text and StyledText. You learned how to create single-line and multiple-line text controls. Text operations such as appending, pasting, and inserting can be easily performed against a text control. When the user keys in text in the text box, you can register listeners to verify the input. StyledText offers many more features than the Text control. You can set different text styles for different regions in the same text area.

# Menus, Toolbars, Cool Bars, and Actions

This chapter teaches you how to use menus, toolbars, and cool bars in SWT. Additionally, you learn how to use the JFace action framework to simplify the task of creating menus and toolbars.

## Using Menus and Menu Items

In SWT, a menu is represented by the `org.eclipse.swt.widgets.Menu` class. A menu may contain many menu items (`org.eclipse.swt.widgets.MenuItem`). Menu items are selectable user interface objects that issue notifications when pressed and released.

### Using Menus

There are different kinds of menus, and the Menu class provides different constructors to create them.

#### Bar Menus

A menu with the `SWT.BAR` style stays at the top of a shell. Bar menus are used as top-level menus for shells. Figure 9-1 shows a menu with two menu items.

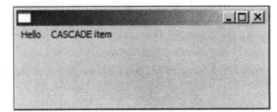

Figure 9-1

To create a bar menu, you can use the following constructor:

```
public Menu(Decorations parent, int style)
```

You need to put the SWT.BAR style bit in the style argument. To set a menu bar to a shell, you need to call the setMenuBar method of the Shell class:

```
public void setMenuBar(Menu menu)
```

The corresponding method to get the menu bar is the getMenuBar method.

The following section provides examples of creating menus.

## Drop-Down Menus

A menu with the SWT.DROP_DOWN style is usually used as a submenu, which is used in conjunction with a menu item with the SWT.CASCADE style. A drop-down menu appears when the user clicks its corresponding parent menu item, as shown in Figure 9-2.

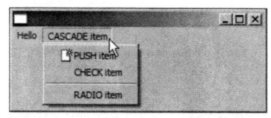

Figure 9-2

To create a drop-down menu, you can use either of the following constructors:

```
public Menu(Menu parentMenu)
public Menu(MenuItem parentItem)
```

The first one constructs a new instance of the menu with the given parent menu and sets the newly created menu style to SWT.DROP_DOWN. The second constructor sets the parent of the new instance to a menu item. The only difference between the two constructors is that they create menu widgets with different types of widgets as their parents. In the former case, the menu is disposed of when the parent menu is disposed of; in the latter case, the menu is disposed of when the parent menu item is disposed of.

After the drop-down menu has been created, you can associate it with a SWT.CASCADE menu item using the setMenu method of the MenuItem class:

```
public void setMenu(Menu menu)
```

## Pop-Up Menus

A pop-up menu, with the SWT.POP_UP style, usually appears when the user right-clicks the corresponding widget, as shown in Figure 9-3.

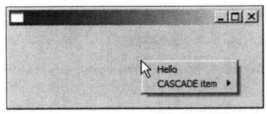

**Figure 9-3**

To create a pop-up menu for a control, you can use the following constructor of the Menu class:

```
public Menu(Control parent)
```

This method creates a menu with the SWT.POP_UP style. After the pop-up menu has been created, you can associate it to a control using the setMenu method of the control class:

```
public void setMenu(Menu menu)
```

The corresponding method to get the pop-up menu of a control is the getMenu method.

## Menu Item Management

Typically, a menu has several menu items as its children. A few methods in the Menu class handle menu item management.

To retrieve all the menu items in a menu, you can use the getItems method:

```
public MenuItem[] getItems()
```

The total number of items can be obtained through the getItemCount method:

```
public int getItemCount()
```

To get a menu item at the specified index, you can use the getItem method:

```
public MenuItem getItem(int index)
```

If the specified index is out of range, an IllegalArgumentException is thrown.

There are two methods to get and set the default menu item. A default menu item is usually highlighted using boldface:

```
public MenuItem getDefaultItem()
public void setDefaultItem(MenuItem item)
```

## Handling Events

Menus can generate two types of events: SWT.HELP and SWT.MENU.

When the user presses F1 on a menu, a help event is generated. The following method can be used to register a HelpListener to a menu:

```
public void addHelpListener(HelpListener listener)
```

Alternatively, you can also use the following code (see Chapter 4):

```
addListener(SWT.HELP, new Listener(...));
```

When a menu appears or disappears, menu events are generated. The following method can be used to add a MenuListener:

```
public void addMenuListener(MenuListener listener)
```

There are two methods in the MenuListener interface that you need to implement:

```
public void menuHidden(MenuEvent e)
public void menuShown(MenuEvent e)
```

## Using MenuItems

A menu item is a selectable user interface object that issues notification when pressed and released.

A menu item may have one and only one style of the following:

❑   SWT.CHECK: A menu item with this style behaves like a checkbox.

❑   SWT.CASCADE: A cascade menu item may have a menu as the submenu. When the user clicks a menu item with the SWT.CASCADE style, instead of issuing notifications, the system opens the menu attached to the menu item.

❑   SWT.PUSH: Menu items with this style behave like push buttons.

❑   SWT.RADIO: A menu item with this style behaves like a radio button.

❑   SWT.SEPARATOR: A menu item with the SWT.SEPARATOR style is a line separator.

The MenuItem class provides two constructors:

```
public MenuItem(Menu parent, int style)
public MenuItem(Menu parent, int style, int index)
```

The first constructor creates a new instance with the given menu as its parent. You specify one and only one of the styles SWT.CHECK, SWT.CASCADE, SWT.PUSH, SWT.RADIO, and SWT.SEPARATOR in the style argument. The second constructor allows you to specify the index at which to place the menu item in the item list maintained by the parent menu.

The following code creates a menu bar, as shown in Figure 9-4.

Figure 9-4

```
Menu menuBar = new Menu(shell, SWT.BAR);

MenuItem itemHello = new MenuItem(menuBar, SWT.PUSH);
itemHello.setText("&Hello");
itemHello.addListener(SWT.Selection, new Listener() {
    public void handleEvent(Event event) {
        System.out.println("HELLO");
    }
});

MenuItem itemCascade = new MenuItem(menuBar, SWT.CASCADE);
itemCascade.setText("&CASCADE item");

Menu menu = new Menu(itemCascade);

MenuItem itemPush = new MenuItem(menu, SWT.PUSH);
itemPush.setText("&PUSH item\tCtrl+P");
itemPush.setAccelerator(SWT.CTRL + 'P');
Image icon = new Image(shell.getDisplay(), "icons/new.gif");
itemPush.setImage(icon);
itemPush.addListener(SWT.Selection, new Listener() {
    public void handleEvent(Event event) {
        System.out.println("item selected: PUSH item");
    }
});

final MenuItem itemCheck = new MenuItem(menu, SWT.CHECK);
itemCheck.setText("CHEC&K item\tCtrl+K");
itemCheck.setAccelerator(SWT.CTRL + 'K');
itemCheck.addListener(SWT.Selection, new Listener() {
    public void handleEvent(Event event) {
        System.out.println("item selected: CHECK item");
        System.out.println("Selection: " + itemCheck.getSelection());
    }
});

new MenuItem(menu, SWT.SEPARATOR);

final MenuItem itemRadio = new MenuItem(menu, SWT.RADIO);
itemRadio.setText("&RADIO item\tCtrl+R");
itemRadio.setAccelerator(SWT.CTRL + 'R');
itemRadio.addListener(SWT.Selection, new Listener() {
    public void handleEvent(Event event) {
        System.out.println("item selected: RADIO item");
        System.out.println("Selection: " + itemRadio.getSelection());
    }
});

itemCascade.setMenu(menu);

shell.setMenuBar(menuBar);
```

The first line of the code creates the menu bar for the shell. A menu item with SWT.PUSH style is added to the menu bar. The setText method of the MenuItem is used to set the text label for the menu item.

We then add an untyped listener to listen for selection events. When the push menu item is pressed, the listener is invoked.

A menu item with the SWT.CASCADE style is then added to the menu bar. A menu with the SWT.DROP_DOWN style is created with the cascade menu item as its parent. We then add a push menu item, a check menu item, a line separator, and a radio menu item to the menu. Finally, we attach the menu to the cascade menu item and set the menu bar to the shell.

Notice that when you specify the text label for a menu item using the setText method, you may include the mnemonic character and accelerator text. Insertion of an ampersand (&) immediately before a character causes the character to be the mnemonic. When the user presses a key sequence matching the mnemonic, the corresponding menu item is selected. To escape the mnemonic character "&", you can double it in the string. Accelerator text is indicated by the \t characters. The text following \t is displayed on platforms that support accelerator text. The accelerator text displays only the acceleration key sequence. To install the acceleration key sequence, you need to call the setAccelerator method:

```
public void setAccelerator(int accelerator)
```

In the preceding code, *Ctrl+K* is assigned to the check menu item in the submenu. When *Ctrl+K* is pressed, even if the submenu is not displayed, a selection event is generated for the check menu item.

In addition to text labels, you can also specify an image label for a menu item using the setImage method:

```
public void setImage(Image image)
```

If a menu item is of the style SWT.CHECK or SWT.RADIO, you can check its selection status through the getSelection method:

```
public boolean getSelection()
```

To modify the selection status for a menu item programmatically, you can use the setSelection method:

```
public void setSelection(boolean selected)
```

Besides selection events, a menu can also generate help events and arm events. An arm event occurs when a menu item is armed (i.e., the user clicks the menu item and the mouse button has not been released yet). The methods to register help listeners and arm listeners are as follows:

```
public void addHelpListener(HelpListener listener)
public void addArmListener(ArmListener listener)
```

At the end of the preceding code, we use setMenu to attach the menu to the cascade menu item:

```
public void setMenu(Menu menu)
```

This method is available only for menu items with the SWT.CASCADE style, and the menu passed must be of the SWT.DROP_DOWN style. Otherwise, exceptions will be thrown.

To enable or disable a menu item, you can use the setEnabled method of the MenuItem class.

## Creating a Text Editor

In this chapter, you are going to create a text editor with basic functions, as shown in Figure 9-5.

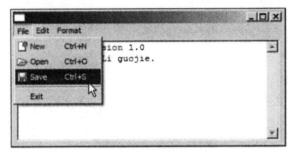

**Figure 9-5**

First, you set up the shell and create a styled text control:

```
public class BasicEditor {
  Display display = new Display();
  Shell shell = new Shell(display);

  // The control used for text displaying and editing.
  StyledText text;

  // Is there any changes since last saving action?
  boolean hasUnsavedChanges;

  // The file associated with current text content.
  File file;

  // The recent directory
  private String lastOpenDirectory;

  // The name of this program.
  public static final String APP_NAME = "BasicEditor v1.0";

  public BasicEditor() {
      shell.setLayout(new GridLayout());

      text =
              new StyledText(
              shell,
              SWT.MULTI
                  | SWT.WRAP
                  | SWT.BORDER
                  | SWT.H_SCROLL
                  | SWT.V_SCROLL);
      text.setLayoutData(new GridData(GridData.FILL_BOTH));

      Font font = new Font(shell.getDisplay(), "Courier New", 10, SWT.NORMAL);
      text.setFont(font);
```

```
    text.setText("BasicEditor version 1.0\r\nWritten by Jack Li Guojie. ");
    text.addModifyListener(new ModifyListener() {
    public void modifyText(ModifyEvent e) {
        hasUnsavedChanges = true;
    }
});
```

Then you create the menu bar and menu items as shown here:

```
// Add menus.
Menu menuBar = new Menu(shell, SWT.BAR);

// --- sub menu: File
MenuItem fileMenuItem = new MenuItem(menuBar, SWT.CASCADE);
fileMenuItem.setText("&File");
Menu fileMenu = new Menu(shell, SWT.DROP_DOWN);

MenuItem miNew = new MenuItem(fileMenu, SWT.PUSH);
miNew.setText("&New\tCtrl+N");
miNew.setImage(getImage("new.gif"));
miNew.setAccelerator(SWT.CTRL + 'N');
miNew.addListener(SWT.Selection, new Listener() {
    public void handleEvent(Event event) {
        if(handleChangesBeforeDiscard()) {
            file = null;
            text.setText("");
        }
    }
});

MenuItem miOpen = new MenuItem(fileMenu, SWT.PUSH);
miOpen.setText("&Open\tCtrl+O");
miOpen.setAccelerator(SWT.CTRL + 'O');
miOpen.setImage(getImage("open.gif"));
miOpen.addListener(SWT.Selection, new Listener() {
    public void handleEvent(Event event) {
        if(handleChangesBeforeDiscard())
            loadTextFromFile();
    }
});

MenuItem miSave = new MenuItem(fileMenu, SWT.PUSH);
miSave.setText("&Save\tCtrl+S");
miSave.setImage(getImage("save.gif"));
miSave.setAccelerator(SWT.CTRL + 'S');
miSave.addListener(SWT.Selection, new Listener() {
    public void handleEvent(Event event) {
        saveTextToFile();
    }
});

new MenuItem(fileMenu, SWT.SEPARATOR);

MenuItem miExit = new MenuItem(fileMenu, SWT.PUSH);
```

```
miExit.setText("&Exit");
miExit.addListener(SWT.Selection, new Listener() {
    public void handleEvent(Event event) {
        if(handleChangesBeforeDiscard())
            shell.dispose();
        }
    });

fileMenuItem.setMenu(fileMenu);

// --- sub menu: Edit.
MenuItem editMenuItem = new MenuItem(menuBar, SWT.CASCADE);
editMenuItem.setText("&Edit");

Menu editMenu = new Menu(shell, SWT.DROP_DOWN);

MenuItem miCopy = new MenuItem(editMenu, SWT.PUSH);
miCopy.setText("&Copy\tCtrl+C");
miCopy.setImage(getImage("copy.gif"));
miCopy.setAccelerator(SWT.CTRL + 'C');
miCopy.addListener(SWT.Selection, new Listener() {
    public void handleEvent(Event event) {
        text.copy();
    }
});

MenuItem miCut = new MenuItem(editMenu, SWT.PUSH);
miCut.setText("Cu&t\tCtrl+X");
miCut.setImage(getImage("cut.gif"));
miCut.setAccelerator(SWT.CTRL + 'X');
miCut.addListener(SWT.Selection, new Listener() {
    public void handleEvent(Event event) {
        text.cut();
    }
});

MenuItem miPaste = new MenuItem(editMenu, SWT.PUSH);
miPaste.setText("&Paste\tCtrl+P");
miPaste.setImage(getImage("paste.gif"));
miPaste.setAccelerator(SWT.CTRL + 'P');
miPaste.addListener(SWT.Selection, new Listener() {
    public void handleEvent(Event event) {
        text.paste();
    }
});

editMenuItem.setMenu(editMenu);

// --- sub menu: Format.
MenuItem formatMenuItem = new MenuItem(menuBar, SWT.CASCADE);
formatMenuItem.setText("&Format");

Menu formatMenu = new Menu(shell, SWT.DROP_DOWN);

final MenuItem miWrap = new MenuItem(formatMenu, SWT.CHECK);
```

```
        miWrap.setText("&Wrap\tCtrl+W");
        miWrap.setAccelerator(SWT.CTRL + 'W');
        miWrap.addListener(SWT.Selection, new Listener() {
            public void handleEvent(Event event) {
                text.setWordWrap(miWrap.getSelection());
            }
        });

        formatMenuItem.setMenu(formatMenu);

        // Add the menu bar to the shell.
        shell.setMenuBar(menuBar);
```

Auxiliary functions are omitted for the sake of simplicity. For the complete source file, please refer to BasicEditor.java.

Finally, you open the shell and set up the event loop:

```
        // Set up the event loop.
        while (!shell.isDisposed()) {
            if (!display.readAndDispatch()) {
                // If no more entries in event queue
                display.sleep();
            }
        }

        display.dispose();
    }
```

# Using ToolBars and ToolItems

A toolbar is able to lay out selectable tool bar items. A menu bar accepts menu items as its children only. Similarly, you can add tool items only to a toolbar.

## Using ToolBars

You can add a menu bar only to a shell; however, you can assign a toolbar to any widget of the type org.eclipse.swt.widgets.Composite.

To assign a toolbar for a composite, you simply pass the composite to the constructor of the ToolBar class.

```
    public ToolBar(Composite parent, int style)
```

### ToolBar Styles

You can specify the style information in the constructor of the ToolBar class. Possible styles are as follows:

❑    SWT.WRAP: If the style is set, a toolbar may wrap the tool items into different rows when the horizontal dimension is not enough for all the items displayed in one row.

❑  SWT.RIGHT: By default, the image of a tool item is display above its text label. Setting this style puts the text label to the right of the image. If the vertical client area is limited, you should consider setting this style.

❑  SWT.HORIZONTAL, SWT.VERTICAL: These two styles specify the orientation of a toolbar. By default, a toolbar is laid out horizontally. To lay out the toolbar vertically, you can specify the SWT.VERTICAL style.

❑  SWT.FLAT, SWT.SHADOW_OUT: These two styles are used to specify the appearance of a toolbar.

### Accessing ToolItems

The ToolBar class provides several methods to enable you to access the tool items of a toolbar easily.

You can use the getItem method to get a tool item at the specified index:

```
public ToolItem getItem(int index)
```

There is another getItem method with signature public ToolItem getItem(Point point), which returns the tool item at the given point in the toolbar or null if no such item exists.

To get all the items in a toolbar, you can call the getItems method:

```
public ToolItem[] getItems()
```

If you need to know the index of a particular tool item in the item list, you can use the indexOf method:

```
public int indexOf(ToolItem item)
```

The total number of items in a toolbar can be obtained through the getItemCount method:

```
public int getItemCount()
```

Finally, if a toolbar has the SWT.WRAP style set, you can get the number of rows in the toolbar by using the getRowCount method:

```
public int getRowCount()
```

Of course, if the toolbar does not have SWT.WRAP style set, the preceding method always returns 1.

## Using ToolItems

A tool item is a selectable user interface object representing a button in a toolbar.

You can create a tool item on a toolbar using the following constructor of the ToolItem class:

```
public ToolItem(ToolBar parent, int style)
```

The first argument specifies the toolbar that this tool item resides on. Style information is stored in the second argument. The complete list of styles is introduced shortly.

Another constructor in the `ToolItem` class enables you to specify the index at which to place the tool item in the item list maintained by the parent toolbar:

```
public ToolItem(ToolBar parent, int style, int index)
```

## Styles of ToolItems

Different kinds of menu items were introduced in the preceding section. Similarly, there are different kinds (styles) of tool items.

A tool item can have one and only one style of the following styles:

- ❑ SWT.PUSH: Tool items with this style behave like push buttons.

- ❑ SWT.CHECK: A tool item with this style behaves like a checkbox.

- ❑ SWT.RADIO: A tool item with this style behaves like a radio button.

- ❑ SWT.SEPARATOR: A tool item with SWT.SEPARATOR style is an item separator. Additionally, you can set a control for an item separator.

- ❑ SWT.DROP_DOWN: With this style set, a tool item is displayed as a button with an arrow. Usually, you add a selection listener to a tool item with the DROP_DOWN style and display a UI component (e.g., a menu) when the tool item is selected.

## Creating ToolItems

In the preceding section, I introduced five different styles of tool items. In this section, you create tool items with different styles.

You are going to create a toolbar, as shown in Figure 9-6.

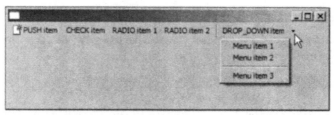

**Figure 9-6**

First, you create the toolbar and its tool items except the last one:

```
ToolBar toolBar = new ToolBar(shell, SWT.FLAT | SWT.WRAP | SWT.RIGHT);

ToolItem itemPush = new ToolItem(toolBar, SWT.PUSH);
itemPush.setText("PUSH item");
Image icon = new Image(shell.getDisplay(), "icons/new.gif");
itemPush.setImage(icon);

ToolItem itemCheck = new ToolItem(toolBar, SWT.CHECK);
```

```
        itemCheck.setText("CHECK item");

        ToolItem itemRadio1 = new ToolItem(toolBar, SWT.RADIO);
        itemRadio1.setText("RADIO item 1");

        ToolItem itemRadio2 = new ToolItem(toolBar, SWT.RADIO);
        itemRadio2.setText("RADIO item 2");

        ToolItem itemSeparator = new ToolItem(toolBar, SWT.SEPARATOR);

        ToolItem itemDropDown = new ToolItem(toolBar, SWT.DROP_DOWN);
        itemDropDown.setText("DROP_DOWN item");
```

You can use the setText method of the ToolItem class to set a text label for a tool item.

You can do several things when configuring a ToolItem:

❑   You can set its text label:

```
public void setText(String string)
```

❑   You can set its image label:

```
public void setImage(Image image)
```

❑   You can set its hot image (i.e., the one that shows up when the mouse is over the item):

```
public void setHotImage(Image image)
```

❑   You can set its disabled image:

```
public void setDisabledImage(Image image)
```

❑   You can set the mnemonic for the item by using the ampersand (&) character in the text of the tool.

❑   You can set the tooltip text:

```
public void setToolTipText(String string)
```

❑   You can enable and disable the tooltip text:

```
public void setEnabled(boolean enabled)
```

Now let's make the last ToolItem, the drop-down one, more functional. Remember the skeleton structure you gave it before:

```
ToolItem itemDropDown = new ToolItem(toolBar, SWT.DROP_DOWN);
    itemDropDown.setText("DROP_DOWN item");
```

Now let's flesh that out by giving the drop-down tool some menu items to display when a user clicks the drop-down arrow at the right edge of the tool:

```
final ToolItem itemDropDown = new ToolItem(toolBar, SWT.DROP_DOWN);
itemDropDown.setText("DROP_DOWN item");
itemDropDown.setToolTipText("Click here to see a drop down menu ...");

final Menu menu = new Menu(shell, SWT.POP_UP);
new MenuItem(menu, SWT.PUSH).setText("Menu item 1");
new MenuItem(menu, SWT.PUSH).setText("Menu item 2");
new MenuItem(menu, SWT.SEPARATOR);
new MenuItem(menu, SWT.PUSH).setText("Menu item 3");

itemDropDown.addListener(SWT.Selection, new Listener() {
    public void handleEvent(Event event) {
        if(event.detail == SWT.ARROW) {
            Rectangle bounds = itemDropDown.getBounds();
            Point point = toolBar.toDisplay(
                bounds.x, bounds.y + bounds.height);
            menu.setLocation(point);
            menu.setVisible(true);
        }
    }
});
```

This tool item is created with the SWT.DROP_DOWN style. Then you create a pop-up menu to display the menu of options for the drop-down tool. You plan to display this menu when the small arrow of the tool item is pressed. A selection listener is added and the menu is set to visible only when the arrow is pressed.

Then you register selection listeners for the tool items:

```
Listener selectionListener = new Listener() {
    public void handleEvent(Event event) {
        ToolItem item = (ToolItem)event.widget;
        System.out.println(item.getText() + " is selected");
        if( (item.getStyle() & SWT.RADIO) != 0 ||
            (item.getStyle() & SWT.CHECK) != 0 )
            System.out.println("Selection status: " + item.getSelection());
    }
};

itemPush.addListener(SWT.Selection, selectionListener);
itemCheck.addListener(SWT.Selection, selectionListener);
itemRadio1.addListener(SWT.Selection, selectionListener);
itemRadio2.addListener(SWT.Selection, selectionListener);
itemDropDown.addListener(SWT.Selection, selectionListener);
```

Because the second-to-last tool item is a plain separator, you do not register the listener to it. For tool items with SWT.RADIO style or SWT.CHECK style, you use the getSelection method to check their selection status:

```
public boolean getSelection()
```

To set selection status programmatically, you can use the setSelection method of the ToolItem class.

Finally, you pack the toolbar and enable it to resize automatically when the shell resizes:

```
toolBar.pack();

shell.addListener(SWT.Resize, new Listener() {
    public void handleEvent(Event event) {
        Rectangle clientArea = shell.getClientArea();
        toolBar.setSize(toolBar.computeSize(clientArea.width, SWT.DEFAULT));
    }
});
```

## Adding Controls to a ToolBar

You can add controls to a toolbar by using menu items with the SWT.SEPARATOR style. In fact, only tool items with the SWT.SEPARATOR style are capable of holding controls.

You are going to modify the code in the last section to add a text control to the toolbar (see Figure 9-7).

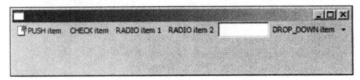

Figure 9-7

```
ToolItem itemSeparator = new ToolItem(toolBar, SWT.SEPARATOR);
Text text = new Text(toolBar, SWT.BORDER | SWT.SINGLE);
text.pack();
itemSeparator.setWidth(text.getBounds().width);
itemSeparator.setControl(text);
```

The code highlighted in bold is the newly added part. First, a text control is created. You then set the width of the separator to the preferred width of the text control. The setControl method of the ToolItem class is used to associate a control with a tool item with the SWT.SEPARATOR style.

```
public void setControl(Control control)
```

The corresponding method to get the control from a separator is the getControl method:

```
public Control getControl()
```

## Adding a Toolbar for the Text Editor

Now, you can add a toolbar to our sample application (see Figure 9-8).

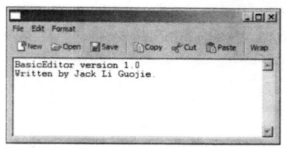

Figure 9-8

```
MenuItem miWrap = null;

public BasicEditor() {
    shell.setLayout(new GridLayout());

    // Add a tool bar.
    ToolBar toolBar = new ToolBar(shell, SWT.FLAT | SWT.RIGHT );
    ToolItem tiNew = new ToolItem(toolBar, SWT.PUSH);
    tiNew.setText("&New");
    tiNew.setImage(getImage("new.gif"));
    tiNew.addListener(SWT.Selection, new Listener() {
        public void handleEvent(Event event) {
            if(handleChangesBeforeDiscard())  {
                file = null;
                text.setText("");
            }
        }
    });

    ToolItem tiOpen = new ToolItem(toolBar, SWT.PUSH);
    tiOpen.setText("&Open");
    tiOpen.setImage(getImage("open.gif"));
    tiOpen.addListener(SWT.Selection, new Listener() {
        public void handleEvent(Event event) {
            if(handleChangesBeforeDiscard())
                loadTextFromFile();
        }
    });

    ToolItem tiSave = new ToolItem(toolBar, SWT.PUSH);
    tiSave.setText("&Save");
    tiSave.setImage(getImage("save.gif"));
    tiSave.addListener(SWT.Selection, new Listener() {
        public void handleEvent(Event event) {
            saveTextToFile();
        }
    });

    new ToolItem(toolBar, SWT.SEPARATOR);

    ToolItem tiCopy = new ToolItem(toolBar, SWT.PUSH);
```

```
        tiCopy.setText("&Copy");
        tiCopy.setImage(getImage("copy.gif"));
        tiCopy.addListener(SWT.Selection, new Listener() {
            public void handleEvent(Event event) {
                text.copy();
            }
        });

        ToolItem tiCut = new ToolItem(toolBar, SWT.PUSH);
        tiCut.setText("Cu&t");
        tiCut.setImage(getImage("cut.gif"));
        tiCut.addListener(SWT.Selection, new Listener() {
            public void handleEvent(Event event) {
                text.cut();
            }
        });

        ToolItem tiPaste = new ToolItem(toolBar, SWT.PUSH);
        tiPaste.setText("&Paste");
        tiPaste.setImage(getImage("paste.gif"));
        tiPaste.addListener(SWT.Selection, new Listener() {
            public void handleEvent(Event event) {
                text.paste();
            }
        });

        new ToolItem(toolBar, SWT.SEPARATOR);

        final ToolItem tiWrap = new ToolItem(toolBar, SWT.CHECK);
        tiWrap.setText("&Wrap");
        tiWrap.addListener(SWT.Selection, new Listener() {
            public void handleEvent(Event event) {
                text.setWordWrap(tiWrap.getSelection());
                miWrap.setSelection(tiWrap.getSelection());
            }
        });

        toolBar.pack();

        text =
            new StyledText(
                shell,
                SWT.MULTI
                    | SWT.WRAP
                    | SWT.BORDER
                    | SWT.H_SCROLL
                    | SWT.V_SCROLL);
        text.setLayoutData(new GridData(GridData.FILL_BOTH));
...
```

A toolbar must be added before you add any child control to the composite. Otherwise, the toolbar and child controls may overlap. If that happens, you have to insert this code before you set up the menus for the application. Otherwise, your menu will overlap the toolbar and you'll never have access to your tools.

The toolbar provides the exact same functions as the menu bar. Because both the menu item `miWrap` and the tool item `tiWrap` control the wrap property of the text widget, you need to synchronize both items.

# Using CoolBars and CoolItems

A cool bar provides an area for dynamically positioning the items that it contains. The resizable and repositionable nature of a cool bar is useful if you need to have a lot of items available to the user. Because a cool bar enables the user to customize its cool items, you could find it in almost any SWT/JFace GUI. In SWT, the class `org.eclipse.swt.widgets.CoolBar` is used to represent cool bars. You can add only an instance of the `org.eclipse.swt.widgets.CoolItem` class to cool bars.

## Creating a CoolBar with CoolItems

You can use the following constructor of the `CoolBar` class to create cool bars:

```
public CoolBar(Composite parent, int style)
```

The `CoolBar` class itself does not support any special style; however, you can use the styles inherited from its ancestor classes, such as `SWT.BORDER` and `SWT.H_SCROLL`.

After a cool bar is created, you can add cool items to it by directly creating cool items with the cool bar as their parent. There are two constructors of the `CoolItem` class:

```
public CoolItem(CoolBar parent, int style)
public CoolItem(CoolBar parent, int style, int index)
```

`SWT.DROP_DOWN` is the only style that can be specified while creating cool items. If this style is set, an arrow indicator is shown on the cool item when there is not enough space for the cool item to display the control embedded. When the user clicks the arrow indicator, a selection event with `SWT.ARROW` as the detail is generated. You can register a selection listener and react accordingly, such as by displaying a menu.

A cool item wraps a control. You can use the following method to set and get the control for a cool item:

```
public Control getControl()
public void setControl(Control control)
```

The following code creates a cool bar, as shown in Figure 9-9:

Figure 9-9

```
Display display = new Display();
Shell shell = new Shell(display);

shell.setLayout(new GridLayout());

CoolBar coolBar = new CoolBar(shell, SWT.NONE);

coolBar.setLayoutData(new GridData(GridData.FILL_HORIZONTAL));

// cool item with a text field.
CoolItem textItem = new CoolItem(coolBar, SWT.NONE);

Text text = new Text(coolBar, SWT.BORDER | SWT.DROP_DOWN);
text.setText("TEXT");
text.pack();

Point size = text.getSize();
textItem.setControl(text);
textItem.setSize(textItem.computeSize(size.x, size.y));

// cool item with a label.
CoolItem labelItem = new CoolItem(coolBar, SWT.NONE);

Label label = new Label(coolBar, SWT.NONE);
label.setText("LABEL");
label.pack();

size = label.getSize();
labelItem.setControl(label);
labelItem.setSize(textItem.computeSize(size.x, size.y));

// cool item with a button.
CoolItem buttonItem = new CoolItem(coolBar, SWT.NONE | SWT.DROP_DOWN);

Composite composite = new Composite(coolBar, SWT.NONE);
composite.setLayout(new GridLayout(2, true));

Button button1 = new Button(composite, SWT.PUSH);
button1.setText("Button 1");
button1.pack();

Button button2 = new Button(composite, SWT.PUSH);
button2.setText("Button 2");
button2.pack();

composite.pack();

size = composite.getSize();
buttonItem.setControl(composite);
buttonItem.setSize(buttonItem.computeSize(size.x, size.y));
...
```

For each of the three cool items, you first create the cool item. Then the control to be wrapped by the cool item is created with the cool bar as the control's parent. After that, you resize the cool item according to the preferred size of the control.

The following is a utility method that helps you to create a cool item with the given control on a cool bar. The size of the cool item is adjusted according to the size of the control.

```
/**
 * Creates a cool item with the given control and adds the cool item to the
 * specified cool bar.
 *
 * @param control
 * @param coolItemStyle -
 *               should be SWT.NONE or SWT.DROP_DOWN.
 * @param coolBar
 * @return the cool item created.
 */
public static CoolItem addControlToCoolBar(
    Control control,
    int coolItemStyle,
    CoolBar coolBar) {
    CoolItem coolItem = new CoolItem(coolBar, coolItemStyle);
    Point size = control.getSize();
    if (size.x == 0 && size.y == 0) {
        // The control size has not been set yet.
        // Pack the control and recalculate its size.
        control.pack();
        size = control.getSize();
    }

    coolItem.setControl(control);
    coolItem.setSize(coolItem.computeSize(size.x, size.y));

    return coolItem;
}
```

## Saving and Loading the Display State of a CoolBar

A cool bar allows the user to reposition the cool items on it. An appealing GUI application should be able to restore the customization made by the user when the application is restarted.

The CoolBar class provides several methods that you can use to save and load the display state of a cool bar.

The getItemOrder method returns an array of zero-relative integers that map the creation order of the cool items to the order in which they are currently being displayed.

```
public int[] getItemOrder()
```

The getWrapIndices method returns an array of integers describing the indices of items in the cool bar that begin on a new row.

```
public int[] getWrapIndices()
```

The indices are given in the order in which they are currently being displayed. Because the first item always has the index value 0, it does not count as a wrap index. If there are two rows in the cool bar, this method returns a one-element array.

Figure 9-10 is the initial shell displayed by the code in the preceding section.

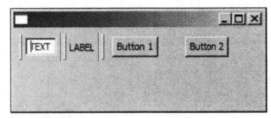

**Figure 9-10**

The initial item order and wrap indices are as follows:

```
Item order: {0, 1, 2}
Wrap indices: {}
```

If the user drops the cool item in the middle (i.e, the label), as shown in Figure 9-11, the new item order and wrap indices are as follows:

```
Item order: {0, 2, 1}
Wrap indices: {2}
```

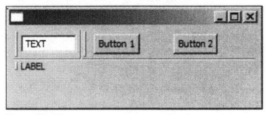

**Figure 9-11**

The getItemSizes method returns the sizes of all items in a cool bar as an array of Points:

```
public Point[] getItemSizes()
```

Now you can implement the saving and loading mechanism.

You can simply insert the following code in the code list in the preceding section to support cool bar state saving and loading:

```
// Code to create the cool bar.
...
try {
    setState(coolBar, new File("coolbar.state"));
} catch (IOException e1) {
    e1.printStackTrace();
}

shell.addListener(SWT.Close, new Listener() {
    public void handleEvent(Event event) {
        try {
            saveState(coolBar, new File("coolbar.state") );
        } catch (IOException e) {
            e.printStackTrace();
        }
    }
});

// shell.pack();
shell.open();
...
```

Just before the shell is opened, you load the state and set it to the cool bar using our custom method setState. When the shell is about to close, you save the state information using the saveState method.

The following is the implementation of the two custom methods you used in the preceding code:

```
// Save the display state of the given cool bar in the specified file.
private void saveState(CoolBar coolBar, File file) throws IOException {
    DataOutputStream out = new DataOutputStream(new FileOutputStream(file));

    try {
        // Orders of items.
        int[] order = coolBar.getItemOrder();
        out.writeInt(order.length);
        for(int i=0; i<order.length; i++)
            out.writeInt(order[i]);

        // Wrap indices.
        int[] wrapIndices = coolBar.getWrapIndices();
        out.writeInt(wrapIndices.length);
        for(int i=0; i<wrapIndices.length; i++)
            out.writeInt(wrapIndices[i]);

        // Sizes.
        Point[] sizes = coolBar.getItemSizes();
```

```
                  out.writeInt(sizes.length);
                  for(int i=0; i<sizes.length; i++) {
                       out.writeInt(sizes[i].x);
                       out.writeInt(sizes[i].y);
                  }
         } finally {
              out.close();
         }


    }

    // Sets the display state for a cool bar, using the saved information in the given
    file.
    private void setState(CoolBar coolBar, File file) throws IOException {
         if(! file.exists())
              throw new IOException("File does not exist: " + file);

         DataInputStream in = new DataInputStream(new FileInputStream(file));

         try {
              // Order
              int size = in.readInt();
              int[] order = new int[size];
              for(int i=0; i<order.length; i++)
                   order[i] = in.readInt();

              // Wrap indices.
              size = in.readInt();
              int[] wrapIndices = new int[size];
              for(int i=0; i<wrapIndices.length; i++)
                   wrapIndices[i] = in.readInt();

              // Sizes.
              size = in.readInt();
              Point[] sizes = new Point[size];
              for(int i=0; i<sizes.length; i++)
                   sizes[i] = new Point(in.readInt(), in.readInt());

              coolBar.setItemLayout(order, wrapIndices, sizes);
         } finally {
              in.close();
         }
    }
```

In our setState method, the setItemLayout method of the CoolBar class is used to set the display
state for the cool bar:

```
public void setItemLayout(int[] itemOrder, int[] wrapIndices, Point[] sizes)
```

# Using Actions and ContributionManagers

The following is the code to create a menu item and a tool item for text wrapping in the text editor:

```
MenuItem miWrap = null;
...

final ToolItem tiWrap = new ToolItem(toolBar, SWT.CHECK);
tiWrap.setText("&Wrap");
tiWrap.addListener(SWT.Selection, new Listener() {
    public void handleEvent(Event event) {
        text.setWordWrap(tiWrap.getSelection());
        miWrap.setSelection(tiWrap.getSelection());
    }
});
...

miWrap = new MenuItem(formatMenu, SWT.CHECK);
miWrap.setText("&Wrap\tCtrl+W");
miWrap.setAccelerator(SWT.CTRL + 'W');
miWrap.addListener(SWT.Selection, new Listener() {
    public void handleEvent(Event event) {
        text.setWordWrap(miWrap.getSelection());
        tiWrap.setSelection(miWrap.getSelection());
    }
});
```

Both the menu item and the tool item perform the exact same operation—when the menu item or the tool item is hit by the user, the wrap property of the text control is set. However, in the preceding code, we have created redundant code to set the operation for both of the items. This is error prone. Furthermore, we also added code to perform synchronization. When the operation is more complex and there are more items to be associated with the same operations, problems occur frequently due to redundant code and extra synchronization code.

JFace provides the actions framework to solve this problem elegantly.

Instead of creating tool items or menu items, you create actions that represent non-UI commands that can be triggered by the user. You then add those actions to contribution managers, which are capable of rendering proper UI objects to represent such actions. In this way, UI creation is greatly simplified and you need to focus only on business logic. Two common managers are MenuManagers and ToolBarManagers. As you'll see, using these managers removes duplication from your text editor application.

## Creating Actions

First, let's create our first action object:

```
// Action: set text wrapping property.
Action actionWrap =
    new Action(
        "&Wrap", IAction.AS_CHECK_BOX) {
        public void run() {
            text.setWordWrap(isChecked());
        }
};
actionWrap.setAccelerator(SWT.CTRL + 'W');
```

In the preceding code, the action object is created with this constructor of the Action class:

```
protected Action(String text, int style)
```

You specify the text label for this action in the first argument. The style of the UI objects that will be created based on this action is specified in the second argument. Possible styles of an action are as follows:

- ❑ AS_CHECK_BOX: This style indicates the UI objects representing the action should be checkboxes or toggle buttons.

- ❑ AS_DROP_DOWN_MENU: The UI objects representing this action should be drop-down menus.

- ❑ AS_PUSH_BUTTON: The UI objects representing this action should be push buttons or push items.

- ❑ AS_RADIO_BUTTON: Radio buttons or radio items should be used to represent this action.

- ❑ AS_UNSPECIFIED: This style indicates the action style is unset. The SWT UI toolkit determines the proper types of UI objects to be created at runtime. By default, the UI objects representing this action should be push buttons or push items. If the setChecked method of the Action class is called, the action style will be AS_CHECK_BOX. Similarly, if setMenuCreator is called, the action style will be AS_DROP_DOWN_MENU.

You then override the run method of the Action class. The run method is called when the action is triggered by the user.

The action is mapped to the specified accelerator keycode by using the setAccelerator method.

```
public void setAccelerator(int keycode)
```

You can set the accelerator keycode in the text label. For example, if the text label &Wrap in the preceding code is replaced by &Wrap\tCtrl+W, you do not have to make the call to the method setAccelerator. The accelerator keycode is extracted from the text set automatically.

The following code creates the rest of the actions:

```
// Action: create new text.
Action actionNew =
    new Action(
        "&New",
        ImageDescriptor.createFromFile(null, "icons/new.gif")) {
        public void run() {
            if (handleChangesBeforeDiscard()) {
                file = null;
                text.setText("");
            }
        }
    };
actionNew.setAccelerator(SWT.CTRL + 'N');

// Action: open a text file.
Action actionOpen =
    new Action(
        "&Open",
        ImageDescriptor.createFromFile(null, "icons/open.gif")) {
```

```
            public void run() {
                if (handleChangesBeforeDiscard())
                    loadTextFromFile();
            }
    };
actionOpen.setAccelerator(SWT.CTRL + 'O');

// Action: save the text to a file.
Action actionSave =
    new Action(
        "&Save\tCtrl+S",
        ImageDescriptor.createFromFile(null, "icons/save.gif")) {
        public void run() {
            saveTextToFile();
        }
    };


// Action: copy selected text.
Action actionCopy =
    new Action(
        "&Copy",
        ImageDescriptor.createFromFile(null, "icons/copy.gif")) {
        public void run() {
            text.copy();
        }
    };
actionCopy.setAccelerator(SWT.CTRL + 'C');

// Action: cut the selected text.
Action actionCut =
    new Action(
        "Cu&t",
        ImageDescriptor.createFromFile(null, "icons/cut.gif")) {
        public void run() {
            text.cut();
        }
    };
actionCut.setAccelerator(SWT.CTRL + 'X');

// Action: paste the text on clipboard.
Action actionPaste =
    new Action(
        "&Paste",
        ImageDescriptor.createFromFile(null, "icons/paste.gif")) {
        public void run() {
            text.paste();
        }
    };
actionPaste.setAccelerator(SWT.CTRL + 'P');

// Action: exit.
Action actionExit = new Action("&Exit\tCtrl+X") {
```

```
        public void run() {
            if (handleChangesBeforeDiscard())
                shell.dispose();
        }
    };
```

This constructor of the `Action` class allows you to specify an image label for the action:

```
    protected Action(String text, ImageDescriptor image)
```

You can also use the `setImageDescriptor` method to set the image:

```
    public void setImageDescriptor(ImageDescriptor newImage)
```

Additionally, two methods enable you to set the hover image and the disabled image for the action:

```
    public void setHoverImageDescriptor(ImageDescriptor newImage)
    public void setDisabledImageDescriptor(ImageDescriptor newImage)
```

Finally, you can use the `setToolTipText` method to set the tooltip text for the action:

```
    public void setToolTipText(String toolTipText)
```

## Creating Menus with MenuManagers

A `MenuManager` is a special type of `ContributionManager`. A contribution manager maintains a list of contribution items and manages them. A menu manager renders itself and its contribution items in a menu control.

The following is the complete code to create the bar menu and to set it to the shell for the text editor application:

```
    // Add menus.
    MenuManager barMenuManager = new MenuManager();

    MenuManager fileMenuManager = new MenuManager("&File");
    MenuManager editMenuManager = new MenuManager("&Edit");
    MenuManager formatMenuManager = new MenuManager("&Format");

    barMenuManager.add(fileMenuManager);
    barMenuManager.add(editMenuManager);
    barMenuManager.add(formatMenuManager);

    fileMenuManager.add(actionNew);
    fileMenuManager.add(actionOpen);
    fileMenuManager.add(actionSave);
    fileMenuManager.add(new Separator());

    fileMenuManager.add(actionExit);

    editMenuManager.add(actionCopy);
```

```
    editMenuManager.add(actionCut);
    editMenuManager.add(actionPaste);

    formatMenuManager.add(actionWrap);

    // Add the menu bar to the shell.
    barMenuManager.updateAll(true);
  shell.setMenuBar(barMenuManager.createMenuBar((Decorations)shell));
```

The guiding principle here is that you need to create a MenuManager for the menu bar and for each menu on the menu bar. Remember that you created an Action for each menu item. When you have the MenuManager created for each menu, you simply call add() on the manager to add each action to it. The updateAll method builds the menu control from the contribution items and does so recursively for all submenus.

```
    public void updateAll(boolean force)
```

The force flag indicates whether the update should be performed even if the menu manager is not *dirty* (i.e., needs to be updated).

The createMenuBar method creates and returns a menu bar with the given decorations:

```
    public Menu createMenuBar(Decorations parent)
```

Note that the Decorations class is the direct superclass of the Shell class, and it provides the appearance and behavior of shells.

To create a pop-up menu, you can use the createContextMenu method:

```
    public Menu createContextMenu(Control parent)
```

## Creating Toolbars with ToolBarManagers

A ToolBarManager renders itself into a toolbar control.

Here is the code to create the toolbar for the text editor using ToolBarManager:

```
    // Add a toolbar.
    ToolBar toolBar = new ToolBar(shell, SWT.FLAT | SWT.RIGHT);
    ToolBarManager toolBarManager = new ToolBarManager(toolBar);

    toolBarManager.add(actionNew);
    toolBarManager.add(actionOpen);
    toolBarManager.add(actionSave);

    toolBarManager.add(new Separator());

    toolBarManager.add(actionCopy);
    toolBarManager.add(actionCut);
```

```
    toolBarManager.add(actionPaste);

    toolBarManager.add(new Separator());

    toolBarManager.add(actionWrap);

    toolBarManager.update(true);
```

First, a toolbar control is created. You then associate this toolbar with a `ToolBarManager`. Action objects are then added to the toolbar manager. You can also add separators by using `add(new Separator())`. Finally, you need to update the control managed by the toolbar manager using the `update` method.

```
    public void update(boolean force)
```

After the menu bar and the toolbar are created, you can then add other controls to the shell. The complete code is in the file `BasicEditor2.java`. When you run this version of the text editor, you will find that those menus and tool items work as usual. However, the code for this version is much more concise and manageable than the code used in the previous version.

# Summary

In this chapter, you learned how to use menus, toolbars, and cool bars. To add a menu bar for a shell, you first create a menu with the `SWT.BAR` style and set the shell as its parent. Then you can add menu items and submenus to the menu bar. When a menu item is hit, a selection event occurs. You can register event listeners to listen to selection events. A sample application showed you how to create menu items with different styles. A toolbar is capable of laying out selectable toolbar items. Similar to a menu item, a tool item can be of a particular style, such as a push button style or a checkbox style. You can use a tool item with a separator style to add a control to a toolbar. If you want items to be positioned dynamically, you need a cool bar. The user can change the display order of cool items on a cool bar by dragging them to new places. Sometimes, managing menus, toolbars, and cool bars is tedious and error-prone. Fortunately, with JFace actions and contribution managers, you can manage menus, toolbars, and cool bars easily. The end of this chapter showed you how to use `Actions` and `ContributionManagers` to rewrite the sample application to make the code more maintainable.

# 10

# Tables

Tables are very useful for handling tabular data. In this chapter, you learn how to use the SWT `Table` control to display, navigate, and edit data. Additionally, the JFace `TableViewer` is introduced to help you simplify these tasks by enabling you to take advantage of MVC programming.

## Using Tables

In SWT, the `org.eclipse.swt.widgets.Table` class represents a table. A table may have many columns and rows. The `TableColumn` class represents a column in a table, and the `TableItem` class represents a row in a table. The labels of data to be presented in the table are stored in `TableItems`. `TableColumns` are lightweight objects that can be used to specify the properties of each column, such as the column width, column header, and so on.

To create a table, you follow these basic steps:

1. Construct a `Table` instance and set its property.
2. Define columns by using `TableColumn` objects.
3. Add rows by creating `TableItem` objects.

### Creating a Table

The only constructor in the `Table` class is:

```
public Table(Composite parent, int style)
```

You specify the parent composite in the first argument and styles in the second argument.

Possible styles that you can specify for a table are as follows:

❏ SWT.SINGLE, SWT.MULTI: By default, at most one row in a table is allowed to be selected at any time. If SWT.MULTI is specified, more than one row can be selected at the same time. You can specify only one of these two styles.

❏ SWT.CHECK: If this style is set, a checkbox is displayed in the first column of each row. You can use the getChecked method of the TableItem class to check whether the checkbox associated with this item is checked. You probably want to use this style if you need to perform operations on multiple items "selected" by the user.

❏ SWT.FULL_SELECTION: By default, you can select a table item only by clicking its cell in the first row. Setting this style enables you to select a row by clicking any cell in the row.

❏ SWT.HIDE_SELECTION: If you want the selection hidden when the table control does not have focus, you can set this style.

In this chapter, we are going to develop a simple bug tracking system, as shown in Figure 10-1. A table is used to display all the bugs maintained by this system.

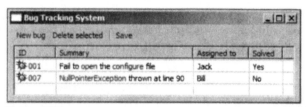

**Figure 10-1**

You create the main table in the user interface using the following code:

```
Table table = new Table(shell, SWT.BORDER | SWT.FULL_SELECTION);
```

Then you make the grid line and the table header visible:

```
table.setLinesVisible(true);
table.setHeaderVisible(true);
```

The header text displayed in Figure 10-1 is provided by TableColumn instances.

## Defining Table Columns

To define a table column, you simply create an instance of the TableColumn class. There are two constructors in the TableColumn class.

```
public TableColumn(Table parent, int style)
public TableColumn(Table parent, int style, int index)
```

You can specify the alignment of the cell label in the style argument. Possible values are SWT.LEFT, SWT.CENTER, and SWT.RIGHT. The first constructor appends a new column in the table, while the second constructor allows you to specify the index at which to place the column.

Optionally, you can set a text label and an image label for a column by using the setText method and the setImage method.

```
public void setText(String string)
public void setImage(Image image)
```

The text label and the image label will be displayed as the column header if the table is configured to display a table header.

You can set the width of a column by using the setWidth method:

```
public void setWidth(int width)
```

To enable or disable the user to resize a column, you can use the setResizable method.

```
public void setResizable(boolean resizable)
```

Even if a column is set to be not resizable, you can still resize it in your code.

Now you can add the required columns for our bug tracking system:

```
TableColumn tcID = new TableColumn(table, SWT.LEFT);
tcID.setText("ID");

TableColumn tcSummary = new TableColumn(table, SWT.NULL);
tcSummary.setText("Summary");

TableColumn tcAssignedTo = new TableColumn(table, SWT.NULL);
tcAssignedTo.setText("Assigned to");

TableColumn tcSolved = new TableColumn(table, SWT.NULL);
tcSolved.setText("Solved");

tcID.setWidth(60);
tcSummary.setWidth(200);
tcAssignedTo.setWidth(80);
tcSolved.setWidth(50);
```

# Adding Data into a Table

To add a row of data to a table, you simply need to create an instance of TableItem with the table as the parent composite.

## Creating TableItems

You can use the two constructors of the TableItem class to create table rows:

```
public TableItem(Table parent, int style)
public TableItem(Table parent, int style, int index)
```

You specify the target table in the first argument. Because `TableItem` does not support any styles, you simply pass `SWT.NULL` in the second argument. The first constructor appends a `TableItem` in the list of rows of a table. The second constructor allows you to insert a `TableItem` at the given index in the list of rows.

## Setting Text Labels and Image Labels for Cells in a TableItem

A table row contains as many cells as the number of columns in the table. You can set the text label and the image label for a certain cell in the row using the `setText` method and the `setImage` method:

```
public void setText(int index, String string)
public void setImage(int index, Image image)
```

You specify the cell index in the first argument in the preceding methods.

The `TableItem` class provides several convenient methods to set labels for cells.

The following methods set the text label and the image label for the first cell (`index = 0`) in a `TableItem`:

```
public void setText(String string)
public void setImage(Image image)
```

If you want to specify labels for multiple cells in one call, you can use the following methods:

```
public void setText(String[] strings)
public void setImage(Image[] images)
```

To get the text label and the image label of a cell in a `TableItem`, you can use the following methods:

```
public String getText(int index)
public Image getImage(int index)
```

In both of the preceding methods, you specify the index of the target cell in the argument.

## Setting Background and Foreground Colors for Cells in a TableItem

To set the background and foreground colors for an entire row of a table, you can use the following methods:

```
public void setBackground(Color color)
public void setForeground(Color color)
```

If the passed argument is `null`, the background color (or foreground color) will be set to the system default.

Similarly, you can use the following methods to set the background and foreground colors for a particular cell in a row:

```
public void setBackground(int index, Color color)
public void setForeground(int index, Color color)
```

With the usage of `TableItems` introduced in the preceding text, you are ready to add bug information into the main table of the bug tracking application:

```
...
loadBugs();

...
private void loadBugs() {
    // Load bugs from a file.
    DataInputStream in = null;

    try {
        File file = new File("bugs.dat");
        if (!file.exists())
            return;
        in = new DataInputStream(new FileInputStream(file));

        while (true) {
            String id = in.readUTF();
            String summary = in.readUTF();
            String assignedTo = in.readUTF();
            boolean solved = in.readBoolean();

            TableItem item = new TableItem(table, SWT.NULL);
            item.setImage(bugIcon);
            item.setText(
                new String[] {
                    id,
                    summary,
                    assignedTo,
                    solved ? "Yes" : "No" });
        }
    } catch (IOException ioe) {
        // Ignore.
    } finally {
        try {
            if(in != null)
                in.close();
        } catch (IOException e) {
            e.printStackTrace();
        }
    }
}
```

The `loadBugs` function tries to load bug information from a file. If a bug record is successfully loaded, a new `TableItem` is created with the information provided in the record.

To enable the user to create new `TableItems`, you add an action in a toolbar.

```
Action actionAddNew = new Action("New bug") {
    public void run() {
        // Append.
        TableItem item = new TableItem(table, SWT.NULL);
        item.setImage(bugIcon);
        table.select(table.getItemCount() - 1);
    }
};


...
ToolBar toolBar = new ToolBar(shell, SWT.RIGHT | SWT.FLAT);

ToolBarManager manager = new ToolBarManager(toolBar);
manager.add(actionAddNew);
manager.update(true);
...
```

When the action is invoked, an empty `TableItem` is created and appended to the table. The `select` method selects the newly created `TableItem` in the table.

## Removing TableItems

The `Table` class provides four methods to help you remove `TableItems` from a table:

```
public void remove(int index)
public void remove(int[] indices)
public void remove(int start, int end)
public void removeAll()
```

You can use the first method to remove the `TableItem` at the specified index. The second and third methods are capable of removing multiple `TableItems`. Finally, the last method can be used to remove all the `TableItems` from a table.

You add the following action to enable the user to remove the selection `TableItem`.

```
...
Action actionDelete = new Action("Delete selected") {
    public void run() {
        int index = table.getSelectionIndex();
        if (index < 0) {
            System.out.println("Please select an item first. ");
            return;
        }
        MessageBox messageBox = new MessageBox(shell, SWT.YES | SWT.NO);
        messageBox.setText("Confirmation");
        messageBox.setMessage(
            "Are you sure to remove the bug with id #"
                + table.getItem(index).getText(0));
        if (messageBox.open() == SWT.YES) {
            table.remove(index);
        }
    }
};
...
manager.add(actionDelete);
```

The `getSelectionIndex` method returns the currently selected `TableItem` in a table. If a `TableItem` is selected, a confirmation message box pops up. If the user confirms the deletion, the selected `TableItem` is removed using the `remove(int index)` method.

## Handling Selections

You can add a selection listener to a table for selection events.

The following selection listener simply listens for selection events and prints out the first selected `TableItem`:

```
table.addListener(SWT.Selection, new Listener() {
    public void handleEvent(Event event) {
        System.out.println("Selected: " + table.getSelection()[0]);
    }
});
```

When the user clicks the second row in the table (see Figure 10-1), the following line is displayed:

```
Selected: TableItem {007}
```

The `getSelection` method returns all the selected `TableItems`:

```
public TableItem[] getSelection()
```

If no `TableItem` is selected currently, an empty array is returned. If a table has the `SWT.SINGLE` style, then at most one `TableItem` is selected at any time.

You can get the indices of all the selected `TableItems` using the `getSelectionIndices` method:

```
public int[] getSelectionIndices()
```

The `getSelectionIndex` returns the index of the currently selected `TableItem`:

```
public int getSelectionIndex()
```

If no `TableItem` is selected, the method returns -1. In the case of `SWT.MULTI` tables, this method returns the selected item, which has the focus.

To get the total number of selected items, you can use the `getSelectionCount` method:

```
public int getSelectionCount()
```

You can use the following methods to make selections programmatically:

```
public void select(int index)
public void select(int[] indices)
public void select(int start, int end)
public void selectAll()
```

The deselection counterparts of the preceding selection methods are as follows:

```
public void deselect(int index)
public void deselect(int[] indices)
public void deselect(int start, int end)
public void deselectAll()
```

Finally, there are `setSelection` methods:

```
public void setSelection(int index)
public void setSelection(int[] indices)
public void setSelection(int start, int end)
public void setSelection(TableItem[] items)
```

The `setSelection` methods first clear any existing selection and then make the selection. For example, `setSelection(int index)` is equivalent to:

```
table.deselectAll()
table.select(index)
```

For a table with the `SWT.CHECK` style, when the user clicks the checkboxes in front of `TableItems`, selection events are generated. The `detail` field of such event objects has the value `SWT.CHECK`. You can get and set the check status of a table item using the following methods:

```
public boolean getChecked()
public void setChecked(boolean checked)
```

## Using TableEditors

You can use table editors to let the user edit data in a table on the fly, as shown in Figure 10-2.

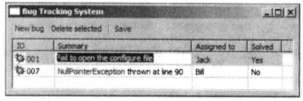

Figure 10-2

To add editing functions to a table, first you need to create a `TableEditor` (`org.eclipse.swt.custom.TableEditor`) based on the table. A table editor manages controls that can be used to edit data. A control managed by a table editor usually appears superimposed above a cell in a table and tracks with the moving and resizing of the cell.

Let's enable the cells in the first three columns to accept user input using the `Text` controls.

First, you need to create a `TableEditor`:

```
final TableEditor editor = new TableEditor(table);
```

Then you add the following MouseDown listener to the table:

```
table.addListener(SWT.MouseDown, new Listener() {
    public void handleEvent(Event event) {
        // Locate the cell position.
        Point point = new Point(event.x, event.y);
        final TableItem item = table.getItem(point);
        if (item == null)
            return;
        int column = -1; // The column that the cell belongs to.
        for (int i = 0; i < table.getColumnCount(); i++) {
            Rectangle rect = item.getBounds(i);
            if (rect.contains(point))
                column = i;
        }
        if (column < 0 || column >= 3)
            return;

        // Cell position located, now open the table editor.

        final Text text = new Text(table, SWT.NONE);
        text.setText(item.getText(column));

        editor.horizontalAlignment = SWT.LEFT;
        editor.grabHorizontal = true;

        editor.setEditor(text, item, column);

        final int selectedColumn = column;
        Listener textListener = new Listener() {
            public void handleEvent(final Event e) {
                switch (e.type) {
                    case SWT.FocusOut :
                        item.setText(selectedColumn, text.getText());
                        text.dispose();
                        break;
                    case SWT.Traverse :
                        switch (e.detail) {
                            case SWT.TRAVERSE_RETURN :
                                item.setText(selectedColumn, text.getText());

                            case SWT.TRAVERSE_ESCAPE :
                                text.dispose();
                                e.doit = false;
                        }
                        break;
                }
            }
        };

        text.addListener(SWT.FocusOut, textListener);
        text.addListener(SWT.Traverse, textListener);

        text.setFocus();
    }
});
```

When a mouse down event is generated, the listener is notified. First, the cell that the mouse pointer is pointing to is determined. If the cell is not in one of the first three columns, nothing happens. However, if it is, a Text control is created with the table as its parent composite. You then configure the table editor. The properties of table editors that can be configured are:

❑ horizontalAlignment, verticalAlignment: These fields specify how the editor should be aligned relative to the cell horizontally and vertically. Possible values for horizontalAlignment are SWT.LEFT, SWT.CENTER, and SWT.RIGHT. Possible values for verticalAlignment are SWT.TOP, SWT.CENTER, and SWT.BOTTOM.

❑ grabHorizontal, grabVertical: These two properties specify whether the editor should be sized to use the entire width and the entire height of the cell.

❑ minimumWidth, minimumHeight: You can specify the minimum width and the minimum height of the editor by using these properties. The default value for both is 0.

After the properties of the editor have been configured, you then set the control for the editor by using the setEditor method:

```
public void setEditor(Control editor, TableItem item, int column)
```

This method specifies the control to be displayed over the given cell.

The text control is displayed and focused on.

Notice that we also add a listener to the text control for focus out events and traverse events. When the user clicks outside the cell currently being edited or navigates to another cell, the content of the text control is set as the table item text and the text control is disposed of.

Similarly, you can use check buttons to enable the user to edit the cells in the fourth column (see Figure 10-3).

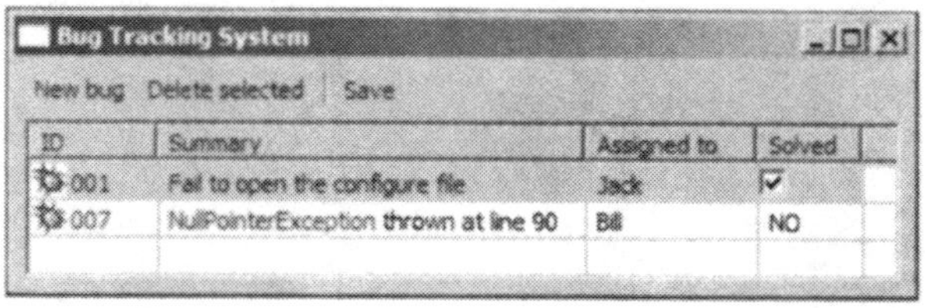

**Figure 10-3**

```
table.addListener(SWT.MouseDown, new Listener() {
    public void handleEvent(Event event) {
        // Locate the cell position.
        Point point = new Point(event.x, event.y);
        final TableItem item = table.getItem(point);
        if (item == null)
            return;
        int column = -1;
        for (int i = 0; i < table.getColumnCount(); i++) {
            Rectangle rect = item.getBounds(i);
            if (rect.contains(point))
```

```
                    column = i;
        }
        if (column != 3)
            return;

        // Cell position located, now open the table editor.

        final Button button = new Button(table, SWT.CHECK);
        button.setSelection(item.getText(column).equalsIgnoreCase("YES"));

        editor.horizontalAlignment = SWT.LEFT;
        editor.grabHorizontal = true;

        editor.setEditor(button, item, column);

        final int selectedColumn = column;
        Listener buttonListener = new Listener() {
            public void handleEvent(final Event e) {
                switch (e.type) {
                    case SWT.FocusOut :
                        item.setText(selectedColumn, button.getSelection()
                                        ? "YES" : "NO");
                        button.dispose();
                        break;
                    case SWT.Traverse :
                        switch (e.detail) {
                            case SWT.TRAVERSE_RETURN :
                                item.setText(selectedColumn,
                                    button.getSelection()? "YES" : "NO");

                            case SWT.TRAVERSE_ESCAPE :
                                button.dispose();
                                    e.doit = false;
                        }
                        break;
                }
            }
        };

        button.addListener(SWT.FocusOut, buttonListener);
        button.addListener(SWT.Traverse, buttonListener);

        button.setFocus();

    }
});
```

## Sorting a Table by Column

In order to present the data in a well-organized manner, you need to improve the table with the ability to sort any column.

The following is a utility function that sorts the table items in a table by the given column in the ascending order of the item text:

```java
/**
 * Sorts the given table by the specified column.
 * @param columnIndex
 */
public static void sortTable(Table table, int columnIndex) {
    if(table == null || table.getColumnCount() <= 1)
        return;
    if(columnIndex < 0 || columnIndex >= table.getColumnCount())
        throw new IllegalArgumentException(
            "The specified column does not exist. ");

    final int colIndex = columnIndex;
    Comparator comparator = new Comparator() {
        public int compare(Object o1, Object o2) {
            return ((TableItem)o1).getText(colIndex).
                compareTo(((TableItem)o2).getText(colIndex));
        }

        public boolean equals(Object obj) {
            return false;
        }
    };

    TableItem[] tableItems = table.getItems();
    Arrays.sort(tableItems, comparator);

    for(int i=0; i<tableItems.length; i++) {
        TableItem item = new TableItem(table, SWT.NULL);
        for(int j=0; j<table.getColumnCount(); j++) {
            item.setText(j, tableItems[i].getText(j));
            item.setImage(j, tableItems[i].getImage(j));
        }
        tableItems[i].dispose();
    }
}
```

The function first validates the passed arguments. Then it creates a comparator, which is used during the sorting process. The getItems() method of the Table class returns an array of the TableItems. The returned array is not the actual structure used by the table, so modifying the returned array does not modify the table in any way. The array of table items is then sorted with the comparator. Now the array is sorted, and you can duplicate table items from the array in order. Once a table item is duplicated, the old table item is disposed of. As a result, the newly created table item is added to the table, while the disposed table item is removed from the table.

Like most other applications, you let the user sort the table by a certain column when the user clicks the column header. To do that, you simply need to add selection listeners to all the columns:

```
Listener sortListener = new Listener() {
    public void handleEvent(Event event) {
        if(! (event.widget instanceof TableColumn))
            return;
        TableColumn tc = (TableColumn)event.widget;
        sortTable(table, table.indexOf(tc));
        System.out.println("The table is sorted by column #" +
                table.indexOf(tc));
    }
};

for(int i=0; i<table.getColumnCount(); i++)
    ((TableColumn)table.getColumn(i)).addListener(SWT.Selection, sortListener);
```

The indexOf(TableColumn tc) method of the Table class returns the index of the specified table column. The table items are then sorted with this column.

Now, when you click the "Assigned to" column header in the table, the table items are sorted with this column (see Figure 10-4). 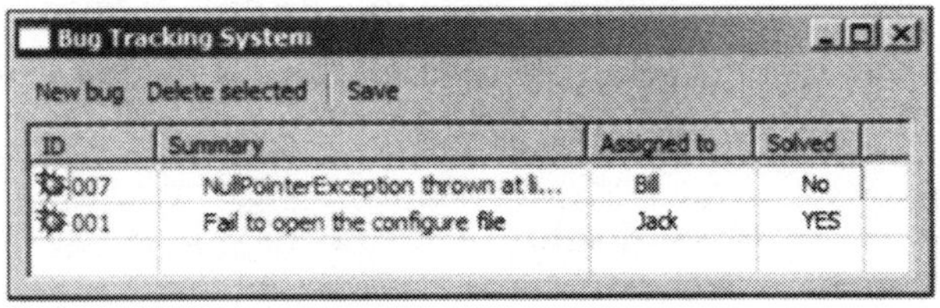

**Figure 10-4**

# Using TableViewers

The JFace viewer framework provides the TableViewer class for you to program with tables using an MVC approach. You learned how to use a ListViewer in Chapter 7. Programming a TableViewer is very similar to programming a ListViewer. The basic steps are as follows:

1. Create domain-specific model objects.
2. Create TableViewers.
3. Set content providers and content.
4. Set label providers (optional).
5. Set cell editors.
6. Add selection listeners (optional).
7. Add filters (optional).
8. Set sorters (optional).
9. Handle events (optional).

Note that the only difference between programming with TableViewers and with ListViewers is that TableViewers can have cell editors (see Step 5) whereas ListViewers don't.

We are going to rewrite the bug tracking application using a TableViewer.

# Creating Domain-Specific Model Objects

In previous sections, we simply read the data from a file into TableItem directly. However, here it's better to create a class to represent a bug and a collection to represent the collection of all the bugs.

```java
/**
 * Represents a bug report.
 *
 */
public static class Bug {
    // For the sake of simplicity, all variables are public.
    public String id;
    public String summary;
    public String assignedTo;
    public boolean isSolved;

    public Bug(String id, String summary, String assignedTo, boolean isSolved)
    {
        this.id = id;
        this.summary = summary;
        this.assignedTo = assignedTo;
        this.isSolved = isSolved;
    }

    // Loads bug reports from a file.
    public static Vector loadBugs(File file) {
        Vector v = new Vector();
        // Load bugs from a file.
        DataInputStream in = null;

        try {
            if (!file.exists())
                return v;
            in = new DataInputStream(new FileInputStream(file));

            while (true) {
                String id = in.readUTF();
                String summary = in.readUTF();
                String assignedTo = in.readUTF();
                boolean solved = in.readBoolean();
                v.add(new Bug(id, summary, assignedTo, solved));
            }

        } catch (IOException ioe) {
            // Ignore.
        } finally {
            try {
                if (in != null)
                    in.close();
```

```
            } catch (IOException e) {
                e.printStackTrace();
            }
        }

        return v;
    }
}

Vector bugs;
```

A class named Bug is created to represent a bug report, and we will use a Vector to contain all the bugs.

## Creating a TableViewer

You can create a TableViewer using any of the constructors of the TableViewer class:

```
public TableViewer(Composite parent)
public TableViewer(Composite parent, int style)
public TableViewer(Table table)
```

The first two constructors create the TableViewer instance and the associated Table control automatically. The third constructor creates a TableViewer based on an existing Table control. We are going to the use the third constructor here:

```
Table table;
TableViewer tableViewer;

String[] colNames = new String[]{"ID", "Summary", "Assigned to", "Solved"};

table = new Table(shell, SWT.BORDER | SWT.FULL_SELECTION);

TableColumn tcID = new TableColumn(table, SWT.LEFT);
tcID.setText(colNames[0]);

TableColumn tcSummary = new TableColumn(table, SWT.NULL);
tcSummary.setText(colNames[1]);

TableColumn tcAssignedTo = new TableColumn(table, SWT.NULL);
tcAssignedTo.setText(colNames[2]);

TableColumn tcSolved = new TableColumn(table, SWT.NULL);
tcSolved.setText(colNames[3]);

tcID.setWidth(60);
tcSummary.setWidth(200);
tcAssignedTo.setWidth(80);
tcSolved.setWidth(50);

tableViewer = new TableViewer(table);

tableViewer.getTable().setLinesVisible(true);
tableViewer.getTable().setHeaderVisible(true);
tableViewer.getTable().setLayoutData(new GridData(GridData.FILL_BOTH));
```

We first create the table with four columns. Then, the table viewer is created. You can use the `getTable` method of the `TableViewer` class to get the table embedded by a table viewer.

```
public Table getTable()
```

# Setting the Content Provider

A `Vector` of `Bugs` is used as the input to the table viewer, so you need to set the content provider for the table viewer as follows:

```
// Sets the content provider.
tableViewer.setContentProvider(new IStructuredContentProvider() {
    public Object[] getElements(Object inputElement) {
        Vector v = (Vector)inputElement;
        return v.toArray();
    }

    public void dispose() {
        System.out.println("Disposing ...");
    }

    public void inputChanged(
        Viewer viewer,
        Object oldInput,
        Object newInput) {
            System.out.println("Input changed: old=" +
                oldInput + ", new=" + newInput);
    }
});
```

You can use the following code to load data into the table viewer:

```
bugs = Bug.loadBugs(new File("bugs.dat"));
tableViewer.setInput(bugs);
```

For details on content providers, please refer to Chapter 7.

# Setting the Label Provider

A label provider maps an element of the viewer's model to an optional image and optional text string used to display the element in the viewer's control. In Chapter 7, we set a `LabelProvider` to the `ListViewer`. However, for `TableViewers`, you should use an instance of `ITableLabelProvider`. If you use `ILabelProvider`, this label provider provides the text label and image label for the first column only, and any remaining columns are blank.

The following is the code to set a label provider for the table viewer:

```
// Sets the label provider.
tableViewer.setLabelProvider(new ITableLabelProvider() {
    public Image getColumnImage(Object element, int columnIndex) {
        if(columnIndex == 0)
            return bugIcon;
```

```
            return null;
    }

    public String getColumnText(Object element, int columnIndex) {
        Bug bug = (Bug)element;
        switch(columnIndex) {
            case 0:
                return bug.id;
            case 1:
                return bug.summary;
            case 2:
                return bug.assignedTo;
            case 3:
                return bug.isSolved ? "YES" : "NO";
        }
        return null;
    }

    public void addListener(ILabelProviderListener listener) {
    }

    public void dispose() {
    }

    public boolean isLabelProperty(Object element, String property) {
        return false;
    }

    public void removeListener(ILabelProviderListener listener) {
    }
});
```

The `getColumnImage` returns the image label for the given element at the specified column, and `getColumnText` returns the text label.

## Setting Cell Editors

When programming with table control directly, we use tedious code to support cell editing. The task is simplified significantly in `TableViewer`.

To enable cell editing, you first set cell editors for the table viewer:

```
// Sets cell editors.

String[] colNames = new String[]{"ID", "Summary", "Assigned to", "Solved"};
tableViewer.setColumnProperties(colNames);

CellEditor[] cellEditors = new CellEditor[4];

cellEditors[0] = new TextCellEditor(table);
cellEditors[1] = cellEditors[0];
cellEditors[2] = cellEditors[0];
cellEditors[3] = new CheckboxCellEditor(table);

tableViewer.setCellEditors(cellEditors);
```

First, you set the column property name for each column in the table using the `setColumnProperties` method. A column property name is used to identify the column in cell modifiers (discussed shortly).

Then you set a cell editor for each column in the table. A cell editor is an instance of the `org.eclipse` `.jface.viewers.CellEditor` class. The `CellEditor` class itself is abstract, and there are several concrete implementations of the `CellEditor` class:

❑ `CheckboxCellEditor`: This editor can be used to edit Boolean values.

❑ `ComboBoxCellEditor`: A combo box editor presents list items in a combo box.

❑ `ColorCellEditor`: A color editor manages a color field.

❑ `TextCellEditor`: Text editors are used to manage text entry fields.

In the preceding code, we set a `TextCellEditor` for the first three columns and a `CheckboxCellEditor` for the last column using the `setCellEditors` method of the `TableViewer` class.

```
public void setCellEditors(CellEditor[] editors)
```

Setting cell editors alone does not make a cell editor function; you have to set a cell modifier for the table viewer. A cell modifier is used to access the data model, and it offers the following functions:

❑ Checks whether a property of the element is editable or not

❑ Gets the current value of a property of the element

❑ Stores the new value to the element

The following is code to set a cell modifier for our bug tracking application:

```
tableViewer.setCellModifier(new ICellModifier() {
    public boolean canModify(Object element, String property) {
        return true;
    }

    public Object getValue(Object element, String property) {
        // Gets the index first.
        int index = -1;
        for(int i=0; i<colNames.length; i++) {
            if(colNames[i].equals(property)) {
                index = i;
                break;
            }
        }
        Bug bug = (Bug)element;

        switch(index) {
            case 0:
                return bug.id;
            case 1:
                return bug.summary;
            case 2:
                return bug.assignedTo;
```

```
            case 3:
                return new Boolean(bug.isSolved);
        }

        return null;
    }

    public void modify(Object element, String property, Object value) {
        System.out.println("Modify: " + element + ", " + property + ", " + value);
        // Get the index first.
        int index = -1;
        for(int i=0; i<colNames.length; i++) {
            if(colNames[i].equals(property)) {
                index = i;
                break;
            }
        }
        Bug bug = null;
        if(element instanceof Item) {
            TableItem item = (TableItem)element;
            bug = (Bug)item.getData();
        }else{
            bug = (Bug)element;
        }
        switch(index) {
            case 0:
                bug.id = (String)value;
                break;
            case 1:
                bug.summary = (String)value;
                break;
            case 2:
                bug.assignedTo = (String)value;
                break;
            case 3:
                bug.isSolved = ((Boolean)value).booleanValue();
                break;
        }

        tableViewer.update(bug, null);
    }
});
```

You need to implement three methods in the interface org.eclipse.jface.viewers.ICellModifier. All the methods have an argument named property. The value of the property argument is one of the column property names set in the previous section using the setColumnProperties method.

The canModify method checks whether the specified property of the given element can be modified. The getValue method is usually queried by cell editors to set their initial values. It returns the value for the given property of the specified element as an object.

The modify method is called when the user modifies a value in a cell editor. The element argument passed can be the model element itself or a TableItem representing it; thus you use the if-else clause to handle this situation. After the model element to be edited is determined, you update the model object and then notify the table viewer to update its corresponding representation.

For more details on viewer updating and refreshing, please consult Chapter 7.

## Column-Wise Sorting Using Sorters

You can use `ViewerSorters` to implement the column-wise sorting function:

```java
// Sorter.
class BugSorter extends ViewerSorter {
    private String property;
    private int propertyIndex;

    public BugSorter(String sortByProperty) {
        for(int i=0; i<colNames.length; i++) {
            if(colNames[i].equals(sortByProperty)) {
                this.property = sortByProperty;
                this.propertyIndex = i;
                return;
            }
        }

        throw new IllegalArgumentException("Unrecognized property: " +
                    sortByProperty);
    }

    /* (non-Javadoc)
     * @see org.eclipse.jface.viewers.ViewerSorter#compare(Viewer, Object, Object)
     */
    public int compare(Viewer viewer, Object e1, Object e2) {
        Bug bug1 = (Bug)e1;
        Bug bug2 = (Bug)e2;

        switch(propertyIndex) {
            case 0:
                return bug1.id.compareTo(bug2.id);
            case 1:
                return bug1.summary.compareTo(bug2.summary);
            case 2:
                return bug1.assignedTo.compareTo(bug2.assignedTo);
            case 3:
                if(bug1.isSolved == bug2.isSolved)
                    return 0;

                if(bug1.isSolved)
                    return 1;
                else
                    return -1;
            default:
                return 0;
```

```
            }

        }

    }


    ...
    // Setting sorters.
    tcID.addListener(SWT.Selection, new Listener() {
        public void handleEvent(Event event) {
            tableViewer.setSorter(new BugSorter(colNames[0]));
        }
    });

    tcSummary.addListener(SWT.Selection, new Listener() {
        public void handleEvent(Event event) {
            tableViewer.setSorter(new BugSorter(colNames[1]));
        }
    });

    tcAssignedTo.addListener(SWT.Selection, new Listener() {
        public void handleEvent(Event event) {
            tableViewer.setSorter(new BugSorter(colNames[2]));
        }
    });

    tcSolved.addListener(SWT.Selection, new Listener() {
        public void handleEvent(Event event) {
            tableViewer.setSorter(new BugSorter(colNames[3]));
        }
    });
```

First, we create a class to extend the ViewerSort class. The compare method is overridden. Then we add a selection listener to each table column. When a table column is selected, rows of the table viewer are sorted according to the values of cells in that column.

## Adding a Filter

In this section, we are going to use a filter to filter out solved bugs (see Figure 10-5).

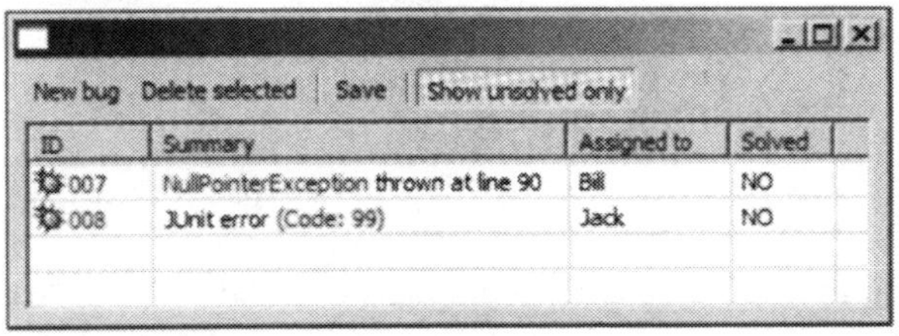

Figure 10-5

The code to implement the filter is very simple, as shown here:

```
final ViewerFilter filter = new ViewerFilter() {
    public boolean select(
        Viewer viewer,
        Object parentElement,
        Object element) {
        if(! ((Bug)element).isSolved)
            return true;
        return false;
    }
};

Action actionShowUnsolvedOnly = new Action("Show unsolved only") {
    public void run() {
        if(! isChecked())
            tableViewer.removeFilter(filter);
        else
            tableViewer.addFilter(filter);
    }
};
actionShowUnsolvedOnly.setChecked(false);

ToolBar toolBar = new ToolBar(shell, SWT.RIGHT | SWT.FLAT);

ToolBarManager manager = new ToolBarManager(toolBar);
manager.add(actionAddNew);
manager.add(actionDelete);
manager.add(new Separator());
manager.add(actionSave);
manager.add(new Separator());
manager.add(actionShowUnsolvedOnly);

manager.update(true);
```

An inner class with `ViewerFilter` as its parent class is created to filter out solved bug reports. If the "Show unsolved only" button is checked, this filter is applied to the table viewer by using the `addFilter` method. If the button is unchecked, the filter is removed from the table viewer by using the `removeFilter` method.

The complete source code for the bug tracking application implemented with `TableViewer` is in the file `BugTrackerJFace.java`.

# Summary

This chapter showed you how to manipulate tabular data with the SWT `Table` control. You learned how to create a table, define table columns, add data to it, and remove data from it. By adding selection listeners, you can listen to cell selection events. You used table editors to enable the user to edit the table content on the fly. The JFace viewer framework provides the `TableViewer` class, which you can use to program tables through the MVC approach. Using a sample application, you learned about creating a table viewer, setting label providers, setting cell editors, setting a column-wise sorter, adding filters, and so on.

# Trees

Trees are used to display hierarchical information. In this chapter, you learn how to use the SWT Tree control to display and edit a hierarchy of items. When the user clicks the tree, events may occur. Event handling of trees is introduced. Additionally, you learn how to use TreeViewers to program with trees using the MVC approach.

## Using Trees

A tree is represented by the org.eclipse.swt.widgets.Tree class in SWT. It may have a hierarchy of items, which are represented by the org.eclipse.swt.widgets.TreeItem class. After a Tree is created, you can add a tree item to it by creating TableItem instances with the tree itself or with one of the tree items in the tree as the tree item's parent.

## Creating a Tree

The only constructor of the Tree class is as follows:

```
public Tree(Composite parent, int style)
```

You specify the parent composite in the first argument and styles of the tree in the second argument.

Possible styles of trees are:

❑ SWT.SINGLE, SWT.MULTI: By default, at most one item in the tree is allowed to be selected at any time. If SWT.MULTI is set, more than one item can be selected at the same time. At most one of them should be specified.

❑ SWT.CHECK: If this style is set, a checkbox is displayed in the front of each tree item. You can use the getChecked method of the TreeItem class to check whether the checkbox associated with this item is checked. You probably want to use this style if you need to perform operations on multiple items "selected" by the user.

In this chapter, you create a simple file browser, as shown in Figure 11-1.

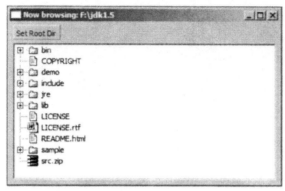

**Figure 11-1**

The main component in the UI is the tree used to display files. The following is the code to create the tree:

```
Display display = new Display();
Shell shell = new Shell(display);

shell.setLayout(new GridLayout());

Tree tree = new Tree(shell, SWT.BORDER);
```

## Using TreeItems

Tree items are fundamental UI elements to build a tree. You can use any of the constructors of the
TreeItem class to create a tree item and add it to a tree.

```
TreeItem(Tree parent, int style)
TreeItem(Tree parent, int style, int index)
TreeItem(TreeItem parentItem, int style)
TreeItem(TreeItem parentItem, int style, int index)
```

The first two constructors create top-level tree items in a tree, and the last two constructors create tree
items at a deeper level with other tree items as their parents. Because TreeItem does not support any
style yet, you can simply put SWT.NULL in the style argument. In the preceding code, the first constructor and the third one append a tree item to the item list, whereas the second one and the last one allow
you to specify the index at which a tree item should be stored in the item list.

In the file browser application, the following code is used to add tree items to the tree:

```
setRootDir(new File("F:/jdk1.5"));

/**
 * Sets the root directory to browse from.
 *
```

```
 * @param root
 */
private void setRootDir(File root) {
    // validates the root first.
    if( (!root.isDirectory()) || (!root.exists()))
        throw new IllegalArgumentException("Invalid root: " + root);

    this.rootDir = root;
    shell.setText("Now browsing: " + root.getAbsolutePath());

    // Remove all the existing items in the tree.
    if (tree.getItemCount() > 0) {
        TreeItem[] items = tree.getItems();
        for (int i = 0; i < items.length; i++) {
            items[i].dispose();
            // Dispose itself and all of its descendants.
        }
    }

    // Adds files under the root to the tree.
    File[] files = root.listFiles();
    for(int i=0; files != null && i < files.length; i++)
        addFileToTree(tree, files[i]);
}


/**
 * Wraps the file in a TreeItem and adds the TreeItem to the Tree.
 *
 * @param parent
 * @param file
 */
private void addFileToTree(Object parent, File file) {
    TreeItem item = null;

    if (parent instanceof Tree)
        item = new TreeItem((Tree) parent, SWT.NULL);
    else if (parent instanceof TreeItem)
        item = new TreeItem((TreeItem) parent, SWT.NULL);
    else
        throw new IllegalArgumentException(
            "parent should be a tree or a tree item: " + parent);

    item.setText(file.getName());
    item.setImage(getIcon(file));

    item.setData(file);

    if (file.isDirectory()) {
        if (file.list() != null && file.list().length > 0)
            new TreeItem(item, SWT.NULL);
    }
}
```

247

When the `setRootDir` method is called, it first disposes of all the existing tree items in the tree and calls the `addFileToTree` method. The `addFileToTree` method creates a `TreeItem` representing the file passed. The `setText` and `setImage` methods are used to set the text label and the image label for the `TreeItem`. You also use the `setData` method to record the file object in the tree item. If the file is a directory and has one or more files under it, a dummy tree item is created for it to display a plus sign in front of the tree item so that the user can click it to browse files under it. When the user tries to expand the tree item, files under the directory are listed and represented using tree items (more details are in the section "Handling Events"). You can recursively build the whole tree completely in one call. However, this operation is very time-consuming. Therefore, we use this optimized approach instead.

In the preceding `setRootDir` method, the `dispose` method of the `TreeItem` class is used to dispose of tree items. As a result, tree items are removed from the tree.

The following are some frequently used methods in the `TreeItem` class. To get the parent of a tree item, you can use the `getParent` method or the `getParentItem` method:

```
public Tree getParent()
public TreeItem getParentItem()
```

If the tree item is a top-level item, the first method returns the tree control and the second method returns `null`. Otherwise, the first method returns the tree control containing the tree item and the second method returns the parent item of the tree item.

The `getItems` method returns all the direct children of a tree item:

```
public TreeItem[] getItems()
```

To get the total number of a tree item's direct children, use the `getItemCount` method:

```
public int getItemCount()
```

To get and set the expand status of a tree item, use the following methods:

```
public boolean getExpanded()
public void setExpanded(boolean expanded)
```

Similarly, you can use these two methods to get and set the check status of a tree item (only applicable to tree items in tables with the `SWT.CHECK` style):

```
public boolean getChecked()
public void setChecked(boolean checked)
```

The `Tree` class provides a few methods to access tree items that it contains.

The following methods return information about top-level tree items in a tree:

```
public int getItemCount()
public TreeItem[] getItems()
```

To get and set the top item displayed in a tree, use the following methods:

```
public TreeItem getTopItem()
public void setTopItem(TreeItem item)
```

Use the `removeAll` method to remove all the tree items from a tree:

```
public void removeAll()
```

## Handling Events

The `Tree` control generates the following events in addition to events inherited from the `Composite` class: `SWT.Selection, SWT.DefaultSelection, SWT.Collapse, and SWT.Expand`. A `SelectionListener` is able to handle `SWT.Selection` and `SWT.DefaultSelection` events, and a `TreeListener` listens for `SWT.Collapse` and `SWT.Expand` events.

To implement the optimized tree building mechanism described in the preceding section, we need a listener to listen for `SWT.Expand` events:

```
tree.addTreeListener(new TreeListener() {
    public void treeCollapsed(TreeEvent e) {
    }

    public void treeExpanded(TreeEvent e) {
        TreeItem item = (TreeItem) e.item;
        TreeItem[] children = item.getItems();

        for (int i = 0; i < children.length; i++)
            if (children[i].getData() == null) // Removes dummy items.
                children[i].dispose();
            else // Child files already added to the tree.
                return;

        File[] files = ((File) item.getData()).listFiles();
        for (int i = 0; files != null && i < files.length; i++)
            buildTree(item, files[i]);
    }
});
```

When the user clicks the plus sign in front of a tree item, an `SWT.Expand` event is generated. As a result, the `treeExpanded` method in the listener is called. First, the tree item being expanded is obtained. We then check the existing child items of this tree item. If the child items are valid, this means they have been constructed properly already. If the child items are dummy ones, you dispose of them and build a tree item for each file under the directory represented by the tree item being expanded.

To enable the user to launch a file from the tree, you add a selection listener as follows:

```
tree.addSelectionListener(new SelectionListener() {
    public void widgetSelected(SelectionEvent e) {
    }
```

```
public void widgetDefaultSelected(SelectionEvent e) {
    TreeItem item = (TreeItem) e.item;
    File file = (File) item.getData();
    if (Program.launch(file.getAbsolutePath())) {
        System.out.println("File has been launched: " + file);
    } else {
        System.out.println("Unable to launch file: " + file);
    }
}
});
```

When the user double-clicks a tree item or presses Enter while a tree item is selected, a default selection event is generated and the `widgetDefaultSelected` method gets called. This method first retrieves the file object from the selected item and tries to launch it using the `launch` method of the `org.eclipse .swt.program.Program` class. For example, when the user default selects the `LICENSE.rtf` file (see Figure 11-2) on Windows, the system opens the file with Microsoft Word.

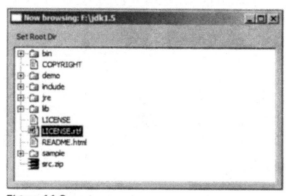

**Figure 11-2**

The `Tree` class provides some methods for you to get and set selection items.

You can use the following two methods to get information about selected items:

```
public int getSelectionCount()
public TreeItem[] getSelection()
```

The `getSelectionCount` method returns the total number of selected items, and the `getSelection` method returns all the selected items as an array.

You can clear the current selection and set new selection items using the `setSelection` method:

```
public void setSelection(TreeItem[] items)
```

The following methods can be used to select/deselect all the tree items in a tree:

```
public void selectAll()
public void deselectAll()
```

## Using TreeEditors

In Chapter 10, you learned how to use TableEditors to implement the cell editing function. A TreeEditor works almost the same as a TableEditor, except a TreeEditor manages controls for editing items in a tree instead of a table.

In this section, we add the file renaming function to our file browser by using a TreeEditor (see Figure 11-3).

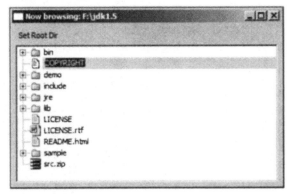

Figure 11-3

First, you create a TreeEditor for the tree:

```
final TreeEditor editor = new TreeEditor(tree);
```

Then, you add the following mouse down listener to the tree:

```
tree.addListener(SWT.MouseDown, new Listener() {
    public void handleEvent(Event event) {
        // Locates the File position in the Tree.
        Point point = new Point(event.x, event.y);
        final TreeItem item = tree.getItem(point);
        if (item == null)
            return;

        final Text text = new Text(tree, SWT.NONE);
        text.setText(item.getText());
        text.setBackground(
            shell.getDisplay().getSystemColor(SWT.COLOR_YELLOW));

        editor.horizontalAlignment = SWT.LEFT;
        editor.grabHorizontal = true;

        editor.setEditor(text, item);

        Listener textListener = new Listener() {
            public void handleEvent(final Event e) {
                switch (e.type) {
```

```
case SWT.FocusOut :
    File renamed = renameFile( (File) item.getData(),
                        text.getText());
    if (renamed != null) {
        item.setText(text.getText());
        item.setData(renamed);
    }
    text.dispose();
    break;

case SWT.Traverse :
    switch (e.detail) {
        case SWT.TRAVERSE_RETURN :
            renamed = renameFile((File) item.getData(),
                            text.getText());
            if (renamed != null) {
                item.setText(text.getText());
                item.setData(renamed);
            }

        case SWT.TRAVERSE_ESCAPE :
            text.dispose();
            e.doit = false;
    }
        break;
        }
    }
};

text.addListener(SWT.FocusOut, textListener);
text.addListener(SWT.Traverse, textListener);

text.setFocus();
    }
});
```

First, the tree item at the point that the user clicks is determined using the getItem(Point point) method of the Tree class. Then we create a Text control and set it as the editor using the setEditor method of the TreeEditor class. The properties of the editor are configured (for more details, see Chapter 10).

A listener is added to the text control to listen for SWT.FocusOut and SWT.Traverse events. If the text control loses focus, you try to rename the file with the new name in the text control using the renameFile method.

```
/**
 * Renames the given file to the specified new name.
 *
 * @param file
```

```
 * @param newName
 * @return the new file name  or <code>null</code> if renaming
 *         fails.
 */
private File renameFile(File file, String newName) {
    File dest = new File(file.getParentFile(), newName);
    if (file.renameTo(dest)) {
        return dest;
    } else {
        return null;
    }
}
```

If the file is successfully renamed, the tree item is updated.

# Using TreeViewer

TreeViewer is the MVC viewer that corresponds to the SWT Tree control. Programming a TreeViewer is very similar to programming other viewers such as ListViewers and TableViewers, which you learned about in previous chapters.

The basic steps for programming a TreeViewer are:

**1.** Create domain-specific model objects.

**2.** Create TreeViewers.

**3.** Set content providers and content.

**4.** Set label providers (optional).

**5.** Add selection listeners (optional).

**6.** Add filters (optional).

**7.** Set sorters (optional).

**8.** Handle events (optional).

Note that, unlike a TableViewer, a TreeViewer does not support direct editing. To make tree items editable, you have to use the same technique used in the preceding section (i.e., you have to add a MouseListener to the TreeItem and respond when a user clicks the mouse button).

In the following sections, we are going to rewrite the file browser application using a tree viewer.

Because the File class is the perfect model class and files in the system are the model objects for the file browser, Step 1 is skipped. You go directly go to Step 2 to create a TreeViewer.

## Creating a TreeViewer

There are three constructors in the `TreeViewer` class that you can use to create `TreeViewers`:

```
TreeViewer(Composite parent)
TreeViewer(Composite parent, int style)
TreeViewer(Tree tree)
```

The first two constructors create a `TreeViewer` on a new tree control under the given parent composite, while the third constructor creates a `TreeViewer` based on an existing tree control. Here is the code to create a tree viewer for the file browser application:

```
TreeViewer treeViewer = new TreeViewer(shell, SWT.BORDER);
treeViewer.getTree().setLayoutData(new GridData(GridData.FILL_BOTH));
```

First the tree viewer is created. The newly created `Tree` control has the `SWT.BORDER` style. You then set the layout data for the tree embedded in the tree viewer. The SWT `Tree` control is obtained through the `getTree` method:

```
public Tree getTree()
```

## Setting the Content Provider

After the `TreeViewer` is created, you then set the content provider for it. A content provider mediates between a viewer's model and the viewer itself. The `TreeViewer` has its own particular type of content provider: `ITreeContentProvider`. You use the following code to set the content provider for the tree viewer:

```
treeViewer.setContentProvider(new ITreeContentProvider() {
    public Object[] getChildren(Object parentElement) {
        File[] files = ((File)parentElement).listFiles();
        if(files == null)
            return new Object[0];
        return files;
    }

    public Object getParent(Object element) {
        return ((File)element).getParentFile();
    }

    public boolean hasChildren(Object element) {
        File file = (File)element;
        File[] files = file.listFiles();
        if(files == null || files.length == 0)
            return false;
        return true;
    }

    public Object[] getElements(Object inputElement) {
        File[] files = ((File)inputElement).listFiles();
```

```
            if(files == null)
                return new Object[0];
            return files;
        }

    public void dispose() {
    }

    public void inputChanged(
        Viewer viewer,
        Object oldInput,
        Object newInput) {
            shell.setText("Now browsing: " + newInput);
    }
});
```

Note that the ITreeContentProvider interface defines three additional methods over the IStructuredContentProvider interface: getChildren, getParent, and hasChildren.

The following line sets the input element:

```
treeViewer.setInput(new File("F:/jdk1.5"));
```

When the setInput method is executed, the inputChanged method in the content provider is called. The tree viewer queries the getElements of the tree content provider for root elements. While adding root elements to the tree, the tree viewer also consults the hasChildren method to check whether an element has any children. When the user expands a tree item, the getChildren method is used to get all the files under the directory represented by it.

## Setting the Label Provider

A label provider maps an element of the viewer's model to an optional image and optional text string used to display the element in the viewer's control. The following is the code to set the label provider for the tree viewer:

```
treeViewer.setLabelProvider(new LabelProvider() {
    public Image getImage(Object element) {
        return getIcon((File)element);
    }

    public String getText(Object element) {
        return ((File)element).getName();
    }
});
```

The getImage method returns an icon (image) representing the file type of the file, and the getText method returns the short form of the file name.

## Setting the Sorter

To organize the files in the file browser, you need to set a sorter to sort the files, as shown in Figure 11-4.

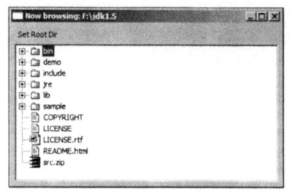

**Figure 11-4**

The code to implement the sorter is shown here:

```
// Sorts the tree in the order that directories go before all normal files
treeViewer.setSorter(new ViewerSorter() {
    public int category(Object element) {
        File file = (File)element;
        if(file.isDirectory())
            return 0;
        else
            return 1;
    }
});
```

In the sorter, only the `category` method of the `ViewerSorter` class is overridden. The `category` method returns the category that the given element belongs to. There are two categories for files here: directories and normal files. The `compare` method of the `ViewerSorter` class compares the elements' categories as computed by the `category` method. Elements within the same category are further subjected to a case-insensitive compare of their label strings computed by the tree viewer's label provider.

## Adding a Filter

In this section, we are going to create a filter to show only the directories, as shown in Figure 11-5.

Here is the code to filter out normal files:

```
final ViewerFilter directoryFilter = new ViewerFilter() {
    public boolean select(
        Viewer viewer,
        Object parentElement,
        Object element) {
            return ((File)element).isDirectory();
    }
};
```

```
Action actionShowDirectoriesOnly = new Action("Show directories only") {
    public void run() {
        if(! isChecked())
            treeViewer.removeFilter(directoryFilter);
        else
            treeViewer.addFilter(directoryFilter);
    }
};
actionShowDirectoriesOnly.setChecked(false);

ToolBar toolBar = new ToolBar(shell, SWT.FLAT);
ToolBarManager manager = new ToolBarManager(toolBar);
manager.add(actionSetRootDir);
manager.add(actionShowDirectoriesOnly);
manager.update(true);
```

If the "Show directories only" button is checked, the filter is added to the tree viewer. As a result, only directories are shown. If the button is unchecked, the filter is removed from the tree viewer so that all kinds of files are displayed.

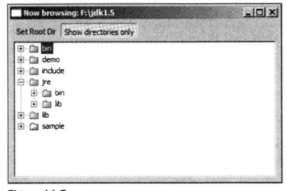

Figure 11-5

# Getting Selections

Let's add the file deletion function to the file browser application, as shown in Figure 11-6.

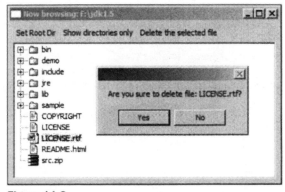

Figure 11-6

257

When the user presses the "Delete the selected file" button, a message box appears. If the user clicks Yes, the application tries to delete the file. The code to implement this function is as follows:

```
Action actionDeleteFile = new Action("Delete the selected file") {
    public void run() {
        IStructuredSelection selection =
            (IStructuredSelection)treeViewer.getSelection();

        File file = (File)selection.getFirstElement();
        if(file == null) {
            System.out.println("Please select a file first.");
            return;
        }

        MessageBox messageBox = new MessageBox(shell, SWT.YES | SWT.NO);
        messageBox.setMessage("Are you sure to delete file: " +
            file.getName() + "?");

        if(messageBox.open() == SWT.YES) {
            File parentFile = file.getParentFile();
            if(file.delete()) {
                System.out.println("File has been deleted. ");
                // Notifies the viewer for update.
                treeViewer.refresh(parentFile, false);
            }else{
                System.out.println("Unable to delete file.");
            }
        }

    }
};
```

If the user clicks the deletion button, the `run` method of the action is invoked. First, the selected element (file) is extracted. If no file is selected, a message is printed out and the function returns. A message box is displayed to ask the user to confirm the deletion. If the file is deleted successfully, you update the tree viewer with the `refresh` method:

```
public void refresh(Object element, boolean updateLabels)
```

This method refreshes the tree viewer starting with the given element.

If you need to listen to selection events generated by the tree, you can simply add an `ISelectionChangedListener` using the `addSelectionChangedListener` method of the `TreeViewer` class:

```
public void addSelectionChangedListener(ISelectionChangedListener listener)
```

With the preceding method, you can register selection listeners that will be invoked when a selection in the tree is made.

# Summary

In this chapter, you learned about the `Tree` control. Trees are powerful UI components for displaying hierarchical data. After a tree is created, you can add an item to it by wrapping the item in a `TreeItem`. Trees are capable of generating selection, collapse, and expand events. You can register proper event listeners to listen to those events. By setting tree editors, you make it possible for the user to edit the data on the fly. To program with trees using the MVC approach, you can use the `TreeViewer` class provided in the JFace viewer framework.

# 12

# Dialogs

Dialogs are UI objects that can be used to acquire particular types of data input from the user. In this chapter, you learn how to use each of the SWT dialogs (except for `PrintDialog`, which is covered in Chapter 17):

❑ `ColorDialog`

❑ `DirectoryDialog`

❑ `FileDialog`

❑ `FontDialog`

❑ `MessageBox`

This chapter first reviews the basics and then teaches you how to create custom dialogs to satisfy your own needs.

This chapter covers only those dialogs available in SWT packages. For dialogs offered by JFace packages, please refer to Chapter 18.

## Dialog Basics

Dialogs are UI objects that can be used to acquire particular types of data input from the user. You use a dialog to:

❑ Create a dialog instance

❑ Configure the dialog (optional)

❑ Open the dialog and wait for input

The possible pseudo code is listed here:

```
Dialog dialog = new Dialog(shell);        // 1) Creates a dialog instance.
dialog.setText("Sample Dialog");          // 2) Configures the title of the dialog
Object value = dialog.open();             // 3) Gets the input from the dialog
...
```

The org.eclipse.swt.widgets.Dialog (abstract) class is the parent class of all SWT dialogs. The Dialog class has two constructors:

```
public Dialog(Shell parent)
public Dialog(Shell parent, int style)
```

To construct a dialog, you must pass a shell as its parent. If the parent is null, an IllegalArgumentException is thrown. The second constructor allows you to specify the style bits for the dialog. You can specify the modality style of the dialog with one of the following styles:

- ❏ SWT.PRIMARY_MODAL: Once the dialog is displayed, the user is not allowed to interact with any ancestor of the dialog.

- ❏ SWT.APPLICATION_MODAL: Once the dialog is displayed, the user is not allowed to interact with any window created by the same application.

- ❏ SWT.SYSTEM_MODAL: Once the dialog is displayed, the user is not allowed to interact with any window on the screen. This includes windows from all other applications.

The first constructor chooses the default modality style as SWT.PRIMARY_MODAL. All the preceding modality styles are hints only because the underlying system may not support them.

Each of the concrete dialogs (e.g., ColorDialog and FileDialog) in SWT has two constructors with exactly the same arguments as those mentioned previously.

You can use the following methods of the Dialog class to get/set the title of the dialog:

```
public String getText()
public void setText(String string)
```

To get the parent shell, you can use the getParent method:

```
public Shell getParent()
```

The following sections cover all dialogs available in SWT.

# Using ColorDialogs and FontDialogs

This section introduces two other types of dialogs: ColorDialog and FontDialog.

## ColorDialogs

ColorDialog allows the user to select a color from the predefined set of available colors. Before opening a color dialog, you can use the setRGB method to set the default selected color:

```
public void setRGB(RGB rgb)
```

If null is passed to setRGB, the system tries to select a default color. The open method of the ColorDialog method returns the selected color as an RGB object or null if the user cancels the selection.

```
public RGB open()
```

## FontDialogs

FontDialog allows the user to select a font with font style, size, and effects. The open method of the FontDialog class returns the selected font as a FontData object or null if the user cancels the selection.

```
public FontData open()
```

You can create a Font object based on the FontData returned. Before opening the dialog, you can optionally set the default selected font using the setFontList method of the FontDialog class:

```
public void setFontList(FontData[] fontData)
```

A font dialog may also support color selection. You can use the following methods to get/set the selected color:

```
public RGB getRGB()
public void setRGB(RGB rgb)
```

## Using ColorDialogs and FontDialogs

To have a better understanding of ColorDialog and FontDialog, let's build a text display application that allows the user to set the foreground color and the text font (see Figure 12-1).

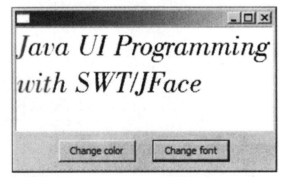

**Figure 12-1**

The corresponding code is as follows:

```
public class FormattedText {
    Display display = new Display();
    Shell shell = new Shell(display);

    // the label used to display the text.
    Label label;

    Button buttonColor;
    Button buttonFont;

    // current selected color.
    Color color;
    // current selected font.
    Font font;

    public FormattedText() {
        label = new Label(shell, SWT.BORDER | SWT.WRAP);
        label.setBackground(display.getSystemColor(SWT.COLOR_WHITE));
        label.setText("Java UI Programming with SWT/JFace");

        buttonColor = new Button(shell, SWT.PUSH);
        buttonColor.setText("Change color");
        buttonColor.addListener(SWT.Selection, new Listener() {
            public void handleEvent(Event event) {
                ColorDialog colorDialog = new ColorDialog(shell);
                if(color != null) // initializes default selected color.
                    colorDialog.setRGB(color.getRGB());
                RGB value = colorDialog.open();
                if(value != null) {
                    if(color != null)
                        color.dispose();
                    color = new Color(display, value);
                    label.setForeground(color);
                }else{
                    System.out.println(
                        "Setting foreground color action canceled.");
                }
            }
        });

        buttonFont = new Button(shell, SWT.PUSH);
        buttonFont.setText("Change font");
        buttonFont.addListener(SWT.Selection, new Listener() {
            public void handleEvent(Event event) {
                FontDialog fontDialog = new FontDialog(shell);
                if(font != null) // initializes default selected font.
                    fontDialog.setFontList(font.getFontData());
                FontData fontData = fontDialog.open();
                if(fontData != null) {
                    if(font != null)
                        font.dispose();
                    font = new Font(display, fontData);
```

```
                    label.setFont(font);
            }else{
                System.out.println("Setting font action canceled.");
            }
        }
    });

    label.setBounds(0, 0, 300, 120);
    buttonColor.setBounds(50, 130, 90, 25);
    buttonFont.setBounds(160, 130, 90, 25);

    shell.setSize(300, 190);
    shell.open();

    // Set up the event loop.
    while (!shell.isDisposed()) {
        if (!display.readAndDispatch()) {
            // If no more entries in event queue
            display.sleep();
        }
    }

    display.dispose();
}

public static void main(String[] args) {
    new FormattedText();
}
}
```

A label is created to display the text. When the change color button is pressed, a color dialog is created. If the currently selected color is known, you use its value to set the default selected color for the dialog. The dialog is displayed when `colorDialog.open()` is executed. If the user selects a color and presses OK, an instance of RGB representing the current selected color is returned. You first dispose of the last selected color and create a new color based on the RGB object returned. After the color object is properly constructed, you then set it as the foreground color of the label using the `setForeground` method of the `Label` class. If the color selection is canceled, a string is displayed to inform the user.

Similarly, when the change font button is pressed, a font dialog is created. Set the default font as the current selected font, if it exists. You cannot directly set the default selected font with a `Font` object; instead you need to use the font data information that the `Font` object contains. The font dialog is then opened. If the user selects a font and clicks OK in the dialog, a `FontData` object representing the selected font is returned. You dispose of the existing `Font` object, if any, and create a new one based on the `FontData` returned. The font of the label is changed through the `setFont` method.

The returned objects from these dialogs, RGBs and FontDatas, are common Java objects that can be garbage collected by the JVM. However, `Color` and `Font` objects are resource-based objects, and you must handle them with care. For a complete discuss of resource-based object management, please refer to Chapter 2.

You may find that the Eclipse IDE uses some fancy color selection buttons, as shown in Figure 12-2.

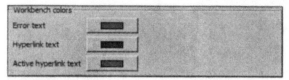

**Figure 12-2**

The implementation class is `org.eclipse.jdt.internal.ui.preferences.ColorEditor`. This class wraps a button displaying the current selected color in a narrow strip. When the button is pressed, a color dialog is displayed for the user to pick the color. The following methods of the `ColorEditor` class can be used to get/set the selected color:

```
public RGB getColorValue()
public void setColorValue(RGB rgb)
```

# Using DirectoryDialogs and FileDialogs

In SWT, there are two kinds of dialogs that you can use to let the user select a file or directory: `DirectoryDialog` and `FileDialog`.

## DirectoryDialogs

A `DirectoryDialog` allows the user to navigate the file system and to select a directory.

Before opening a directory dialog, you can set its initial directory using the `setFilterPath` method of the `DirectoryDialog` class:

```
public void setFilterPath(String string)
```

Optionally, you can provide a description of the purpose of the directory dialog using the `setMessage` method:

```
public void setMessage(String string)
```

The open method of the `DirectoryDialog` class returns the selected directory or `null` if the user cancels the selection:

```
public String open()
```

## FileDialogs

A `FileDialog` allows the user to navigate the file system and to select one or more files. In addition to modality styles, `FileDialog` supports the following styles:

- ❑ SWT.SAVE: This style should be used if you intend to write data into the selected file or files.

- ❑ SWT.OPEN: This style should be used if you intend to read data from the selected file or files.

- ❑ SWT.MULTI: Set this style to enable the user to select multiple files.

Before opening a file dialog, you can set its initial selected directory and initial selected file name using the following methods:

```
public void setFilterPath(String string)
public void setFileName(String string)
```

Both of the preceding methods can take `null` values.

You can use `setFilterExtensions` to set the file extensions that the dialog will use to filter the files. Optionally, you can provide descriptions of the filters using `setFilterNames`:

```
public void setFilterExtensions(String[] extensions)
public void setFilterNames(String[] names)
```

For example, the following code sets three filters, as shown in Figure 12-3:

```
fileDialog.setFilterExtensions(new String[]{"*.rtf", "*.html", "*.*"});
fileDialog.setFilterNames(new String[]{ "Rich Text Format", "HTML Document",
"Any"});
```

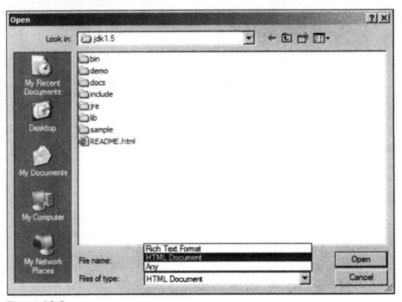

Figure 12-3

When the user selects HTML Document, the second filter, *.html, is applied. As a result, only files ending with ".html" are shown. If the third filter is applied, then files with any extension are shown.

The `open` method returns the absolute path of the first selected file or `null` if the user cancels the selection:

```
public String open()
```

To get the directory that the selected file(s) belongs to, use the `getFilterPath` method:

```
public String getFilterPath()
```

The `getFileNames` method returns the file names of all the selected files as an array:

```
public String[] getFileNames()
```

If you are interested only in the file name of the first selected file, use the `getFileName` method:

```
public String getFileName()
```

Both `getFileNames` and `getFileName` methods return relative file names to the filter path.

## Using DirectoryDialogs and FileDialogs

In this section, we build a simple file selection application (as shown in Figure 12-4). This application simply prints out the selected directories or files.

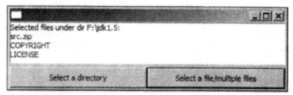

**Figure 12-4**

Here is the code for this application:

```
public class DirFileSelection {
    Display display = new Display();
    Shell shell = new Shell(display);

    // the label used to display selected dir/file.
    Label label;

    Button buttonSelectDir;
    Button buttonSelectFile;

    String selectedDir;
    String fileFilterPath;

    public DirFileSelection() {
        label = new Label(shell, SWT.BORDER | SWT.WRAP);
        label.setBackground(display.getSystemColor(SWT.COLOR_WHITE));
        label.setText("Select a dir/file by clicking the buttons below.");

        buttonSelectDir = new Button(shell, SWT.PUSH);
        buttonSelectDir.setText("Select a directory");
        buttonSelectDir.addListener(SWT.Selection, new Listener() {
```

```
        public void handleEvent(Event event) {
            DirectoryDialog directoryDialog =
                new DirectoryDialog(shell);

            directoryDialog.setFilterPath(selectedDir);
            directoryDialog.setMessage(
                "Please select a directory and click OK");

            String dir = directoryDialog.open();
            if(dir != null) {
                label.setText("Selected dir: " + dir);
                selectedDir = dir;
            }
        }
    });

    buttonSelectFile = new Button(shell, SWT.PUSH);
    buttonSelectFile.setText("Select a file/multiple files");
    buttonSelectFile.addListener(SWT.Selection, new Listener() {
        public void handleEvent(Event event) {
            FileDialog fileDialog = new FileDialog(shell, SWT.MULTI);

            fileDialog.setFilterPath(fileFilterPath);

            fileDialog.setFilterExtensions(
                new String[]{"*.rtf", "*.html", "*.*"});
            fileDialog.setFilterNames(new String[]{
                "Rich Text Format", "HTML Document", "Any"});

            String firstFile = fileDialog.open();

            if(firstFile != null) {
                fileFilterPath = fileDialog.getFilterPath();
                String[] selectedFiles = fileDialog.getFileNames();
                StringBuffer sb = new StringBuffer(
                    "Selected files under dir " +
                    fileDialog.getFilterPath() + ": \n");
                for(int i=0; i<selectedFiles.length; i++) {
                    sb.append(selectedFiles[i] + "\n");
                }
                label.setText(sb.toString());
            }
        }
    });

    label.setBounds(0, 0, 400, 60);
    buttonSelectDir.setBounds(0, 65, 200, 30);
    buttonSelectFile.setBounds(200, 65, 200, 30);

    shell.pack();
    shell.open();

    // Set up the event loop.
    while (!shell.isDisposed()) {
```

```
            if (!display.readAndDispatch()) {
                // If no more entries in event queue
                display.sleep();
            }
        }

        display.dispose();
    }


    public static void main(String[] args) {
        new DirFileSelection();
    }
}
```

When the user presses the directory selection button, a `DirectoryDialog` is created. You then set the initial directory and the description using the `setFilterPath` method and the `setMessage` method, respectively. The dialog is then opened. If the user clicks OK, the selected directory is returned and printed on the label.

If the user presses the file selection button, a `FileDialog` is created. First, the initial directory for the dialog is set. Then, filter extensions and their corresponding descriptions are set using the `setFilterExtensions` method and `setFilterNames`, respectively. The dialog is then opened. If the user selects one or more files and clicks OK, the `open` method returns the absolute path of the first selected file. You then obtain the directory-selected files belonging to the `getFilterPath` method. The file name of each of the selected files is printed on the label.

You might notice that neither `FileDialog` nor `DirectoryDialog` allows the user to select multiple items. The primary reason is that not all platforms support multiple item selection. If you need advanced dialogs for selecting files and directories, you have to create custom dialogs, which you learn about later in this chapter.

# Using MessageBoxes

A message box is used to inform or warn the user.

You can specify the icon and buttons to be displayed on a message box using the following styles:

❑ `SWT.ICON_ERROR`, `SWT.ICON_INFORMATION`, `SWT.ICON_QUESTION`, `SWT.ICON_WARNING`, `SWT.ICON_WORKING`: You can specify one of these in the constructor of the `MessageBox` class. The actual icon displayed on the message box is system-dependent. No more than one of them should be specified. No icon is displayed in the message box if none is specified.

❑ `[SWT.OK] [OK | CANCEL] [YES | NO] [YES | NO | CANCEL] [RETRY | CANCEL] [ABORT | RETRY | IGNORE]`: These groups can be used to specify the buttons to be displayed at the bottom of the message box. For example, if you set `YES | NO | CANCEL`, three buttons will be displayed in the message box — i.e., a button labeled Yes, a button labeled No, and a button labeled Cancel. These groups are the only valid combinations to set buttons. If you specify an invalid combination (e.g., `YES | OK`), buttons may not be displayed properly.

Before opening a message box, you can optionally set a description for it using the `setMessage` method:

```
public void setMessage(String string)
```

This message is displayed below the dialog title and above the buttons.

The `open` method returns the ID of the button selected by the user:

```
public int open()
```

For example, the following code displays a message box, as shown in Figure 12-5.

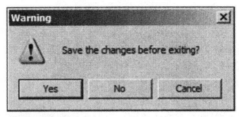

**Figure 12-5**

```
MessageBox messageBox = new MessageBox(shell,
                    SWT.ICON_WARNING | SWT.YES | SWT.NO | SWT.CANCEL);

messageBox.setText("Warning");
messageBox.setMessage("Save the changes before exiting?");

int buttonID = messageBox.open();

switch(buttonID) {
    case SWT.YES:
        // saves changes ...
    case SWT.NO:
        // exits here ...
        break;
    case SWT.CANCEL:
        // cancels the action ...
}
```

First, a message box is created with a warning icon and three buttons. Then, we set the title and the message for this message box. The message box is displayed when the `open` method is called. After the user presses one of buttons, the message box is disposed of and the ID of the button being clicked is returned. We then take proper actions based on the returned value.

Sometimes, a message box is disposed of when the user presses the *Esc* key or clicks the close trim box (i.e., the box with an X at the upper right of the shell) of the dialog instead of clicking any of the buttons. In this case, the returned value is dependent on the button group specified. If there is a `SWT.CANCEL` button in the group, then `SWT.CANCEL` is returned. If there is only one button, i.e, `SWT.OK`, then the returned value is `SWT.OK`.

# Creating Your Own Dialogs

If none of the standard SWT dialogs satisfies your requirements, you can create your own dialogs. In Chapter 5, you learned how to create a dialog shell. To make dialog shells reusable, put dialog shells in classes implementing the `Dialog` class. The `Dialog` class is declared abstract, but there is no abstract method in it.

You use the following code to implement a number input dialog, as shown in Figure 12-6:

```java
public class NumberInputDialog extends Dialog {
    Double value; // the value to be returned.

    /**
     * @param parent
     */
    public NumberInputDialog(Shell parent) {
        super(parent);
    }

    /**
     * @param parent
     * @param style
     */
    public NumberInputDialog(Shell parent, int style) {
        super(parent, style);
    }

    /**
     * Makes the dialog visible.
     *
     * @return
     */
    public Double open() {
        Shell parent = getParent();
        final Shell shell =
            new Shell(parent, SWT.TITLE | SWT.BORDER | SWT.APPLICATION_MODAL);
        shell.setText("NumberInputDialog");

        shell.setLayout(new GridLayout(2, true));

        Label label = new Label(shell, SWT.NULL);
        label.setText("Please enter a valid number:");

        final Text text = new Text(shell, SWT.SINGLE | SWT.BORDER);

        final Button buttonOK = new Button(shell, SWT.PUSH);
        buttonOK.setText("Ok");
        buttonOK.setLayoutData(new GridData(GridData.HORIZONTAL_ALIGN_END));
        Button buttonCancel = new Button(shell, SWT.PUSH);
        buttonCancel.setText("Cancel");
```

```
        text.addListener(SWT.Modify, new Listener() {
            public void handleEvent(Event event) {
                try {
                    value = new Double(text.getText());
                    buttonOK.setEnabled(true);
                } catch (Exception e) {
                    buttonOK.setEnabled(false);
                }
            }
        });

        buttonOK.addListener(SWT.Selection, new Listener() {
            public void handleEvent(Event event) {
                shell.dispose();
            }
        });

        buttonCancel.addListener(SWT.Selection, new Listener() {
            public void handleEvent(Event event) {
                value = null;
                shell.dispose();
            }
        });

        // Prevents ESCAPE from disposing the dialog
        shell.addListener(SWT.Traverse, new Listener() {
            public void handleEvent(Event event) {
                if(event.detail == SWT.TRAVERSE_ESCAPE)
                    event.doit = false;
            }
        });

        text.setText("");
        shell.pack();
        shell.open();

        Display display = parent.getDisplay();
        while (!shell.isDisposed()) {
        if (!display.readAndDispatch())
            display.sleep();
        }

        return value;
    }
}
```

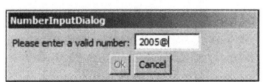

Figure 12-6

The open method first creates all the widgets needed. The dialog class should take care of data validation. To do that, you add a text modify listener to enable the OK button if the input is valid or to disable the button in case of invalid input. When any of the buttons is selected, the dialog should be disposed. If the Cancel button is selected, you set the value to null before disposing of the dialog. To force the user to click one of the buttons, you add a traverse listener to prevent escape from disposing of the dialog. At the end of the open method, you set up an event loop to prevent the method from returning immediately (for more details, see Chapter 4).

The open method returns the input number as a Double object or null if the user clicks the Cancel button. The code that follows is the sample usage of the NumberInputDialog class:

```
public static void main(String[] args) {
    Shell shell = new Shell();
    NumberInputDialog dialog = new NumberInputDialog(shell);
    System.out.println(dialog.open());
}
```

Now, you have created a custom dialog and you can use it to get input from the user.

# Summary

This chapter covered dialogs that are available in SWT packages. The chapter covered the general configuration and usage of dialogs, and I discussed each type of dialog. You use ColorDialog to enable the user to select a color and FontDialog to enable the user to select a font with font style, size, and effects. A sample application showed you how to use ColorDialog and FontDialog. To let the user select a file or directory, you use FileDialog or Directory, respectively. You use MessageBox to inform or warn the user. Finally, if none of the dialogs satisfies your needs, you can create your own dialog by extending the Dialog class.

# Part III: Dynamic Controls

# 13

# Scales, Sliders, and Progress Bars

In this chapter, you learn how to use certain controls to present numerical values. They are:

❑ Scale

❑ Slider

❑ ProgressBar

A scale is a selectable UI component that presents a range of continuous numeric integer values. A slider works much like a scale does, except the appearance of a slider differs from that of a scale. Unlike a scale or a slider, a progress bar is not a selectable UI object but it can be used to display the progress of a lengthy operation.

## Using Scales

A scale is a selectable user interface object presenting a range of continuous numeric integer values. The Scale control can have two styles: SWT.VERTICAL and SWT.HORIZONTAL. These two scale styles are shown in Figure 13-1. The scale at the top has the SWT.HORIZONTAL style, whereas the scale below has the SWT.VERTICAL style. If you do not specify a style when you are creating a scale, the default is SWT.HORIZONTAL.

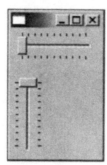

**Figure 13-1**

For a scale with the SWT.HORIZONTAL style, the minimum value is selected when the thumb (the small bar) is on the left end of the scale and the maximum is selected when the thumb is on the right end of the scale. If you rotate a horizontal scale 90 degrees clockwise, you'll get a vertical scale. For a vertical scale, the minimum value is selected when the thumb is on the top end of the scale. Sometimes, this value representation is awkward; the user usually likes to see the maximum value at the top and the minimum at the bottom. You cannot configure a scale to change its value representation behavior, but you can easily create an illusion (an example of this is given later in the chapter).

There is only one constructor in the Scale class:

```
public Scale(Composite parent, int style)
```

The Scale class provides several methods for you to access its minimum and maximum values:

```
public void setMinimum(int value)
public void setMaximum(int value)
public int getMinimum()
public int getMaximum()
```

The default minimum and maximum values on Windows are 0 and 100, respectively.

You can select values on scales through the mouse or the keyboard. When you are using the keyboard, you can use Page Up and Page Down keys for coarse tuning and the down/up arrow keys for fine-tuning. The increment/decrement unit amount for coarse tuning can be gotten and set using the following methods:

```
public int getPageIncrement()
public void setPageIncrement(int pageIncrement)
```

Similarly, you can use the following method to get/set the increment/decrement unit amount for fine-tuning:

```
public int getIncrement()
public void setIncrement(int increment)
```

To get and set the current selected value, you can use the `getSelection` method and the `setSelection` method:

```
public int getSelection()
public void setSelection(int value)
```

Finally, if you need to listen for selection events, you can register one or more selection listeners using the `addListener` method for untyped listeners or the `addSelectionListener` method for typed listeners:

```
public void addSelectionListener(SelectionListener listener)
```

The `detail` field of the `Event` object gives selection details, such as whether the selection is made through the mouse (`SWT.DRAG`) or the keyboard (`SWT.ARROW_DOWN`, `SWT.PAGE_UP`, `SWT.HOME`, and so on).

The following code creates a volume-adjusting utility, as shown in Figure 13-2.

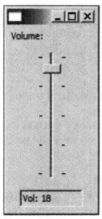

**Figure 13-2**

```
...
Scale scale;
Text value;

shell.setLayout(new GridLayout(1, true));

Label label = new Label(shell, SWT.NULL);
label.setText("Volume:");

scale = new Scale(shell, SWT.VERTICAL);
scale.setBounds(0, 0, 40, 200);

scale.setMaximum(20);
scale.setMinimum(0);
scale.setIncrement(1);
scale.setPageIncrement(5);
```

**279**

```
scale.addListener(SWT.Selection, new Listener() {
    public void handleEvent(Event event) {
        int perspectiveValue =
            scale.getMaximum() - scale.getSelection() + scale.getMinimum();
        value.setText("Vol: " + perspectiveValue);
    }
});

value = new Text(shell, SWT.BORDER | SWT.SINGLE);
...
```

A vertical scale is created in the code. There are 20 levels of volume and an additional level 0 to represent the mute volume. The setIncrement method and the setPageIncrement method are used to config-ure the increment unit amounts for fine-tuning and coarse-tuning. A selection listener is added to listen to selection events. To overcome the awkward value presentation of vertical scales, you use "perspec-tive" values instead of the raw values returned by the getSelection method. When a value is selected, its perspective value is printed in the text field.

# Using Sliders

A slider works exactly as a scale does, except that the appearance of a slider is different.

All the methods of the Scale class introduced previously apply to the Slider class, too. The Slider class offers the following additional methods over the Scale class:

```
public int getThumb()
public void setThumb(int value)
public void setValues(int selection, int minimum, int maximum, int thumb, int
increment, int pageIncrement)
```

The getThumb method and the setThumb method can be used to get/set the thumb size in pixels. However, not all operating systems support the setThumb method. The setValues method is a facade method that you can use to set various values in one call.

```
public void setValues(int selection, int minimum, int maximum, int thumb, int
increment, int pageIncrement)
```

Let's rewrite the volume adjusting program using a slider (see Figure 13-3).

```
...
Slider slider;
Text value;

shell.setLayout(new GridLayout(1, true));

Label label = new Label(shell, SWT.NULL);
label.setText("Volume:");

slider = new Slider(shell, SWT.VERTICAL);
slider.setBounds(0, 0, 40, 200);
```

```
slider.setMaximum(20);
slider.setMinimum(0);
slider.setIncrement(1);
slider.setPageIncrement(5);

slider.setThumb(4);

slider.addListener(SWT.Selection, new Listener() {
    public void handleEvent(Event event) {
        int perspectiveValue =
            slider.getMaximum() - slider.getSelection() + slider.getMinimum();
        value.setText("Vol: " + perspectiveValue);
    }
});

value = new Text(shell, SWT.BORDER | SWT.SINGLE);
...
```

**Figure 13-3**

If you compare the preceding code with the code in the previous section, the only difference (with the exception of variable names and types) is that the setThumb method is highlighted in bold. If you look carefully at the UIs, you may find there is another difference. With the scale version of the volume adjusting program, you can adjust volume from level 0 to 20. However, the slider version allows you to set only levels 4 to 20. The cause of this problem is that the selectable range of a slider is [minimum, maximum - thumbSize]. To fix it, you need to set the maximum value to 24:

```
slider.setMaximum(24);
```

and replace the perspective calculation code with the following line:

```
int perspectiveValue = slider.getMaximum() - slider.getSelection() +
slider.getMinimum() - slider.getThumb();
```

Now, you can select any level from 0 to 20 (see Figure 13-4).

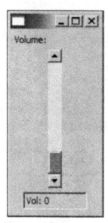

Figure 13-4

# Using ProgressBars

Unlike a scale or a slider, a progress bar is an unselectable UI object that is usually used to display progress of a lengthy operation. In SWT, the ProgressBar class is used to represent a progress bar.

Styles supported by ProgressBar are as follows:

❑    SWT.HORIZONTAL, SWT.VERTICAL: You use one of these styles to specify the orientation of the progress bar to be created. If neither of the two styles is specified, the progress bar is placed horizontally by default. No more than one of these styles should be specified.

❑    SWT.SMOOTH: A progress bar is painted and filled from the minimum value to its selected value. On Windows, by default (i.e., when you specify SWT.NONE in the ProgressBar constructor, which requires a style int), the area is crammed with a series of small rectangles. If this style is set, the area will be filled with a continuous long bar (see Figure 13-5).

❑    SWT.INDETERMINATE: For a progress bar representing the progress of a lengthy operation, you may set this style if the percentage of currently finished work is indeterminate. This style causes the progress bar to display an animation repeatedly. Prior to SWT version 2.1, the org.eclipse.swt.custom.AnimatedProgress class was used to create a progress bar with an animation effect. Since SWT version 2.1, the AnimatedProgress class is deprecated; instead, you should use the ProgressBar class with this style.

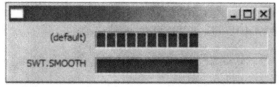

Figure 13-5

To get/set the minimum allowed value for a progress bar, you can use the following methods:

```
public int getMinimum()
public void setMinimum(int value)
```

For the method setMinimum, if the passed argument is less than 0 or larger than the current maximum value, this method ignores the request. The default minimum and maximum values are 0 and 100, respectively.

Similarly, the following are methods to get/set the maximum allowed value:

```
public int getMaximum()
public void setMaximum(int value)
```

If the value passed to setMaximum is not greater than the current minimum value, the request is ignored.

To get and set the current selected value, you can use the following methods:

```
public int getSelection()
public void setSelection(int value)
```

To understand how progress bars work, let's build a simple number counting program, as shown in Figure 13-6.

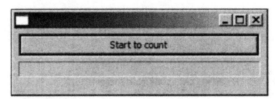

**Figure 13-6**

When the user presses the button, the program starts to count numbers from 0 to 10 and the progress is shown in the progress bar under the button (see Figure 13-7).

**Figure 13-7**

The code to implement the preceding program is as follows:

```
...
Button button = new Button(shell, SWT.BORDER);
button.setText("Start to count");

ProgressBar progressBar = new ProgressBar(shell, SWT.SMOOTH);
progressBar.setMinimum(0);
progressBar.setMaximum(10);

final Thread countThread = new Thread(){
    public void run() {
        for(int i=0; i<=10; i++) {
            final int num = i;
            try {
                Thread.sleep(1000);
            } catch (InterruptedException e) {
                e.printStackTrace();
            }

            shell.getDisplay().asyncExec(new Runnable(){
                public void run() {
                    if(button.isDisposed() || progressBar.isDisposed())
                        return;
                    button.setText("Counting: " + num);
                    progressBar.setSelection(num);
                }
            });
        }
    }
};

button.addListener(SWT.Selection, new Listener() {
    public void handleEvent(Event event) {
        button.setEnabled(false);
        countThread.start();
    }
});
```

First, a button and a progress bar are created. We then set the minimum and maximum values for the progress bar to 0 and 10, respectively. A thread is created to perform the counting task in a separate non-UI thread. A selection listener is added to the button to listen to selection events. If the user clicks the button, the counting thread is triggered to start. When counting each number, the counting thread makes a UI update request using the asyncExec method. For a complete discussion of threading and UI updating, see Chapter 4.

In many cases, you may want to display a string representing the percentage of the job completed in the center of a progress bar (see Figure 13-8).

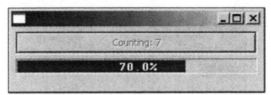

**Figure 13-8**

The simplest approach to implementing this behavior is to add a paint listener to the progress bar and draw the percentage in the graphics context of the progress bar:

```
progressBar.addPaintListener(new PaintListener() {
    public void paintControl(PaintEvent e) {
        // The string to be drawn on the progress bar.
        String string = (progressBar.getSelection() * 1.0 /
          (progressBar.getMaximum()-progressBar.getMinimum()) * 100) + "%";

        Point point = progressBar.getSize();
        Font font = new Font(shell.getDisplay(),"Courier",10,SWT.BOLD);
        e.gc.setFont(font);
        e.gc.setForeground(shell.getDisplay().getSystemColor(SWT.COLOR_WHITE));

        FontMetrics fontMetrics = e.gc.getFontMetrics();
        int stringWidth = fontMetrics.getAverageCharWidth() * string.length();
        int stringHeight = fontMetrics.getHeight();

        e.gc.drawString(string, (point.x-stringWidth)/2 ,
            (point.y-stringHeight)/2, true);

        font.dispose();
    }
});
```

First, the string to be displayed is determined. Then you set the font for the graphics context. To center the string, you need to know its width and height in pixels. To do this, you use the FontMetrics object obtained from the graphics context. The string is then drawn to the progress bar using the drawString method of the graphics context. Finally, the font object is disposed of.

*You do not hard code any value in the paint listener so you can add the paint listener to any SWT progress bars without changing the code.*

You'll also notice that the string in the progress bar looked ugly in the program you just ran (look closely at Figure 13-9).

**285**

**Figure 13-9**

In order for the string to be displayed properly, you have to mark the progress bar to be painted completely, including the background, by using the redraw method:

```
shell.getDisplay().
    asyncExec(new Runnable(){
        public void run() {
            if(button.isDisposed() || progressBar.isDisposed())
                    return;
            button.setText("Counting: " + num);
            progressBar.setSelection(num);
            progressBar.redraw();
        }
    });
```

The new line added is highlighted in bold. Without calling the redraw method, the system will not repaint the background of the progress bar and, as a result, the string may not be displayed clearly (see Figure 13-9).

Now all three controls have been introduced. You use a scale or a slider to let the user select a value from a range of continuous numeric integer values. To display the progress of a lengthy operation, you can use a progress bar.

# Summary

This chapter covered three SWT controls that are capable of presenting numerical values. The controls include Scale, Slider, and ProgressBar. A scale and a slider differ in their appearance; however, both of them function as a selectable UI component presenting a range of continuous numeric integer values. Unlike a scale or a slider, a progress bar is an unselectable UI component that is often used to display the progress of a lengthy operation. The next chapter covers the SWT widgets that have not been covered yet.

# Other Important SWT Components

In this chapter, you learn about the rest of the SWT widgets that have not been covered in previous chapters:

- ❏    `Group`
- ❏    `Sash, SashForm`
- ❏    `TabFolder`
- ❏    `Browser`

Each control is discussed in detail. You learn how to use them through examples.

## Using Groups

A group is a composite that provides an etched border with an optional title. The Group `class` extends the `Composite` class and provides two methods for optional title text handling:

```
public String getText()
public void setText(String string)
```

The `getText` method returns the title or an empty string (not `null`) if the title has not been set yet. You use the `setText` method to set the title for a group. Mnemonics are supported by the group control.

In addition to the styles inherited from the Composite class, you can specify one of the following border shadow styles:

- ❑ SHADOW_ETCHED_IN
- ❑ SHADOW_ETCHED_OUT
- ❑ SHADOW_IN
- ❑ SHADOW_OUT
- ❑ SHADOW_NONE

Shadow styles are just hints and may not be honored by every platform. Groups with different shadow styles are shown in Figure 14-1 (Windows XP) and Figure 14-2 (Red Hat Linux 9).

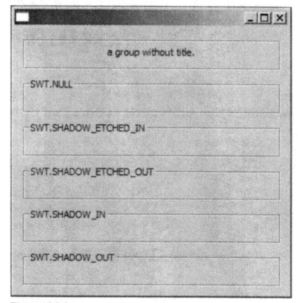

**Figure 14-1**

Figure 14-1 shows that the actual rendered shadows of groups with different styles are all the same on Windows. However, the underlying native UI system on Linux honors the style specified for each group (see Figure 14-2).

Figure 14-2

Groups are useful for organizing the controls logically on a shell and, as a result, make the UI more accessible. For example, the bug report application shown in Figure 14-3 uses two groups to separate controls for input of bug details and those for proxy setting. The corresponding code is shown here:

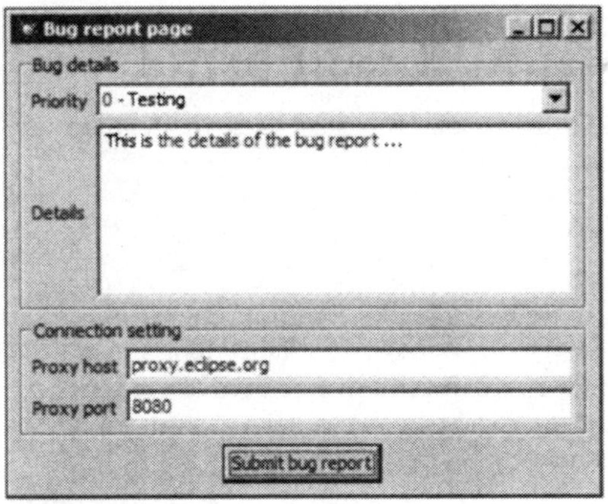

Figure 14-3

```
Display display = new Display();
Shell shell = new Shell(display);

shell.setLayout(new GridLayout(1, true));
shell.setImage(new Image(display, "icons/bug.gif"));
shell.setText("Bug report page");
```

```
Group groupBug = new Group(shell, SWT.NULL);
groupBug.setText("Bug details");
groupBug.setLayout(new GridLayout(2, false));
groupBug.setLayoutData(new GridData(GridData.FILL_BOTH));

new Label(groupBug, SWT.NULL).setText("Priority");
Combo combo = new Combo(groupBug, SWT.BORDER);
combo.setLayoutData(new GridData(GridData.FILL_HORIZONTAL));

new Label(groupBug, SWT.NULL).setText("Details");
Text text = new Text(groupBug, SWT.BORDER | SWT.MULTI);
text.setLayoutData(new GridData(GridData.FILL_BOTH));

Group groupProxy = new Group(shell, SWT.NULL);
groupProxy.setText("Connection setting");
groupProxy.setLayout(new GridLayout(2, false));
groupProxy.setLayoutData(new GridData(GridData.FILL_HORIZONTAL));

new Label(groupProxy, SWT.NULL).setText("Proxy host");
Text textHost = new Text(groupProxy, SWT.SINGLE | SWT.BORDER);
textHost.setLayoutData(new GridData(GridData.FILL_HORIZONTAL));
new Label(groupProxy, SWT.NULL).setText("Proxy port");
Text textPort = new Text(groupProxy, SWT.SINGLE | SWT.BORDER);
textPort.setLayoutData(new GridData(GridData.FILL_HORIZONTAL));

Button button = new Button(shell, SWT.PUSH);
button.setLayoutData(new GridData(GridData.HORIZONTAL_ALIGN_CENTER));
button.setText("Submit bug report");
```

# Using Sashes and SashForms

This section provides a brief introduction to sashes. Then you learn how to use a sash form to place multiple UI components together.

## Using Sashes

Sash represents a selectable user interface object that allows the user to drag a rubber-banded outline of the sash within the parent composite, as shown in Figure 14-4. In SWT GUI programming, a sash widget is rarely used directly. Instead, SashForms should be used to place two or more resizable components together. With basic knowledge of sashes, you can have a better understanding of sash forms, which are covered in the next subsection.

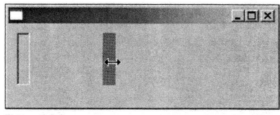

Figure 14-4

The sash in Figure 14-4 is created using the following code:

```
Sash sash = new Sash (shell, SWT.BORDER | SWT.HORIZONTAL);
```

The constructor of the Sash class is as follows:

```
public Sash(Composite parent, int style)
```

In addition to the styles inherited from the Control class, you can specify one of the orientation styles of the Sash class: SWT.HORIZONTAL and SWT.VERTICAL. The orientation styles specify the orientation of the sash divider and imply the direction in which a user can drag that divider. For example, the sash that you saw in Figure 14-4 is created with the SWT.VERTICAL style. This means the divider is vertical and a user can drag it horizontally. On the other hand, sashes with the SWT.HORIZONTAL style can be dragged in the vertical direction only. If none of the orientation styles is specified, the default SWT.HORIZONTAL is used.

The Sash class is a direct subclass of the Control class, and the Sash class provides only two additional methods:

```
public void addSelectionListener(SelectionListener listener)
public void removeSelectionListener(SelectionListener listener)
```

You can use the preceding methods to add or remove a selection listener for a sash. When a sash is dragged, a selection event is generated. The detailed information is contained in the event object passed to each selection listener.

The following code enables a sash to move as the user drags it:

```
sash.addListener (SWT.Selection, new Listener () {
    public void handleEvent (Event e) {
        System.out.println("Selected. ");
        sash.setBounds (e.x, e.y, e.width, e.height);
    }
});
```

It becomes very annoying if you need to handle the sash movement by yourself. Fortunately, you do not have to take care of this for a sash form.

# Using SashForms

SashForms are used extensively in complex UI applications. A SashForm lays out its children in a row or a column and places a sash between adjacent children. The user can drag the sash to adjust the sizes of child controls. A SashForm is a composite that is capable of resizing its children when the user drags the sashes onto it.

## Creating SashForms

The following is the only constructor of the SashForm class:

```
public SashForm(Composite parent, int style)
```

In addition to the styles inherited from the Composite class, the SashForm class supports optional orientation styles: SWT.HORIZONTAL and SWT.VERTICAL. If you want to place all the child controls in a row, you should specify SWT.HORIZONTAL. The SWT.VERTICAL style causes a SashForm to place its children in a column.

For example, the following code creates two SashForms, as shown in Figure 14-5.

```
sashForm = new SashForm(shell, SWT.HORIZONTAL);

Text text1 = new Text(sashForm, SWT.CENTER);
text1.setText("Text in pane #1");
Text text2 = new Text(sashForm, SWT.CENTER);
text2.setText("Text in pane #2");

sashForm2 = new SashForm(sashForm, SWT.VERTICAL);
final Label labelA = new Label(sashForm2, SWT.BORDER | SWT.CENTER);
labelA.setText("Label in pane A");
final Label labelB = new Label(sashForm2, SWT.BORDER |SWT.CENTER);
labelB.setText("Label in pane B");
```

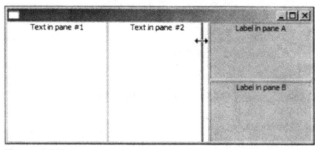

**Figure 14-5**

A SashForm named sashForm is created with the SWT.HORIZONTAL style. Two text widgets are created with the SashForm as their parent. Another SashForm named sashForm2 is created and placed in the first SashForm. With the SWT.VERTICAL styles, sashForm2 places its two children (labelA and lableB) in a column.

To get or set the orientation of a SashForm, you can use the following methods:

```
public int getOrientation()
public void setOrientation(int orientation)
```

Note that although the SashForm class is a subclass of the Composite class, it does not make sense to set a layout manager for a SashForm because it places its children using an internal algorithm. The setLayout method ignores any layout manager passed.

## Resizing a SashForm's Children

By default, a SashForm initially allocates spaces for all its children evenly. If you are developing an IDE, you would let the source code pane occupy much more room than the message pane. You can use the following methods to get and set the percentage of total width (SashForms with the SWT.HORIZONTAL style) or total height (SashForms with the SWT.VERTICAL style) each child will occupy.

```
public int[] getWeights()
public void setWeights(int[] weights)
```

The getWeights method returns an array of integers representing the relative weights of the children. The weight represents the percentage of the space taken by a child control. The weights are returned in the order of the creation of child controls. Correspondingly, you use setWeights to set a weight for each child control. The size of the integer array you pass must be equal to the total number of children of the SashForm; otherwise, an exception is thrown.

The following line changes the initial sizes of child controls of the SashForm in the previous section. (see Figure 14-6):

```
sashForm.setWeights(new int[]{1, 2, 3});
```

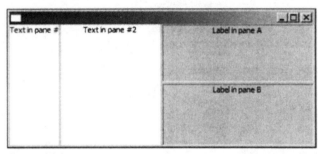

**Figure 14-6**

Because the weights are just relative ratios, setWeights(new int[]{10, 20, 30}) is equivalent to setWeights(new int[]{1, 2, 3}), which means the first component occupies ⅙ of the total available space, the second component occupies ⅓, and the third component occupies ½.

In most applications, you should add functions to save and load the weights of each SashForm so that the user does not have to adjust children in SashForms every time the application is started.

## Maximizing a Control in a SashForm

Sometimes, it is desirable to maximize a control and hide all the others in a SashForm. For example, you may want to hide all other panes except the source code pane so that you can focus on coding. The SashForm class provides the setMaximizedControl method for you to maximize a control:

```
public void setMaximizedControl(Control control)
```

To set all the controls to normal layout, you can call the setMaximizedControl method with null as the argument and the sash form will lay out controls using the normal layout separated by sashes.

Use getMaximizedControl to query the current maximized control:

```
public Control getMaximizedControl()
```

This method returns the current maximized control or `null` if no control is maximized in the `SashForm`.

Let's modify the sample `SashForm` UI application from previous sections, as shown in Figure 14-7.

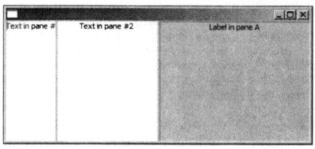

Figure 14-7

```
labelA.addMouseListener(new MouseListener() {
    public void mouseDoubleClick(MouseEvent e) {
        if(sashForm2.getMaximizedControl() == labelA)
            sashForm2.setMaximizedControl(null);
        else
            sashForm2.setMaximizedControl(labelA);
    }

    public void mouseDown(MouseEvent e) {
    }

    public void mouseUp(MouseEvent e) {
    }
});
```

When the label is double-clicked, the mouse listener is invoked. If the label is currently maximized, you set it back to normal; otherwise, you maximize it by calling the `setMaximizedControl` method.

# Using TabFolders and TabItems

With the `TabFolder` class, you can place several controls (usually composites) in the same space. The user can choose the desired control to view by selecting the tab corresponding to the control.

In SWT, the tab items in a tab folder are represented by the `TabItem` class.

## Basic Usages

Follow these basic steps to create a tab folder and add tab pages:

1. Construct an instance of the `TabFolder` class.
2. Create controls to be placed on the tab folder.
3. Create a tab item for each control.

For example, the following code creates the tab folder shown in Figure 14-8:

```
TabFolder tabFolder = new TabFolder(shell, SWT.NULL);
// tab item #1
Button button = new Button(tabFolder, SWT.NULL);
button.setText("This is a button.");

TabItem tabItem1 = new TabItem(tabFolder, SWT.NULL);
tabItem1.setText("item #1");
tabItem1.setImage(icon);
tabItem1.setControl(button);

// tab item #2
Text text = new Text(tabFolder, SWT.MULTI);
text.setText("This is a text control.");

TabItem tabItem2 = new TabItem(tabFolder, SWT.NULL);
tabItem2.setText("item #2");
tabItem2.setImage(icon);
tabItem2.setControl(text);

// tab item #3
Label label = new Label(tabFolder, SWT.NULL);
label.setText("This is a text label.");

TabItem tabItem3 = new TabItem(tabFolder, SWT.NULL);
tabItem3.setText("item #3");
tabItem3.setControl(label);
```

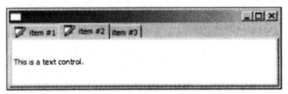

**Figure 14-8**

First, the tab folder is created without any style specified. A button control is then created with the tab folder as its parent. After setting the text for the button, we create a tab item and set the button as its control using the setControl method of the TabItem class. The text and image labels for the tab item are set using the setText method and setImage method, respectively. Similarly, we create two more tab items.

When you create a tab folder, you can optionally supply one of the tab position styles — SWT.TOP and SWT.BOTTOM — in the constructor. If SWT.TOP is specified, the tabs will appear at the top of the tab folder (refer to Figure 14-8). Similarly, SWT.BOTTOM causes the tabs to appear at the bottom of the tab folder, as shown in Figure 14-9. If no style is specified, a tab folder has, by default, the SWT.TOP style.

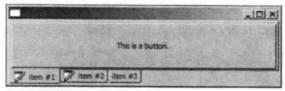

**Figure 14-9**

# Accessing and Selecting TabItems

The `TabFolder` class provides several methods for you to access and select tab items.

To count the total number of tab items contained in a tab folder, use the `getItemCount` method:

```
public int getItemCount()
```

The `getItems` method returns all the tab items in an array:

```
public TabItem[] getItems()
```

You can get the tab item at the specified index position using the `getItem` method:

```
public TabItem getItem(int index)
```

The `getItem` may throw an exception if the given index is out of range. To find the index position of a given tab item in the tab folder, you use the `indexOf` method:

```
public int indexOf(TabItem item)
```

If the tab item is not contained in the tab folder, the `indexOf` method returns -1.

When the user clicks a tab, the tab item corresponding to the tab is selected and a selection event is generated. You use the `getSelection` method to get the current selected tab item.

```
public TabItem[] getSelection()
```

The `getSelection` method returns the current selected tab item in an array of size 1 or an empty array if none of the tab items is selected. If a tab item is selected, you can get it using `getSelection()[0]`. To get the index position of the current selected tab item, you can use the `getSelectionIndex` method:

```
public int getSelectionIndex()
```

The `getSelectionIndex` method returns the index of the selected tab item or -1 if no tab item is selected.

Use the following method to add/remove typed selection listeners:

```
public void addSelectionListener(SelectionListener listener)
public void removeSelectionListener(SelectionListener listener)
```

For example, you can add a selection listener to the tab folder sample application by using the following code:

```
tabFolder.addSelectionListener(new SelectionListener() {
    public void widgetSelected(SelectionEvent e) {
        System.out.println("Selected item index = " +
            tabFolder.getSelectionIndex());
        System.out.println("Selected item = " +
            (tabFolder.getSelection() == null ?
                "null" : tabFolder.getSelection()[0].toString()));
    }

    public void widgetDefaultSelected(SelectionEvent e) {
        widgetSelected(e);
    }
});
```

When the user clicks the middle tab, the following lines are printed out:

```
Selected item index = 1
Selected item = TabItem {item #2}
```

The `TabFolder` class also provides two methods for you to select tab items programmatically:

```
public void setSelection(int index)
public void setSelection(TabItem[] items)
```

For example, to select the middle tab item (index is 1) in the tab folder, you can use either `setSelection(1)` or `setSelection(new TabItem[]{tabItem2})`. Neither of the preceding methods generates selection events. When you call either of them, none of the selection listeners is notified. If this behavior is not desired, you can extend the `TabFolder` class and override the two methods to add some code to notify the selection listeners.

## Customizing TabItems

In addition to the `setControl` method, the `TabItem` class offers several methods for you to customize the appearance of a tab item.

You can use the `setImage` method and the `setText` method to set the image label and the text label for a tab item. The image label and text label are displayed on the tab:

```
public void setImage(Image image)
public void setText(String string)
```

Optionally, you can set the tooltip text for a tab item using the `setToolTipText` method:

```
public void setToolTipText(String string)
```

# Using Browsers

The SWT browser control renders HTML documents. The `org.eclipse.browser` package contains the `Browser` class and classes for event handling. The `Browser` class provides essential web navigation methods and methods for you to add and remove listeners for various events.

This section first shows you how to navigate using the browser control. During navigation, various events can be generated by the browser, and you can register proper event listeners. Finally, you learn how to build a simple web browser using the SWT browser control.

## *Navigation Methods*

You use the `setUrl` method to load a web page for a URL:

```
public boolean setUrl(String url)
```

The preceding method loads the specified URL and returns `true` if the page is loaded successfully or `false` otherwise.

If you need to render the HTML document in memory, you can use the `setText` method:

```
public boolean setText(String html)
```

For example, the following code renders the text "SWT & JFace" in Header 1 format:

```
browser.setText(
    "<html><body>" + "<h1>SWT &amp; JFace </h1>" + "</body/html>");
```

To navigate to the previous session history page, use the `back` method:

```
public boolean back()
```

The `back` method returns `true` if the operation is successful, `false` otherwise. To check whether you can navigate to the previous session history page, you can use the `isBackEnabled` method:

```
public boolean isBackEnabled()
```

Similarly, you can use the `forward` method to navigate to the next session history item and the `isForwardEnabled` method to check whether the forwarding operation is possible:

```
public boolean forward()
public boolean isForwardEnabled()
```

Use the `refresh` method to refresh the current page and the `stop` method to stop any loading and rendering operation:

```
public void refresh()
public void stop()
```

# *Events*

You learned about all the navigation methods in the previous section. When you navigate pages programmatically or use your keyboard or mouse, various events are generated. All the events that the browser control can generate are listed in the following table.

| Events | Listeners | Remarks |
|---|---|---|
| LocationEvent | LocationListener | Fired by a browser when the browser navigates to a different URL. |
| TitleEvent | TitleListener | Generated when the title of the current document is available or when it changes. |
| StatusTextEvent | StatusTextListener | Generated when the status text is changed. |
| ProgressEvent | ProgressListener | Generated when progress is made during loading of a URL or when the loading is completed. |
| WindowEvent | OpenWindowListener<br>CloseWindowListener<br>VisibilityWindowListener | Sent when a new window needs to be created or when a window needs to be closed. (When we are talking about browsers, a window is a browser control.) |

The terms LocationEvent, TitleEvent, StatusTextEvent, and ProgressEvent are easy to understand and handle. For example, the following code creates a shell containing a browser and registers a listener for TitleEvents:

```
Shell shell = new Shell(display);
shell.setLayout(new GridLayout());

Browser browser = new Browser(shell, SWT.BORDER);
browser.addTitleListener(new TitleListener() {
    public void changed(TitleEvent event) {
        shell.setText(event.title + " - powered by SWT");
    }
});
```

When the title of the currently displayed HTML document is available or modified, you display the HTML document title on the top of the shell.

WindowEvents are a little complicated. The Javadoc of the WindowEvent class suggests using the following method to equip an existing browser control with the capability of handling window creating and closing requests:

```
static void initialize(final Display display, Browser browser) {
    browser.addOpenWindowListener(new OpenWindowListener() {
        public void open(WindowEvent event) {
            Shell shell = new Shell(display);
            shell.setText("New Window");
            shell.setLayout(new FillLayout());
            Browser browser = new Browser(shell, SWT.NONE);
            initialize(display, browser);
            event.browser = browser;
        }
    });

    browser.addVisibilityWindowListener(new VisibilityWindowListener() {
        public void hide(WindowEvent event) {
            Browser browser = (Browser)event.widget;
            Shell shell = browser.getShell();
            shell.setVisible(false);
        }

        public void show(WindowEvent event) {
            Browser browser = (Browser)event.widget;
            Shell shell = browser.getShell();
            if (event.location != null) shell.setLocation(event.location);
            if (event.size != null) {
                Point size = event.size;
                shell.setSize(shell.computeSize(size.x, size.y));
            }
            shell.open();
        }
    });

    browser.addCloseWindowListener(new CloseWindowListener() {
        public void close(WindowEvent event) {
            Browser browser = (Browser)event.widget;
            Shell shell = browser.getShell();
            shell.close();
        }
    });
}
```

It is simple to use the preceding method:

```
initialize(shell.getDisplay(), browser);
```

When the user clicks a link with the `target` as `_blank` (for example, `<a href="go.html" target="_blank">Go</a>`) or when a window opening JavaScript code (for example, `window.open`) is executed, the registered `openWindowListener` is invoked. The `open` method first creates a new browser control inside a new shell. The browser field of the event object is set to the newly created browser control — for example, this browser is the "new window." The HTML document is then opened in the new window. If no `OpenWindowListener` provides any browser control to the event object, no new window is constructed. Therefore, the new window opening operation is ignored.

A VisibilityWindowListener is registered to handle window visibility–related events. Note that WindowEvent objects may contain detailed information such as the location and size of the window. For example, the following JavaScript code gives information that will be included in WindowEvent objects.

```
url = "http://www.asprise.com/special/popup.htm";
window.open(url,'PopURL','width=400,height=327,screenX=0,screenY=0,left=0,top=0');
```

To handle window closing events, a CloseWindowListener is registered. If the window needs to be closed, simply close the shell containing the window.

## A Simple Web Browser

In this section, we create a simple Web browser using the SWT browser control (see Figure 14-10).

**Figure 14-10**

This simple Web browser allows the user to navigate Web pages easily and to go backward or forward. Additionally, it supports new window creation.

Create the UI components first:

```
public class SWTBrowser {
    Display display = new Display();
    Shell shell = new Shell(display);

    Text textLocation;

    Browser browser;

    Label labelStatus;
```

```
public SWTBrowser() {
    shell.setLayout(new GridLayout());

    ToolBar toolBar = new ToolBar(shell, SWT.FLAT | SWT.RIGHT);
    final ToolBarManager manager = new ToolBarManager(toolBar);

    Composite compositeLocation = new Composite(shell, SWT.NULL);
    compositeLocation.setLayout(new GridLayout(3, false));
    compositeLocation.setLayoutData(new GridData(GridData.FILL_HORIZONTAL));

    Label labelAddress = new Label(compositeLocation, SWT.NULL);
    labelAddress.setText("Address");

    textLocation = new Text(compositeLocation, SWT.SINGLE | SWT.BORDER);
    textLocation.setLayoutData(new GridData(GridData.FILL_HORIZONTAL));

    Button buttonGo = new Button(compositeLocation, SWT.NULL);
    buttonGo.setImage(new Image(shell.getDisplay(), "icons/web/go.gif"));

    browser = new Browser(shell, SWT.BORDER);
    browser.setLayoutData(new GridData(GridData.FILL_BOTH));

    Composite compositeStatus = new Composite(shell, SWT.NULL);
    compositeStatus.setLayoutData(new GridData(GridData.FILL_HORIZONTAL));
    compositeStatus.setLayout(new GridLayout(2, false));

    labelStatus = new Label(compositeStatus, SWT.NULL);
    labelStatus.setText("Ready");
    labelStatus.setLayoutData(new GridData(GridData.FILL_HORIZONTAL));

    final ProgressBar progressBar =
        new ProgressBar(compositeStatus, SWT.SMOOTH);
```

A label is created to display a status message and a progress bar is created to display page loading progress.

Next, register a selection listener for both the button and the address text field so that the user can navigate to the URL specified in the address text field by clicking the button or simply pressing the Enter key in the text field.

```
Listener openURLListener = new Listener() {
    public void handleEvent(Event event) {
        browser.setUrl(textLocation.getText());
    }
};

buttonGo.addListener(SWT.Selection, openURLListener);
textLocation.addListener(SWT.DefaultSelection, openURLListener);
```

Use the following to add each toolbar item to the toolbar using the `ToolBarManager` created:

```java
// Adds tool bar items using actions.
final Action actionBackward =
    new Action(
        "&Backward",
        ImageDescriptor.createFromFile(
        null,
        "icons/web/backward.gif")) {
        public void run() {
            browser.back();
        }
    };
actionBackward.setEnabled(false); // action is disabled at start up.

final Action actionForward =
    new Action(
        "&Forward",
        ImageDescriptor.createFromFile(
            null,
            "icons/web/forward.gif")) {
        public void run() {
            browser.forward();
        }
    };
actionForward.setEnabled(false); // action is disabled at start up.

Action actionStop =
    new Action(
        "&Stop",
        ImageDescriptor.createFromFile(null, "icons/web/stop.gif")) {
        public void run() {
            browser.stop();
        }
    };

Action actionRefresh =
    new Action(
        "&Refresh",
        ImageDescriptor.createFromFile(
            null,
            "icons/web/refresh.gif")) {
        public void run() {
            browser.refresh();
        }
    };

Action actionHome =
    new Action(
        "&Home",
        ImageDescriptor.createFromFile(null, "icons/web/home.gif")) {
        public void run() {
            browser.setUrl("http://www.eclipse.org");
        }
```

```
        };

    manager.add(actionBackward);
    manager.add(actionForward);
    manager.add(actionStop);
    manager.add(actionRefresh);
    manager.add(actionHome);

    manager.update(true);
    toolBar.pack();
```

Several listeners such as LocationListener and StatusListener are registered to listen for events and to update the controls in the UI:

```
    browser.addLocationListener(new LocationListener() {
        public void changing(LocationEvent event) {
            // Displays the new location in the text field.
            textLocation.setText(event.location);
        }

        public void changed(LocationEvent event) {
            // Update tool bar items.
            actionBackward.setEnabled(browser.isBackEnabled());
            actionForward.setEnabled(browser.isForwardEnabled());
            manager.update(false);
        }
    });

    browser.addProgressListener(new ProgressListener() {
        public void changed(ProgressEvent event) {
            progressBar.setMaximum(event.total);
            progressBar.setSelection(event.current);
        }

        public void completed(ProgressEvent event) {
            progressBar.setSelection(0);
        }
    });

    browser.addStatusTextListener(new StatusTextListener() {
        public void changed(StatusTextEvent event) {
            labelStatus.setText(event.text);
        }
    });

    browser.addTitleListener(new TitleListener() {
        public void changed(TitleEvent event) {
            shell.setText(event.title + " - powered by SWT");
        }
    });
```

Finally, initialize the new window-handling mechanism for the browser by using the `initialize` method in the last section and open the shell.

```
initialize(display, browser);

shell.setSize(500, 400);
shell.open();

while (!shell.isDisposed()) {
    if (!display.readAndDispatch()) {
        // If no more entries in event queue
        display.sleep();
    }
}

display.dispose();
}
```

# Summary

Starting with the simple composite, Group, this chapter introduced several other important SWT controls that were not covered in previous chapters. The SashForm control is very useful for positioning and resizing several adjoining controls. To save the space, you can use a TabFolder to have many controls share the same space and the user can click the tab to access each corresponding control. The Browser control was also discussed. We developed a simple web browser to help you understand the navigation methods and browser event handling mechanism. In the next chapter, you learn about SWT graphics programming.

# 15

# SWT Graphics and Image Handling

In many applications, you need to perform custom drawing. This chapter shows you how to customize drawing and how to perform various operations on images. The first part of this chapter shows you how to perform various drawing operations with graphics context — drawing lines, arcs, shapes, images, and text, and filling shapes. SWT image handling is introduced in the second part. You learn how an image is represented in SWT. You also learn about practical image manipulation techniques.

## Drawing with Graphics Contexts

In SWT, all classes that implement `org.eclipse.swt.graphics.Drawable` are capable of performing drawing operations. The classes include the following:

❑ `Control`

❑ `Image`

❑ `Device` (`Display`, `Printer`)

The basic steps for drawing graphics are as follows:

1. Get a graphics context instance from the target drawable object.

2. Perform drawing operations on the graphics context.

3. Dispose of the graphics context if necessary.

# Getting a Graphics Context

To perform a drawing operation on a drawable object, you need first to obtain or construct a graphics context instance from it. Class `org.eclipse.swt.graphics.GC` represents graphics contexts and supports various drawing capabilities. You then use the graphics context instance to perform the actual drawing operations.

> *Because GC objects employ native OS resources, you need to dispose of them if you created them. See Chapter 2 for details on resource management.*

To get a graphics context instance, you can either obtain an existing one or create an instance.

## Obtaining an Existing Graphics Context

Typically, you obtain an existing graphics context instance from a `PaintEvent` object. We used the following code to display the percentage value in a progress bar in Chapter 13:

```
progressBar.addPaintListener(new PaintListener() {
        public void paintControl(PaintEvent e) {
            // The string to draw.
            String string = (progressBar.getSelection() * 1.0 /
               (progressBar.getMaximum()-progressBar.getMinimum()) * 100) + "%";

            Point point = progressBar.getSize();
            Font font = new Font(shell.getDisplay(),"Courier",10,SWT.BOLD);
            e.gc.setFont(font);
            e.gc.setForeground(
                shell.getDisplay().getSystemColor(SWT.COLOR_WHITE));

            FontMetrics fontMetrics = e.gc.getFontMetrics();
            int stringWidth =
                fontMetrics.getAverageCharWidth() * string.length();
            int stringHeight = fontMetrics.getHeight();

            e.gc.drawString(string, (point.x-stringWidth)/2 ,
                (point.y-stringHeight)/2, true);

            font.dispose();
        }
    });
```

When the progress bar is being painted, the paint listener is invoked with a `PaintEvent` object as the argument. A graphics context instance for the progress bar is stored in the `gc` field of the `PaintEvent` object. We then use the graphics context instance to perform actual drawing operations on the progress bar. After finishing drawing, we do not dispose of the graphics context object because it was not created by us.

After finishing drawing with an existing graphics context instance, you should not dispose of it if you did not create it.

## *Creating a Graphics Context Instance on a Drawable Object*

If you are unable to get an existing graphics context of a drawable object, you can create one. For example, the following code draws an oval on the image on the right side of Figure 15-1.

```
Display display = new Display();
Shell shell = new Shell(display);
shell.setLayout(new GridLayout(2, true));

Image image = new Image(display, "icons/eclipse.gif");

// Clones the image.
Image image2 = new Image(display, image.getImageData());

// Draws an oval
GC gc = new GC(image2);
gc.setForeground(display.getSystemColor(SWT.COLOR_WHITE));
gc.drawOval(10, 10, 90, 40);
gc.dispose();

CLabel label = new CLabel(shell, SWT.NULL);
label.setImage(image);
label.setBounds(10, 10, 130, 130);

CLabel label2 = new CLabel(shell, SWT.NULL);
label2.setImage(image2);
label2.setBounds(150, 10, 130, 130);
```

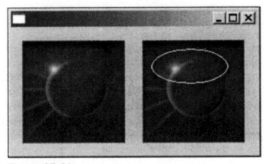

**Figure 15-1**

An image (the Eclipse logo) is created from a GIF file. The other image is obtained by cloning the first image. In order to draw on the second image, we then create a GC object from it. Then we draw a white oval on the graphics context. Because this GC object is created by us, we need to dispose of it after finishing drawing. Finally, two labels are used to display both of the images. In Figure 15-1, you can clearly see there is a white oval on the second image. The method drawOval is covered in the section "Drawing Lines, Arcs, and Shapes."

# Using Canvas

In previous sections, you have seen examples of drawing on controls. SWT provides a class `org.eclipse` `.swt.widgets.Canvas` designed for general graph drawing. `Canvas`, as the name suggests, provides a surface for you to perform arbitrary drawing operations.

As an example, the following code creates a canvas with a rounded rectangle on it (see Figure 15-2).

```
Canvas canvas = new Canvas(shell, SWT.NULL);
canvas.setBounds(10, 10, 200, 100);

canvas.addPaintListener(new PaintListener() {
    public void paintControl(PaintEvent e) {
        e.gc.drawRoundRectangle(10, 10, 180, 80, 10, 10);
    }
});
```

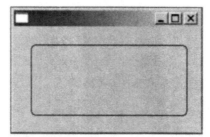

Figure 15-2

While creating a canvas, you may optionally specify one or more of its painting configuration styles:

❑   SWT.NO_BACKGROUND: By default, a canvas is filled with its background color before it paints itself. Sometimes, this can cause screen flickering. You can specify this style to disable background filling; however, if you do so, you are responsible for drawing every pixel of the client area. If you have an image filling the whole client area of the canvas, then it is a good idea to prevent the background from being drawn by specifying this style.

❑   SWT.NO_REDRAW_RESIZE: When a control is resized, it sends a paint event to request itself being redrawn. For potential performance optimization, you can specify this style to disable a canvas from sending a paint event when its size is reduced. However, not all canvases should be created with this style. For example, if you use a rectangle as the border of a canvas, this style should not be used because the border may be rendered incorrectly.

❑   SWT.NO_MERGE_PAINTS: Many native platforms perform UI event optimization. For example, several repaint requests may be merged into one request. By specifying this style, you disable this behavior. In most cases, you should not specify this style because it could reduce the painting performance.

Before using the preceding styles, you should fully understand them. Otherwise, they may introduce many undesired effects to your canvases. For more details, please refer to the Javadoc documentation.

## Drawing Lines, Arcs, and Shapes

In SWT, graphics objects live in a plane defined by Cartesian coordinates, where the origin is at the top-left corner (0, 0), the x axis increases from left to right, and the y axis increases from top to bottom.

Drawing a line is very straightforward with the drawLine method:

```
public void drawLine(int x1, int y1, int x2, int y2)
```

You simply pass the coordinating x and y values of the two end points of the line to the method.

If you need to draw multiple connected straight lines, you can use the drawPolyLine method:

```
public void drawPolyline(int[] pointArray)
```

A *polyline* is a series of connected lines. A polyline can be represented by an array containing the coordinating x and y values of connecting points. Lines are drawn between each consecutive pair and no line is drawn between the first pair and the last pair in the array. For example, the following code draws a right angle, as shown in Figure 15-3.

```
int[] points = new int[3 * 2];
points[0] = 10; // The point at the top.
points[1] = 10;

points[2] = 10; // The point at the left bottom.
points[3] = 100;

points[4] = 100; // the point at the right bottom
points[5] = 100;

gc.drawPolyline(points);
```

Figure 15-3

The `drawPolygon` method works similarly to `drawPolyline` except that the line between the last point and the end point is drawn. If you replace the `gc.drawPolyline` method in the preceding code with `gc.drawPolygon`, you get a right triangle.

You draw the outline of a rectangle with the `drawRectangle` method:

```
public void drawRectangle(int x, int y, int width, int height)
```

You specify the coordinating *x* and *y* values of the top-left corner point and the width and height of the rectangle as the arguments to the `drawRectangle` method. Alternatively, you can put the four parameters into a `Rectangle` object and call the following method:

```
public void drawRectangle(Rectangle rect)
```

To draw an oval, you can use the `drawOval` method:

```
public void drawOval(int x, int y, int width, int height)
```

The resulting drawing is a circle or an ellipse fitting within the rectangle area specified by the arguments.

If you want to draw only a part of an oval (i.e., an arc), you can use the `drawArc` method:

```
public void drawArc(int x, int y, int width, int height, int startAngle, int
arcAngle)
```

The first four parameters specify the oval that the arc belongs to. The last two parameters define which part of the oval the arc occupies. The arc begins at `startAngle` and expands for `arcAngle` degrees. Angle 0 degree is at the three o'clock position and degree values increase counterclockwise.

For example, the arc shown in Figure 15-4 is created with the following code:

```
gc.drawArc(10, 10, 200, 100, 0, -90);
```

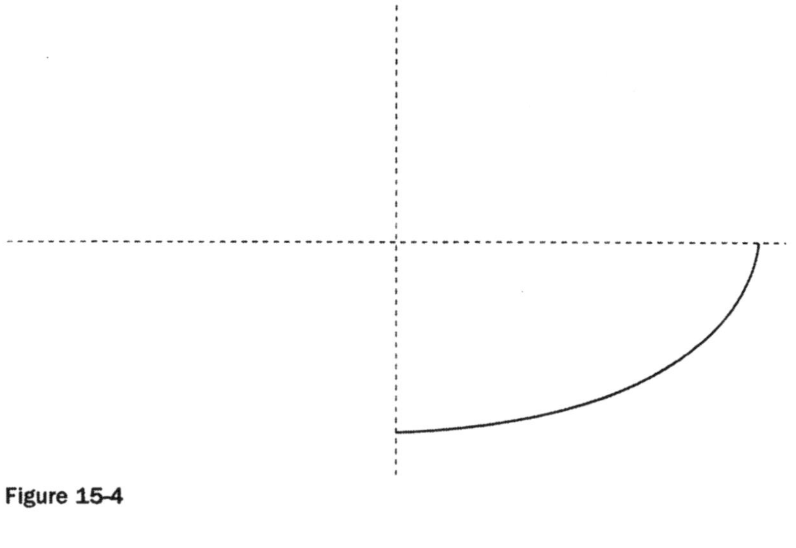

Figure 15-4

The GC class also provides the drawRoundRectangle method for you to draw round-cornered rectangles:

```
public void drawRoundRectangle(int x, int y, int width, int height, int arcWidth,
int arcHeight)
```

The first four parameters define the bound of the rectangle and the last two parameters specify the width and height of the corner arcs.

So far, you have learned about several methods for drawing lines, arcs, and shapes. Before calling the preceding method, you can set the foreground color. Additionally, you can use the following methods to set the line style and line width:

```
public void setLineStyle(int lineStyle)
public void setLineWidth(int lineWidth)
```

Figure 15-5 shows lines with different styles and line widths.

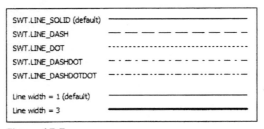

**Figure 15-5**

# Filling Shapes

In previous sections, you have learned how to draw lines, arcs, and shapes with the drawing method of the GC class. There are corresponding filling methods in the GC class that you can use to fill various shapes:

```
public void fillArc(int x, int y, int width, int height, int startAngle, int
arcAngle)
public void fillOval(int x, int y, int width, int height)
public void fillPolygon(int[] pointArray)
public void fillRectangle(int x, int y, int width, int height)
public void fillRectangle(Rectangle rect)
public void fillRoundRectangle(int x, int y, int width, int height, int arcWidth,
int arcHeight)
```

Instead of drawing the outlines of the shapes, the preceding filling methods fill the shapes with the background color of the graphics context. Note that the bottom and right edges of the shapes are not included in filling operations. For example, fillRectangle(0, 0, 200, 100) fills the area within the rectangle [0, 0, 199, 99].

From a programming standpoint, filling shapes is very similar to drawing shapes. For example, by changing `gc.drawArc(10, 10, 200, 100, 0, -90);` with the following code

```
e.gc.setBackground(display.getSystemColor(SWT.COLOR_DARK_GREEN));
e.gc.fillArc(10, 10, 200, 100, 0, -90);
```

you get Figure 15-6 instead of Figure 15-5, as shown in the last section.

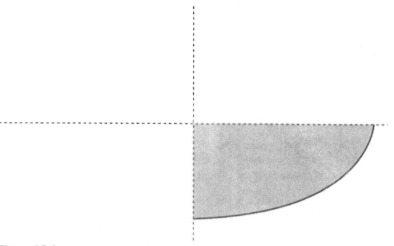

**Figure 15-6**

Because the default background color of the graphics context is the same as the background color of the control, the background color of the graphics context is changed before the `fillArc` method is called (otherwise, you won't be able to see the filled area).

Additionally, you can fill a rectangle with a color gradient using the `fillGradientRectangle` method:

```
public void fillGradientRectangle(int x, int y, int width, int height, boolean vertical)
```

This method fills the specified rectangle with a gradient progressing from the graphics context's foreground color to its background color from left to right or top to bottom.

## Drawing and Copying Images

In SWT, the class `org.eclipse.swt.graphics.Image` represents an image that has been prepared for display. Two methods of the GC class can be used to draw images onto the graphics context:

```
public void drawImage(Image image, int x, int y)
public void drawImage(Image image, int srcX, int srcY, int srcWidth, int srcHeight,
int destX, int destY, int destWidth, int destHeight)
```

The first `drawImage` method draws the specified image in the graphics context at the given coordinates, while the second one provides finer control. With the second `drawImage` method, you can draw a part of the specified image into a rectangle on the graphics context. If the source and destination areas are of differing sizes, the image or a part of the image is resized (stretched or shrunk) to fit the destination rectangle.

For example, the following code draws the same image twice using different methods on a canvas (see Figure 15-7):

```
Canvas canvas = new Canvas(shell, SWT.NULL);

final Image image = new Image(display, "icons/eclipse.gif");

canvas.addPaintListener(new PaintListener() {
    public void paintControl(PaintEvent e) {
        e.gc.drawImage(image, 10, 10);
        e.gc.drawImage(image, 0, 0, 100, 100, 200, 10, 200, 50);
    }
});
```

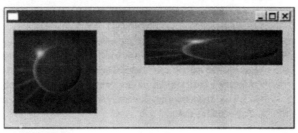

**Figure 15-7**

The `GC` class provides the `copyArea` method for you to copy a rectangular area of the graphics context onto another position:

```
public void copyArea(int srcX, int srcY, int width, int height, int destX, int
destY)
```

Additionally, you can copy a rectangular area of the graphics context onto an image using the following method:

```
public void copyArea(Image image, int x, int y)
```

The following is a handy method I wrote to capture a control into an image file using the `copyArea` method:

```
/**
 * Captures the specified control and saves the result into a file
 * in the BMP format.
 * @param control
 * @param fileName
```

```
*/
public static void captureControl(Control control, String file) {
    GC gc = new GC(control);
    Image image = new Image(control.getDisplay(),
                            control.getSize().x, control.getSize().y);

    gc.copyArea(image, 0, 0);
    ImageLoader loader = new ImageLoader();
    loader.data = new ImageData[] { image.getImageData() };
    loader.save(file, SWT.IMAGE_BMP);
    gc.dispose();
}
```

See the section "Image Handling" for information on saving images.

## Drawing Text

You use one of the GC drawString methods to render text:

```
public void drawString(String string, int x, int y)
public void drawString(String string, int x, int y, boolean isTransparent)
```

The first drawString method draws the specified string with the graphics context's font and foreground color and fills the background of the rectangular area with the graphics context's background color. The x and y coordinates of the top-left corner of the rectangular area is specified in the x and y parameters. The second method allows you to specify whether the background of the rectangular area should be filled or not. If isTransparent is set to true, the rectangular area will not be filled, otherwise, it will be filled with the graphics context's background color.

The following code renders two strings on the canvas, as shown in Figure 15-8:

```
final Canvas canvas = new Canvas(shell, SWT.NO_BACKGROUND);

final Image image = new Image(display, "icons/eclipse.gif");
canvas.addPaintListener(new PaintListener() {
    public void paintControl(PaintEvent e) {
        Rectangle size = image.getBounds();
        // Draws the background image.
        e.gc.drawImage(image, 0, 0, size.width, size.height, 0, 0,
                       canvas.getSize().x, canvas.getSize().y);

        Font font = new Font(display, "Tahoma", 18, SWT.BOLD);
        e.gc.setFont(font);
        e.gc.setForeground(display.getSystemColor(SWT.COLOR_WHITE));
        e.gc.setBackground(display.getSystemColor(SWT.COLOR_BLUE));

        String english = "SWT rocks!";
        String chinese = "\u4e2d\u6587\u6c49\u5b57\u6d4b\u8bd5";

        e.gc.drawString(english, 10, 10);
```

```
        e.gc.drawString(chinese, 10, 80, true);

        font.dispose();
    }
});
```

**Figure 15-8**

You may notice that the rectangular area occupied by the English string is filled with the background color of the graphics context, whereas the Chinese string is drawn transparently without background filling. (On many operating systems, you need to install Chinese packages in order to read Chinese characters.)

The limitation of the drawString methods is that they are unable to handle layout characters such as a tab (\t) and carriage return (\n) correctly. To solve this problem, the GC class provides another set of methods to render text:

```
public void drawText(String string, int x, int y)
public void drawText(String string, int x, int y, boolean isTransparent)
public void drawText(String string, int x, int y, int flags)
```

The first two methods work in the same way as their drawString counterparts except drawText methods expands text layout characters. The third drawText method allows you to have finer control over text rendering by configuring the flags parameter. The flags parameter should be a combination of the following:

- ❑ SWT.DRAW_DELIMITER: Processes line delimiters and draws multiple lines
- ❑ SWT.DRAW_TAB: Expands tabs
- ❑ SWT.DRAW_MNEMONIC: Draws mnemonic character decorations
- ❑ SWT.DRAW_TRANSPARENT: Leaves the background transparent

In some cases, it is desirable to determine the size of the rectangular area to be occupied by a string or text before it is drawn so that you can align it or center it. The GC class provides three methods for you to do so:

```
public Point stringExtent(String string)
public Point textExtent(String string)
public Point textExtent(String string, int flags)
```

The following sample code draws text in the center of a canvas:

```
canvas.addPaintListener(new PaintListener() {
    public void paintControl(PaintEvent e) {
        String text = "Text to be drawn in the center";
        Point textSize = e.gc.textExtent(text);
        e.gc.drawText(text,
            (canvas.getSize().x - textSize.x)/2,
            (canvas.getSize().y - textSize.y)/2);
    }
});
```

# Advanced Techniques

This section introduces several advanced drawing techniques, including clipping, XOR, and double buffering.

## Clipping

Clipping is a technique used to limits the extent of a drawing. By default, a graphics context is clipped to the bounds of the corresponding drawable object. By modifying the clipping area of the graphics context, you can create some special graphical effects. For example, the follow code results in the clipping effect shown in Figure 15-9.

```
final Canvas canvas = new Canvas(shell, SWT.NULL);
final Image image = new Image(display, "icons/eclipse.gif");
canvas.addPaintListener(new PaintListener() {
    public void paintControl(PaintEvent e) {
        Region region = new Region(); // A triangle region.
        region.add(new int[]{60, 10, 10, 100, 110, 100});
        e.gc.setClipping(region);

        e.gc.drawImage(image, 0, 0);
    }
});
```

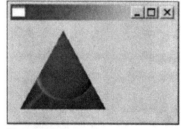

Figure 15-9

Once the clipping region is set, any drawing that occurs outside the region will be ignored. There are several setClipping methods in the GC class:

```
public void setClipping(int x, int y, int width, int height)
public void setClipping(Rectangle rect)
public void setClipping(Region region)
```

The first two methods support a rectangle as the clipping area, whereas the third method accepts any `Region` object.

## XOR

When you draw anything on a graphics context, the pixel values making up the drawable object are set with new values. If the graphics context mode is set to XOR, then the color of the pixels on the drawable surface is determined by XORing the color values of the source being drawn and the existing color values.

For example, Figure 15-10 shows three ovals drawn in XOR mode. The code is as follows.

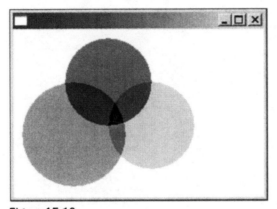

**Figure 15-10**

```
final Canvas canvas = new Canvas(shell, SWT.NULL);
canvas.setBackground(display.getSystemColor(SWT.COLOR_WHITE));

canvas.addPaintListener(new PaintListener() {
    public void paintControl(PaintEvent e) {
        e.gc.setXORMode(true);

        e.gc.setBackground(display.getSystemColor(SWT.COLOR_GREEN));
        e.gc.fillOval(60, 10, 100, 100); // Top

        e.gc.setBackground(display.getSystemColor(SWT.COLOR_RED));
        e.gc.fillOval(10, 60, 120, 120); // left bottom

        e.gc.setBackground(display.getSystemColor(SWT.COLOR_BLUE));
        e.gc.fillOval(110, 60, 100, 100); // right bottom

    }
});
```

Because XOR is a bitwise operation, it is hard to perceive it visually.

## *Double Buffering*

If you experience flickering during drawing, you can use a *double buffering* technique to reduce it. Double buffering works in this way: Instead of drawing graphics directly to the graphics context of a canvas, you draw graphics objects on an image and then draw the image to the canvas. Because intermediate states of drawing will not appear, flicker is greatly reduced.

The following code shows a sample implementation of double buffering:

```
final Canvas doubleBufferedCanvas = new Canvas(shell, SWT.NO_BACKGROUND);

doubleBufferedCanvas.addPaintListener(new PaintListener() {
    public void paintControl(PaintEvent e) {
        // Creates new image only when absolutely necessary.
        Image image = (Image) doubleBufferedCanvas .getData("double-buffer-image");
        if (image == null
            || image.getBounds().width != canvas.getSize().x
            || image.getBounds().height != canvas.getSize().y) {
            image =
                new Image(
                    display,
                    canvas.getSize().x,
                    canvas.getSize().y);
            doubleBufferedCanvas.setData("double-buffer-image", image);
        }

        // Initializes the graphics context of the image.
        GC imageGC = new GC(image);
        imageGC.setBackground(e.gc.getBackground());
        imageGC.setForeground(e.gc.getForeground());
        imageGC.setFont(e.gc.getFont());

        // Fills the background.
        Rectangle imageSize = image.getBounds();
        imageGC.fillRectangle(0, 0, imageSize.width + 1, imageSize.height + 1);

        // Performs actual drawing here ...
        imageGC.drawRoundRectangle(10, 10, 200, 100, 5, 5);


        // Draws the buffer image onto the canvas.
        e.gc.drawImage(image, 0, 0);

        imageGC.dispose();
    }
});
```

An image is created with its size equal to the size of the canvas. The drawing operations are performed on the image. After the drawing is done, you draw the image to the canvas and dispose of the graphics context object of the buffered image.

# Image Handling

This section introduces how images are represented in SWT and covers image operations such as alpha blending and scaling. It also demonstrates techniques to display GIF animations.

## Image Basics

In SWT, the `org.eclipse.swt.graphics.Image` class represents a graphical image that is ready to be displayed on specific devices, such as monitors and printers. The easiest way to create an image is by loading it from an image file. For example, the following code loads an image and sets it to be the icon image of a shell.

```
Image image = new Image(shell.getDisplay(), "icons/icon.gif");
shell.setImage(image);
```

Behind the scenes, an instance of `org.eclipse.swt.graphics.ImageLoader` is used to load the data from the specified file. Currently, the following image file formats are supported:

- Windows bitmap (*.bmp)
- Windows icon (*.ico)
- JPEG (*.jpg, *.jpeg)
- Graphics Interchange Format (*.gif)
- Portable Network Graphics (*.png)
- Tag Image File Format (*.tif, *.tiff)

An image loader first creates a data model for the image to be loaded. The image data model is represented by the `org.eclipse.swt.graphics.ImageData` class and it is device-independent. After the image data model has been properly prepared, you are ready to construct the device-dependent `Image` instance with one of the constructors of the `Image` class — for example, `public Image(Device device, ImageData data)`. SWT then employs the underlying native graphics system to render the image to a screen or a printer.

To get a copy of the image data of an image, you can call the `getImageData` method:

```
public ImageData getImageData()
```

You can manipulate an image data object and create new images with the modified image data object. Finally, you can save those images using the `save` methods of the `ImageLoader` class:

```
public void save(OutputStream stream, int format)
public void save(String filename, int format)
```

You can output the image into an output stream or a file in one of the following formats:

- `SWT.IMACE_BMP`: Windows bitmap format
- `SWT.IMAGE_BMP_RLE`: Windows bitmap format with RLE compression
- `SWT.IMAGE_GIF`: GIF format

❑  SWT.IMAGE_ICO: Windows icon format

❑  SWT.IMAGE_JPEG: JPEG format

❑  SWT.IMAGE_PNG: PNG format

For example, the following code loads a GIF image and saves it into a file in Windows bitmap format:

```
Image image = new Image(display, "icons/icon.gif");
ImageLoader loader = new ImageLoader();
loader.data = new ImageData[] { image.getImageData() };
loader.save("icon.bmp", SWT.IMAGE_BMP);
```

In SWT, images use native resources and, therefore, must be disposed of properly. However, image model objects, i.e. instances of ImageData, are pure Java objects that can be managed by a Java runtime garbage collector, so you do not have to dispose of them by yourself. See Chapter 4 for details on SWT resource management.

Next, we are going to have a closer look at the image model ImageData.

# ImageData and PaletteData

Instances of ImageData represent image model objects, which describe images in a device-independent way. An image data object stores the image width and height, and also pixel values for all coordinates. Internally, a byte array is used to record each raw pixel value. Another important property of an image is its *depth*, which specifies the number of bits used to represent a pixel value. For example, a black and white image has depth value 1. Zero (0) represents white and 1 represents black, and each pixel requires only 1 bit to represent. Similarly, a depth value of 16 results in $2^{16}$, which equals 65,536 different color values per pixel.

In order to get the actual color value for a pixel, a *palette* must be used to map the raw pixel value into a color value. In SWT, the class org.eclipse.swt.graphics.PaletteData is used to represent a palette. There are two kinds of palettes: direct and indexed.

## Direct Palettes

In a direct palette, each pixel value comprises three components: red, green, and blue. Masks are used to get each component from a pixel value. For example, you can use the following code to get each component of a pixel value:

```
int pixelValue = imageData.getPixel(50, 50);
int redComponent = pixelValue & imageData.palette.redMask;
int greenComponent = pixelValue & imageData.palette.greenMask;
int blueComponent = pixelValue & imageData.palette.blueMask;
```

The pixel value at the specified coordinates can be obtained using the getPixel method of the ImageData class. The palette field of an ImageData instance stores palettes used to translate pixel values to colors. For a direct palette, you can get the masks by accessing its fields directly. By using bitwise AND operations, you get each individual component.

In order to display each pixel onscreen, SWT needs to create device-dependent `Color` instances based on the red, blue, and green components obtained previously:

```
Color color = new Color(display, redComponent, greenComponent, blueComponent);
```

Because SWT frees you from doing tedious work on image display, this chapter does not go into detail about color management. You focus on `ImageData` and `PaletteData` instead.

When you load an image from a file, the image loader creates the `ImageData` object with an associated `PaletteData` object. Here, you are going to learn how to create an image from scratch. To create an image, all you need to do is to construct a proper `ImageData` object. Before you can create an `ImageData` instance, you have to set up a palette. Suppose you want the image to have depth value of 24 (each pixel value is stored in 24 bits). First, you need to allocate storage space for each red, green, and blue component in 24 bits. One possible plan is to allocate the first 8 bits for the red component, a second 8 bits for the green component, and the last 8 bits for the blue component. So the masks for red, green, and blue components are 0xFF0000, 0x00FF00, 0x0000FF, respectively. A direct palette can be constructed easily with these three masks:

```
PaletteData paletteData = new PaletteData(0xFF0000, 0x00FF00, 0x0000FF);
```

Now, you are ready to create image data objects. After an image data instance is constructed, you can set pixel values for it. For example, the following code creates an image with a blue *T* on a yellow background, as shown in Figure 15-11:

```
PaletteData paletteData = new PaletteData(0xFF0000, 0x00FF00, 0x0000FF);
ImageData imageData = new ImageData(100, 100, 24, paletteData);

for(int i=0; i<100; i++) { // each column.
    for(int j=0; j<100; j++) { // each row.
        if(j < 30 || (i > 35 && i < 65))
            imageData.setPixel(i, j, 0xFF);
        else
            imageData.setPixel(i, j, 0xFFFF00);
    }
}

final Image image= new Image(display, imageData);
```

Figure 15-11

## Indexed Palettes

In a direct palette, the pixel values are recorded directly. However, for an indexed palette, each pixel value stores a reference to an indexed color palette. For example, suppose you have two colors available on the indexed color palette: red [index=0], blue [index=1]. If a pixel has a stored value of 1, the corresponding color is blue. The following code re-creates the big *T* image with an indexed palette:

```
PaletteData paletteData2 = new PaletteData(new RGB[] {
    new RGB(0, 0, 255), // blue
    new RGB(255, 255, 0) // yellow
});

ImageData imageData2 = new ImageData(100, 100, 1, paletteData2);

for (int i = 0; i < 100; i++) { // each column.
    for (int j = 0; j < 100; j++) { // each row.
        if (j < 30 || (i > 35 && i < 65))
            imageData2.setPixel(i, j, 0);
        else
            imageData2.setPixel(i, j, 1);
    }
}

final Image image = new Image(display, imageData2);
```

An indexed palette with only two colors — blue and yellow — is created. You then create an image data object with this indexed palette. Because this palette has only two colors, the depth value is 1. When calling the setPixel method, the index of the color is used instead of the actual color value.

An indexed palette can have only 1, 2, 4, or 8 bit depths. A direct palette should be used when the bit-depth value is larger than 8.

To check whether a palette is direct or indexed, you can query the field isDirect of a PaletteData object:

```
public boolean isDirect
```

If this field is true, it is a direct palette. Otherwise, it is an indexed palette.

Regardless of palette type, you can always get the correct RGB value from a pixel value using the getRGB method of the PaletteData class:

```
public RGB getRGB(int pixel)
```

The most common usage is:

```
RGB color = imageData.palette.getRGB(imageData.getPixel(50, 50));
```

With this knowledge of ImageData and PaletteData, you are now ready to manipulate images.

## *Transparency and Alpha Blending*

You can specify a particular color in an image to appear transparent by setting the field `transparentPixel` of the `ImageData` class.

For example, the image on the left of Figure 15-12 has no color set to be transparent, whereas the right image has the white color as the transparent color.

**Figure 15-12**

The corresponding code is as follows:

```
ImageData imageData = new ImageData("icons/eclipse.jpg");

final Image image = new Image(display, imageData);

imageData.transparentPixel = imageData.palette.getPixel(new RGB(255, 255, 255));

final Image image2 = new Image(display, imageData);

final Canvas canvas = new Canvas(shell, SWT.NULL);
canvas.addPaintListener(new PaintListener() {
    public void paintControl(PaintEvent e) {
        e.gc.drawImage(image, 10, 20);
        e.gc.drawImage(image2, 200, 20);
    }
});
```

First, the image data object is created from a JPEG file. Because JPEG does not support transparency, the default value of the field `transparentPixel` must be -1, which means no transparent color. The image on the left is created with this image data. Note that the image simply clones the specified image data; any subsequent change on the image data will not affect the image. Then we set the transparent color of the image data to be white. The `getPixel` method of the `PaletteData` class returns the pixel value corresponding to the specified color regardless of the type of the palette. After setting the transparent color, another image is created. The two images are then displayed within a canvas.

You may notice that some "white" regions still show on the second image because those colors are not pure white. To remove such ugly regions, you need to convert off-white pixels to pure white. You iterate over each pixel to replace the off-white color with pure white, as shown here:

```
RGB white = new RGB(255, 255, 255);
for(int i=0; i<imageData.width; i++) {
    for(int j=0; j<imageData.height; j++) {
```

```
        RGB rgb = imageData.palette.getRGB(imageData.getPixel(i, j));

        int threshold = 220;
        if(rgb.red > threshold && rgb.green > threshold && rgb.blue > threshold)
            imageData.setPixel(i, j, imageData.palette.getPixel(white));
    }
}

imageData.transparentPixel = imageData.palette.getPixel(new RGB(255, 255, 255));

final Image image2 = new Image(display, imageData);
```

As shown in Figure 15-13, most of the off-white regions are removed. By modifying the pixel values, you can create many kinds of graphical effects.

Figure 15-13

In the preceding example, we set pixels with certain colors to be completely transparent. A pixel may have a certain level of transparency between opaque and completely transparent. The value specifying the level of transparency of a pixel is called an *alpha* value. You can assign an alpha value for each pixel in the image. The following sample code creates a fade-in effect, as shown in Figure 15-14:

```
ImageData imageData = new ImageData("icons/eclipse.jpg");

byte[] alphaValues = new byte[imageData.height * imageData.width];
for(int j=0; j<imageData.height; j++) {
    for(int i=0; i<imageData.width; i++) {
        alphaValues[j*imageData.width + i] =
                    (byte) (255 - 255 * i / imageData.width);
    }
}

imageData.alphaData = alphaValues;

final Image image = new Image(display, imageData);

canvas.addPaintListener(new PaintListener() {
    public void paintControl(PaintEvent e) {
        e.gc.drawImage(image, 10, 10);
    }
});
```

**Figure 15-14**

We first create a byte array with a size equal to the number of pixels in the image data object. The alpha value for each pixel is then set. The valid range of an alpha value is [0, 255], with 0 representing completely transparent and 255 representing opaque. After that, we assign the byte array to the `alphaData` field of the image data object. An image is created with the image data and drawn on a canvas.

If you want all the pixels of an image data object to share the same alpha value, simply set the field `alpha` of the image data object.

## Image Scaling

In the first section of this chapter, we used a GC object to resize and draw an image. Here, you learn another way to resize an image: through the `scaleTo` method of the `ImageData` class:

```
public ImageData scaledTo(int width, int height)
```

The `scaleTo` method stretches or shrinks the image data to the specified size and the resized image data object is returned. You can then use the returned image data object to create images. For example, the following code resizes an image into a 100 × 100 image:

```
ImageData imageData = new ImageData("icons/eclipse.jpg");

ImageData imageData2 = imageData.scaledTo(100, 100);
Image image2 = new Image(display, imageData2);
```

## Displaying Animation

SWT does not support native GIF animation. To display GIF animation, you have to create a thread and display each frame after a certain delay.

The following code snippet shows how to display GIF animation in SWT:

```
ImageLoader imageLoader = new ImageLoader();
final ImageData[] imageDatas = imageLoader.load("icons/eclipse-ani.gif");

final Image image = new Image(display, imageDatas[0].width, imageDatas[0].height);
final Canvas canvas = new Canvas(shell, SWT.NULL);

canvas.addPaintListener(new PaintListener() {
    public void paintControl(PaintEvent e) {
```

```
            e.gc.drawImage(image, 0, 0);
    }
});

final GC gc = new GC(image);

final Thread thread = new Thread() {
    int frameIndex = 0;
    public void run() {
        while (!isInterrupted()) {
            frameIndex %= imageDatas.length;
            final ImageData frameData = imageDatas[frameIndex];

            display.asyncExec(new Runnable() {
                public void run() {
                    Image frame =
                        new Image(display, frameData);
                    gc.drawImage(frame, frameData.x, frameData.y);
                    frame.dispose();
                    canvas.redraw();
                }
            });

            try {
                // delay
                Thread.sleep(imageDatas[frameIndex].delayTime * 10);
            } catch (InterruptedException e) {
                return;
            }

            frameIndex += 1;
        }

    }
};

shell.addShellListener(new ShellAdapter() {
    public void shellClosed(ShellEvent e) {
        thread.interrupt();
    }
});

shell.setSize(400, 200);
shell.open();

thread.start();
```

First, the GIF file is loaded using an image loader. Each frame in the GIF animation is represented by an ImageData object. We then create an image (this image will be referred to as the canvas image), which is used to draw an animation frame onto. A canvas is used to display the canvas image. A thread is created to draw frames on the canvas image repeatedly. When a frame is drawn on the canvas image, the canvas is set to be redrawn to display the updated frame. After each frame is drawn, the thread sleeps for the delay time associated with the frame. A shell listener is used to interrupt the animation thread when the shell is closed. Finally, open the shell and start the animation thread.

# Summary

In the first part of chapter, you learned how to draw lines, arcs, shapes, images, and text with graphics context. You learned about double buffering to reduce screen flicker. The second part focused on SWT images. `ImageData` and `PaletteData` are two main classes that are used to represent the image model. You saw how to manipulate an image by modifying its associated image data object. The chapter also covered such topics as transparency and GIF animation. In the next chapter, you learn how to use the drag-and-drop feature to make the UI more accessible.

# 16

# Drag and Drop and the Clipboard

There are two approaches for exchanging data within an application and between applications: drag and drop (DND) and the clipboard.

This chapter shows you how to enable your applications to supply data and to accept data in the drag-and-drop process, and how to use the clipboard to exchange data within an application or between different applications. Through practical examples, you learn how to equip your applications with DND and clipboard functions.

## Using Drag and Drop

SWT supports native drag and drop. You can drag data from a control to another location in the same control, to a different control within the same application, or to a different application.

A *drag source* provides the data in a drag-and-drop transfer. It is also the object that originates a DND operation. The drag source specifies the types of data and a set of operations that a control supports. Each control may have no more than one drag source object associated with it. Drag source listeners are used to listen for drag events, supply the content of data being transferred and, optionally, to update the control UI after transfer.

A *drop target* identifies the control over which data can be dropped (transferred). More specifically, a drop target specifies the types of data that can be dropped on the control and a set of operations that can be performed. Each control may have no more than one drop source object associated with it. Drop target listeners listen for drop events and control the dropping process.

A successful drag and drop will not happen unless the drop target can "understand" the data supplied by the drag source. In SWT, *transfer* objects provide the data translation mechanism. They are capable of converting between a Java representation of data (a Java object) and a platform-specific representation of data and vice versa.

The rest of this section steps you through a word jumble program in order to provide a detailed look at DND. The game is shown in Figure 16-1. The program randomly scrambles the letters of a word, and the goal is to unscramble the word in the second row by dragging the letters from the first row and organizing them in the correct order.

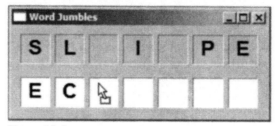

**Figure 16-1**

In this program, controls (probably labels) in the first row are drag sources, whereas controls in the second row are drag targets. In the next few sections, you learn how to add the drag-and-drop mechanism.

## Creating Drag Sources

First, create two labels in row 1 and row 2 for each letter in the word:

```
String word = "ECLIPSE";

Label[] labelsRowOne;
Label[] labelsRowTwo;

shell.setText("Word Jumbles");
labelsRowOne = new Label[word.length()];
labelsRowTwo = new Label[word.length()];

int width = 40;

for (int i = 0; i < word.length(); i++) {
    final Label labelRowOne = new Label(shell, SWT.BORDER);
    labelsRowOne[i] = labelRowOne;
    labelRowOne.setBounds(10 + width * i, 10, width - 5, width - 5);
    labelRowOne.setFont(font);
    labelRowOne.setText(word.charAt(randomPermutation[i]) + "");
    labelRowOne.setAlignment(SWT.CENTER);

    setDragSource(labelRowOne);

    final Label labelRowTwo = new Label(shell, SWT.BORDER);
    labelsRowTwo[i] = labelRowTwo;
    labelRowTwo.setBounds(10 + width * i, 20 + width, width - 5, width - 5);
    labelRowTwo.setBackground(display.getSystemColor(SWT.COLOR_WHITE));
    labelRowTwo.setFont(font);
    labelRowTwo.setAlignment(SWT.CENTER);

    setDropTarget(labelRowTwo);
}
```

The setDragSource method should be implemented to specify a drag source for the label passed. The following is a possible implementation:

```
public void setDragSource(final Label label) {
    // Allows text to be moved only.
    int operations = DND.DROP_MOVE;
    final DragSource dragSource = new DragSource(label, operations);

    // Data should be transferred in plain text format.
    Transfer[] formats = new Transfer[] { TextTransfer.getInstance()};
    dragSource.setTransfer(formats);

    dragSource.addDragListener(new DragSourceListener() {
        public void dragStart(DragSourceEvent event) {
            // Disallows drags if text is not available.
            if (label.getText().length() == 0)
                event.doit = false;
        }

        public void dragSetData(DragSourceEvent event) {
            // Provides the text data.
            if (TextTransfer.getInstance().isSupportedType(event.dataType))
                event.data = label.getText();
        }

        public void dragFinished(DragSourceEvent event) {
            // Removes the text after the move operation.
            if (event.doit == true || event.detail == DND.DROP_MOVE) {
                label.setText("");
            }
        }
    });

    label.addDisposeListener(new DisposeListener() {
        public void widgetDisposed(DisposeEvent e) {
            dragSource.dispose();
        }
    );
}
```

First, construct a drag source object with the label and include the allowed operations as the arguments with the constructor of the DragSource class:

```
public DragSource(Control control, int style)
```

Next, specify the control that the user clicks to initiate the drag in the first argument and the allowed operations in the second argument. Following is a list of all of possible operations:

- ❏ DND.DROP_NONE: No drag-and-drop operation performed
- ❏ DND.DROP_COPY: A copy of the data in the drag source is added to the drop target
- ❏ DND.DROP_MOVE: A copy of the data in the drag source is added to the drop target and the original data is removed from the drag source
- ❏ DND.DROP_LINK: The drop target makes a link to the data in the drag source

In this case, you can allow only the move operation. If multiple operations are allowed, you can bitwise OR the desired operations. For example, to allow copy and move operations, you specify DND.DROP_COPY | DND.DROP_MOVE in the second argument of the constructor of the DragSource class.

Now that you have specified the allowed operation, you are ready to specify the data types that the drag source can provide with the setTransfer method of the DragSource class:

```
public void setTransfer(Transfer[] transferAgents)
```

Currently, several data types are implemented in the org.eclipse.swt.dnd package, as described in the following table.

| Data Type | Corresponding Java Type | Example |
|---|---|---|
| TextTransfer (plain text) | String | Hello World |
| RTFTransfer (rich text file) | String | {\rtf1\ansi\deff0 \f0\fs60 Hello, World!} |
| FileTransfer (a list of files) | String[] | File file1 = new File("C:\file1\ "); File file2 = new File("C:\WINDOWS\file2"); new String[] {file1.getAbsolutePath(), file2.getAbsolutePath() }; |

Here, the data to be transferred is available only in the plain text format (TextTransfer). You may notice that setTransfer allows you to specify more than one data type. For example, setTransfer(new Transfer[] {TextTransfer.getInstance(), RTFTransfer.getInstance()}) states that the control can provide data in two types, plain text and RTF text. So in which format should the data be prepared when the drop target sends a request? You'll get an answer to this question very soon when you learn about the drag source listener.

The drag source itself cannot handle data transfer. To do that, you need to use a drag source listener. A drag source listener listens for drag events and acts accordingly. There are three methods in the DragSourceListner interface:

```
public void dragStart(DragSourceEvent event)
public void dragSetData(DragSourceEvent event)
public void dragFinished(DragSourceEvent event)
```

## dragStart()

The dragStart method is called when the user initiates a drag-and-drop operation. The initiating action taken by the user is platform-specific. For example, on Windows, the user initiates a DND operation by pressing down with the left mouse button and dragging. However, on Motif, the user does it by pressing down the middle button of the mouse. In this drag source listener, you cancel the DND operation (if the text of the label is empty) by setting the doit field to FALSE on the drag source event object. Otherwise, DND operations are allowed.

## dragSetData()

The `dragSetData` method may be called multiple times when the drop target requests data. The type of data requested by the drop target is stored in the `dataType` field of the `DragSourceEvent` object. The drag source can then use this information to provide data in the correct format. If the data type request is supported by the drag source, the drag source provides the data to the drop target by storing the data in the `data` field of the drag source event object. Because transfer classes are implemented in a platform-dependent way, you cannot access the members of transfer classes directly to make your application portable. Rather, you should always use the following pattern to perform type checking:

```
if ([Transfer class].getInstance().isSupportedType(event.dataType))
...
```

In the preceding code, `[Transfer class]` can be any of the following: `TextTransfer`, `RFTTransfer`, or `FileTransfer`.

## dragFinished()

When the drag-and-drop operation finishes, the `dragFinished` method is called. A DND operation finishes when the user drops the data on a valid control, drops the data on an invalid control, or terminates the DND operation by pressing the Escape key. If the operation is performed, the `doit` field of the drag source event object is `true`; otherwise it is `false`. Additionally, you can check the type of operation performed by querying the `detail` field of the event object. In the game program, the text is removed only if a move operation has been performed.

Because instances of `DragSource` and `DropTarget` classes use native operating system resources, you should dispose of them when they are not in use anymore. To do that, you add a `dispose` listener to the label so that the drag source object associated with the label is disposed of when the label is about to be disposed of.

You have now finished coding the drag source part. To test it, you can run the program and drag a letter in the first row onto a text editor such as Microsoft Word. However, you cannot drop a letter on any of the labels in the second row. To enable the labels on the second row to accept data, you need to create drop targets with them.

# Creating Drop Targets

After implementing the `setDragSource` method, we are going to implement the `setDropTarget` method as used in `setDropTarget(labelRowTwo)`. Creating a drop target for a control is very similar to creating a drag source on a control, as you saw in the preceding section. First, you need to create the drop target object with the control and allowed operations as the argument. Then you set data types that the drop target accepts. After that, you need to register a drop listener to handle drop events. Here is the code for the `setDropTarget` method:

```
public void setDropTarget(final Label label) {
    int operations = DND.DROP_MOVE;
    final DropTarget dropTarget = new DropTarget(label, operations);

    // Data should be transferred in plain text format.
    Transfer[] formats = new Transfer[] { TextTransfer.getInstance()};
```

```
    dropTarget.setTransfer(formats);

    dropTarget.addDropListener(new DropTargetListener() {
        public void dragEnter(DropTargetEvent event) {
            // Does not accept any drop if the label has text on it.
            if(label.getText().length() != 0)
                event.detail = DND.DROP_NONE;
        }

        public void dragLeave(DropTargetEvent event) {
        }

        public void dragOperationChanged(DropTargetEvent event) {
        }

        public void dragOver(DropTargetEvent event) {
        }

        public void drop(DropTargetEvent event) {
            if (TextTransfer.getInstance().isSupportedType(event.currentDataType)){
                String text = (String) event.data;
                label.setText(text);
                // Checks the result.
                check();
            }
        }

        public void dropAccept(DropTargetEvent event) {
        }
    });

    label.addDisposeListener(new DisposeListener() {
        public void widgetDisposed(DisposeEvent e) {
            dropTarget.dispose();
        }
    });
}
```

As you learned earlier, setting allowed operations and data types for a drop target is very similar to setting them for a drag source. Let's skip the first part and look at the drop target listener in detail.

## Overview of Methods in DropTargetListener

As the user drags the cursor into, over, and out of a control designated as a drop target, various drop target events are generated, and the corresponding methods in drop target listeners are invoked. Six methods are declared in the `DropTargetListener` interface:

```
public void dragEnter(DropTargetEvent event)
public void dragOperationChanged(DropTargetEvent event)
public void dragOver(DropTargetEvent event)
public void dropAccept(DropTargetEvent event)
public void dragLeave(DropTargetEvent event)
public void drop(DropTargetEvent event)
```

The first four methods may be invoked before the drop happens. You can use them to

❑ Set the type of data that should be transferred in the currentDataType field of the drop target event object.

❑ Change the operation to be performed by modifying the detail field of the event object. (You can stop the drop from happening by setting the detail field to DND.DROP_NONE.)

❑ Set the visual feedback effects on the drop target control (except the dropAccept method).

The drop method is called when the data is being dropped. You learn about each method in detail next.

## dragEnter()

The dragEnter method is invoked when the dragging cursor enters the drop target boundary. The currentDataType field of the event object is determined by the first transfer type specified in the setTransfer() method that matches a data type provided by the drag source. You can change the default data type by setting the currentDataType field of the event object. The dataTypes field of the event object contains all the data types that the drag source can provide. The value of the currentDataType must be one of the types in the dataTypes.

The detail field of the event object specifies the operation to be performed. The operation is determined by the modifier keys pressed by the user. If no keys are pressed, the detail field of the event object has the value as DND.DROP_DEFAULT. You can modify a drop operation by changing the detail field to the desired operation. In my code, if the label has text on it, you disable the drop operation by setting the detail field to DND.DROP_NONE. The detail field value can be only DND.DROP_NONE or an operation supported by the drag source (stored in the operations field of the event object).

If the drop target control is a tree or a table, you can optionally specify visual feedback effects for it by setting the feedback field of the event object with the values listed in the following table.

| Feedback | Description |
| --- | --- |
| DND.FEEDBACK_EXPAND | The item currently under the cursor is expanded to allow the user to select a drop target from a sub item. (Applies to trees) |
| DND.FEEDBACK_INSERT_AFTER | An insertion mark is shown after the item under the cursor. (Applies to tables and trees) |
| DND.FEEDBACK_INSERT_BEFORE | An insertion mark is shown before the item under the cursor. (Applies to tables and trees) |
| DND.FEEDBACK_NONE | No feedback effect is shown. |
| DND.FEEDBACK_SCROLL | The widget is scrolled up or down to allow the user to drop on items that are not currently visible. (Applies to tables and trees) |
| DND.FEEDBACK_SELECT | The item under the cursor is selected. (Applies to tables and trees) |

The default value of the feedback field is DND.FEEBACK_SELECT.

### dragOperationChanged()

During a drag operation, the dragOperationChanged method is called when the operation being performed has changed. The cause of the change is usually that the user changes the modifier keys while dragging. For example, on Windows, pressing the Ctrl key indicates a copy operation (DND.DROP_COPY) and pressing both the Ctrl and Shift keys indicates a link operation (DND.DROP_LINK). With no modifier, the default operation (DND.DROP_DEFAULT) is requested.

Similar to the dragEnter method, you can change the operation, data type, and visual feedback for the drop target in this method.

### dragOver()

The dragOver method is called constantly when the cursor is moving over the drop target. Like the dragEnter and dragOperationChanged method, you can modify the operation, data type, and visual feedback for the drop target in this method.

### dragAccept()

The dragAccept method is invoked when the drop is about to be performed. This method provides the last chance to specify the operation and to define the current data type.

### dragLeave()

The dragLeave method may be called in any the following cases:

❑    The cursor has left the drop target.

❑    The drop operation has been cancelled.

❑    The data is about to be dropped.

You cannot modify any field of the event object in this method.

### drop()

In the drop method, the data is being dropped. The data field of the event object contains the data as a Java object. For more details on data type and Java object mapping, please refer to the table in the section "Creating Drag Sources." In the word jumbles program, you check the data type and then set the text to the label. Even in this method, you can cancel a drop operation by setting the detail field of the event object to DND.DROP_NONE.

You have now completed the word jumbles program. With the knowledge gained during development of this simple program, you are ready to create more complex applications. In the next section, you learn how to build an easy-to-use bookmark organizer by taking advantage of SWT drag and drop.

## The Bookmark Organizer

In this section, you build a bookmark organizer as shown in Figure 16-2. The bookmark organizer allows you to reorganize Internet Explorer's bookmarks. To use the program, first you need to export your IE bookmarks as an HTML file. The bookmark organizer can load all the bookmarks contained in the exported HTML file. You can then reorganize your bookmarks by drag and drop — i.e., you can copy or move a bookmark to any folder through drag and drop.

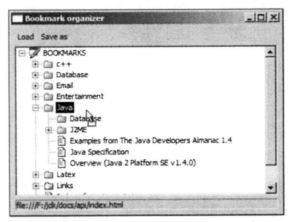

**Figure 16-2**

## Constructing the UI

First, construct the basic UI objects and implement the data parsing and saving mechanism.

```java
/**
 * Represents a bookmark.
 *
 */
class Bookmark {
    public String name;
    public String href;
    public String addDate;
    public String lastVisited;
    public String lastModified;
}

/**
 *
 */
public class BookmarkOrganizer {
    private static String folderLinePrefix = "<DT><H3 FOLDED";
    private static String urlLinePrefix = "<DT><A HREF";
    private static Pattern folderPattern = Pattern.compile("\"(\\d+)\">(.*)<");
    // the pattern used to extract HREF, DATE and other information.
    private static Pattern urlPattern =
        Pattern.compile("\"(.*)\".*\"(.*)\".*\"(.*)\".*\"(.*)\">(.*)<");

    private static String KEY_ADD_DATE = "ADD_DATE";
    private static String KEY_HREF = "HREF";
    private static String KEY_LAST_VISITED = "LAST_VISITED";
    private static String KEY_LAST_MODIFIED = "LAST_MODIFIED";

    Display display = new Display();
    Shell shell = new Shell(display);

    Tree tree;
```

```
    Label label;

    TreeItem rootItem;

    Image iconRoot = new Image(display, "icons/icon.gif");
    Image iconFolder = new Image(display, "icons/folder.gif");
    Image iconURL = new Image(display, "icons/file.gif");

    TreeItem dragSourceItem;

    public BookmarkOrganizer() {
        shell.setText("Bookmark organizer");
        shell.setLayout(new GridLayout(1, true));

        ToolBar toolBar = new ToolBar(shell, SWT.FLAT);
        ToolItem itemOpen = new ToolItem(toolBar, SWT.PUSH);
        itemOpen.setText("Load");
        itemOpen.addListener(SWT.Selection, new Listener() {
            public void handleEvent(Event event) {
                FileDialog dialog = new FileDialog(shell, SWT.OPEN);
                String file = dialog.open();
                if (file != null) {
                    // removes existing items.
                    TreeItem[] items = rootItem.getItems();
                    for (int i = 0; i < items.length; i++)
                        items[i].dispose();

                    loadBookmark(new File(file), rootItem);
                    setStatus("Bookmarks loaded successfully");
                }
            }
        });

        ToolItem itemSave = new ToolItem(toolBar, SWT.PUSH);
        itemSave.setText("Save as");
        itemSave.addListener(SWT.Selection, new Listener() {
            public void handleEvent(Event event) {
                FileDialog dialog = new FileDialog(shell, SWT.SAVE);
                String file = dialog.open();
                if (file != null) {
                    try {
                        BufferedWriter writer =
                            new BufferedWriter(new FileWriter(file));
                        saveBookmark(writer, rootItem);
                        writer.close();
                        setStatus(
                            "Bookmarks saved successfully to file: " + file);
                    } catch (IOException e) {
                        e.printStackTrace();
                    }
                }
            }
```

```
        });

        tree = new Tree(shell, SWT.BORDER);
        tree.setLayoutData(new GridData(GridData.FILL_BOTH));
        rootItem = new TreeItem(tree, SWT.NULL);
        rootItem.setText("BOOKMARKS");
        rootItem.setImage(iconRoot);

        label = new Label(shell, SWT.BORDER);
        label.setLayoutData(new GridData(GridData.FILL_HORIZONTAL));

        tree.addSelectionListener(new SelectionAdapter() {
            public void widgetSelected(SelectionEvent e) {
                TreeItem item = (TreeItem) e.item;
                Bookmark bookmark = (Bookmark) item.getData();
                if (bookmark != null) {
                    setStatus(bookmark.href);
                } else if (item.getData(KEY_ADD_DATE) != null) { // folder.
                    setStatus("Folder: " + item.getText());
                }
            }
        });


        // Specifies drag and drop support here ....



        shell.setSize(400, 300);
        shell.open();

        // Sets up the event loop.
        while (!shell.isDisposed()) {
            if (!display.readAndDispatch()) {
                // If no more entries in event queue
                display.sleep();
            }
        }

        display.dispose();
    }

/**
 * Writes the bookmark(s) into the given buffered writer.
 * @param writer
 * @param item
 * @throws IOException
 */
private void saveBookmark(BufferedWriter writer, TreeItem item)
    throws IOException {
    ...
}

/**
```

```
 * Loads the bookmarks from the specified file.
 * This method parses the specified file line by line to extract all folders
 * and urls contained in the file and wrap them into tree items.
 * @param file
 * @param rootItem
 */
private void loadBookmark(File file, TreeItem rootItem) {
    TreeItem parent = rootItem;

    try {
        BufferedReader reader = new BufferedReader(new FileReader(file));
        String line = null;
        while ((line = reader.readLine()) != null) {
            line = line.trim();
            if (line.startsWith(folderLinePrefix)) { // a folder.
                // using regex to find any folder contained in the line.
                Matcher matcher = folderPattern.matcher(line);
                if (matcher.find()) {
                    String addDate = matcher.group(1);
                    String name = matcher.group(2);

                    TreeItem item = new TreeItem(parent, SWT.NULL);
                    item.setText(name);
                    item.setData(KEY_ADD_DATE, addDate);
                    item.setImage(iconFolder);
                    parent = item;
                }
            } else if (line.startsWith(urlLinePrefix)) { // a url
                // using regex to find any URL contained in the line.
                Matcher matcher = urlPattern.matcher(line);
                if (matcher.find()) {
                    Bookmark bookmark = new Bookmark();
                    bookmark.href = matcher.group(1);
                    bookmark.addDate = matcher.group(2);
                    bookmark.lastVisited = matcher.group(3);
                    bookmark.lastModified = matcher.group(4);
                    bookmark.name = matcher.group(5);

                    TreeItem item = new TreeItem(parent, SWT.NULL);
                    item.setText(bookmark.name);
                    item.setData(bookmark);
                    item.setImage(iconURL);


                }
            } else if (line.equals("</DL><p>")) { // folder boundary.
                parent = parent.getParentItem();
            }
        }
    } catch (FileNotFoundException e) {
        e.printStackTrace();
    } catch (IOException e) {
        e.printStackTrace();
    }
```

```
    }

    private void setStatus(String message) {
        label.setText(message);
    }

    public static void main(String[] args) {
        new BookmarkOrganizer();
    }
}
```

First, declare the tree to be used to display bookmarks. Then add the toolbar and toolbar items to the shell. One toolbar item is used to load bookmark information from a file, and the other one saves the bookmarks on the tree into a file. A tree control is created so that bookmarks can be displayed on it. The `loadBookmark` method creates a tree item for each bookmark folder and bookmark when loading bookmark information from the file. The `Bookmark` class is used to represent a book. An instance of `Bookmark` is associated with its tree item through the `setData` method of the `TreeItem` class.

Let's take a moment to think of a way to implement the drag-and-drop mechanism. Our goal here is to enable the user to drag a bookmark (represented by a tree item) to any of the folders. Remember that only a control can be used to create a drag source or a drop target, so we cannot directly create drag sources or drop targets based on tree items because `TreeItem` is not a subclass of `Control`. The only possible candidate here is the tree control itself. Clearly, we need to create a drag source and a drop target based on the exact same control — the tree control.

Then you determine the proper format of data being transferred. Obviously, the data to be transferred is a `Bookmark` object. As you learned in previous sections, only three transfer types are available in the SWT DND package: `TextTransfer`, `RTFTransfer`, and `FileTransfer`. None of the existing transfer classes is capable of directly transferring an instance of the `Bookmark` object. There are two possible ways to overcome this:

❏   "Embedding" an instance of `Bookmark` in a string. For example, for a bookmark {`"Eclipse"`, `"http://www.eclipse.org"`, `ADD_DATE=" 1045048972"`, `LAST_VISIT="1083069965"` `LAST_MODIFIED="1045048972"`}, we can embed it in a string object as: `Eclipse| http:// www.eclipse.org|1045048972|1083069965`. Both the drag source listener and the drop target listener should understand the string format.

❏   Creating our own transfer type by extending the `ByteArrayTransfer` class.

Both approaches can do the job. In the following section, you use the latter method.

## Creating a Custom Transfer Type

Create a class named `BookmarkTransfer` to handle `Bookmark` object transfer:

```
public class BookmarkTransfer extends ByteArrayTransfer {
    private static final String BOOKMARK_TRANSFER_NAME = "BOOKMARK";
    private static final int BOOKMARK_TRANSFER_ID =
        registerType(BOOKMARK_TRANSFER_NAME);
    private static final BookmarkTransfer instance = new BookmarkTransfer();

    public static BookmarkTransfer getInstance() {
```

```
        return instance;
    }

    /*
     * (non-Javadoc)
     *
     * @see org.eclipse.swt.dnd.Transfer#getTypeIds()
     */
    protected int[] getTypeIds() {
        return new int[] { BOOKMARK_TRANSFER_ID };
    }

    /*
     * (non-Javadoc)
     *
     * @see org.eclipse.swt.dnd.Transfer#getTypeNames()
     */
    protected String[] getTypeNames() {
        return new String[] { BOOKMARK_TRANSFER_NAME };
    }

    /*
     * (non-Javadoc)
     *
     * @see org.eclipse.swt.dnd.Transfer#javaToNative(java.lang.Object,
     *       org.eclipse.swt.dnd.TransferData)
     */
    protected void javaToNative(Object object, TransferData transferData) {
        if (object == null || !(object instanceof Bookmark))
            return;

        Bookmark bookmark = (Bookmark) object;

        if (isSupportedType(transferData)) {
            try {
                // Writes data to a byte array.
                ByteArrayOutputStream stream = new ByteArrayOutputStream();
                DataOutputStream out = new DataOutputStream(stream);
                out.writeUTF(bookmark.name);
                out.writeUTF(bookmark.href);
                out.writeUTF(bookmark.addDate);
                out.writeUTF(bookmark.lastVisited);
                out.writeUTF(bookmark.lastModified);
                out.close();

                super.javaToNative(stream.toByteArray(), transferData);
            } catch (IOException e) {
                e.printStackTrace();
            }
        }
    }

    /*
     * (non-Javadoc)
```

```
    *
    * @see org.eclipse.swt.dnd.Transfer#nativeToJava(TransferData)
    */
protected Object nativeToJava(TransferData transferData) {
    if (isSupportedType(transferData)) {
        byte[] raw = (byte[]) super.nativeToJava(transferData);
        if (raw == null)
            return null;
        Bookmark bookmark = new Bookmark();

        try {
            ByteArrayInputStream stream = new ByteArrayInputStream(raw);
            DataInputStream in = new DataInputStream(stream);
            bookmark.name = in.readUTF();
            bookmark.href = in.readUTF();
            bookmark.addDate = in.readUTF();
            bookmark.lastVisited = in.readUTF();
            bookmark.lastModified = in.readUTF();
            in.close();
        } catch (IOException e) {
            e.printStackTrace();
            return null;
        }

        return bookmark;
    } else {
        return null;
    }
}

}
```

The getTypeIds method returns the platform-specific IDs of the data types and can be converted using this transfer agent, and the getTypesNames method returns the names of the data types supported by the transfer agent. The javaToNative method in the preceding class is used to convert a Java object to a platform-specific representation. First, you write the Bookmark object into a byte array. Then you call the javaToNative method of the ByteArrayTransfer class, which is capable of converting a Java byte array into a platform-specific representation and writes the native code to the TransferData object. In this way, you don't have to care about the platform-specific data transformation; those methods that are defined in the ByteArrayTransfer class (which is the superclass for all transfer types such as TextTransfer, RTFTransfer, and FileTransfer) do all the dirty work. The nativeToJava method coverts the native data representation into a Bookmark object.

Now, we can equip the tree control with drag-and-drop functionality.

## Adding Drag-and-Drop Support

First, create a drag source on the tree control:

```
TreeItem dragSourceItem;

...

final DragSource dragSource =
```

```
    new DragSource(tree, DND.DROP_MOVE | DND.DROP_COPY | DND.DROP_LINK);
dragSource.setTransfer(new Transfer[] { BookmarkTransfer.getInstance()});

dragSource.addDragListener(new DragSourceAdapter() {
    public void dragStart(DragSourceEvent event) {
        TreeItem[] selection = tree.getSelection();
        // Only a URL bookmark can be dragged.
        if (selection.length > 0 && selection[0].getData() != null) {
            event.doit = true;
            dragSourceItem = selection[0];
        } else {
            event.doit = false;
        }
    };

    public void dragSetData(DragSourceEvent event) {
        if (BookmarkTransfer
            .getInstance()
            .isSupportedType(event.dataType))
            event.data = dragSourceItem.getData();
    }

    public void dragFinished(DragSourceEvent event) {
        if (event.detail == DND.DROP_MOVE)
            dragSourceItem.dispose();
        dragSourceItem = null;
    }

});
```

The drag source is created with BookmarkTransfer as its only supported transfer type. A class member named dragSourceItem is used to record the dragged item. Items other than bookmark items, such as folder items, are not allowed to be dragged, as they are restricted in the dragStart method. The dragSetData method simply verifies the requested data type and sends the Bookmark object associated with the dragged item. If the drop operation is the move operation, you remove the dragged item by calling its dispose method.

After setting the drag source, you need to create a drop target based on the tree control:

```
final DropTarget dropTarget =
    new DropTarget(tree, DND.DROP_MOVE | DND.DROP_COPY | DND.DROP_LINK);
dropTarget.setTransfer(new Transfer[] { BookmarkTransfer.getInstance()});

dropTarget.addDropListener(new DropTargetAdapter() {

    public void dragOver(DropTargetEvent event) {
        event.feedback =
            DND.FEEDBACK_EXPAND
                | DND.FEEDBACK_SCROLL
                | DND.FEEDBACK_SELECT;
    }

    public void dropAccept(DropTargetEvent event) {
```

```
            // can only drop into to a folder
            if (event.item == null
                || ((TreeItem) event.item).getData() != null)
                event.detail = DND.DROP_NONE;
        }

    public void drop(DropTargetEvent event) {
        try {
            if (event.data == null) {
                event.detail = DND.DROP_NONE;
                return;
            }

            TreeItem item =
                new TreeItem((TreeItem) event.item, SWT.NULL);
            Bookmark bookmark = (Bookmark) event.data;
            item.setText(bookmark.name);
            item.setImage(iconURL);
            item.setData(bookmark);
        } catch (RuntimeException e) {
            e.printStackTrace();
        }
    }
});
```

Like the drag source, the drop target supports the BookmarkTransfer type only. A drop target listener is added after the drop target is created. The feedback field of the event object is configured in the dropOver method to have the tree control exhibiting visual effects such as selection and expansion. The dropAccept method specifies that only a folder item can accept a bookmark drop. Finally, the drop method performs the actual drop. Notice that you use a try-catch statement to catch all exceptions. In the current SWT release, DND wraps all event listener code in an exception block. If an event listener throws an exception, no error will be reported and the DND operation is set to DND.DROP_NONE. I advise you to wrap your complex code in drag-and-drop listeners in exception blocks so that you can easily figure out what happens in case of error.

Now, the bookmark organizer is completed. You can load your bookmarks, organize them, and save the results in a new file.

# Using the Clipboard

Drag and drop allows the user to transfer data from an application to itself or to other applications instantly. Sometimes, it is desirable to perform the transfer operation at a later point in time. In this case, you can use the clipboard as the temporary holder for the transfer data.

## Putting Data on the Clipboard

The clipboard provides a virtual space to place data in multiple formats. For example, the following code places data in plain text format as well as rich text format:

```
ToolBar toolBar = new ToolBar(shell, SWT.FLAT);
ToolItem itemCopy = new ToolItem(toolBar, SWT.PUSH);
ToolItem itemPaste = new ToolItem(toolBar, SWT.PUSH);
itemCopy.setText("Copy");
itemPaste.setText("Paste");

itemCopy.addListener(SWT.Selection, new Listener() {
    public void handleEvent(Event event) {
        Clipboard clipboard = new Clipboard(display);
        String plainText = "Hello World";
        String rtfText = "{\\rtf1\\b Hello World}";
        TextTransfer textTransfer = TextTransfer.getInstance();
        RTFTransfer rftTransfer = RTFTransfer.getInstance();

        clipboard.setContents(new String[]{plainText, rtfText}, new
Transfer[]{textTransfer, rftTransfer});

        clipboard.dispose();
    }
});
```

When the item labeled "Copy" is hit, a `Clipboard` object is created with the following constructor:

```
public Clipboard(Display display)
```

The data to be placed on the clipboard is prepared in two formats. The `setContents` of the `Clipboard` class is used to place the data onto the clipboard:

```
public void setContents(Object[] data, Transfer[] dataTypes)
```

Once the data is placed on the clipboard, all previous data available on the clipboard is cleared. Because the data is available in multiple formats, the target application may choose the format it supports best. For example, when you hit the Copy tool item and do a paste in Microsoft Word, you see the text "Hello World" displayed in bold. This is because Microsoft Word gets the data in rich text format. Now, if you open the Notepad application and do a paste, you will see that the text "Hello World" does not appear in bold because Notepad is not able to display RTF text and it gets data in plain text format only.

On all systems except GTK, the data you place on the clipboard lasts even after your application is closed.

*Because a **Clipboard** object allocates native system resources, you have to dispose of it after use.*

## Getting Data from the Clipboard

In the preceding section, you learned how to put data on the clipboard. Now you learn how to get data from the clipboard. Because the data on the clipboard may be available in multiple formats, you need to check the availability of your desired format. If the format is supported, you can get the data in that format directly. If the desired format is not supported, you may have to consider using an alternate format.

For example, the follow code checks the availability of the RTF format and gets the data in both plain text format and RTF format:

```
itemPaste.addListener(SWT.Selection, new Listener() {
    public void handleEvent(Event event) {
        Clipboard clipboard = new Clipboard(display);

        TransferData[] transferDatas = clipboard.getAvailableTypes();

        for(int i=0; i<transferDatas.length; i++) {
            // Checks whether RTF format is available.
            if(RTFTransfer.getInstance().isSupportedType(transferDatas[i])) {
                System.out.println("Data is available in RTF format");
                break;
            }
        }

        String plainText =
                (String)clipboard.getContents(TextTransfer.getInstance());
        String rtfText = (String)clipboard.getContents(RTFTransfer.getInstance());

        System.out.println("PLAIN: " + plainText + "\n" + "RTF: " + rtfText);

        clipboard.dispose();
    }
});
```

The getAvailableTypes method returns available data formats in an array:

```
public TransferData[] getAvailableTypes()
```

To check whether a format is supported, you need use the Transfer.isSupportedType method, as shown in the preceding code.

You use the getContents method to get the data in a specified format:

```
public Object getContents(Transfer transfer)
```

The getContents method returns the data in the given type or null if no data of the type is available.

# Summary

In this chapter, the SWT drag-and-drop mechanism was discussed. A drag source provides data in a DND process, while a drop target consumes the data. Drag source listeners and drop target listeners are used extensively to perform various actions in DND. If none of the existing data types is suitable for your data transfer, you can create your own data transfer type. You learned that the clipboard is a handy tool for holding data temporarily and then transferring it at a later point in time. DND and the clipboard are particularly useful for text editing applications. In such applications, you can persist the editing by saving to disks or printing to printers. In the next chapter, you learn about SWT printing support in detail.

# 17

# Printing

SWT offers developers a compact printing API. You can add the printing functionality to your existing programs easily. This chapter introduces you to basic printing mechanisms and then uses a real world example to guide you step by step through coding for printing and print preview. Finally, you learn about multiple-page printing and pagination.

## Printing Fundamentals

In SWT, the `org.eclipse.swt.printing` package contains classes used for printing support. Currently, there are only three classes within this package:

- ❑   PrintDialog
- ❑   Printer
- ❑   PrinterData

A print job is described by an instance of `PrinterData`. The `PrinterData` instance is a lightweight Java object that specifies the target printer and the scope and type of printing desired. For example, the number of pages and copies can be specified in `PrinterData` objects. In most of these cases, you bring up a print dialog (represented by the `PrintDialog` class) and let the user select the target printer and configure various settings. A `PrinterData` object, with all the information specified by the user in the print dialog, is returned when a print dialog is closed. To perform the printing operation, you have to initiate a `Printer` instance and create a GC on the printer and then draw on the printer GC using the usual graphics calls.

For example, the following code prints the text "Eclipse" on the selected printer:

```
PrintDialog dialog = new PrintDialog(shell);

// Opens a dialog and lets user select the
// target printer and configure various settings.
PrinterData printerData = dialog.open();
if(printerData != null) { // If a printer is selected
    // Creates a printer.
    Printer printer = new Printer(printerData);

    // Starts the print job.
    if(printer.startJob("Text")) {
        GC gc = new GC(printer);

        // Starts a new page.
        if(printer.startPage()) {
            gc.drawString("Eclipse", 200, 200);

            // Finishes the page.
            printer.endPage();
        }

        gc.dispose();

        // Ends the job.
        printer.endJob();
    }

    // Disposes the printer object after use.
    printer.dispose();

    System.out.println("Print job done.");
}
```

First, select the target printer and configure the print job settings in the print dialog. The print job is represented by the `PrinterData` object returned. A `Printer` instance is created with the `PrinterData` object. To start the print job, call the `startJob` method of the `Printer` class with the job name (a meaningful string) as the argument. If the job has been successfully started, a graphics context based on the printer is obtained. After that, you can start a new page by calling the `startPage` method. If the `startPage` method succeeds, draw the text on the printer. The `endPage` method is used to indicate that the current page is finished printing. To end the print job, invoke the `endJob` method of the `Printer` class. Finally, dispose of the `Printer` object because it employs native operating resources.

The preceding code prints only a single page. You can use the obtained `Printer` object to print multiple pages. The printing process is illustrated in Figure 17-1.

In the sample code, you use a printer dialog to let the user select the target printer. The following section discusses many other ways to select the target printer.

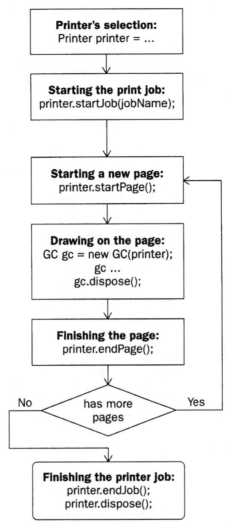

Figure 17-1

# Selecting the Target Printer

As you have seen in the preceding sample code, instances of the Printer class are used to perform the printing job. The Printer class has two constructors:

```
public Printer()
public Printer(PrinterData data)
```

The default constructor creates an instance representing the default printer. If there is no printer available, the default constructor throws an exception. The other constructor allows you to select a specific printer by using a `PrinterData` object.

To obtain a `PrinterData` instance, you can create one using one of the constructors of the `PrinterData` object:

```
public PrinterData()
public PrinterData(String driver, String name)
```

The default constructor creates an instance representing the default constructor. Similar to the default constructor of the `Printer` class, this default constructor throws an exception if there is no printer available. If the driver and name of the printer are known, you can use the other constructor to create an instance representing the corresponding printer. As mentioned before, an instance of `PrinterData` also contains print job control information such as the number of pages and copies. You can set such control parameters through the fields of the `PrinterData` class:

❑ public boolean `collate`: Specifies whether or not the printer should collate the printed paper

❑ public int `copyCount`: Specifies the number of copies to print

❑ public boolean `printToFile`; public String `fileName`: The `printToFile` field specifies whether or not the print job should go to a file. If the `printToFile` is set to `true`, you can use the `fileName` field to set the name of the file in which the job will be printed.

❑ public in `scope`; public int `startPage`; public int `endPage`: The scope filed defines the scope of the print job, which may be expressed in one of the following values: `PrinterData.ALL_PAGES` (printing all pages in current document), `PrinterData.SELECTION` (printing the current selection only), or `PrinterData.PAGE_RANGE` (printing the range of pages specified by the `startPage` field and the `endPage` field).

During printing, you can access the associated `PrinterData` instance of the printer by calling the `getPrinterData` method of the `Printer` class:

```
public PrinterData getPrinterData()
```

Besides constructing a `PrinterData` object by calling the constructors of the `PrinterData` class directly, you can use a print dialog to get an instance of `PrinterData` representing the user selection. For example, the following code brings up a print dialog (in Windows), as shown in Figure 17-2.

```
PrintDialog dialog = new PrintDialog(shell);
PrinterData printerData = dialog.open();

if(printerData != null) { // If a printer is selected
    Printer printer = new Printer(printerData);
    ...
}
```

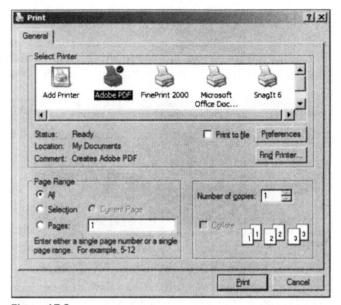

**Figure 17-2**

The user may select the target printer and configure the print settings in the print dialog. After the user hits the Print button (or equivalent buttons on other platforms), the open method of the PrintDialog class returns a PrinterData object containing all the information about the selected printer and print control settings. You can then use the PrinterData object to construct a Printer instance. On the other hand, if the user hits the Cancel button, a null object is returned by the open method. So you must make sure the returned PrinterData object is not null in order to initiate a proper Printer object.

To get all the printers on the system as an array of PrinterData object, you can use the getPrinterList method of the Printer class:

```
public static PrinterData getDefaultPrinterData()
```

You can iterate the array and select the desired PrinterData object to create the Printer instance.

After a Printer object is obtained, you can perform various printing operations on it.

# Basic Printing

With a valid Printer object, you can create a graphics context on it and then draw on the graphics context using the various graphics calls introduced in Chapter 15.

# The Image Viewer Application

In the first section, you saw a very simple example that prints a word on a selected printer. In practical printing, you have to consider many issues such as margin settings and DPI effects. In this section, you learn how to perform proper printing with an image viewer application, as shown in Figure 17-3.

Figure 17-3

The user can load an image using the Open tool item. The image is displayed on a canvas at the center of the shell. Our task here is to implement a print behavior so that when the user presses the Print tool item, the image currently being displayed is printed on the selected printer properly:

```
ToolItem itemPrint = new ToolItem(toolBar, SWT.PUSH);
itemPrint.setText("Print");
itemPrint.addListener(SWT.Selection, new Listener() {
    public void handleEvent(Event event) {
        print();
    }
});

/**
 * Lets the user select a printer and prints the image on it.
 *
 */
void print() {
    PrintDialog dialog = new PrintDialog(shell);
    // Prompts the printer dialog to let the user select a printer.
    PrinterData printerData = dialog.open();

    if (printerData == null) // the user cancels the dialog
        return;
    // Loads the printer.
    Printer printer = new Printer(printerData);

    ...

}
```

When the Print tool item is selected, the print method is invoked. The printer selection part is very straightforward. You need to insert the actual printing procedure at the point marked by the ellipsis. To print the image properly on the printer, you first calculate the page margins. Then, you need to properly resize the image so that the image can be printed on the printer with the correct size.

## Setting the Page Margins

Without proper page margins, objects may be printed close to the edges of the page, which can look ugly and unprofessional. In order to position and align objects correctly on the page, you have to set the page margins before performing the actual printing.

For the image viewer application, you want to print the image on the page with margins equal to 1 inch for each side (see Figure 17-4).

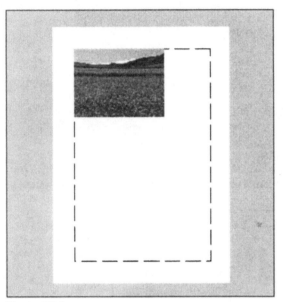

**Figure 17-4**

Before setting the page margins, you need to know the size of the page.

The getBounds method of the Printer class returns the physical size of the page in pixels:

```
public Rectangle getBounds()
```

However, not every part of the physical page can be printed on. The printable area of the page can be determined by using the getClientArea method:

```
public Rectangle getClientArea()
```

Additionally, you can use the computeTrim method to determine the physical horizontal and vertical offsets for the printable area:

```
Rectangle trim = printer.computeTrim(0, 0, 0, 0);
```

The horizontal offset is trim.x and trim.y is the vertical offset relative to the upper-left corner of the physical page.

Suppose 1 inch of margin at each side is desired; the positions of those margins can be calculated as follows:

```
double marginLeft = 1.0; // in inches
double marginRight = 1.0;
double marginTop = 1.0;
double marginBottom = 1.0;

Rectangle clientArea = printer.getClientArea();
Rectangle trim = printer.computeTrim(0, 0, 0, 0);

Point dpi = printer.getDPI();

// The origin of the coordinate is the upper left corner of the client area.
int leftMargin = (int) (marginLeft * dpi.x) - trim.x;
int rightMargin = clientArea.width + trim.width - (int) (marginRight * dpi.x) -
trim.x;
int topMargin = (int) (marginTop * dpi.y) - trim.y;
int bottomMargin = clientArea.height + trim.height - (int) (marginBottom * dpi.y) -
trim.y;
```

Because setting margins is necessary in almost every application with printing support, it is a good idea to create a utility class so that you can reuse it later. Here is the `PrintMargin` class:

```
/**********************************************************************
 * All Right Reserved. Copyright (c) 1998, 2004 Jackwind Li Guojie
 *
 * Created on 2004-5-2 18:55:02 by JACK $Id$
 *
 **********************************************************************/

package com.asprise.books.javaui.ch17;

import org.eclipse.swt.graphics.Point;
import org.eclipse.swt.graphics.Rectangle;
import org.eclipse.swt.printing.Printer;

/**
 * Contains margin information (in pixels) for a print job.
 *
 */
public class PrintMargin {
    // Margin to the left side, in pixels
    public int left;
    //  Margins to the right side, in pixels
    public int right;
    //  Margins to the top side, in pixels
    public int top;
    //  Margins to the bottom side, in pixels
    public int bottom;

    private PrintMargin(int left, int right, int top, int bottom) {
        this.left = left;
        this.right = right;
```

```
        this.top = top;
        this.bottom = bottom;
}

/**
 * Returns a PrintMargin object containing the true border margins for the
 * specified printer with the given margin in inches.
 * Note: all four sides share the same margin width.
 * @param printer
 * @param margin
 * @return
 */
static PrintMargin getPrintMargin(Printer printer, double margin) {
    return getPrintMargin(printer, margin, margin, margin, margin);
}

/**
 * Returns a PrintMargin object containing the true border margins for the
 * specified printer with the given margin width (in inches) for each side.
 */
static PrintMargin getPrintMargin(
    Printer printer,
    double marginLeft,
    double marginRight,
    double marginTop,
    double marginBottom) {
    Rectangle clientArea = printer.getClientArea();
    Rectangle trim = printer.computeTrim(0, 0, 0, 0);

    //System.out.println(printer.getBounds() + " - " + clientArea + "" +
    // trim);
    Point dpi = printer.getDPI();

    int leftMargin = (int) (marginLeft * dpi.x) - trim.x;
    int rightMargin =
        clientArea.width
            + trim.width
            - (int) (marginRight * dpi.x)
            - trim.x;
    int topMargin = (int) (marginTop * dpi.y) - trim.y;
    int bottomMargin =
        clientArea.height
            + trim.height
            - (int) (marginBottom * dpi.y)
            - trim.y;

    return new PrintMargin(
        leftMargin,
        rightMargin,
        topMargin,
        bottomMargin);
}

public String toString() {
```

```
            return "Margin { "
                + left
                + ", "
                + right
                + "; "
                + top
                + ", "
                + bottom
                + " }";
        }
    }
```

With the `PrintMargin` class, you can easily get the page margins with the following code:

```
PrintMargin margin = PrintMargin.getPrintMargin(printer, 1.0);
```

Now that the page margins have been calculated, you are ready to print the image on the page.

## Printing the Image

Here is the code to print the image:

```
if (image == null) // If no image is loaded, do not print.
    return;

final Point printerDPI = printer.getDPI();
final Point displayDPI = display.getDPI();

final PrintMargin margin = PrintMargin.getPrintMargin(printer, 1.0);

Thread printThread = new Thread() {
    public void run() {
        if (!printer.startJob(fileName)) {
            System.err.println("Failed to start print job!");
            printer.dispose();
            return;
        }

        GC gc = new GC(printer);

        if (!printer.startPage()) {
            System.err.println("Failed to start a new page!");
            gc.dispose();
            return;
        } else {
            int imageWidth = image.getBounds().width;
            int imageHeight = image.getBounds().height;

            // Handles DPI conversion.
            // '1.0' is used to make the result a double
            // to achieve better precision.
            double dpiScaleFactorX = printerDPI.x * 1.0 / displayDPI.x;
```

```
                double dpiScaleFactorY = printerDPI.y * 1.0 / displayDPI.y;

                // If the image is too large to draw on a page, reduces its
                // width and height proportionally.
                double imageSizeFactor =
                    Math.min(1, (margin.right - margin.left) * 1.0 /
                                (dpiScaleFactorX * imageWidth));
                imageSizeFactor = Math.min(imageSizeFactor,
                                (margin.bottom - margin.top) * 1.0 /
                                (dpiScaleFactorY * imageHeight));

                // Draws the image to the printer.
                gc.drawImage(
                    image,
                    0,
                    0,
                    imageWidth,
                    imageHeight,
                    margin.left,
                    margin.top,
                    (int) (dpiScaleFactorX * imageSizeFactor * imageWidth),
                    (int) (dpiScaleFactorY * imageSizeFactor * imageHeight));
                gc.dispose();
            }

        printer.endPage();
        printer.endJob();

        printer.dispose();
        System.out.println("Printing job done!");
        }
    };
printThread.start();
```

A new thread is used to execute the print job because the print task may take considerable time. You learned about printing fundamentals in the first section. In the next section, you learn about image drawing. In order to better understand the code in the preceding section, you need to know about measuring the resolution of the output device, better known as *dpi*.

## DPI Conversion

The measurement of *dots per inch* (dpi) specifies the number of dots (pixels) per linear inch. Different devices may have different dpi values. For example, my laptop screen has a dpi value of 96 × 96 (horizontally and vertically), whereas my high-resolution printer has 1200 × 1200 dpi. Let's say an image is 96 pixels wide. The image appears 1 inch wide on my screen, although it is only 0.08 inch wide when it is output on the printer! In order to print the image properly, you would have to scale the image using the following formula:

```
imageOnPrinterWidth = imageWidth * printer.getDPI().x / display.getDPI().x;
imageOnPrinterHeight = imageHeight * printer.getDPI().y / display.getDPI().y;
```

Note that the getDPI methods of the Printer class and the Display class return the dpi values of the printer and the screen, respectively.

Sometimes, the image is too large to be displayed on the page. In this case, you need to scale it to fit the print page.

After the new image size has been determined, the image can be printed to the page easily with the `drawImage` method of the `GC` class.

Finally, you can end the print job and dispose of the printer object.

## Providing the Print Preview

The print preview feature allows the user to select the target printer, configure various parameters such as page margins, and preview the print layout, as shown in Figure 17-5.

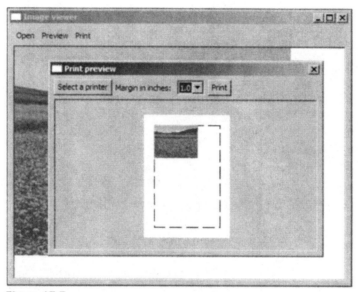

Figure 17-5

There are many ways to implement the print preview. The most straightforward technique is to create the print preview as an image with the size equal to that of the print page and print the objects on the image. However, this approach may cause performance problems, especially when the print page is large and the printer resolution is high.

With the knowledge gained in previous sections, you can easily provide the print preview in a canvas with proper image scaling and drawing operations. Here is the implementation of the print preview dialog:

```
public class ImagePrintPreviewDialog extends Dialog {
    ImageViewer viewer;
    Shell shell;
    Canvas canvas;
    Printer printer;
    PrintMargin margin;
```

```
    Combo combo;

public ImagePrintPreviewDialog(ImageViewer viewer) {
    super(viewer.shell);
    this.viewer = viewer;
}

public void open() {
    shell =
        new Shell(
            viewer.shell,
            SWT.DIALOG_TRIM | SWT.APPLICATION_MODAL | SWT.RESIZE);
    shell.setText("Print preview");
    shell.setLayout(new GridLayout(4, false));

    final Button buttonSelectPrinter = new Button(shell, SWT.PUSH);
    buttonSelectPrinter.setText("Select a printer");
    buttonSelectPrinter.addListener(SWT.Selection, new Listener() {
        public void handleEvent(Event event) {
            PrintDialog dialog = new PrintDialog(shell);
            // Prompts the printer dialog to let the user select a printer.
            PrinterData printerData = dialog.open();

            if (printerData == null) // the user cancels the dialog
                return;
            // Loads the printer.
            final Printer printer = new Printer(printerData);
            setPrinter(
                printer,
                Double.parseDouble(
                    combo.getItem(combo.getSelectionIndex())));
        }
    });

    new Label(shell, SWT.NULL).setText("Margin in inches: ");
    combo = new Combo(shell, SWT.READ_ONLY);
    combo.add("0.5");
    combo.add("1.0");
    combo.add("1.5");
    combo.add("2.0");
    combo.add("2.5");
    combo.add("3.0");
    combo.select(1);
    combo.addListener(SWT.Selection, new Listener() {
        public void handleEvent(Event event) {
            double value =
                Double.parseDouble(
                    combo.getItem(combo.getSelectionIndex()));
            setPrinter(printer, value);
        }
    });

    final Button buttonPrint = new Button(shell, SWT.PUSH);
    buttonPrint.setText("Print");
```

```
           buttonPrint.addListener(SWT.Selection, new Listener() {
               public void handleEvent(Event event) {
                   if (printer == null)
                       viewer.print();
                   else
                       viewer.print(printer, margin);
                   shell.dispose();
               }
           });

           canvas = new Canvas(shell, SWT.BORDER);
           GridData gridData = new GridData(GridData.FILL_BOTH);
           gridData.horizontalSpan = 4;
           canvas.setLayoutData(gridData);
           canvas.addPaintListener(new PaintListener() {
               public void paintControl(PaintEvent e) {
                   int canvasBorder = 20;

                   if (printer == null || printer.isDisposed())
                       return;
                   Rectangle rectangle = printer.getBounds();
                   Point canvasSize = canvas.getSize();

                   double viewScaleFactor =
                       (canvasSize.x - canvasBorder * 2) * 1.0 / rectangle.width;
                   viewScaleFactor =
                       Math.min(
                           viewScaleFactor,
                           (canvasSize.y - canvasBorder * 2)
                               * 1.0
                               / rectangle.height);

                   int offsetX =
                       (canvasSize.x - (int) (viewScaleFactor * rectangle.width))
                           / 2;
                   int offsetY =
                       (canvasSize.y - (int) (viewScaleFactor * rectangle.height))
                           / 2;

                   e.gc.setBackground(
                       shell.getDisplay().getSystemColor(SWT.COLOR_WHITE));
                   // draws the page layout
                   e.gc.fillRectangle(
                       offsetX,
                       offsetY,
                       (int) (viewScaleFactor * rectangle.width),
                       (int) (viewScaleFactor * rectangle.height));

                   // draws the margin.
                   e.gc.setLineStyle(SWT.LINE_DASH);
                   e.gc.setForeground(
                       shell.getDisplay().getSystemColor(SWT.COLOR_BLACK));

                   int marginOffsetX =
                       offsetX + (int) (viewScaleFactor * margin.left);
```

```
            int marginOffsetY =
                offsetY + (int) (viewScaleFactor * margin.top);
        e.gc.drawRectangle(
            marginOffsetX,
            marginOffsetY,
            (int) (viewScaleFactor * (margin.right - margin.left)),
            (int) (viewScaleFactor * (margin.bottom - margin.top)));

        if (viewer.image != null) {
            int imageWidth = viewer.image.getBounds().width;
            int imageHeight = viewer.image.getBounds().height;

            double dpiScaleFactorX =
                printer.getDPI().x
                    * 1.0
                    / shell.getDisplay().getDPI().x;
            double dpiScaleFactorY =
                printer.getDPI().y
                    * 1.0
                    / shell.getDisplay().getDPI().y;

            double imageSizeFactor =
                Math.min(
                    1,
                    (margin.right - margin.left)
                        * 1.0
                        / (dpiScaleFactorX * imageWidth));
            imageSizeFactor =
                Math.min(
                    imageSizeFactor,
                    (margin.bottom - margin.top)
                        * 1.0
                        / (dpiScaleFactorY * imageHeight));

            e.gc.drawImage(
                viewer.image,
                0,
                0,
                imageWidth,
                imageHeight,
                marginOffsetX,
                marginOffsetY,
                (int) (dpiScaleFactorX
                    * imageSizeFactor
                    * imageWidth
                    * viewScaleFactor),
                (int) (dpiScaleFactorY
                    * imageSizeFactor
                    * imageHeight
                    * viewScaleFactor));

        }

    }
```

```
            });

        shell.setSize(400, 400);
        shell.open();
        setPrinter(null, 1.0);

        // Set up the event loop.
        while (!shell.isDisposed()) {
            if (!shell.getDisplay().readAndDispatch()) {
                // If no more entries in event queue
                shell.getDisplay().sleep();
            }
        }
    }

    /**
     * Sets target printer.
     *
     * @param printer
     */
    void setPrinter(Printer printer, double marginSize) {
        if (printer == null) {
            printer = new Printer(Printer.getDefaultPrinterData());
        }
        this.printer = printer;
        margin = PrintMargin.getPrintMargin(printer, marginSize);
        canvas.redraw();
    }
}
```

A canvas is used to display the print preview. When the target printer or print parameters are changed, the canvas is forced to update.

In the image view application, you add the following code to bring up the print preview dialog:

```
ToolItem itemPrintPreview = new ToolItem(toolBar, SWT.PUSH);

itemPrintPreview.setText("Preview");
itemPrintPreview.addListener(SWT.Selection, new Listener() {
    public void handleEvent(Event event) {
        ImagePrintPreviewDialog dialog =
            new ImagePrintPreviewDialog(ImageViewer.this);
        dialog.open();
    }
});
```

# Text Printing and Pagination

In Chapter 9, you learned how to create a simple text editor that's based on the StyledText control. The text editor enables the user to load text from a file, edit the text, and save the text into a file. Here, you add the print feature to the editor (see Figure 17-6).

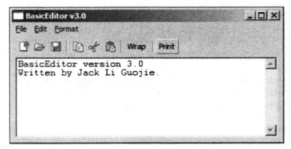

Figure 17-6

When the Print toolbar item is pressed, the application prints the content of the text box to a selected printer. You can either implement the printing feature by yourself or you can simply invoke the print methods of the StyledText class. Here, you learn how to implement text printing from scratch and then how to use existing print methods in the StyledText class.

First, create an Action object and add it to the toolbar:

```
Action actionPrint = new Action("&Print@Ctrl+P") {
    public void run() {
        printText(text.getText());
    }
};

...

toolBarManager.add(new Separator());
toolBarManager.add(actionPrint);
```

When the toolbar item is hit, the printText function is invoked. The following is the implementation of the printText method:

```
int x;
int y;
int lineHeight; // The height of each line.
PrintMargin margins; // Page margins
int pageNumber = 1;
int lineNumber = 1;

void printText(String text) {
    PrintDialog dialog = new PrintDialog(shell);
    PrinterData printerData = dialog.open();
    if(printerData == null)
        return;
    Printer printer = new Printer(printerData);
    if(! printer.startJob("text"))
        return;

    GC gc = new GC(printer);

    margins = PrintMargin.getPrintMargin(printer, 1.0);
```

```
        x = margins.left;
        y = margins.top;

        StringBuffer buffer = new StringBuffer();

        Font font = new Font(printer, "Arial", 12, SWT.NORMAL);
        gc.setFont(font);
        lineHeight = gc.getFontMetrics().getHeight();

        printer.startPage();
        // prints page number at the bottom margin.
        String page = "- " + pageNumber + " -";
        gc.drawString(page, (margins.right - margins.left - gc.textExtent(page).x) / 2
    + margins.left, margins.bottom + gc.textExtent(page).y);

        for(int index = 0; index <text.length();) {
            char c = text.charAt(index);

            switch(c) {
                case '\r':
                    if(index < text.length() - 1 && text.charAt(index + 1) == '\n') {
                        printNewLine(printer, gc, buffer.toString());
                        buffer.setLength(0);
                        index += 2;
                    }
                    break;

                case '\t':
                case ' ':
                    if(gc.textExtent(buffer.toString() + ' ').x > margins.right -
    margins.left) {
                        printNewLine(printer, gc, buffer.toString());
                        buffer.setLength(0);
                    }
                    buffer.append(c);

                    if(index < text.length() - 1 &&
                        (!Character.isWhitespace(text.charAt(index + 1)))) {
                        // Looks ahead a word to see whether the line should wrap here.
                        String word = readWord(text, index + 1);
                        if(gc.textExtent(buffer.toString() + word).x >
                                margins.right - margins.left) {
                            printNewLine(printer, gc, buffer.toString());
                            buffer.setLength(0);
                        }
                    }
                    index += 1;
                    break;

                default:
                    buffer.append(c);
                    index += 1;
            }
```

```
        }

    if(buffer.length() > 0)
        printNewLine(printer, gc, buffer.toString());

    if(y + lineHeight <= margins.bottom)
        printer.endPage();
    printer.endJob();

    gc.dispose();
    font.dispose();
    printer.dispose();
}

/**
 * Prints the new line to page. If there is not enough vertical space,
 * a new page is started.
 * @param printer
 * @param line
 * @param x
 * @param y
 */
void printNewLine(Printer printer, GC gc, String line) {
    System.out.println("Line: " + line);
    if(y + lineHeight > margins.bottom) {
        printer.endPage();
        x = margins.left;
        y = margins.top;

        pageNumber ++;
        lineNumber = 1;

        // prints page number at the bottom margin.
        String page = "- " + pageNumber + " -";
        gc.drawString(page,
                (margins.right - margins.left - gc.textExtent(page).x) / 2 +
                margins.left, margins.bottom + gc.textExtent(page).y);
    }
    gc.drawString(line, x, y);
    y += lineHeight;
}

/**
 * Reads a word from the given text starting from the offset.
 * @param text
 * @param offset
 * @return
 */
String readWord(String text, int offset) {
    StringBuffer sb = new StringBuffer();
    int index = offset;
    char c = 0;

    while(index < text.length()) {
```

```
        c = text.charAt(index);
        if(Character.isWhitespace(c))
            break;

        sb.append(c);
        index += 1;
    }

    return sb.toString();
}
```

When the printText method is invoked, it first prompts the print dialog. If a printer is selected by the user, the GC object for the printer is created and the page margins are set. You might notice that a font is set as the font of the graphics context:

```
Font font = new Font(printer, "Arial", 12, SWT.NORMAL);
gc.setFont(font);
```

The font is created on the printer device instead of the display object (i.e., the computer screen). If you use a font created on the display, the final text output might look strange because the dpi value for the printer is usually different from that of the display.

After the font has been set properly, you iterate each character in the text. If a line is too long to be displayed, it should be wrapped or broken into multiple lines. You use a very simple line-breaking algorithm — if the word next to a white space does not fit into the space that's provided, the line should be broken.

The printNewLine function is used to print out lines on the printer. This function first checks whether there is enough space for a new line. If there is not enough room for a new line, a new page is started. Subsequent lines are then printed on the new page. The page number is printed at the bottom margin of each page. The final printed work is shown in Figure 17-7.

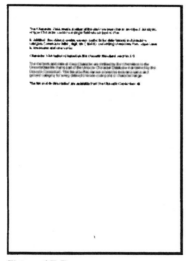

**Figure 17-7**

In addition to implementing your own print procedure, you can simply call one of the `print` methods of the `StyledText` class:

```
public Runnable print(Printer printer)
public void print()
public Runnable print(Printer printer, StyledTextPrintOptions options)
```

The first method creates a `Runnable` object that can be executed to perform the print task on the specified printer. The second method prints the text content on the default printer within the UI thread. The last print method allows you to control the print job with a `StyledTextPrintOptions` object. For example, you can use the following code to print the text content with "SWT" as the page header and the page number as the page footer:

```
StyledTextPrintOptions options = new StyledTextPrintOptions();
options.header = "SWT";
options.footer = "- <page> -";
options.jobName = "Text";

Runnable runnable = text.print(new Printer(), options);
runnable.run();
```

Note that the <page> tag in the footer will be replaced by the page number during printing.

If you need advanced control over the printing from a `StyledText` control, you can use the `printText` method as a starting point to create your own custom printing.

# Summary

Printing is a convenient way to generate a permanent copy of your work. This chapter showed you how to equip your applications with printing support. Beginning with the fundamental process of printing, this chapter covered comprehensive SWT printing topics. You can print images, shapes, and text on the printer through the graphics context object of the printer. Because the screen may have a dpi value that is different from the printer, you should take this issue into consideration when printing objects on the printer. The task of setting page margins is greatly simplified with the utility class that was discussed. Finally, the chapter introduced text printing and pagination.

# 18

# JFace Windows and Dialogs

In this chapter, you learn how to use the JFace window framework (org.eclipse.jface.window) to simplify window creation and management tasks. This chapter also discusses JFace dialogs. JFace provides various dialogs in package org.eclipse.jface.dialogs that enable you to communicate with the user easily. For example, you can use an input dialog to get input from the user and a progress monitor dialog to display the progress of a lengthy operation to the user.

## JFace Windows

In almost every UI application, you need to create and manage one or more windows. In previous chapters, you learned that in order to create a window, you need to create a shell first and then add the menu, toolbar, and other controls to the shell. Finally, you set up the event loop and show the shell. This creation procedure is quite tedious. Fortunately, with the org.eclipse.jface.window package, such window creation and management tasks are greatly simplified. With the JFace window framework, you are freed from performing low-level shell manipulation. For example, instead of coding the event loop, you simply set the block on an open property of a JFace window to run the event loop for the window.

This section first introduces several important classes in the org.eclipse.jface.window package. Then it shows you how to create an application window easily by extending the ApplicationWindow class. With ApplicationWindow, you can run a lengthy operation and display the progress status easily. Finally, management of multiple windows with WindowsManager is briefly discussed.

### org.eclipse.jface.window.Window

The org.eclipse.jface.window.Window class is the superclass of all JFace application window and dialog classes. To create a JFace window, you simply follow these basic steps:

1. Create an instance of a concrete subclass of the `Window` class.
2. Configure the window if necessary, e.g., set the icon image for the window. (Optional)
3. Call the `create` method to create the shell and widget tree. (Optional)
4. Open the shell by invoking the `open` method (the widget tree will be created if it has not been created).

For example, the following code opens a window, as shown in Figure 18-1.

```java
public static void main(String[] args) {
    Window window = new ApplicationWindow(null);
    window.setBlockOnOpen(true);
    int returnStatus = window.open();
}
```

**Figure 18-1**

# Application Windows

The `org.eclipse.jface.window.ApplicationWindow` class represents a high level "main window," and it has built-in support for an optional menu bar, an optional toolbar, an optional cool bar and an optional status line.

Only one constructor is in the `ApplicationWindow` class:

```java
public ApplicationWindow(Shell parentShell)
```

You can pass the parent shell as the argument. If the window is a top-level window, you simply pass `null` to the constructor.

Before opening the window, you can set the block on open behavior through the `setBlockOnOpen` method, which is inherited from the `Window` class:

```java
public void setBlockOnOpen(boolean shouldBlock)
```

If the block on open property is set to `true`, an event loop is run internally so that the `open` method of the `Window` class will not return until the window is closed. For top-level windows and dialogs, you should set this property to `true`. By default, a window does not block on open.

To open a window, you need to invoke the `open` method of the `Window` class:

```java
public int open()
```

The `open` method returns an integer code, which indicates the user's action if the window is a dialog.

You use the `close` method to close a window:

```
public boolean close()
```

The `close` method disposes of the shell.

JFace does not hide the underlying shell control. You can use the `getShell` method of the `Window` class to get the wrapped shell instance:

```
public Shell getShell()
```

The `ApplicationWindow` class is designed to be subclassed. In particular, you need to override one or more of the following methods to customize it:

- ❑ `protected Control createContents(Composite parent)`: If this method is not overridden, by default, a blank `Composite` control is placed on the shell. You place the widget tree creation code in this method. The returned control will be remembered and returned when the `getControl` method is called.

- ❑ `protected MenuManager createMenuManager()`: You override the `createMenuManager` to create a menu manager for this application window.

- ❑ `protected StatusLineManager createStatusLineManager()`: If a status line is desired, you override this method to create one.

- ❑ `protected ToolBarManager createToolBarManager(int style)`: You override the `createToolBarManager` to supply a toolbar manager for this application window.

- ❑ `protected CoolBarManager createCoolBarManager(int style)`: A cool bar manager can be supplied by overriding this method.

The `createContents` method is invoked when the window is about to be created. However, the last four methods in the preceding list will *not* be called unless their corresponding `add` methods are invoked. For example, you need to invoke the `addMenuBar` method to configure this application window to have a menu bar. The complete mapping is described in the following table.

| Item | The Configuration Method | The Supplier Method |
|------|--------------------------|---------------------|
| The menu bar | `addMenuBar()` | `createMenuManager()` |
| The toolbar | `addToolBar(int style)` | `createToolBarManager(int style)` |
| The cool bar | `addCoolBar(int style)` | `createCoolBarManager(int style)` |
| The status line | `addStatusLine()` | `createStatusLineManager()` |

To add an item to the window, you have to override its supplier method and invoke the configuration method.

To become familiar with the ApplicationWindow class, let's create a simple file viewer, as shown in Figure 18-2.

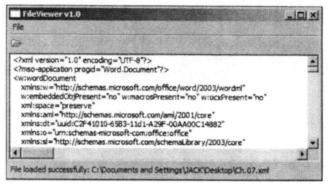

**Figure 18-2**

When the user clicks the toolbar item or the menu item, a file dialog opens. If a file is selected in the dialog, its content is displayed in the text area.

A class named FileViewer is created to extend the ApplicationWindow class:

```java
public class FileViewer extends ApplicationWindow {

    // The text control used to display the file content.
    Text text;
    public FileViewer(Shell parentShell) {
        super(parentShell);
        addMenuBar();
        addStatusLine();
        addToolBar(SWT.FLAT);
    }

    /* (non-Javadoc)
     * @see org.eclipse.jface.window.Window#createContents(Composite)
     */
    protected Control createContents(Composite parent) {
        getShell().setText("FileViewer v1.0");
        setStatus("Ready");

        text = new Text(parent,
                        SWT.MULTI | SWT.BORDER | SWT.H_SCROLL | SWT.V_SCROLL);
        text.setSize(300, 200);
        return text;
    }

    Action actionOpenFile = new Action("Open",
                ImageDescriptor.createFromFile(null, "icons/open.gif")) {
        public void run() {
            FileDialog dialog = new FileDialog(getShell(), SWT.OPEN);
            final String file = dialog.open();
```

```
            if(file != null) {
                try {
                    String content = readFileAsAString(new File(file));
                    text.setText(content);
                    setStatus("File loaded successfully: " + file);
                } catch (IOException e) {
                    e.printStackTrace();
                    setStatus("Failed to load file: " + file);
                }
            }
        }
    }
);

/* (non-Javadoc)
 * @see org.eclipse.jface.window.ApplicationWindow#createMenuManager()
 */
protected MenuManager createMenuManager() {
    MenuManager menuManager = new MenuManager("");

    MenuManager fileMenuManager = new MenuManager("&File");
    fileMenuManager.add(actionOpenFile);

    menuManager.add(fileMenuManager);

    return menuManager;
}

/* (non-Javadoc)
 * @see org.eclipse.jface.window.ApplicationWindow#createStatusLineManager()
 */
protected StatusLineManager createStatusLineManager() {
    return super.createStatusLineManager();
}

/* (non-Javadoc)
 * @see org.eclipse.jface.window.ApplicationWindow#createToolBarManager(int)
 */
protected ToolBarManager createToolBarManager(int style) {
    ToolBarManager toolBarManager = new ToolBarManager(style);
    toolBarManager.add(actionOpenFile);

    return toolBarManager;
}

public static void main(String[] args) {
    ApplicationWindow viewer = new FileViewer(null);
    viewer.setBlockOnOpen(true);
    viewer.open();
}

/**
 * Reads the content of a file into a String.
 * @param file file to be read
 * @return
```

```
 * @throws IOException
 */
public static String readFileAsAString(File file) throws IOException {
    ...

}

}
```

The text control is created in the `createContents` method. The passed argument to this method is the shell wrapped by the application window and the shell has its special layout. You should not replace the shell's layout. An action object is created to represent the file selection and loading process. Then a menu bar and a toolbar are created in the `createMenuManager` method and the `createToolBarManager` method, respectively. The action has been added to both the menu bar and the toolbar. Additionally, a status line is created to display the status at the bottom of the window. To add a special item such as a menu bar or toolbar, you have to invoke the corresponding configuration (`add`) method. In the constructor of the `FileViewer` class, you invoke the corresponding configuration methods for the menu bar, the toolbar, and the status line.

The `main` method creates an instance of the `FileViewer` class, sets block on the open property, and opens the window.

*For more details on menu managers and toolbar managers, please refer to Chapter 9.*

## Running Time-Consuming Operations with Application Windows

Time-consuming procedures, such as file transferring and network downloading, should not be run in the main (UI) thread. (In Chapter 4, you learned how to use separate threads to perform such operations.) By implementing the `IRunnableContext` interface, the `ApplicationWindow` class supports running long-running operations in the main thread or a separate thread, and showing the progress in the status line. Additionally, the user may terminate the operation optionally.

The steps to execute a lengthy operation with an `ApplicationWindow` are as follows:

❑   Creating an `IRunnableWithProgress` object with an `IProgressMonitor` instance to reflect progress

❑   In the `run` method, calling `beginTask` at the start of the lengthy operation

❑   Double each element of work, calling `worked()` on the monitor with an integer to reflect the number of units just completed

❑   Calling `done()` on the monitor when you're finished

Let's extend the file viewer application by adding a feature that counts the number of lines. First, you create an `IRunnableWithProgress` instance to represent the number of lines in the counting procedure:

```
String content;
String lineDelimiter;

IRunnableWithProgress runnableWithProgress = new IRunnableWithProgress() {
```

```java
public void run(IProgressMonitor monitor)
    throws InvocationTargetException, InterruptedException {
    System.out.println("Running from thread: " +
                        Thread.currentThread().getName());

    getShell().getDisplay().syncExec(new Runnable() {
        public void run() {
            content = text.getText();
            lineDelimiter = text.getLineDelimiter();
        }
    });

    monitor.beginTask("Counting total number of lines", content.length());
    int lines = 1;
    for(int i=0; i<content.length(); i++) {
        if(monitor.isCanceled()) {
            // checks whether the operation has been cancelled.
            monitor.done();
            System.out.println("Action cancelled");
            return;
        }

        // Checks the existence of the line delimiter.
        if(i + lineDelimiter.length() < content.length()) {
            if(lineDelimiter.equals(
                content.substring(i, i+lineDelimiter.length()))) {
                lines ++;
            }
        }

        monitor.worked(1);

        // sleeps for 1ms on purpose so that you see the progress clearly.
        Thread.sleep(1);
    }

    monitor.done();
    System.out.println("Total number of lines: " + lines);
    }
};
```

The only method declared in the IRunnableWithProgress interface is the run method. The IProgressMonitor passed as the argument is used to report operation progress. It is likely that the operation is run in a thread different from the main UI thread so the syncExec method is used to access the text control.

The methods in the IProgressMonitor interface that are invoked in the preceding code are as follows:

❑  public void beginTask(String name, int totalWork): This method notifies the progress monitor that the main task is starting. You specify the name of the task and the total work units as the arguments.

❑  public void worked(int work): If certain units of work have been performed, you can use the worked method to notify the progress monitor. The passed argument represents an installment, as opposed to the cumulative amount.

**379**

❏   public void done(): Invoke the done method when the operation is completed.

❏   public boolean isCanceled(): Use this method to check whether the user cancels the current operation.

❏   public void setCanceled(boolean value): To cancel or resume the operation, you can use the setCanceled method.

In the preceding code, if the user cancels the operation, the run method returns immediately. Otherwise, after the total number of lines has been calculated, the number of lines is printed.

The run method of the ApplicationWindow class can be used to execute the IRunnableWithProgress object:

```
public void run(boolean fork, boolean cancelable, IRunnableWithProgress runnable)
        throws InvocationTargetException, InterruptedException
```

To run the operation in a separate thread, set the fork argument to true. If the operation can be canceled by the user, you need to set the cancelable to true so that a cancel button will be displayed next to the progress bar.

To level the user, invoke the run method, wrap it in an action object, and add the action to the menu bar and the toolbar:

```
Action actionCount = new Action("Count", ImageDescriptor.createFromFile(null,
"icons/run.gif")) {
    public void run() {
        try {
            FileViewer.this.run(true, true, runnableWithProgress);
        } catch (InvocationTargetException e) {
            e.printStackTrace();
        } catch (InterruptedException e) {
            e.printStackTrace();
        }
    }
};

...

MenuManager toolsMenuManager = new MenuManager("&Tools");
toolsMenuManager.add(actionCount);
menuManager.add(toolsMenuManager);

...

toolBarManager.add(actionCount);
...
```

When the counting action is invoked, the UI appears, as shown as Figure 18-3.

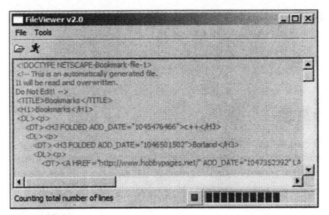

**Figure 18-3**

The operation progress is displayed on a progress bar. The cancel button sits on the right of the progress bar. The user can press the cancel button to cancel the operation. While running the operation, the application window is disabled—you cannot close the window, and the text control on the window is disabled, too.

## Multiple Windows Management with WindowManagers

A window manager is used to remember a group of windows (application windows, dialogs, and so on). A window manager can also contain other window managers. This kind of organization enables you to close all the windows managed (or more accurately, remembered) by a window manager and its sub-window managers.

The two constructors in the WindowManager class are as follows:

```
public WindowManager()
public WindowManager(WindowManager parent)
```

The first constructor creates a top-level window manager, and the second one creates a window manager with another window manager as its parent.

To add a window into a window manager, use the add method:

```
public void add(Window window)
```

Use the remove method to remove a window from a window manager:

```
public final void remove(Window window)
```

*If a window is disposed, it is automatically removed from its window manager.*

To close all the windows managed by a window manager and all of its descendent managers, you use the `close` method of the `WindowManager` class:

```
public boolean close()
```

# JFace Dialogs

In Chapter 12, you learned about SWT built-in dialogs, such as `FileDialog`, `MessageBox`, and so on. You also learned how to create your own custom dialogs. Before creating your own dialog type, you might like to check whether there is a suitable one in the `org.eclipse.jface.dialogs` package. There are a number of dialogs in the `org.eclipse.jface.dialogs` package from which to choose.

The steps to create a dialog are very similar to those to create a window:

1.  Create an instance of a concrete subclass of the `org.eclipse.jface.dialogs.Dialog` class.
2.  Open the dialog (in modal state) by invoking the `open` method.

The following sections show you how to use various JFace dialogs.

## Using MessageDialogs

A message dialog is used to show a message to the user. The only constructor of the `MessageDialog` class is:

```
public MessageDialog(Shell parentShell, String dialogTitle, Image dialogTitleImage,
    String dialogMessage, int dialogImageType, String[] dialogButtonLabels, int
    defaultIndex)
```

You specify the parent shell of this dialog in the `parentShell` parameter. You can set the dialog title and dialog title image in the `dialogTitle` and `dialogTitleImage` parameters, respectively. The message shown on the dialog can be set through the `dialogMessage` parameter. Optionally, you may configure the image displayed along with the message on the dialog with the `dialogImageType` parameter. The following is the list of valid values for the `dialogImageType` parameter:

❑ `MessageDialog.NONE`: You set the dialog image type to NONE to indicate that no image should be displayed on the dialog.

❑ `MessageDialog.ERROR`: If you are displaying an error message, you should set the dialog image type to ERROR so that an error icon will be displayed on the dialog.

❑ `MessageDialog.INFORMATION`: Setting the dialog image type to INFORMATION results in an information icon (such as the letter *i* in a circle) displayed on the dialog.

❑ `MessageDialog.QUESTION`: If you are asking the user a question, you may set the dialog image type to QUESTION to display a question icon on the dialog.

❑ `MessageDialog.WARNING`: To display a warning sign, you set the dialog image type to WARNING.

Below the message and optional dialog image, you can display an array of buttons. You specify the labels for the buttons in the `dialogButtonLabels` parameter. To make a button the default button, you need to specify its index as the value of the `defaultIndex` parameter.

For example, to display the dialog shown in Figure 18-4, you need to create a `MessageDialog` with the following code:

```
MessageDialog dialog =
    new MessageDialog(
        getShell(),
        "Select your favorite Java UI framework",
        null,
        "Which one of the following is your favorite Java UI framework?",
        MessageDialog.QUESTION,
        new String[] { "AWT", "Swing", "SWT/JFace" },
        2);

int answer = dialog.open();

switch (answer) {
    case -1: // if the user closes the dialog without clicking any button.
        System.out.println("No selection");
        break;

    case 0 :
        System.out.println("Your selection is: AWT");
        break;
    case 1 :
        System.out.println("Your selection is: Swing");
        break;
    case 2 :
        System.out.println("Your selection is: SWT/JFace");
        break;

}
```

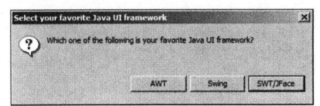

**Figure 18-4**

Three buttons corresponding to three Java UI frameworks are displayed at the bottom of the dialog. The third button is set to be the default button. When the user clicks any button, the `open` method returns the index of the button clicked. If the user disposes of the dialog by pressing the Esc key or hitting the close trim, the value `-1` is returned by the `open` method.

The constructor of the `MessageDialog` class is very powerful; however, it is quite annoying to display a simple message to inform the user with the following tedious code:

```
MessageDialog dialog =
    new MessageDialog(
        getShell(),
        "Message",
        null,
        "This is a message",
        MessageDialog.INFORMATION,
        new String[] { "OK" },
        0);
dialog.open();
```

Fortunately, the `MessageDialog` class provides several class methods to handle situations like that. For example, with the `openInformation` method, displaying the same message is simple:

```
MessageDialog.openInformation(getShell(), "Message", "This is a message");
```

The following table provides a complete list of such utility methods.

| Message Type | Method | Remarks |
|---|---|---|
| Information | MessageDialog.openInformation | This method displays a dialog showing the information message. |
| Question | MessageDialog.openQuestion | This method creates and opens a dialog with two buttons: YES and NO. If the YES button is pressed, Boolean value `true` is returned, `false` otherwise. |
| Warning | MessageDialog.openWarning | This method displays a dialog showing the warning message. |
| Error | MessageDialog.openError | This method displays a dialog showing the error message. |
| Confirm | MessageDialog.openConfirm | Two buttons, OK and Cancel, are displayed on the dialog. The open method returns `true` if the OK button is clicked, `false` otherwise. |

## Using InputDialogs

An input dialog uses a text field to solicit an input string from the user.

The constructor of the `InputDialog` is as follows:

```
public InputDialog(Shell parentShell, String dialogTitle, String dialogMessage,
    String initialValue, IInputValidator validator)
```

The dialog's parent shell, title, and message can be specified in the first three arguments. You have the option to supply the initial value for the text field through the initialValue argument. To allow only a valid string input, you can set a validator for the last argument.

For example, the following code creates the dialog shown in Figure 18-5:

```
IInputValidator validator = new IInputValidator() {
    public String isValid(String newText) {
        if(newText.equalsIgnoreCase("SWT/JFace") ||
                newText.equalsIgnoreCase("AWT") ||
                newText.equalsIgnoreCase("Swing"))
            return null;
        else
            return "The allowed values are: SWT/JFace, AWT, Swing";
    }
};

InputDialog dialog = new InputDialog(getShell(), "Question", "What's your favorite
Java UI framework?", "SWT/JFace", validator);

if(dialog.open() == Window.OK) {
    System.out.println("Your favorite Java UI framework is: " + dialog.getValue());
}else{
    System.out.println("Action cancelled");
}
```

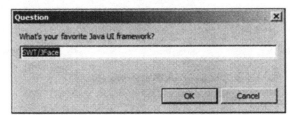

Figure 18-5

An input validator implementing the IInputValidator interface is created first. The isValid method is used to validate the input string. If the input string is valid, the isValid method returns null, or the error message otherwise. This error message will be displayed under the text field on the dialog.

The dialog is created with the validator. If the user clicks OK, the open method returns the value Window.OK and the input string can be obtained through the getValue method of the InputDialog class.

## Using ProgressMonitorDialogs

A progress monitor dialog can be used to execute a long-running operation and display the progress. In the first part of this chapter, you saw how to use application windows to execute time-consuming operations. Alternatively, you can use a ProgressMonitorDialog to perform the execution.

The steps to create and use a progress monitor dialog are as follows:

1. Create an instance of the `PrgressMonitorDialog` class with its constructor `ProgressMonitorDialog(Shell parent)`.

2. Execute the task with the run method: `run(boolean fork, boolean cancelable, IRunnableWithProgress runnable)`.

The following code creates a progress monitor dialog (see Figure 18-6) and executes a simple number counting task:

```
IRunnableWithProgress runnableWithProgress = new IRunnableWithProgress() {
    public void run(IProgressMonitor monitor)
        throws InvocationTargetException, InterruptedException {
        monitor.beginTask("Number counting", 10);
        for(int i=0; i<10; i++) {
            if(monitor.isCanceled()) {
                monitor.done();
                return;
            }

            System.out.println("Count number: " + i);
            monitor.worked(1);
            Thread.sleep(500); // 0.5s.
        }
        monitor.done();
    }
};

ProgressMonitorDialog dialog = new ProgressMonitorDialog(getShell());
try {
    dialog.run(true, true, runnableWithProgress);
} catch (InvocationTargetException e) {
    e.printStackTrace();
} catch (InterruptedException e) {
    e.printStackTrace();
}
```

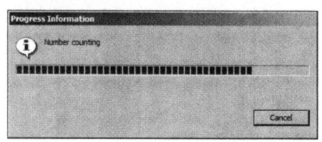

**Figure 18-6**

The user may click the Cancel button to cancel the operation. When the operation is complete, the dialog closes automatically.

# Summary

This chapter introduced you to the JFace windows framework and JFace dialogs. You can use the `ApplicationWindow` class to simplify the task of creating and managing windows. If you need to manage multiple windows, you can use the `WindowManager` class to help you group windows and close all the windows with a single call. Dialogs are special windows that are used for narrow-focused communication with the user. JFace provides several dialogs that you can use to create various dialogs with minimal code. The next chapter covers JFace wizards. These wizards are very useful for guiding the user through the steps to complete complex tasks.

# Part IV: Application Development

# 19

# JFace Wizards

Wizards are great tools to guide the user through tedious tasks. In many other UI toolkits, you have to code a wizard framework. JFace saves you the trouble by providing a solid wizard framework. This chapter introduces you to the JFace wizard framework with a sample application. You learn how to do the following:

❑    Create a wizard

❑    Add wizard pages to a wizard

❑    Run a wizard

❑    Persist dialog settings

## JFace Wizard Basics

Wizards are used heavily in the Eclipse IDE. You use wizards to create your projects and Java classes in Eclipse. The JFace wizard framework provides an effective mechanism to guide the user in completing complex and tedious tasks.

In JFace, a wizard is represented by the IWizard interface. The Wizard class provides an abstract base implementation of the IWizard interface. To create your own wizards, you usually extend the Wizard class instead of implementing the IWizard interface from scratch.

A wizard consists of one or more wizard pages, which are represented by the IWizardPage interface. The WizardPage class provides an abstract implementation of the IWizardPage interface. You can easily create wizard pages by extending the WizardPage class.

In order to run a wizard, you need a *wizard container*. Represented by the IWizardContainer interface, a wizard container is used to display wizard pages and provide a page navigation mechanism. WizardDialog is a ready-to-use wizard container. The layout of a wizard dialog is shown in Figure 19-1. The current wizard page title, description, and image are shown at the top of the dialog. The wizard page content is displayed in the center. If you need to run a time-consuming task, you can optionally configure the dialog to display a progress indicator below the wizard page content. At the bottom of the dialog, there are several navigation buttons that the user can use to navigate among multiple wizard pages.

Building a custom wizard involves the following steps:

1. Subclass the Wizard class, implement addPages, and override methods, such as performFinish.

2. Create wizard pages by subclassing the WizardPage class.

3. Run a wizard in a wizard container.

4. Load and save dialog settings (optional).

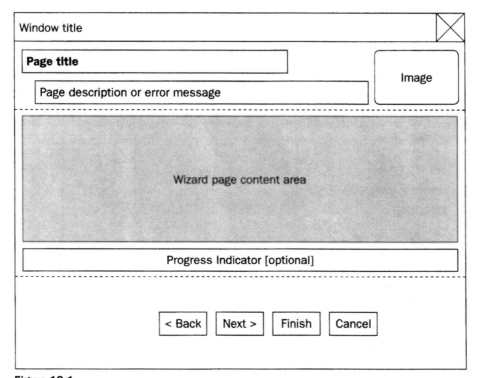

**Figure 19-1**

In this chapter, you learn how to use the wizard framework through a hotel reservation sample application (see Figure 19-2). The hotel reservation wizard gathers the user's reservation details, information about the user, and payment information, and stores all the information in a model data object. The wizard consists of three wizard pages. The first page gathers the basic room reservation details. The second page collects the user's information, such as the user's name, phone number, e-mail address, and so on. The last page queries the user for payment information.

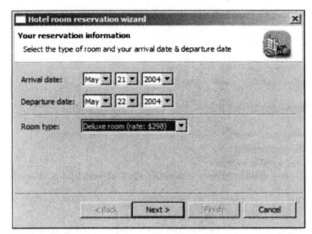

Figure 19-2

# Creating a JFace Wizard

Before creating the wizard, you first construct a class to model the data:

```java
// The data model.
class ReservationData {
    Date arrivalDate;
    Date departureDate;
    int roomType;

    String customerName;
    String customerPhone;
    String customerEmail;
    String customerAddress;

    int creditCardType;
    String creditCardNumber;
    String creditCardExpiration;

    public String toString() {
        StringBuffer sb = new StringBuffer();
        sb.append("** HOTEL ROOM RESERVATION DETAILS *\n");
        sb.append("Arrival date:\t" + arrivalDate.toString() + "\n");
        sb.append("Departure date:\t" + departureDate.toString() + "\n");
        sb.append("Room type:\t" + roomType + "\n");
        sb.append("Customer name:\t" + customerName + "\n");
        sb.append("Customer email:\t" + customerEmail + "\n");
        sb.append("Credit card no.:\t" + creditCardNumber + "\n");

        return sb.toString();
    }
}
```

Then you create the wizard by extending the Wizard class:

```java
public class ReservationWizard extends Wizard {

    // the model object.
    ReservationData data = new ReservationData();

    public ReservationWizard() {

        setWindowTitle("Hotel room reservation wizard");
        setNeedsProgressMonitor(true);
        setDefaultPageImageDescriptor(
                ImageDescriptor.createFromFile(null, "icons/hotel.gif"));

    }


    // Overrides org.eclipse.jface.wizard.IWizard#addPages()
    public void addPages() {
        addPage(new FrontPage());
        addPage(new CustomerInfoPage());
        addPage(new PaymentInfoPage());
    }


    // Overrides org.eclipse.jface.wizard.IWizard#performFinish()
    public boolean performFinish() {
        try {
            // puts the data into a database ...
            getContainer().run(true, true, new IRunnableWithProgress() {
                public void run(IProgressMonitor monitor)
                    throws InvocationTargetException, InterruptedException {
                    monitor.beginTask("Store data", 100);
                    monitor.worked(40);

                    // stores the data, and it may take long time.

                    System.out.println(data);

                    Thread.sleep(2000);
                    monitor.done();
                }
            });
        } catch (InvocationTargetException e) {
            e.printStackTrace();
        } catch (InterruptedException e) {
            e.printStackTrace();
        }

        return true;
    }


    // Overrides org.eclipse.jface.wizard.IWizard#performCancel()
    public boolean performCancel() {
        boolean ans = MessageDialog.openConfirm(getShell(), "Confirmation",
                        "Are you sure to cancel the task?");
```

```
        if(ans)
            return true;
        else
            return false;
    }
 }
```

The model data object is created first. Within the constructor of the class, you call several methods to configure the wizard:

- ❑ public void setWindowTitle(String newTitle): This method sets the window title for the container that hosts this wizard to the specified string.

- ❑ public void setNeedsProgressMonitor(boolean b): The setNeedsProgressMonitor method specifies whether a progress monitor is needed for this wizard. Because we need to execute a time-consuming procedure (storing the model data) later, we configure the wizard with a progress monitor.

- ❑ public void setDefaultPageImageDescriptor(ImageDescriptor imageDescriptor): This method sets the default page image for the wizard. This image descriptor will be used to obtain an image for pages with no image of their own.

The ReservationWizard class overrides three methods from the Wizard class.

## Adding Wizard Pages with addPages()

The addPages method is called before the wizard opens. The Wizard implementation does nothing. In the ReservationWizard class, you override this method to add three wizard pages with the addPage method:

```
public void addPage(IWizardPage page)
```

The addPage method appends the specified wizard page at the end of the page list. Implementation of those wizard page classes is discussed later in the chapter.

## Finish Processing with performFinish()

The performFinish method is invoked when the user clicks the Finish button. Because this method is declared as abstract, you have to implement it. You can return a Boolean flag to indicate whether the finish request is granted or not. If the finish request is accepted (i.e., performFinish returns true), the wizard is closed. Otherwise, the wizard remains open.

In the reservation wizard, the performFinish method tries to store the model data into a database. Because this procedure may take considerable time, it is put into an IRunnableWithProgress object and executed through the wizard container. During the execution, the progress monitor shows the progress. The getContainer method simply returns the container hosting the wizard:

```
public IWizardContainer getContainer()
```

Notice that the Finish button is not always in the enabled status. It is enabled only if the canFinish method (in the Wizard class) returns true:

```
public boolean canFinish()
```

The default implementation of this method returns true only if every wizard page in the wizard is completed. (Wizard page completion is covered later in the chapter.) You can override this method to modify the default behavior.

# Cancel Processing with performCancel()

Similar to the performFinished method, the performCancel method is executed when the Cancel button is clicked. The wizard implementation of the performCancel method simply returns true to indicate that the cancel request is accepted. The ReservationWizard class overrides the performCancel method to display a confirmation dialog to the user. If the user confirms the cancel action, the performCancel method returns true and the wizard closes. Otherwise, the performCancel method returns false and the cancel request is rejected.

The Cancel button is always enabled when the wizard is open.

So far, this chapter had covered the methods used and overridden in the ReservationWizard class. In addition to those methods, the Wizard class provides many methods to access wizard pages.

# Accessing Wizard Pages

The getPageCount method returns the number of pages in the wizard:

```
public int getPageCount()
```

To retrieve all the wizard pages as an array, you can use the getPages method:

```
public IWizardPage[] getPages()
```

The getPage method allows you to get an individual page by its name:

```
public IWizardPage getPage(String name)
```

The first page to be displayed in the wizard can be obtained through the getStartingPage method:

```
public IWizardPage getStartingPage()
```

The getNextPage method returns the successor of the specified wizard page or null if none:

```
public IWizardPage getNextPage(IWizardPage page)
```

Similarly, the getPreviousPage returns the predecessor of the given page or null if none:

```
public IWizardPage getPreviousPage(IWizardPage page)
```

To obtain the currently displayed wizard page from a container, you can use the `getCurrentPage` method of the `IWizardPage` interface:

```
public IWizardPage getCurrentPage()
```

The data model and wizard have been created. The next step is to create all the wizard pages used in the wizard.

# Creating Wizard Pages

The first wizard page (refer to Figure 19-2) gathers basic reservation information—arrival date, departure date, and room type.

The following is the implementation of the first wizard page:

```java
public class FrontPage extends WizardPage {
    Combo comboRoomTypes;

    Combo comboArrivalYear;
    Combo comboArrivalMonth;
    Combo comboArrivalDay;
    Combo comboDepartureYear;
    Combo comboDepartureMonth;
    Combo comboDepartureDay;

    FrontPage() {
        super("FrontPage");
        setTitle("Your reservation information");
        setDescription(
            "Select the type of room and your arrival date & departure date");
    }

    /* (non-Javadoc)
     * @see org.eclipse.jface.dialogs.IDialogPage#createControl(Composite)
     */
    public void createControl(Composite parent) {
        Composite composite = new Composite(parent, SWT.NULL);
        GridLayout gridLayout = new GridLayout(2, false);
        composite.setLayout(gridLayout);

        new Label(composite, SWT.NULL).setText("Arrival date: ");

        Composite compositeArrival = new Composite(composite, SWT.NULL);
        compositeArrival.setLayout(new RowLayout());

        String[] months = new String[]{"Jan", "Feb", "Mar", "Apr", "May", "Jun",
                "Jul", "Aug", "Sep", "Oct", "Nov", "Dec"
        };

        Calendar calendar = new GregorianCalendar(); // today.
```

```
((ReservationWizard)getWizard()).data.arrivalDate = calendar.getTime();

comboArrivalMonth = new Combo(compositeArrival,SWT.BORDER | SWT.READ_ONLY);
for(int i=0; i<months.length; i++)
    comboArrivalMonth.add(months[i]);
comboArrivalMonth.select(calendar.get(Calendar.MONTH));

comboArrivalDay = new Combo(compositeArrival, SWT.BORDER | SWT.READ_ONLY);
for(int i=0; i<31; i++)
    comboArrivalDay.add("" + (i+1));
comboArrivalDay.select(calendar.get(Calendar.DAY_OF_MONTH)-1);

comboArrivalYear = new Combo(compositeArrival, SWT.BORDER | SWT.READ_ONLY);
for(int i=2004; i<2010; i++)
    comboArrivalYear.add("" + i);
comboArrivalYear.select(calendar.get(Calendar.YEAR)-2004);

calendar.add(Calendar.DATE, 1); // tomorrow.
((ReservationWizard)getWizard()).data.departureDate = calendar.getTime();


new Label(composite, SWT.NULL).setText("Departure date: ");

Composite compositeDeparture =
        new Composite(composite, SWT.NULL | SWT.READ_ONLY);
compositeDeparture.setLayout(new RowLayout());

comboDepartureMonth =
        new Combo(compositeDeparture, SWT.NULL | SWT.READ_ONLY);
for(int i=0; i<months.length; i++)
    comboDepartureMonth.add(months[i]);
comboDepartureMonth.select(calendar.get(Calendar.MONTH));

comboDepartureDay =
        new Combo(compositeDeparture, SWT.NULL | SWT.READ_ONLY);
for(int i=0; i<31; i++)
    comboDepartureDay.add("" + (i+1));
comboDepartureDay.select(calendar.get(Calendar.DAY_OF_MONTH)-1);

comboDepartureYear =
        new Combo(compositeDeparture, SWT.NULL | SWT.READ_ONLY);
for(int i=2004; i<2010; i++)
    comboDepartureYear.add("" + i);
comboDepartureYear.select(calendar.get(Calendar.YEAR)-2004);

// draws a line.
Label line = new Label(composite, SWT.SEPARATOR | SWT.HORIZONTAL);

GridData gridData = new GridData(GridData.FILL_HORIZONTAL);
gridData.horizontalSpan = 2;
line.setLayoutData(gridData);

new Label(composite, SWT.NULL).setText("Room type: ");
comboRoomTypes = new Combo(composite, SWT.BORDER | SWT.READ_ONLY);
```

```
            comboRoomTypes.add("Standard room (rate: $198)");
            comboRoomTypes.add("Deluxe room (rate: $298)");
            comboRoomTypes.select(0);

            Listener selectionListener = new Listener() {
                public void handleEvent(Event event) {
                    int arrivalDay = comboArrivalDay.getSelectionIndex() + 1;
                    int arrivalMonth = comboArrivalMonth.getSelectionIndex();
                    int arrivalYear = comboArrivalYear.getSelectionIndex() + 2004;

                    int departureDay = comboDepartureDay.getSelectionIndex() + 1;
                    int departureMonth = comboDepartureMonth.getSelectionIndex();
                    int departureYear = comboDepartureYear.getSelectionIndex() + 2004;

                    setDates(arrivalDay, arrivalMonth, arrivalYear,
                            departureDay, departureMonth, departureYear);
                }
            };

            comboArrivalDay.addListener(SWT.Selection, selectionListener);
            comboArrivalMonth.addListener(SWT.Selection, selectionListener);
            comboArrivalYear.addListener(SWT.Selection, selectionListener);
            comboDepartureDay.addListener(SWT.Selection, selectionListener);
            comboDepartureMonth.addListener(SWT.Selection, selectionListener);
            comboDepartureYear.addListener(SWT.Selection, selectionListener);

            comboRoomTypes.addListener(SWT.Selection, new Listener() {
                public void handleEvent(Event event) {
                    ((ReservationWizard)getWizard()).data.roomType =
                            comboRoomTypes.getSelectionIndex();
                }
            });

            setControl(composite);
    }

    // validates the dates and update the model data object.
    private void setDates(int arrivalDay, int arrivalMonth, int arrivalYear, int
departureDay, int departureMonth, int departureYear) {
            Calendar calendar = new GregorianCalendar();
            calendar.set(Calendar.DAY_OF_MONTH, arrivalDay);
            calendar.set(Calendar.MONTH, arrivalMonth);
            calendar.set(Calendar.YEAR, arrivalYear);

            Date arrivalDate = calendar.getTime();

            calendar.set(Calendar.DAY_OF_MONTH, departureDay);
            calendar.set(Calendar.MONTH, departureMonth);
            calendar.set(Calendar.YEAR, departureYear);

            Date departureDate = calendar.getTime();

            System.out.println(arrivalDate + " - " + departureDate);
```

```
        if(! arrivalDate.before(departureDate)) { // arrival date is before dep.
date.
            setErrorMessage("The arrival date is not before the departure date");
            setPageComplete(false);
        }else{
            setErrorMessage(null); // clear error message.
            setPageComplete(true);
            ((ReservationWizard)getWizard()).data.arrivalDate = arrivalDate;
            ((ReservationWizard)getWizard()).data.departureDate = departureDate;
        }
    }
}
```

The FrontPage class extends the WizardPage class and overrides the createControl method.

The createControl method will be called when the wizard is created. Within this method, the widget tree is created. Also, you call the setControl method to set the top-level control for this page. Selection event listeners are registered for the combos on the page. When an element in a combo is selected, the corresponding property in the model data object is updated. For arrival and departure dates, you use a function named setDates to validate the input and update the model object, if necessary.

In case of error (for example, the user sets the arrival data after the departure date), setErrorMessage is used to notify the wizard container to display an error message (see Figure 19-3):

```
public void setErrorMessage(String newMessage)
```

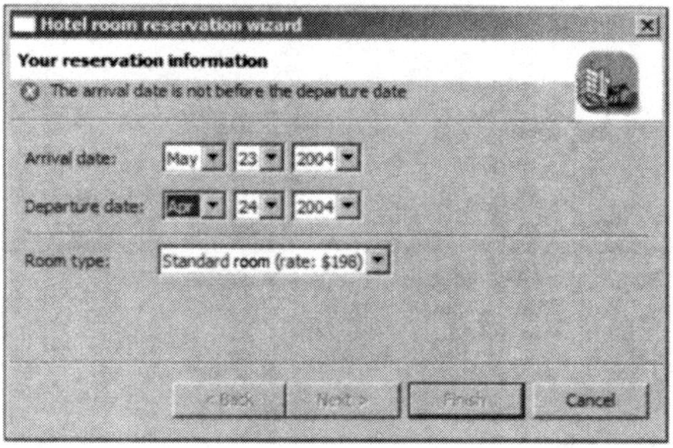

**Figure 19-3**

To remove the error message, you can call setErrorMessage with null as the argument.

In order to let the user resolve the error before proceeding to the next page or clicking the Finish button, you set the completion status of this page to true:

```
public void setPageComplete(boolean complete)
```

You can check the completion status by using the isPageCompleted method:

```
public boolean isPageComplete()
```

The Next button is enabled only if canFlipToNextPage returns true:

```
public boolean canFlipToNextPage()
```

The WizardPage implementation of this method returns true only when the page is completed and the next page exists. You may override this method to modify this behavior.

In the constructor of the FrontPage class, you called several methods to configure the wizard page. There are several methods that you can use to configure the wizard pages:

- ❑ public void setTitle(String title): The setTitle method sets the title for this wizard page. The title of the page will be displayed at the top of the container (refer to Figure 19-1).

- ❑ public void setDescription(String description): This method provides a description for this wizard page.

- ❑ public void setMessage(String newMessage, int newType): The setMessage method allows you to set the message for this page and specify the message type. Valid values for message type are: IMessageProvider.NONE, IMessageProvider.INFORMATION, IMessageProvider.WARNING, and IMessageProvider.ERROR. The message will be displayed under the title of the page.

- ❑ public void setErrorMessage(String newMessage): This method sets the error message for the wizard page.

- ❑ public void setImageDescriptor(ImageDescriptor image): This method sets a custom image for the wizard page. Otherwise, the default image for this wizard will be used if it exists.

The two other wizard pages, CustomerInfoPage and PaymentInfoPage, can be implemented in similar ways.

# Running a Wizard

You've created the wizard and added wizard pages. Now you are ready to run it in a wizard container. The following code shows the reservation wizard in a WizardDialog:

```
ReservationWizard wizard = new ReservationWizard();
WizardDialog dialog = new WizardDialog(getShell(), wizard);
dialog.setBlockOnOpen(true);
dialog.open();
```

First, an instance of the ReservationWizard class is created. The wizard instance is then used to create a WizardDialog object. After configuring the dialog, you bring the dialog up by calling its open method.

After the wizard dialog is open, you can then fill in necessary information and navigate among wizard pages using the Back and Next buttons. After entering all the required information correctly, you can finish your reservation by clicking Finish or you can cancel the task by clicking Cancel.

# Loading and Saving Dialog Settings

If the user uses a wizard regularly, have the wizard *remember* some dialog settings so that the user does not have to key in certain information repeatedly. In the hotel reservation dialog, customer information such as name, phone number, and e-mail address should be saved after the wizard is closed and loaded when the wizard is opened again.

The JFace wizard framework has built-in support for dialog setting persistence. The IDialogSettings interface represents a storage mechanism for making settings persistent. You can store a collection of key-value pairs in such stores. The key must be a string, and the values can be either a string or an array of strings. If you need to store other primitive types, such as int and double, you store them as strings and use some convenient functions declared in the interface to perform conversion. The DialogSettings class is a concrete implementation of the IDailogSettings interface. A DialogSettings store persists the settings in an XML file.

Usually, the dialog settings should be loaded before the wizard is opened and they should be saved when the wizard is closed. The following code is used in the sample wizard to load and save dialog settings:

```
public class ReservationWizard extends Wizard {

    static final String DIALOG_SETTING_FILE = "userInfo.xml";

    static final String KEY_CUSTOMER_NAME = "customer-name";
    static final String KEY_CUSTOMER_EMAIL = "customer-email";
    static final String KEY_CUSTOMER_PHONE = "customer-phone";
    static final String KEY_CUSTOMER_ADDRESS = "customer-address";

    // the model object.
    ReservationData data = new ReservationData();

    public ReservationWizard() {
        setWindowTitle("Hotel room reservation wizard");
        setNeedsProgressMonitor(true);
        setDefaultPageImageDescriptor(ImageDescriptor.createFromFile(null,
"icons/hotel.gif"));

        DialogSettings dialogSettings = new DialogSettings("userInfo");
        try {
            // loads existing settings if any.
            dialogSettings.load(DIALOG_SETTING_FILE);
        } catch (IOException e) {
            e.printStackTrace();
        }

        setDialogSettings(dialogSettings);

    }


    /* (non-Javadoc)
     * @see org.eclipse.jface.wizard.IWizard#performFinish()
     */
    public boolean performFinish() {
```

```
        if(getDialogSettings() != null) {
            getDialogSettings().put(KEY_CUSTOMER_NAME, data.customerName);
            getDialogSettings().put(KEY_CUSTOMER_PHONE, data.customerPhone);
            getDialogSettings().put(KEY_CUSTOMER_EMAIL, data.customerEmail);
            getDialogSettings().put(KEY_CUSTOMER_ADDRESS, data.customerAddress);
            try {
                // Saves the dialog settings into the specified file.
                getDialogSettings().save(DIALOG_SETTING_FILE);
            } catch (IOException e1) {
                e1.printStackTrace();
            }
        }

        ...

    return true;
    }
    ...
}
```

In the preceding list, code in bold is the code inserted to support dialog setting persistence. A `DialogSettings` object is created with the section name `userInfo`. The `load` method of the `DialogSettings` class is used to load settings from an XML file:

```
public void load(String fileName) throws IOException
```

After the `DialogSettings` instance is created and loaded with existing settings, the `setDialogSettings` method of the `Wizard` class is invoked to register the dialog settings instance to the wizard:

```
public void setDialogSettings(IDialogSettings settings)
```

When the `DialogSettings` instance is registered, you can access it from wizard pages easily with the `getDialogSettings` method of the `WizardPage` class.

Finally, the dialog settings are saved to the file before the wizard closes with the `save` method of the `DialogSettings` class. The data stored in the XML file looks like the following:

```
<?xml version="1.0" encoding="UTF-8"?>
<section name="userInfo">
    <item key="customer-name" value="Jack"/>
    <item key="customer-phone" value="(++65) 9488 82xx"/>
    <item key="customer-email" value="jack@asprise.com"/>
    <item key="customer-address" value="No. 50 ..."/>
</section>
```

Here is the code to obtain persisted dialog settings and use them to fill the UI fields in the `CustomerInfoPage` class:

```
public class CustomerInfoPage extends WizardPage {
    Text textName;
    Text textPhone;
    Text textEmail;
```

```
    Text textAddress;

public CustomerInfoPage() {
    super("CustomerInfo");
    setTitle("Customer Information");

    setPageComplete(false);
}

/*
 * (non-Javadoc)
 *
 * @see org.eclipse.jface.dialogs.IDialogPage#createControl(Composite)
 */
public void createControl(Composite parent) {
    Composite composite = new Composite(parent, SWT.NULL);
    composite.setLayout(new GridLayout(2, false));

    ...

    if (getDialogSettings() != null) {
            textName.setText(
                getDialogSettings().get(
                    ReservationWizard.KEY_CUSTOMER_NAME));
            textPhone.setText(
                getDialogSettings().get(
                    ReservationWizard.KEY_CUSTOMER_PHONE));
            textEmail.setText(
                getDialogSettings().get(
                    ReservationWizard.KEY_CUSTOMER_EMAIL));
            textAddress.setText(
                getDialogSettings().get(
                    ReservationWizard.KEY_CUSTOMER_ADDRESS));

    }

    setControl(composite);
}

private boolean validDialogSettings() {
    if(getDialogSettings().get(ReservationWizard.KEY_CUSTOMER_NAME) == null ||
    getDialogSettings().get(ReservationWizard.KEY_CUSTOMER_ADDRESS)== null||
    getDialogSettings().get(ReservationWizard.KEY_CUSTOMER_EMAIL)== null ||
    getDialogSettings().get(ReservationWizard.KEY_CUSTOMER_PHONE) == null)
        return false;
    return true;
}
}
```

In the preceding code, if a specific record is available in the dialog settings store, it is used to fill the corresponding text field.

# Summary

You should now know how to create a wizard, add wizard pages to it, and run it. The JFace wizard framework greatly simplifies the task of creating wizards. There are many such useful frameworks in JFace. The next chapter discusses JFace text, which is another important JFace framework.

# Creating a Text Editor with JFace Text

The JFace text framework provides numerous functionalities to enable developers to create, display, and edit text documents. This chapter provides a brief overview of the JFace text framework and then shows you how to create a basic, custom text editor with JFace text. Then you learn how to extend and improve the functionality of the custom text editor by adding two add-ons: content assist and syntax highlighting.

## Overview of the JFace Text Framework

This section provides an overview of the JFace text framework. First, it surveys the packages of the JFace text framework. After that, I discuss important classes and show how they fit into the MVC scenario.

### JFace Text Package Organization

The classes contained in the JFace text framework are organized into the following packages:

- ❏ `org.eclipse.jface.text`
- ❏ `org.eclipse.jface.text.contentassist`
- ❏ `org.eclipse.jface.text.formatter`
- ❏ `org.eclipse.jface.text.information`
- ❏ `org.eclipse.jface.text.presentation`
- ❏ `org.eclipse.jface.text.reconciler`

- ❑   org.eclipse.jface.text.rules
- ❑   org.eclipse.jface.text.source
- ❑   org.eclipse.ui.editors.text
- ❑   org.eclipse.ui.texteditor

The org.eclipse.jface.text package is the main package, which provides a framework for creating, displaying, and manipulating text documents. The org.eclipse.jface.text.contentassist, org.eclipse.jface.text.formatter, org.eclipse.jface.text.information, org.eclipse .jface.text.presentation, and org.eclipse.jface.text.reconciler packages provide various add-ons for a text viewer. The org.eclipse.jface.text.rules package contains classes that handle rule-based text scanning. The org.eclipse.jface.text.source package provides utility classes handling text annotations. Finally, the two subpackages of the org.eclipse.ui package provide many ready-to-use text editors.

When programming JFace text, you need to add the following jar files into your Java path:

- ❑   $ECLIPSE_HOME/plugins/org.eclipse.jface.text_x.x.x/jfacetext.jar
- ❑   $ECLIPSE_HOME/plugins/org.eclipse.text_x.x.x/text.jar
- ❑   $ECLIPSE_HOME/plugins/org.eclipse.ui.editors_x.x.x/editors.jar
- ❑   $ECLIPSE_HOME/plugins/org.eclipse.ui.workbench.texteditor_x.x.x/
     texteditor.jar

## Models, Views, and Controllers in JFace Text Framework

As mentioned in Chapter 2, the JFace text framework is model-view-controller based. Within the JFace text framework, a text document is modeled as an IDocument (model). To view or edit an IDocument document, you need an ITextViewer (controller), which turns a StyledText widget (view) into a document-based text component. Usually, you do not have to implement the IDocument and ITextViewer interfaces from scratch because the framework provides many abstract as well as concrete implementations of these interfaces. Built on ITextViewer and its descendant classes, many editor-related classes in the org.eclipse.ui.texteditor and org.eclipse.ui.editors.text packages also act in the controller role. Such classes include AbstractTextEditor and TextEditor, which act as the controller and manage the view (through ITextViewer) and the model.

All of these classes are illustrated in Figure 20-1.

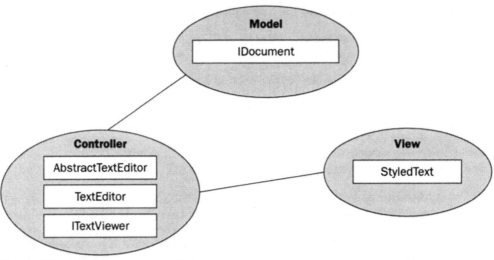

Figure 20-1

## Model-Related Classes

Classes used to represent the model in MVC are as follows.

### IDocument, AbstractDocument, Document

The IDocument interface represents text providing support for text manipulation, partition, search, and document change event notification. You use the setContent method to set the content of the document:

```
public void set(String text)
```

It's very important to understand *document partitioning*. A partition is a certain part of the document. The whole document can be viewed as a sequence of non-overlapping partitions. The following XML document is a simple example:

```
<!-- Information about the author of this book -->
<author>
    <name>Jack Li Guojie</name>
</author>
```

You can partition it into a comment partition and several XML tag partitions. One of the advantages of document partitioning is that you can manipulate partitions in different ways according to their types. For example, you might set different foreground colors for a comment partition and an XML tag partition. The process of dividing a document into non-overlapping partitions is called document partitioning. Usually, you need a *document partitioner* to perform the task. You use the following method to set a partitioner for a document:

```
public void setDocumentPartitioner(IDocumentPartitioner partitioner)
```

**409**

You learn more details about document partitioning in the following section.

The JFace text framework provides several classes implementing the IDocument interface — for example, AbstractDocument and Document. These classes provide functions such as text storing and document management.

### IDocumentPartitioner, IPartitionTokenScanner, DefaultPartitioner

An IDocumentPartitioner is capable of dividing a document into a set of disjointed partitions. A partition is represented by the ITypedRegion interface. The ITypedRegion interface defines the content type, offset (to the beginning of the document), and the length of a partition. Once the document changes, the document partitioner is invoked to update the partition.

In most cases, a document partitioner uses a scanner to scan the document from the beginning to the end to perform partitioning. Such a scanner is represented by the IPartitionTokenScanner interface. A partition token scanner returns tokens representing partitions. The RuleBasedPartitionScanner class is a concrete implementation of the IPartitionTokenScanner interface. A rule-based partition scanner performs document partitioning according to the specified predicate rules. For example, the following code creates a rule-based partition scanner that is capable of scanning for XML comment partitions:

```
String XML_COMMENT = "XML Comment";
IToken xmlComment = new Token(JNLP_COMMENT);
IPredicateRule[] rules = new IPredicateRule[1];

rules[0] = new MultiLineRule("<!--", "-->", XML_COMMENT);

RuleBasedPartitionScanner scanner = new RuleBasedPartitionScanner();
scanner.setPredicateRules(rules);
```

Now you can use the scanner to build a document partitioner with the DefaultPartitioner class:

```
IDocumentPartitioner partitioner =
                new DefaultPartitioner(scanner, new String[]{XML_COMMENT});
```

The scanner built before is used as the first argument of the DefaultPartitioner constructor. The second argument specifies all the legal content types supported by the scanner. In our case, the XML comment type is the only content type. Now, you can use the setDocumentPartitioner method of the IDocument interface to set the document partitioner.

## Controller-Related Classes

Classes used as the controller in MVC include the following.

### ITextViewer, TextViewer

An ITextViewer enables a text widget to support model documents mentioned in the preceding subsection. You can register various listeners on a text viewer to listen for text change events. A text viewer supports a set of plugins: undo manager, double-click behavior, auto indentation, and text hover. Implementing the ITextViewer is complicated and error prone; usually, you should use or extend classes implementing the ITextViewer class in the framework. The TextViewer class is a concrete implementation of the ITextViewer interface.

## ISourceViewer, SourceViewer, SourceViewerConfiguration

The ISourceViewer interface extends the ITextViewer interface by providing visual annotation support, visual range indication, and explicit configuration support. The SourceViewer class provides a concrete implementation of the ISourceViewer interface. A SourceViewer uses a small strip shown on the left of the viewer as the annotation presentation area and a small strip shown on the right of the viewer as the overview presentation area.

The SourceViewerConfiguration class bundles all the configuration options for a source viewer. You can pass an instance of this class to the configure method of ISouceViewer to configure a source viewer. Configurations bundled in the SourceViewerConfiguration class include:

- ❏ **Annotation hover:** Represented by IAnnotationHover, provides the information to be displayed on a hover pop-up window that appears over the presentation area of annotations. The default value is null.

- ❏ **Auto indentation strategy:** Represented by IAutoIndentStrategy, specifies how to perform auto indentation when manipulating text of certain type. By default, an instance of DefaultAutoIndentStrategy is returned.

- ❏ **Content assist:** Represented by IContentAssistant, provides support on interactive content completion. The default value is null.

- ❏ **Content formatter:** Represented by IContentFormatter, formats ranges within the document. The default value is null.

- ❏ **Double-click strategy:** Represented by ITextDoubleClickStrategy, defines the reaction of a text viewer to mouse double-click event. By default, an instance of DefaultTextDoubleClickStrategy is returned.

- ❏ **Information control creator:** Represented by IInformationControlCreator, is factory-creating information controls for the given source viewer. By default, an instance of DefaultInformationControl is returned.

- ❏ **Information presenter:** Represented by IInformationPresenter, determines and shows information requested for the current cursor position. The default value is null.

- ❏ **Overview annotation hover:** Represented by IAnnotationHover, provides information to be shown in a hover pop-up window when requested for the overview ruler of the source viewer. By default, the implementation returns the general annotation hover.

- ❏ **Presentation reconciler:** Represented by IPresentationReconciler, defines and maintains the representation of a text viewer's document in the presence of changes applied to the document. The default value is null.

- ❏ **Model reconciler:** Represented by IReconciler, defines and maintains a model of the content in the presence of changes applied to the document. The default value is null.

- ❏ **Tab width:** Defines the visual width of the tab character, and the default value is 4.

- ❏ **Text hover:** Represented by ITextHover, provides the information to be shown in a text hover pop-up window when requested for a certain content type. The default value is null.

- ❏ **Undo manager:** Represented by IUndoManager, monitors the text viewer and keeps a history of the changes applied to the viewer. By default, an instance of DefaultUndoManager with history length equal to 25 is used.

To modify a default configuration, you have to extend the SourceViewerConfiguration class and re-implement the corresponding get method. Later in this chapter, you will see how to equip an editor with a content assistant by configuring a subclass of SourceViewerConfiguration to the editor.

### AbstractTextEditor, TextEditor, IDocumentProvider

An AbstractTextEditor controls and manages the source viewer and the document.

The source viewer (represented by SourceViewer) is created and maintained by an AbstractTextEditor. Thus, you cannot set the source viewer for the text editor. However, with the SourceViewerConfiguration class, you can configure the source viewer wrapped by the text editor with the following method:

```
protected void setSourceViewerConfiguration(SourceViewerConfiguration
configuration)
```

Note that the setSourceViewerConfiguration method is protected; you need to call it in a subclass of the AbstractTextEditor class.

An AbstractTextEditor requests a document through a document provider. A document provider is represented by the IDocumentProvider interface, which maps between domain elements and documents. A text editor employs document providers to bridge the gap between input elements and documents. For example, the FileDocumentProvider is capable of providing documents from file resources. A text editor may request a document from a document provider through the getDocument method of the IDocumentProvider interface:

```
public IDocument getDocument(Object element)
```

In the simplest case, a text editor invokes the getDocument method with a file as the argument, and the document provider retrieves the file content and returns a document based on it.

The TextEditor class is a full-fledged implementation of the AbstractTextEditor class. You can easily create your own custom editors by extending the TextEditor class.

So far, you have learned a lot about a number of classes and interfaces. In the next section, you learn how to use those classes to create a custom editor.

# Creating a Basic Custom Editor

Here you create a custom editor for Java Network Launching Protocol (JNLP) files. Java Web Start technology relies on JNLP files for application provisioning, runtime configuration, and so on. For more details on Java Web Start and JNLP files, refer to Chapter 3. This JNLP editor enables the user to create and edit JNLP files. Additionally, it supports syntax highlighting, content assist, and content formatting (see Figure 20-2).

**Figure 20-2**

First, create the JNLPEditor class by extending the TextEditor class:

```
public class JNLPEditor extends TextEditor {

    private ColorManager colorManager;

    public JNLPEditor() {
        super();
        colorManager = new ColorManager();
        // setSourceViewerConfiguration(new JNLPConfiguration(colorManager));
        setDocumentProvider(new JNLPDocumentProvider());
    }

    public void dispose() {
        colorManager.dispose();
        super.dispose();
    }

}
```

Note that the ColorManager class is used to manage the creation and disposal of various colors, which will be used when you implement the syntax highlighting feature. For now, because you are implementing only a plain text editor without advanced features such as content assist, you do not need to set a custom SourceViewerConfiguration for the source viewer. The setDocumentProvider method is called to set an instance of JNLPDocumentProvider as the document provider for this editor.

Here is the implementation of the JNLPDocumentProvider class:

```java
public class JNLPDocumentProvider extends FileDocumentProvider {

    protected IDocument createDocument(Object element) throws CoreException {
        IDocument document = super.createDocument(element);
        if (document != null) {
            IDocumentPartitioner partitioner =
                new DefaultPartitioner(
                    new JNLPPartitionScanner(),
                    new String[] {
                        JNLPPartitionScanner.JNLP_TAG,
                        JNLPPartitionScanner.JNLP_COMMENT });
            partitioner.connect(document);
            document.setDocumentPartitioner(partitioner);
        }
        return document;
    }
}
```

The JNLPDocumentProvider class extends the FileDocumentProvider class. A FileDocumentProvider
loads a file into an IDocument instance through the createDocument method. Next, you set a document
partitioner for this document. The document partitioner is created from a scanner, JNLPPartitionScanner.

The following code displays the JNLPPartitionScanner class:

```java
public class JNLPPartitionScanner extends RuleBasedPartitionScanner {
    public final static String JNLP_COMMENT = "JNLP_COMMENT";
    public final static String JNLP_TAG = "JNLP_TAG";

    public JNLPPartitionScanner() {

        IToken comment = new Token(JNLP_COMMENT);
        IToken tag = new Token(JNLP_TAG);

        IPredicateRule[] rules = new IPredicateRule[2];

        rules[0] = new MultiLineRule("<!--", "-->", comment);
        rules[1] = new TagRule(tag);

        setPredicateRules(rules);
    }
}

class TagRule extends MultiLineRule {

    public TagRule(IToken token) {
        super("<", ">", token);
    }

    protected boolean sequenceDetected(
        ICharacterScanner scanner,
        char[] sequence,
        boolean eofAllowed) {
```

```
        int c = scanner.read();
        if (sequence[0] == '<') {
            if (c == '?') {
                // aborts in case of a processing instruction
                scanner.unread();
                return false;
            }
            if (c == '!') {
                scanner.unread();
                // aborts in case of a comment
                return false;
            }
        } else if (sequence[0] == '>') {
            scanner.unread();
        }
        return super.sequenceDetected(scanner, sequence, eofAllowed);
    }
}
```

The `JNLPPartitionScanner` is created as a subclass of the `RuleBasedPartitionScanner`.
`JNLPPartitionScanner` is capable of detecting two kinds of partitions: JNLP comments and JNLP tags.
A `MultipleLineRule` detects patterns beginning with a given sequence and ending with another given
sequent, which may span multiple lines. The first rule is created with the following statement:

```
rules[0] = new MultiLineRule("<!--", "-->", comment)
```

This rule means that a comment starts with `<!--` and ends with `-->`. As for the tag rule, a tag should
begin with `<` and end with `>`. However, entries such as `<!-- comment -->` and `<?xml ... ?>` are not
valid tags. You extend the `MultiLineRule` class and override the `sequenceDetected` method to
exclude such invalid tags.

Now you are ready to run the JNLP editor. You can create and edit JNLP files using the editor. Next, you
modify the JNLP editor with syntax highlighting.

# Syntax Highlighting

The steps to equip the JNLP editor with syntax highlighting are as follows:

1. Create a custom source viewer configuration class by extending the
   `SourceViewerConfiguration` class.

2. Override the `getPresentationReconciler` method to return a proper
   `IPresentationReconciler` object.

3. Configure an instance of this custom source viewer configuration to the editor through the
   `setSourceViewerConfiguration` method of the `TextEditor` class.

Step 1 and Step 3 require minimum effort. Let's focus on Step 2. An `IPresentationReconciler` defines
and maintains the representation of a text viewer's document in the presence of changes applied to the
document. The presentation reconciler keeps track of changes. It sends each change to *presentation damagers*

to compute damages and passes these damages to *presentation repairers* to construct text presentations. By applying the newly constructed text presentations, the presentation reconciler maintains the text viewer and the document synchronized.

A presentation damager is represented by the `IPresentationDamager` interface and a presentation repairer is represented by the `IPresentationRepairer` interface. The damage can be computed through the `getDamageRegion` method of the `IPresentationDamager` interface. To rebuild a damaged region, the presentation reconciler calls the `createPresentation` method of the `IPresentationDamager`. A presentation damager and repairer pair is assumed to be specific for a particular document content type (partition type).

The presentation reconciler implementation for the JNLP editor is as follows:

```java
public class JNLPConfiguration extends SourceViewerConfiguration {
    private ColorManager colorManager = new ColorManager();

    public JNLPConfiguration(ColorManager colorManager) {
        this.colorManager = colorManager;
    }

    PresentationReconciler reconciler;

    public IPresentationReconciler getPresentationReconciler(
                                        ISourceViewer sourceViewer) {
        if(reconciler != null)
            return reconciler;

        reconciler = new PresentationReconciler();


        // 1) Damager and repairer for JNLP tags.
        RuleBasedScanner scanner = new RuleBasedScanner();

        IToken stringColor =
            new Token(
              new
                TextAttribute(colorManager.getColor(IJNLPColorConstants.STRING)));

        IRule[] rules = new IRule[2];

        // the rule for double quotes
        rules[0] = new SingleLineRule("\"", "\"", stringColor, '\\');
        // The white space rule.
        IWhitespaceDetector whitespaceDetector = new IWhitespaceDetector() {
            public boolean isWhitespace(char c) {
                return (c == ' ' || c == '\t' || c == '\n' || c == '\r');
            }
        };

        rules[1] = new WhitespaceRule(whitespaceDetector);

        scanner.setRules(rules);
        scanner.setDefaultReturnToken(
```

```
            new Token(
                new TextAttribute(
                    colorManager.getColor(IJNLPColorConstants.TAG))));

    DefaultDamagerRepairer dr =
        new DefaultDamagerRepairer(scanner);

    reconciler.setDamager(dr, JNLPPartitionScanner.JNLP_TAG);
    reconciler.setRepairer(dr, JNLPPartitionScanner.JNLP_TAG);

    // 2) Damager and repairer for JNLP default content type.
    IToken procInstr =
        new Token(
            new TextAttribute(
                colorManager.getColor(IJNLPColorConstants.PROC_INSTR)));

    rules = new IRule[2];
    // the rule for processing instructions
    rules[0] = new SingleLineRule("<?", "?>", procInstr);
    // the rule for generic whitespace.
    rules[1] = new WhitespaceRule(whitespaceDetector);


    scanner = new RuleBasedScanner();
    scanner.setRules(rules);
    scanner.setDefaultReturnToken(
    new Token(
        new TextAttribute(
            colorManager.getColor(IJNLPColorConstants.DEFAULT))));

    dr = new DefaultDamagerRepairer(scanner);
    reconciler.setDamager(dr, IDocument.DEFAULT_CONTENT_TYPE);
    reconciler.setRepairer(dr, IDocument.DEFAULT_CONTENT_TYPE);

    return reconciler;
    }

        ...

}
```

First, you construct an instance of `PresentationReconciler` if it does not exist yet. Then you try to create a damager and repairer pair for the JNLP tag content type. Basically, you want to highlight a tag using the color blue and highlight the strings within the tag using green. A rule-based scanner is created to scan the tag for strings (it should be highlighted in green) and white space (no color). You have seen how a partition scanner returns the partition type as a string. Here the rule-based scanner returns the color (wrapped in a `TextAttribute` object) used to highlight the text. The following rule

```
 IToken stringColor = new Token(
        new TextAttribute(colorManager.getColor(IJNLPColorConstants.STRING)));
```

```
rules[0] = new SingleLineRule("\"", "\"", stringColor, '\\');
```

**417**

states that the double quoted strings within tags should be highlighted in a certain color (green). After setting rules for the scanner, you set the default return token for the scanner with the `setDefaultReturnToken` method:

```
scanner.setDefaultReturnToken(new Token(
        new TextAttribute(colorManager.getColor(IJNLPColorConstants.TAG))));
```

The preceding code instructs the presentation that text within a tag (other than strings and white spaces) should appear in a special color to identify the tag (blue).

Now you are ready to create the pair and register the pair to the reconciler:

```
DefaultDamagerRepairer dr = new DefaultDamagerRepairer(scanner);

reconciler.setDamager(dr, JNLPPartitionScanner.JNLP_TAG);
reconciler.setRepairer(dr, JNLPPartitionScanner.JNLP_TAG);
```

The `DefaultDamagerRepairer` class is a standard implementation of a syntax-driven presentation damager and repairer. It uses a token scanner to determine the damage and repair presentation. After an instance of `DefaultDamagerRepairer` is created with the scanner constructed previously, you register the pair for JNLP tag content type; if a JNLP tag partition changes, the damager and repairer are used to handle the change and rebuild the presentation.

Similarly, you construct a damager and repairer pair and register it to the presentation reconciler for the default content type.

After the `getPresentationReconciler` method is properly implemented, you set the source viewer configuration for the JNLP editor with an instance of `JNLPConfiguration`:

```
public class JNLPEditor extends TextEditor {
    private ColorManager colorManager;

    public JNLPEditor() {
        super();
        colorManager = new ColorManager();
        setSourceViewerConfiguration(new JNLPConfiguration(colorManager));
        setDocumentProvider(new JNLPDocumentProvider());
    }

    ...
}
```

If you run the editor now, you will find that documents are highlighted, and as you change the content, the syntax highlighting changes accordingly.

# Providing Content Assistance

In the previous section, you learned how to equip the JNLP editor with syntax highlighting. In this section, you learn how to add another advanced feature to the editor: content assistant. Content assistant increases the user's productivity by automatically inserting appropriate text and reducing typographical errors (typos).

As you saw with syntax highlighting, content assistant is configured through the getContentAssistant method within a subclass of SourceViewerConfiguration. Because you have already created the JNLPConfiguration class, you are going to override the getContentAssistant method in it.

The getContentAssistant method returns an instance of type IContentAssistant. An IContentAssistant provides support on interactive content completion. It is capable of proposing, displaying, and inserting completions of the content at the viewer's cursor position. A content assistant uses a list of IContentAssistantProcessor objects to find appropriate content completion proposals. Each IContentAssistantProcessor is registered for a particular type of document content type. For example, if the cursor is in a certain type, only the corresponding IContentAssistantProcessor will be queried for content completion proposals. Usually, you do not have to implement the IContentAssistant interface; instead, you can use its default implementation—ContentAssistant. You need to implement an IContentAssistantProcessor and register it to the content assistant for the corresponding content type.

The following code shows the implementation of the getContentAssistant method in the JNLPConfiguration class:

```
public class JNLPConfiguration extends SourceViewerConfiguration {

    ...

    /*
     * (non-Javadoc)
     * @seeSourceViewerConfiguration#getContentAssistant(ISourceViewer)
     */
    public IContentAssistant getContentAssistant(ISourceViewer sourceViewer) {
        ContentAssistant assistant = new ContentAssistant();

        IContentAssistProcessor processor = new JNLPCAProcessor();

        assistant.setContentAssistProcessor(
            processor,
            JNLPPartitionScanner.JNLP_TAG);

        assistant.setContentAssistProcessor(
            processor,
            IDocument.DEFAULT_CONTENT_TYPE);

        assistant.enableAutoActivation(true);
        assistant.setAutoActivationDelay(500); // 0.5 s.

        return assistant;
    }
    ...
}
```

First, you create an instance of ContentAssistant. Then you create an instance of IContentAssistantProcessor and register it to two content types. The enableAutoActivation method is invoked to enable the auto activation. When the user types a certain character (one of the characters in the array returned by the getCompletionProposalAutoActivationCharacters method of IContentAssistantProcessor), after a specified delay, content assistant is activated automatically. The amount of time delay is configured through the setAutoActivationDelay method of the ContentAssistant class.

Here is the implementation of the content assistant processor:

```java
public class JNLPCAProcessor implements IContentAssistProcessor {

    // Proposed parts before the cursor
    final static String[] PARTS1 =
        {
            "<?xml version=\"1.0\" encoding=\"utf-8\"?>\n",
            "<jnlp spec=\"1.0+\" codebase=\"\" href=\"\">",
            "<information>",
            "<title>",
            "<vendor>",
            "<homepage href=\"",
            "<description>",
            "<icon href=\"",
            "<security>",
            "<resources>",
            "<j2se version=\"",
            "<jar href=\"",
            "<application-desc main-class=\"" };

    // Proposed parts after the cursor
    final static String[] PARTS2 =
        {
            "",
            "\n</jnlp>",
            "\n</information>",
            "</title>",
            "</vendor>",
            "\"/>",
            "</description>",
            "\"/>",
            "\n</security>",
            "\n</resources>",
            "\"/>",
            "\"/>",
            "\"/>" };

    /*
     * (non-Javadoc)
     * @see IContentAssistProcessor#computeCompletionProposals(ITextViewer, int)
     */
    public ICompletionProposal[] computeCompletionProposals(
        ITextViewer viewer,
        int documentOffset) {

        IDocument document = viewer.getDocument();

        // computes the tag starting part.
        StringBuffer sb = new StringBuffer();
```

```
        int offset = documentOffset;
        for (;;) {
            char c;
            try {
                c = document.getChar(--offset);
            } catch (BadLocationException e) {
                sb.setLength(0);
                break;
            }
            if (c == '>' || Character.isWhitespace(c)) {
                sb.setLength(0);
                break;
            }
            sb.append(c);
            if (c == '<') {
                sb = sb.reverse();
                break;
            }
        }

        String startingPart = sb.toString();
        ArrayList list = new ArrayList();
        if (startingPart.length() > 0) {
            for (int i = 0; i < PARTS1.length; i++) {
                if (PARTS1[i].startsWith(startingPart)) {
                    String completeText = PARTS1[i] + PARTS2[i];
                    int cursorPos = PARTS1[i].length();
                    CompletionProposal proposal =
                        new CompletionProposal(
                            completeText,
                            documentOffset - startingPart.length(),
                            startingPart.length(),
                            cursorPos);
                    list.add(proposal);
                }
            }
        }

        ICompletionProposal[] proposals = new ICompletionProposal[list.size()];
        list.toArray(proposals);

        return proposals;
}

/*
 * (non-Javadoc)
 * @see IContentAssistProcessor#computeContextInformation(ITextViewer, int)
 */
public IContextInformation[] computeContextInformation(
    ITextViewer viewer,
    int documentOffset) {
    return null;
}

/*
```

```
 * (non-Javadoc)
 * @see IContentAssistProcessor#getCompletionProposalAutoActivationCharacters()
 */
public char[] getCompletionProposalAutoActivationCharacters() {
    return new char[] { '<' };
}


/*
 * (non-Javadoc)
 * @see IContentAssistProcessor#getContextInformationAutoActivationCharacters()
 */
public char[] getContextInformationAutoActivationCharacters() {
    return null;
}


/*
 * (non-Javadoc)
 * @see IContentAssistProcessor#getErrorMessage()
 */
public String getErrorMessage() {
    return null;
}


/*
 * (non-Javadoc)
 *
 * @see IContentAssistProcessor#getContextInformationValidator()
 */
public IContextInformationValidator getContextInformationValidator() {
    return null;
}


}
```

Two string arrays are defined first. The first string array lists the first parts (which will be inserted before the cursor if the user selects the completion proposal) of all the possible proposals, and the second string array lists the other parts (which will be inserted after the cursor).

When the user presses *Ctrl+spacebar* or content assistant automatically activates, computeCompletionProposals is invoked to retrieve all the possible proposals. The preceding implementation first checks the existing part of the tag. Strings in the first string array, starting with the existing part, are considered to be suitable completion proposals. A CompletionProposal instance is created for each candidate pair of strings. Finally, the computeCompletionProposals method returns all the completion proposals in an array.

The getCompletionProposalAutoActivationCharacters method returns all characters that, when entered by the user, should automatically trigger the presentation of possible completions. In our case, only the tag opening character < is used with auto activation characters.

Now you can try out the content assistant feature in the JNLP editor.

# Running the Editor

You have completed the JNLP editor. Now you are going to deploy it as an Eclipse plug-in. Here is the main plug-in class:

```java
public class JNLPEditorPlugin extends AbstractUIPlugin {
    //The shared instance.
    private static JNLPEditorPlugin plugin;
    //Resource bundle.
    private ResourceBundle resourceBundle;

    /**
     * The constructor.
     */
    public JNLPEditorPlugin(IPluginDescriptor descriptor) {
        super(descriptor);
        plugin = this;
        try {
            resourceBundle= ResourceBundle.getBundle(
                    "com.asprise.books.javaui.ch20.JNLPEditorPluginResources");
        } catch (MissingResourceException x) {
            x.printStackTrace();
            resourceBundle = null;
        }
    }

    /**
     * Returns the shared instance.
     */
    public static JNLPEditorPlugin getDefault() {
        return plugin;
    }

    /**
     * Returns the workspace instance.
     */
    public static IWorkspace getWorkspace() {
        return ResourcesPlugin.getWorkspace();
    }

    /**
     * Returns the string from the plugin's resource bundle,
     * or 'key' if not found.
     */
    public static String getResourceString(String key) {
        ResourceBundle bundle= JNLPEditorPlugin.getDefault().getResourceBundle();
        try {
            return (bundle!=null ? bundle.getString(key) : key);
        } catch (MissingResourceException e) {
            return key;
        }
    }

    /**
```

```
        * Returns the plugin's resource bundle,
        */
       public ResourceBundle getResourceBundle() {
           return resourceBundle;
       }
   }
```

Here is the code for the plug-in descriptor:

```xml
<?xml version="1.0" encoding="UTF-8"?>
<plugin
   id="JNLPEditor"
   name="JNLPEditor Plug-in"
   version="1.0.0"
   provider-name="Jack Li Guojie"
   class="com.asprise.books.javaui.ch20.JNLPEditorPlugin">

   <runtime>
      <library name="JNLPEditor.jar">
         <export name="*"/>
      </library>
   </runtime>
   <requires>
      <import plugin="org.eclipse.core.resources"/>
      <import plugin="org.eclipse.ui"/>
      <import plugin="org.apache.xerces"/>
   </requires>

   <extension
         point="org.eclipse.ui.editors">
      <editor
            name="Java Web Start JNLP Editor"
            icon="icons/sample.gif"
            extensions="jnlp"

contributorClass="org.eclipse.ui.texteditor.BasicTextEditorActionContributor"
            class="com.asprise.books.javaui.ch20.JNLPEditor"
            id="com.asprise.books.javaui.ch20.JNLPEditor">
      </editor>
   </extension>

</plugin>
```

By copying the plug-in descriptor and binary code to the appropriate plug-in directory of the Eclipse IDE, you are ready to run the editor. You can double-click a JNLP file from the resource explorer to invoke the JNLP editor.

The editor runs well within Eclipse workbench. What about running the editor in stand-alone mode? Unfortunately, the TextEditor class (directly or indirectly) makes reference to other classes of Eclipse workbench. However, you can spend some time modifying the source code and removing the dependency on Eclipse workbench.

# Summary

The JFace text framework is very powerful and complex. This chapter introduced you to essential concepts regarding JFace text, such as document partitioning, presentation damager and repairer, and so forth. The sample JNLP editor project walked you through the process of creating a custom text editor. You learned to create a basic editor, add syntax highlighting, and provide a content assistant. In the next chapter, you learn about another UI framework called Eclipse Forms, which enables you to create flat, web-like user interfaces.

# 21

# Eclipse Forms

Eclipse Forms provides a framework for creating flat, web-like user interfaces. This chapter shows you how to use the Eclipse Forms frame. You learn how to use the toolkit to create basic forms or scrollable forms. The chapter introduces Eclipse Forms custom widgets, such as hyperlinks, form texts, sections, and so on. Also, two Eclipse Forms layout managers are discussed at the end of this chapter.

## Introduction to Eclipse Forms

A new Eclipse version 3.0 feature, Eclipse Forms, provides a convenient API for creating polished, web-like user interfaces. Eclipse Forms is used extensively in the Eclipse Plug-in Development Environment (PDE). Figure 21-1 shows a PDE Eclipse Forms–based plug-in descriptor file editor. If you take a close look, you might notice a few features of Eclipse Forms:

- ❑ SWT controls, such as buttons and texts, are polished to adapt them to forms.

- ❑ Some of the forms, including the one shown in Figure 21-1, are scrollable.

- ❑ Some controls on forms, such as labels, are wrapped to fill the provided width.

- ❑ Other features are included such as hyperlinks, sections, and so on.

Eclipse Forms uses a toolkit to adapt common SWT controls to the form environment. Additionally, it provides many custom controls — e.g., hyperlinks and sections designed to fit into forms. A new layout manager is created to lay out controls in a form with proper wrapping.

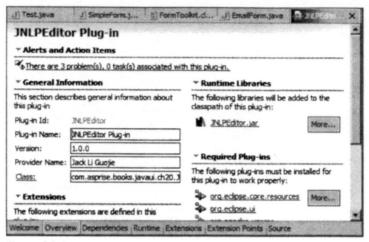

Figure 21-1

Before you begin programming with Eclipse Forms, you need to add the forms.jar (under the folder $ECLIPSE_HOME/plugins/org.eclipse.ui.forms_3.x.x) into your Java path. The following are the main packages of Eclipse Forms:

❑ org.eclipse.ui.forms: This package contains many UI management utility classes.

❑ org.eclipse.ui.forms.editor: If you are developing Eclipse plug-ins, you can use classes in this package to create multi-page editors.

❑ org.eclipse.ui.forms.events: This package contains new events created to support custom form widgets.

❑ org.eclipse.ui.forms.widgets: Custom form widgets, layout managers, and a form toolkit are defined in this package.

## Creating a Basic Form

The following sample application (an e-mail message composition form) shows you how to create a basic form. The completed e-mail message composition form is shown in Figure 21-2.

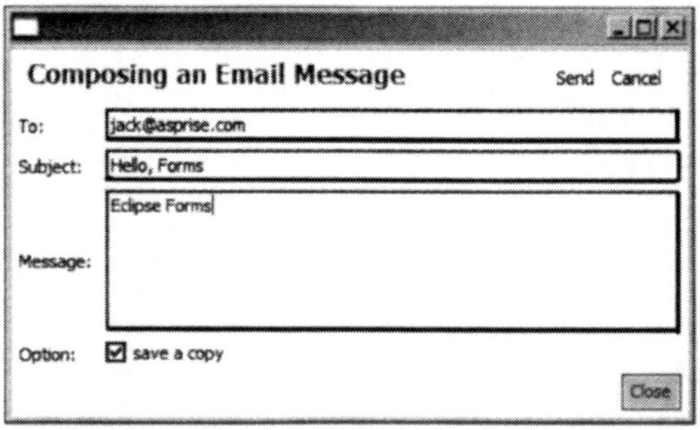

Figure 21-2

The following are the steps you follow to create the form:

1.  Set up a form toolkit.
2.  Create a form instance.
3.  Set the form title (optional).
4.  Add form body content.
5.  Add toolbar items and menus (optional).

First, let's create the application window by subclassing the `ApplicationWindow` class:

```java
public class EmailForm extends ApplicationWindow {
    /**
     * @param parentShell
     */
    public EmailForm(Shell parentShell) {
        super(parentShell);
    }

    public static void main(String[] args) {
        EmailForm emailForm = new EmailForm(null);
        emailForm.setBlockOnOpen(true);
        emailForm.open();
    }

}
```

Next, override the `createContents` method to create the form:

```java
protected Control createContents(Composite parent) {
    Composite composite = new Composite(parent, SWT.NULL);
    composite.setLayout(new FillLayout());

    // Sets up the toolkit.
    FormToolkit toolkit = new FormToolkit(getShell().getDisplay());

    // Creates a form instance.
    Form form = toolkit.createForm(composite);
    form.setLayoutData(new GridData(GridData.FILL_BOTH));

    // Sets title.
    form.setText("Composing an Email Message");

    // Adds body contents.
    form.getBody().setLayout(new GridLayout(2, false));
    Label label = toolkit.createLabel(form.getBody(), "To: ", SWT.NULL);
    Text textTo = toolkit.createText(form.getBody(), "");
    textTo.setLayoutData(new GridData(GridData.FILL_HORIZONTAL));

    label = toolkit.createLabel(form.getBody(), "Subject: ", SWT.NULL);
    Text textSubject = toolkit.createText(form.getBody(), "");
```

```
    textSubject.setLayoutData(new GridData(GridData.FILL_HORIZONTAL));

    label = toolkit.createLabel(form.getBody(), "Message: ", SWT.NULL);
    Text textMessage = toolkit.createText(form.getBody(), "");
    textMessage.setLayoutData(new GridData(GridData.FILL_BOTH));

    label = toolkit.createLabel(form.getBody(), "Option: ", SWT.NULL);
    Button buttonOption = toolkit.createButton(
                            form.getBody(), "save a copy", SWT.CHECK);

    Button buttonClose = toolkit.createButton(form.getBody(), "Close", SWT.PUSH);
    GridData gridData = new GridData();
    gridData.horizontalSpan = 2;
    gridData.horizontalAlignment = GridData.END;
    buttonClose.setLayoutData(gridData);

    // Adds toolbar items.
    form.getToolBarManager().add(new Action("Send") {
        public void run() {
            System.out.println("Sending email ...");
        }
    });

    form.getToolBarManager().add(new Action("Cancel") {
        public void run() {
            System.out.println("Cancelled.");
        }
    });

    form.updateToolBar();


    return composite;
}
```

A composite is created to contain the form to be created. Before creating the form, you construct a FormToolkit. A form toolkit is capable of creating SWT controls adapted to work in Eclipse Forms. Besides creating the form-adapted versions of common SWT controls, a form toolkit is also responsible for creating custom form widgets.

The following code creates a Form instance:

```
Form form = toolkit.createForm(composite);
```

Form is a custom control that renders an optional title and a body composite. In Figure 21-2, the form title and toolbar items are displayed in the top of the form. All the widgets under the title are in the form's body composite. You can use the following methods of the Form class to get and set the form title:

```
public java.lang.String getText()
public void setText(java.lang.String text)
```

The body composite of the form can be obtained through the `getBody` method of the `Form` class:

```
public org.eclipse.swt.widgets.Composite getBody()
```

Initially, no layout manager is associated with the body composite of a form. You have to set a proper manager for it. Here, you use a `GridLayout` manager. You can add various controls on the body of the form.

Instead of creating those controls directly, you call various factory methods of the toolkit to create them. The factory methods of the `FormToolkit` class create controls and configure their appearance in order to adapt them to the form environment. Instead of using

```
Text textTo = new Text(form.getBody(), SWT.NULL);
```

you use the following code so that the text control is adapted to the form properly:

```
Text textTo = toolkit.createText(form.getBody(), "");
```

What happens if an SWT control does not have a corresponding factory method in the `FormToolkit` class? In this case, you create the control first and then use it as the argument to call the `adapt` method of the `FormToolkit` class. The `adapt` method adjusts colors of the control to match the form. For example, the following code creates a `Combo` control on a form:

```
Combo combo = new Combo(form.getBody(), SWT.DROP_DOWN);
toolkit.adapt(combo);
```

After creating all the necessary controls, you add two toolbar items. The `getToolBarManager` method returns the toolbar manager used by the form:

```
public org.eclipse.jface.action.IToolBarManager getToolBarManager()
```

Next. use the toolbar manager to add actions. For more details, see Chapter 9. After adding toolbar items, the `updateToolBar` method is invoked to notify the system that the toolbar has been updated.

When you run the program, the UI should look similar to the one that appeared in Figure 21-2.

## Customizing Forms

If you resize the e-mail composition form, you might notice that the form is not scrollable. To make the form scrollable, you need to use `ScrolledForm` instead of `Form`. In the preceding code, you can replace the line:

```
Form form = toolkit.createForm(composite);
```

with

```
ScrolledForm form = toolkit.createScrolledForm(composite);
```

Now if you reduce the size of the window to less than the minimum size required by the form, scrollbars appear and you can use them to navigate the form.

The `ScrolledForm` class embeds a `Form` in itself and provides scrolling support.

To set the background color of a form, use the `setBackground` method:

```
public void setBackground(org.eclipse.swt.graphics.Color bg)
```

Use the `setBackgroundImage` method to set the background image to be rendered behind the title:

```
public void setBackgroundImage(org.eclipse.swt.graphics.Image backgroundImage)
```

If the image is too small, it will be tiled as many times as needed to fill the title area.

# Using Custom Form Controls

In the last section, you built an e-mail composition form using common SWT controls such as labels, text fields, and buttons. Eclipse Forms provides a set of custom controls tailored for forms. This section introduces you to custom controls such as form texts, hyperlinks, sections, and so on. All of the custom form controls are subclasses of the `org.eclipse.swt.widgets` control class, which allows you to mix custom controls with common SWT controls. Let's begin with hyperlinks.

## Using Hyperlinks

On the World Wide Web, a hyperlink is a reference to a hypertext document or other resource. A Web browser usually displays a hyperlink in a special color or style. A hyperlink in Eclipse Forms looks like a common hyperlink and it generates events when it is clicked.

### Creating a Basic Hyperlink

The `Hyperlink` class represents a hyperlink in Eclipse Forms. For example, the following code creates a link, as shown in Figure 21-3:

```
Hyperlink hyperlink = toolkit.createHyperlink(
                    form.getBody(), "This is a hyperlink to Eclipse.org", SWT.NULL);
hyperlink.setHref("http://www.eclipse.org");
hyperlink.setForeground(getShell().getDisplay().getSystemColor(SWT.COLOR_BLUE));
hyperlink.addHyperlinkListener(new IHyperlinkListener() {
    public void linkEntered(HyperlinkEvent e) {
        System.out.println("Mouse entered.");
    }

    public void linkExited(HyperlinkEvent e) {
        System.out.println("Mouse left.");
    }

    public void linkActivated(HyperlinkEvent e) {
        System.out.println("Hyperlink activated.");
        System.out.println("HREF = " + e.getHref());
    }
});
```

**Figure 21-3**

First, an instance of the `Hyperlink` class is created with the `createHyperlink` method of the
`FormToolkit` class:

```
public Hyperlink createHyperlink(Composite parent, String text, int style)
```

You specify the composite containing the hyperlink, displayed text, and style of the hyperlink in the
first, second, and third arguments, respectively. Then you set the object associated with this hyperlink
through the `setHref` method:

```
public void setHref(java.lang.Object href)
```

In the Web environment, a hyperlink's reference is usually a Uniform Resource Identifier (URI).
However, for an Eclipse Forms hyperlink, its reference object can be any Java object.

By default, the foreground color for a hyperlink is black. You call the `setForeground` method of the
`Hyperlink` class to set the hyperlink's foreground color to blue. A hyperlink is capable of generating
`HyperlinkEvents`. Then you add an `IHyperlinkListener` to listen to such events.

When the mouse pointer enters the hyperlink client area or keyboard focus switches to the hyperlink,
the `linkEntered` method of the hyperlink listener is invoked. The `linkExited` method is called
when the mouse pointer exits the hyperlink client area or keyboard focus switches from the hyperlink.
If the user clicks the hyperlink or presses the Enter key while the hyperlink has keyboard focus, the
`linkActivated` method is called. All of the three methods are called with a `HyperlinkEvent` object
as the argument. You can obtain the object associated with the hyperlink through the `getHref` method
of the `HyperlinkEvent` class:

```
public java.lang.Object getHref()
```

By default, the text of a hyperlink is underlined. You can use the `setUnderlined` method to control this
behavior:

```
public void setUnderlined(boolean underlined)
```

Sometimes, you need to display an image in a hyperlink. In this case, you need the `ImageHyperlink`
class.

## Creating ImageHyperlinks

The `ImageHyperlink` class extends `Hyperlink` by adding the capability to render an image relative
to the optional text. Additionally, an image hyperlink supports the display of custom images for hover
and active states.

The following code creates an image hyperlink below the hyperlink that you created in the last section (see Figure 21-4):

```
ImageHyperlink imageHyperlink = toolkit.createImageHyperlink(
                                        form.getBody(), SWT.NULL);
imageHyperlink.setText("This is an image hyperlink.");
imageHyperlink.setForeground(
            getShell().getDisplay().getSystemColor(SWT.COLOR_BLUE));
imageHyperlink.setImage(new Image(getShell().getDisplay(), "icons/eclipse0.gif"));
imageHyperlink.addHyperlinkListener(new HyperlinkAdapter() {
    public void linkActivated(HyperlinkEvent e) {
        System.out.println("Image hyperlink activated.");
    }
});
```

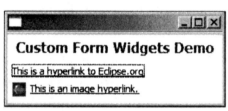

**Figure 21-4**

You might notice that the procedure is very similar to that of creating a text hyperlink. First, an instance of ImageHyperlink is created. Then you call the setText method to set text for this hyperlink. If you want to display an image only, you do not need call this method. The setImage method is used to set the image to be displayed on the hyperlink:

```
public org.eclipse.swt.graphics.Image getImage()
```

If you need the hyperlink to display different images in hover and active states, you can use the following methods to set them:

```
public void setHoverImage(org.eclipse.swt.graphics.Image hoverImage)
public void setActiveImage(org.eclipse.swt.graphics.Image activeImage)
```

Finally, you add a hyperlink listener for this image hyperlink. Instead of implementing the IHyperlinkListener interface, you can simply extend the HyperlinkAdapter class and override the desired methods only.

## Managing Multiple Hyperlinks with HyperlinkGroups

You can use the HyperlinkGroup class to manage a group of hyperlinks. A HyperlinkGroup tracks hyperlink activation and updates normal and active colors of all the links belonging to this group. Use the add method of the HyperlinkGroup class to add a hyperlink to a group:

```
public void add(Hyperlink link)
```

Use the following methods to change the appearance of all the hyperlinks in a group:

```
public void setBackground(org.eclipse.swt.graphics.Color bg)
public void setForeground(org.eclipse.swt.graphics.Color fg)
public void setActiveBackground(org.eclipse.swt.graphics.Color newActiveBackground)
public void setActiveForeground(org.eclipse.swt.graphics.Color newActiveForeground)
```

For example, the following code adds both the text hyperlink and the image hyperlink created previously into a hyperlink group and uses the group to manage both hyperlinks:

```
HyperlinkGroup group = new HyperlinkGroup(getShell().getDisplay());
group.add(hyperlink);
group.add(imageHyperlink);

group.setActiveBackground(getShell().getDisplay().getSystemColor(SWT.COLOR_YELLOW))
;
group.setActiveForeground(getShell().getDisplay().getSystemColor(SWT.COLOR_RED));
group.setForeground(getShell().getDisplay().getSystemColor(SWT.COLOR_BLUE));
```

# Using FormTexts

The FormText control is a powerful read-only text control that is capable of rendering styled text. One of the advantages of FormText over the Label control is that FormText is able to wrap text to fill the provided width.

## Rendering Normal Text

The following code renders normal text using FormText, as shown in Figure 21-5:

```
form.getBody().setLayout(new TableWrapLayout());

FormText text = toolkit.createFormText(form.getBody(), true);

text.setText(
  "Eclipse is a kind of universal tool platform - an open extensible " +
  "IDE for anything and nothing in particular. For more details, please " +
  "visit http://www.eclipse.org for more details.",
  false,
  false);
```

Figure 21-5

In order to enable `FormText` to wrap text, its containing composite must use a layout manager that supports wrap. In the preceding code, `TableWrapLayout` is used as the layout manager for the form body. More details on `TableWrapLayout` are covered later in this chapter.

An instance of `FormText` is created and returned through the `createFormText` method of the `FormToolkit` class:

```
public FormText createFormText(Composite parent, boolean trackFocus)
```

Specify the containing composite for the `FormText` in the first argument. If there are hyperlinks in the text and you want the toolkit to monitor focus transfer so that the hyperlink in focus is visible, you should set the `trackFocus` to `true`; otherwise, set it to `false`.

After the `FormText` instance is constructed, set the content text for it through the `setText` method of the `FormText` class:

```
public void setText(java.lang.String text, boolean parseTags, boolean expandURLs)
```

Specify the text content for the `FormText` instance in the first argument. You can provide the text content in either plain text format or XML format. For XML format, you set `parseTags` to `true`; otherwise, set it to `false`. If `expandURLs` is set to `true`, all hyperlinks within the content text will be parsed and displayed as `Hyperlink` instances.

When you resize the window, you might notice that the text is wrapped properly to fit the width provided. A URL link is included in the text content; the next section shows how to make the `FormText` parse it and display it as a hyperlink.

## Automatically Parsing URLs

In this section, you learn how to use `TextForm` to parse URLs into hyperlinks and capture events generated by those hyperlinks.

The following code extends the code in the preceding section by adding automaticly the URL parsing feature:

```
form.getBody().setLayout(new TableWrapLayout());
FormText text = toolkit.createFormText(form.getBody(), true);

HyperlinkGroup group = new HyperlinkGroup(form.getDisplay());
group.setForeground(form.getDisplay().getSystemColor(SWT.COLOR_BLUE));
group.setActiveForeground(form.getDisplay().getSystemColor(SWT.COLOR_BLUE));

text.setHyperlinkSettings(group);

text.setText(
    "Eclipse is a kind of universal tool platform - an open extensible " +
    "IDE for anything and nothing in particular. For more details, please " +
    "visit http://www.eclipse.org web site.",
    false,
    true);

text.addHyperlinkListener(new HyperlinkAdapter() {
```

```
    public void linkActivated(HyperlinkEvent e) {
        System.out.println("Link activated: " + e.getHref());
    }
});
```

The first two lines are exactly the same as the code in the last section. A HyperlinkGroup instance is constructed and set to the FormText object. All the hyperlinks automatically parsed and constructed later will belong to this group. You can configure the appearance of the hyperlinks through the HyperlinkGroup object. Then you call the setText method of the FormText class. By setting the third argument to true, you configure the FormText instance to automatically parse and construct hyperlinks from URLs (see Figure 21-6).

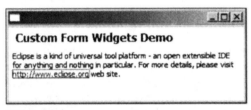

**Figure 21-6**

Hyperlinks are useful only if you can listen for events they generate. In order to listen for all the events generated from all the hyperlinks within the text, you add a hyperlink listener to the FormText object through the addHyperlinkListener method. When one of the hyperlinks generates an event, the hyperlink listener is notified. The getHref method of the HyperlinkEvent object passed to the listener returns a text string representing the corresponding URL of the hyperlink.

## Rendering XML Text

FormText is capable of parsing and displaying XML tags. It supports only a very limited subset of HTML tags. For example, the following code renders the XML text, as shown in Figure 21-7.

```
form.getBody().setLayout(new TableWrapLayout());
FormText text = toolkit.createFormText(form.getBody(), true);

Image image = new Image(form.getDisplay(), "icons/eclipse0.gif");
text.setImage("eclipse", image);
text.setText(
    "<form>"
        + "<p><img href=\"eclipse\"/> Eclipse Projects: </p>"
        + "<li><b>Platform</b> - Eclipse frameworks</li>"
        + "<li><b>JDT</b> - Java development tools</li>"
        + "<li><b>PDE</b> - Plug-in development environment</li>"
        + "</form>",
    true,
    false);
```

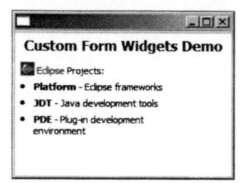

**Figure 21-7**

You might notice that FormText renders the text much as a Web browser does. However, there are a number of differences. For FormText, the root tag for the XML text must be form. FormText is not a Web browser, and it cannot automatically retrieve images from the Internet. In the preceding code, you create an image first and then register it with the FormText instance with a key (i.e., "eclipse"). In the XML text, you reference the image using its key through the href attribute of the img tag.

Currently, the FormText class supports only the following tags:

❑   p: Used to define paragraphs. It may have vspace as an attribute. If vspace is set to true, additional vertical space is added.

❑   li: Used to define unordered list items. It may have the following attributes: vspace, style (valid values: bullet, text, and image), value, indent, and bindent.

❑   img: Used to render an image. The href attribute is a key to the image registered with the FormText instance through the setImage method.

❑   a: Used to render a hyperlink. The href attribute defines the href value for the hyperlink.

❑   b: Used to decorate the enclosed text with **bold**.

❑   br: Used to force a line break.

❑   span: Used to set the color and the font for the enclosed text. It may have a color attribute and a font attribute.

As you can see, only a subset of HTML tags is supported by the FormText control. If you need to render HTML documents, use the Browser control (see Chapter 14 for more details).

## Using ExpandableComposites

An expandable composite is capable of expanding or collapsing a single client control. An expansion toggle item and a title acting as a hyperlink are displayed at the top of an expandable composite. The client control is displayed below the title when expanded or hidden when collapsed.

The following code creates an expandable composite with FormText as its client (see Figure 21-8):

```
form.getBody().setLayout(new TableWrapLayout());

ExpandableComposite ec1 =
    toolkit.createExpandableComposite(
        form.getBody(),
        ExpandableComposite.TREE_NODE | ExpandableComposite.EXPANDED);
ec1.setText("This is the title");

FormText text = toolkit.createFormText(ec1, false);
text.setText(
    "This is a long text. The user can show or hide this text "
        + "by expanding or collapsing the expandable composite.",
    false,
    false);
ec1.setClient(text);

ec1.addExpansionListener(new ExpansionAdapter() {
    public void expansionStateChanged(ExpansionEvent e) {
        // resizes the application window.
        getShell().pack(true);
    }
});
```

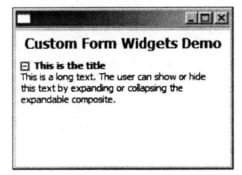

Figure 21-8

First, an instance of the ExpandableComposite class is created and obtained through the createExpandableComposite method of the FormToolkit class. You can define the toggle item in the second argument of the method. The TREE_NODE style creates the toggle control as a tree widget, while the TWISTIE creates a triangle-style toggle item. The EXPANDED style specifies that the expandable composite should be expanded initially.

The setText method of the ExpandableComposite class is used to set the title for the expandable composite. The client control, a FormText instance, is then created and set to the expandable composite. When the user expands or collapses an expandable composite, expansion events are generated. An expansion listener is added to the expandable to listen for expansion events and resize its containing window accordingly.

**439**

# Using Sections

A section is an expandable composite. It extends an expandable composite by displaying a separate, optional description below the separator.

For example, the following code creates a section, as shown in Figure 21-9:

```
form.getBody().setLayout(new TableWrapLayout());

Section section = toolkit.createSection(form.getBody(), Section.DESCRIPTION |
        Section.TREE_NODE | Section.EXPANDED);

section.setText("This is the title");
toolkit.createCompositeSeparator(section);
section.setDescription("-= This is a description -=");

FormText text = toolkit.createFormText(section, false);
text.setText(
    "This is a long text. The user can show or hide this text "
        + "by expanding or collapsing the expandable composite.",
    false,
    false);
section.setClient(text);
```

**Figure 21-9**

Use the createSection method of the FormToolkit class to create a Section instance. The DESCRIPTION style causes the description to be displayed under the separator. You use the setText method to set the title for the section. The separator between the title and the description is created with the createCompositeSeparator method of the FormToolkit class. The description text is set with the setDescription method of the Section class. Finally, the client control is created and set to the section.

# Using Form Layout Managers

Eclipse Forms provides two additional layouts that aren't provided by SWT: `TableWrapLayout` and `ColumnLayout`.

## Using TableWrapLayout

`TableWrapLayout` is a layout manager that attempts to positions controls using a two-pass auto-layout HTML table algorithm recommended by the W3C. You can view the `TableWrapLayout` manager as the layout manager used by a browser to lay out HTML tables. For more details on the W3C's HTML table auto-layout algorithm, please visit `www.w3.org/TR/html4/appendix/notes.html#h-B.5.2.2`.

`TableWrapLayout` behaves much like `GridLayout`, except for the following differences:

❑ `TableWrapLayout` is wrap-sensitive. It divides the space across columns to avoid excess wrapping for some controls.

❑ `GridLayout` distributes excess horizontal and vertical space to controls; however, `TableWrapLayout` fills only the horizontal space.

❑ `TableWrapLayout` works well only if all the controls that need to wrap have the appropriate style, i.e., `SWT.WRAP`. By default, all Eclipse Forms custom widgets have the `SWT.WRAP` style set.

Aside from the behavior differences just described, the usage of `TableWrapLayout` is very similar to that of `GridLayout`. For example, the following code lays out the controls, as shown in Figure 21-10.

```java
TableWrapLayout layout = new TableWrapLayout();
layout.numColumns = 2;
form.getBody().setLayout(layout);

Color color = form.getDisplay().getSystemColor(SWT.COLOR_YELLOW);

Label label = toolkit.createLabel(form.getBody(), "Some text spans over two columns
in the first row. ", SWT.WRAP);
TableWrapData data = new TableWrapData();
data.colspan = 2;
label.setLayoutData(data);
label.setBackground(color);

label = toolkit.createLabel(form.getBody(), "Some text in the first column of the
second row. and here it goes on and on ... ... ... ... ", SWT.WRAP);
label.setBackground(color);
label = toolkit.createLabel(form.getBody(), "Some text in the second column of the
second row. ", SWT.WRAP);
label.setBackground(color);
```

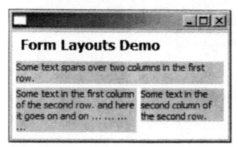

**Figure 21-10**

First, create an instance of the `TableWrapLayout` class. The total number of columns is set to 2 through the `numColumns` field of the `TableWrapLayout` object. The layout object is then set to the form body.

The first label is created through the `createLabel` method of the `FormToolkit` class. Note that the `SWT.WRAP` style is specified for the label. The configuration layout data class for `TableWrapLayout` is the `TableWrapData` class. Because you want the first label to span the whole row, you create a `TableWrapData` object with `colsSpan` equal to 2 and set this layout data object to the label.

Then you create the other two labels. By default, those two labels have `colsSpan` and `rowsSpan` both equal to 1.

If you look carefully at Figure 21-10, the widths for the second label and the third label are different because `TableWrapLayout` tries to avoid excess wrapping for the labels. Because the text string in the second label is much longer than the text string in the third label, the layout avoids excess wrapping by distributing more horizontal space to the second label.

## Using ColumnLayouts

`ColumnLayout` arranges child controls in vertical columns. All the columns are set to be identical in size. `ColumnLayout` adapts the number of columns to the parent composite width. The number of columns increases as the parent composite width increases. It also tries to avoid large gaps at the end of the last column.

For example, the following code shows how `ColumnLayout` works:

```
ColumnLayout layout = new ColumnLayout();
layout.maxNumColumns = 4;
form.getBody().setLayout(layout);

Color color = form.getDisplay().getSystemColor(SWT.COLOR_YELLOW);

Label label = null;
for(int i=0; i<10; i++) {
    label = toolkit.createLabel(form.getBody(), "Text label #" + i);
}
```

First, you create an instance of the `ColumnLayout` class. By default, the maximum and the minimum values for the number columns are 3 and 1, respectively. Here, you set the maximum number of columns allowed to 4 through the `maxNumColumns` field. Then you set the column layout as the layout manager for the form body. Finally, ten labels are added to the form body.

Initially, the screen output looks like Figure 21-11.

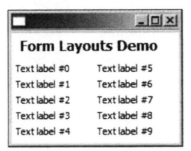

**Figure 21-11**

As the user resizes the window, the layout varies the number of columns (see Figure 21-12).

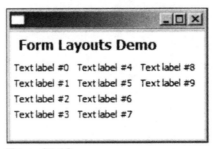

**Figure 21-12**

# Summary

This chapter walked you through the Eclipse Forms framework. First, it showed you how to create forms. You can use the form toolkit to create a form easily. If you need a scrollable form, you can use `ScrolledForm`. A form can contain common SWT widgets. Furthermore, the Eclipse Forms framework provides many custom widgets such as hyperlinks, form texts, and sections. Form text is a very powerful control that is capable of displaying plain text as well as XML text. You learned about many types of layout managers in Chapter 6. The Eclipse Forms framework provides two additional layout managers: `TableWrapLayout` and `ColumnLayout`. You can use Eclipse Forms in every platform that SWT supports. SWT also supports many native features of underlying platforms. In the next chapter, you learn about OLE automation on Windows platforms.

# 22

# Programming OLE in Windows

SWT is integrated tightly with the underlying system. In this chapter, you learn how to embed OLE documents and ActiveX controls in SWT widgets on Windows platforms. As an example, we embed a Microsoft Word document in an SWT application. The chapter walks you through the steps to embed an OLE document: creating the OLE container, creating an OLE site for the OLE document, activating the OLE object, and deactivating the OLE object. You also learn how to save changes made to the OLE document and execute basic commands. OLE automation gives you much more control over an OLE document or ActiveX control. This chapter shows you how to get/set property values and invoke complex methods.

## Introduction

*Component Object Model* (COM), also known as *ActiveX*, is a software architecture enabling cross-software communication mainly for Windows platforms. With COM technology, you can mix and integrate all kinds of software parts together at runtime. The precursor to ActiveX was *object linking and embedding (OLE)*. In 1996, Microsoft renamed some parts of OLE relating to the Internet as ActiveX, and then renamed all OLE technologies into ActiveX. In 1997, the entire framework was renamed COM. The terminology here becomes a little confusing. In this chapter, *OLE documents* refers to a compound document technology, as used in Microsoft Office, and general software components such as Web browsers are referred to as *ActiveX controls*.

In SWT, package `org.eclipse.swt.ole.win32` provides a set of classes that allow you to integrate OLE documents and ActiveX controls into SWT widgets.

## *OleFrame*

The `OleFrame` class, a subclass of `org.eclipse.swt.widgets.Composite`, represents an OLE container. `OleFrame` offers the following functions:

❏ Positioning and sizing the OLE document or ActiveX control

❏ Inserting menu items from the application into the OLE document's menu

❏ Activating and deactivating the OLE document's menu

❏ Positioning the OLE document's menu

❏ Translating accelerator keystrokes intended for the OLE document or ActiveX control

## *OleClientSite, OleControlSite*

While `OleFrame` provides a UI container for an OLE document or ActiveX control, `OleClientSite` and `OleControlSite` provide sites for the embedded OLE documents and ActiveX controls, respectively.

`OleClientSite` handles interactions with a particular OLE document. It provides the following functions:

❏ Creating the in-place editor for a blank document or opening an existing document

❏ Laying out the editor

❏ Activating and deactivating the document

❏ Saving changes made to the document

Although `OleClientSite` is a subclass of the `Composite` class, it does not make sense to add any control to it.

Extending the `OleClientSite` class, `OleControlSite` provides a site to handle an ActiveX control within a container. It provides the following additional features over those provided by `OleClientSite`:

❏ Handling events from the ActiveX control

❏ Notifying of property changes from the ActiveX control

❏ Providing simplified access to well-known properties of the ActiveX control, such as color and font

❏ Exposing ambient properties of the container to the ActiveX control

In the next section you learn how to use `OleClientSite` and `OleControlSite` to embed a Microsoft Word OLE document into an SWT application.

# Embedding a Microsoft Word OLE Document into an SWT Application

In this section, you learn how to embed a typical OLE document—Microsoft Word—into SWT widgets. First, an OLE document or ActiveX control container is created. You can use the container to contribute menus to the OLE document or ActiveX control's menu. The site used to manage the embedded OLE document or ActiveX control is constructed in the container. At this point, the OLE document or ActiveX control is still invisible. You need to activate it to make it visible (see Figure 22-1). When the OLE document or ActiveX control is visible, you can perform actions and make changes to it. The changes made to an OLE document can be saved to a file.

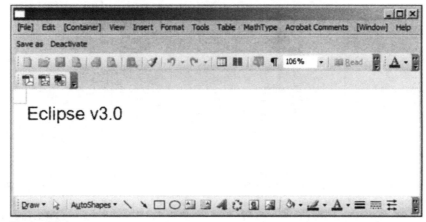

Figure 22-1

## Creating the OLE Container

In SWT, OleFrame represents an OLE container. It is responsible for positioning an OLE document or ActiveX control and managing menus. The following code creates an OLE container and contributes various menus to the embedded OLE document:

```
OleFrame oleFrame;

/*
 * (non-Javadoc)
 *
 * @see
org.eclipse.jface.window.Window#createContents(org.eclipse.swt.widgets.Composite)
 */
protected Control createContents(Composite parent) {
    Composite composite = new Composite(parent, SWT.NULL);
    composite.setLayout(new FillLayout());

    oleFrame = new OleFrame(composite, SWT.NULL);

    if (getMenuBarManager() != null) {
```

```
        MenuItem windowMenu =
            new MenuItem(getMenuBarManager().getMenu(), SWT.CASCADE);
        windowMenu.setText("[Window]");

        MenuItem containerMenu =
            new MenuItem(getMenuBarManager().getMenu(), SWT.CASCADE);
        containerMenu.setText("[Container]");

        MenuItem fileMenu =
            new MenuItem(getMenuBarManager().getMenu(), SWT.CASCADE);
        fileMenu.setText("[File]");

        oleFrame.setWindowMenus(new MenuItem[] { windowMenu });
        oleFrame.setContainerMenus(new MenuItem[] { containerMenu });
        oleFrame.setFileMenus(new MenuItem[] { fileMenu });
    }

    ...

    // creates client site here ...

    return composite;
}
```

The program main class extends the `ApplicationWindow` class and overrides the `createContents` method. After the instance of `OleFrame` is created, you can make various menus available to the embedded OLE document. When the embedded OLE document is activated, it displays its menu bar above the application's menu bar, if any. In Figure 22-1, the menu bar of the embedded OLE document is shown on the top. The application's toolbar is shown below the menu bar. The embedded OLE document is displayed below the application's toolbar. The following methods can be used to make various menus available to the embedded OLE document or ActiveX control's menu bar:

```
public void setFileMenus(MenuItem[] fileMenus)
public void setContainerMenus(MenuItem[] containerMenus)
public void setWindowMenus(MenuItem[] windowMenus)
```

The available menus are merged into the menu bar of the embedded OLE document, as shown in Figure 22-1. One or more menus can be inserted into any of the following possible locations:

❑ **File:** Far left

❑ **Container:** Middle

❑ **Window:** Far right, just before Help

After the OLE container is created, you are ready to create a site for the OLE document.

## *Creating an OLE Site*

You use a site to manage the embedded OLE document or ActiveX control. To embed an OLE document, you use the `OleClientSite` class. If you embed an OLE document, the entire corresponding application is embedded, including the content part, toolbars, menu bar, and so on. You use the `OleControlSite` class to embed an ActiveX control. For an ActiveX control, only the content part is shown, and you need to manage the behavior of the content through the API exposed by the ActiveX control.

*You can determine whether a COM object supports the OLE document behavior by the interfaces it implements. If it implements the* **IOleDocument** *interface, the COM object supports OLE document behavior; otherwise, it does not. Similarly, all COM objects supporting ActiveX control behavior implement the IOleControl interface. If a COM object implements both interfaces, it supports OLE document as well as ActiveX control behaviors.*

The Microsoft Word COM object supports both the OLE document and ActiveX control behaviors. So either OleClientSite or OleControlSite can be used. In this case, you can use the OleClientSite class to embed Microsoft Word as an OLE document:

```
OleClientSite clientSite;

protected Control createContents(Composite parent) {
    ...
    // creates the OLE container ...
    ...

    clientSite =
        new OleClientSite(oleFrame, SWT.NONE, new File("icons/test.doc"));

    // activates the OLE object here ...

    return composite;
}
```

You can create an instance of OleClientSite from the OLE document's *ProgramID* or from a *storage file*. The ProgramID of an OLE document is a string that identifies the corresponding application. For example, Microsoft Word has ProgramID "Word.Document". You can find ProgramIDs for all the programs in the system registry.

The following code constructs an instance of OleClientSite for Microsoft Word from its ProgramID:

```
OleClientSite clientSite = new OleClientSite(oleFrame, SWT.NULL, "Word.Document");
```

You create the OleClientSite object from a storage file. A storage file is a structured file written in application-specific format. For example, a Word storage file contains the text content, text format and styles, and other information.

If you want to embed Microsoft Word as an ActiveX control, you can use the following code:

```
clientSite = new OleControlSite(oleFrame, SWT.NULL, "Word.Document");
```

Now the site for the OLE document is created. However, it is still invisible. You need to activate it to make it visible.

# Activating the OLE Object

Activating an OLE object is often referred to as *in-place activation*. In-place activation allows the user to manipulate the OLE object without switching to its corresponding original application. For example, you can edit the embedded document without starting Microsoft Word.

To activate an OLE document or ActiveX control, you call the doVerb method of the OleClientSite class or the OleControlSite class:

```
public int doVerb(int verb)
```

You can specify the action code in the argument using one of the following values:

- ❑ OLE.OLEIVERB_PRIMARY: Specifies the action that occurs when the user double-clicks the OLE object. If the OLE object supports in-place activation, this verb usually activates it in place.

- ❑ OLE.OLEIVERB_SHOW: Instructs the OLE object to show itself for editing or viewing. It is called to display newly inserted objects for initial editing and to show link resources.

- ❑ OLE.OLEIVERB_OPEN: Instructs the OLE object (either supporting in-place activation or not) to open itself for editing in a window separate from that of its container. If the OLE object does not support in-place activation, this verb has the same effect as OLE.OLEIVERB_SHOW.

- ❑ OLE.OLEIVERB_HIDE: Causes the OLE object to remove its UI from view. This applies only to objects supporting in-place activation.

- ❑ OLE.OLEIVERB_UIACTIVATE: Activates the OLE object in place, along with its full set of UI tools.

- ❑ OLE.OLEIVERB_INPLACEACTIVATE: Activates the OLE object in place without displaying UI tools such as menus and toolbars. Single-clicking the OLE object causes it to negotiate the display of its UI tools with the container. If the container refuses, the OLE object remains active but without its tools displayed.

- ❑ OLE.OLEIVERB_DISCARDUNDOSTATE: Used to instruct objects to discard any undo state that they may be maintaining without deactivating the OLE object.

Here, you simply invoke the doVerb method with OLE.OLEIVERB_SHOW to activate the OLE object:

```
protected Control createContents(Composite parent) {
    ...
    // creates OLE container and the client site.
    ...

    clientSite.doVerb(OLE.OLEIVERB_SHOW);

    return composite;
}
```

Now the embedded Word OLE document is displayed (see Figure 22-1). If the Word document does not exist or it cannot be read, an exception will be thrown. You can add code to catch this exception.

## *Deactivating the OLE Object*

In the preceding section, you learned about how to activate the OLE object with the doVerb method. If you place several OLE documents or ActiveX controls in an application, it is desirable to have only one OLE object in an "active" state at a time. For deactivated OLE objects, their content parts are visible but the toolbars and menus are removed.

You can use the deactivateInPlaceClient method on the OleClientSite or OleControlSite class to deactivate an OLE document or ActiveX control:

```
public void deactivateInPlaceClient()
```

In the sample application, you add a deactivation action:

```
protected ToolBarManager createToolBarManager(int style) {
    ToolBarManager manager = new ToolBarManager(style);

    ...

    Action actionDeactivate = new Action("Deactivate") {
        public void run() {
            clientSite.deactivateInPlaceClient();
        }
    };

    manager.add(actionDeactivate);

    ...

    return manager;
}
```

When the Deactivate toolbar item is pressed, the OLE document is deactivated, as shown in Figure 22-2.

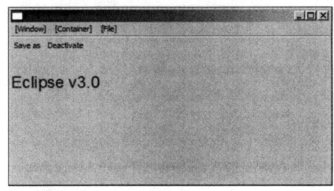

**Figure 22-2**

Note that the menus and toolbars belonging to the OLE document are removed. You can reactivate the OLE document by clicking its content area.

# Saving Changes

If you run the sample application, you might notice that the embedded Microsoft Word document does not save changes to the file nor does it display any dialog to ask you to save changes. Your code has to handle the task of saving changes.

The changes made to OLE documents can be saved either in storage files or ordinary files. A storage file contains structured data specific to the OLE object. For example, the test.doc file that is used to create the client site is a Microsoft Word storage file. An ordinary file does not contain OLE object–specific information. For example, an XML file is an ordinary file that does not specific any OLE objects.

You use the save method of the OleClientSite class to save the current document into a file:

```
public boolean save(File file, boolean includeOleInfo)
```

You specify the target file in the first argument. If you want to save the file into an OLE storage file, you set the includeOleInfo as true; otherwise, false. This method returns true if the document is saved successfully or false otherwise.

The following code provides a "Save as" action for the user to save the changed document into a file:

```
protected ToolBarManager createToolBarManager(int style) {
    ToolBarManager manager = new ToolBarManager(style);

    Action actionSaveAs = new Action("Save as") {
        public void run() {
            FileDialog dialog = new FileDialog(getShell(), SWT.SAVE);
            String path = dialog.open();
            if (path != null) {
                if (clientSite.save(new File(path), true)) {
                    System.out.println("Saved to file successfully.");
                } else {
                    System.err.println("Failed to save to file");
                }
            }
        }
    };

    manager.add(actionSaveAs);

    ...

    return manager;
}
```

You can use the isDirty method to check whether there is any change made to the document:

```
public boolean isDirty()
```

# *Executing Common Commands*

You can use the exec method to send a predefined set of comments to OLE documents and ActiveX controls provided that they support the IOleCommandTarget interface. Some of the well-known commands are:

- ❑ OLE.OLECMDID_OPEN: Open a file.
- ❑ OLE.OLECMDID_NEW: Create a new file.
- ❑ OLE.OLECMDID_SAVE: Save the document into the file.
- ❑ OLE.OLECMDID_SAVEAS: Save the document into another file.
- ❑ OLE.OLECMDID_PRINT: Print.
- ❑ OLE.OLECMDID_CUT: Cut the selected text.
- ❑ OLE.OLECMDID_SPELL: Perform spelling check.
- ❑ OLE.OLECMDID_ZOOM: Zoom the view.
- ❑ OLE.OLECMDID_FIND: Do a search.

You can check the status of a command on an OLE object through the queryStatus method:

```
public int queryStatus(int cmd)
```

You pass the command id as the argument. This method returns the status of the specified command as a bitwise OR'd combination of the following:

- ❑ OLE.OLECMDF_SUPPORTED
- ❑ OLE.OLECMDF_ENABLED
- ❑ OLE.OLECMDF_LATCHED
- ❑ OLE.OLECMDF_NINCHED

If a command is enabled, you can then invoke the exec method to execute the command:

```
public int exec(int cmdID, int options, Variant in, Variant out)
```

You specify the command id in the first argument. The behavior of the specified command can be configured through options. Valid values for options are: OLE.OLECMDEXECOPT_DODEFAULT, OLE.OLECMDEXECOPT_PROMPTUSER, OLE.OLECMDEXECOPT_DONTPROMPTUSER, OLE.OLECMDEXECOPT_SHOWHELP.

Parameters passed to the command can be specified in the in argument through a Variant object. The Variant class provides a general OLE mechanism for passing data of different types via a common interface. You can use the out argument to obtain the values returned from the command.

The exec method returns OLE.S_OK if the command is executed successfully.

As an example, the following code creates the spell check action using the `exec` method:

```
protected ToolBarManager createToolBarManager(int style) {
    ...

    Action actionSpellCheck = new Action("Spell check") {
        public void run() {
            if((clientSite.queryStatus(OLE.OLECMDID_SPELL) & OLE.OLECMDF_ENABLED)
                    != 0) {
                clientSite.exec(OLE.OLECMDID_SPELL,
                                    OLE.OLECMDEXECOPT_PROMPTUSER, null, null);
            }
        }
    };

    manager.add(actionSpellCheck);

    return manager;
}
```

First, the status of the spell check command is checked. If the command is enabled, it is executed through the `exec` method.

The `exec` method can be used only to execute common commands. To access a much richer set of commands, OLE automation should be used.

# OLE Automation

In the previous section, you learned how to use the `exec` method to execute simple commands. OLE automation provides a generic mechanism for accessing functionalities specific to a particular ActiveX control or OLE document. Only those OLE documents and ActiveX controls supporting the `IDispatch` interface can provide OLE automation support. OLE automation allows you to get and set properties and invoke methods of an OLE document or ActiveX control.

OLE automation can be used to simplify the user's tasks. For example, you are developing an e-mail client application. This application allows the user to compose e-mail messages in Microsoft Word and then send them out. Before sending a message, the user has to check the spelling to catch and correct any spelling errors. If the user forgets to perform the spelling check, the e-mail is sent out with possible spelling errors. With OLE automation, you can call the spelling check function of Word to perform the spelling check automatically when the user clicks the Send button. This simple feature protects the user from any embarrassing spelling errors.

## Listing OLE Automation Properties and Methods

Before getting/setting property values and invoking methods, you need to know the property or method name and its semantics. You can use the following method to inspect properties and methods supported by an OLE document or ActiveX control:

```
/*
 * Copyright (c) 2000, 2003 IBM Corp. All rights reserved. This file is made
 * available under the terms of the Common Public License v1.0 which
 * accompanies this distribution, and is available at
 * http://www.eclipse.org/legal/cpl-v10.html
 */

/*
 * OLE and ActiveX example snippet: browse the typelibinfo for a program id
 *
 * For a list of all SWT example snippets see
 * http://dev.eclipse.org/viewcvs/index.cgi/%7Echeckout%7E/platform-swt-
home/dev.html#snippets
 */
import org.eclipse.swt.*;
import org.eclipse.swt.internal.ole.win32.*;
import org.eclipse.swt.ole.win32.*;
import org.eclipse.swt.widgets.*;

public class Main {

    public static void main(String[] args) {
        if (args.length == 0) {
            System.out.println("Usage: java Main <program id>");
            return;
        }

        String progID = args[0];

        Shell shell = new Shell();

        OleFrame frame = new OleFrame(shell, SWT.NONE);
        OleControlSite site = null;
        OleAutomation auto = null;
        try {
            site = new OleControlSite(frame, SWT.NONE, progID);
            auto = new OleAutomation(site);
        } catch (SWTException ex) {
            System.out.println("Unable to open type library for " + progID);
            return;
        }

        TYPEATTR typeattr = auto.getTypeInfoAttributes();
        if (typeattr != null) {
            if (typeattr.cFuncs > 0)
                System.out.println("Functions for " + progID + " :\n");
            for (int i = 0; i < typeattr.cFuncs; i++) {
                OleFunctionDescription data = auto.getFunctionDescription(i);
                String argList = "";
                int firstOptionalArgIndex =
                    data.args.length - data.optionalArgCount;
                for (int j = 0; j < data.args.length; j++) {
                    argList += "[";
                    if (j >= firstOptionalArgIndex)
```

```
                                argList += "optional, ";
                        argList += getDirection(data.args[j].flags)
                                + "] "
                                + getTypeName(data.args[j].type)
                                + " "
                                + data.args[j].name;
                        if (j < data.args.length - 1)
                                argList += ", ";
                }
                System.out.println(
                        getInvokeKind(data.invokeKind)
                                + " (id = "
                                + data.id
                                + ") : "
                                + "\n\tSignature   : "
                                + getTypeName(data.returnType)
                                + " "
                                + data.name
                                + "("
                                + argList
                                + ")"
                                + "\n\tDescription : "
                                + data.documentation
                                + "\n\tHelp File   : "
                                + data.helpFile
                                + "\n");
        }

        if (typeattr.cVars > 0)
                System.out.println("\n\nVariables for " + progID + " :\n");
        for (int i = 0; i < typeattr.cVars; i++) {
                OlePropertyDescription data = auto.getPropertyDescription(i);
                System.out.println(
                        "PROPERTY (id = "
                                + data.id
                                + ") :"
                                + "\n\tName : "
                                + data.name
                                + "\n\tType : "
                                + getTypeName(data.type)
                                + "\n");
        }
    }

    auto.dispose();
    shell.dispose();
}

private static String getTypeName(int type) {
    switch (type) {
        case OLE.VT_BOOL :
            return "boolean";
        case OLE.VT_R4 :
            return "float";
```

```
        case OLE.VT_R8 :
            return "double";
        case OLE.VT_I4 :
            return "int";
        case OLE.VT_DISPATCH :
            return "IDispatch";
        case OLE.VT_UNKNOWN :
            return "IUnknown";
        case OLE.VT_I2 :
            return "short";
        case OLE.VT_BSTR :
            return "String";
        case OLE.VT_VARIANT :
            return "Variant";
        case OLE.VT_CY :
            return "Currency";
        case OLE.VT_DATE :
            return "Date";
        case OLE.VT_UI1 :
            return "unsigned char";
        case OLE.VT_UI4 :
            return "unsigned int";
        case OLE.VT_USERDEFINED :
            return "UserDefined";
        case OLE.VT_HRESULT :
            return "int";
        case OLE.VT_VOID :
            return "void";

        case OLE.VT_BYREF | OLE.VT_BOOL :
            return "boolean **";
        case OLE.VT_BYREF | OLE.VT_R4 :
            return "float **";
        case OLE.VT_BYREF | OLE.VT_R8 :
            return "double **";
        case OLE.VT_BYREF | OLE.VT_I4 :
            return "int **";
        case OLE.VT_BYREF | OLE.VT_DISPATCH :
            return "IDispatch **";
        case OLE.VT_BYREF | OLE.VT_UNKNOWN :
            return "IUnknown **";
        case OLE.VT_BYREF | OLE.VT_I2 :
            return "short **";
        case OLE.VT_BYREF | OLE.VT_BSTR :
            return "String **";
        case OLE.VT_BYREF | OLE.VT_VARIANT :
            return "Variant **";
        case OLE.VT_BYREF | OLE.VT_CY :
            return "Currency **";
        case OLE.VT_BYREF | OLE.VT_DATE :
            return "Date **";
        case OLE.VT_BYREF | OLE.VT_UI1 :
            return "unsigned char **";
        case OLE.VT_BYREF | OLE.VT_UI4 :
```

457

```
                    return "unsigned int **";
            case OLE.VT_BYREF | OLE.VT_USERDEFINED :
                return "UserDefined **";
        }
        return "unknown " + type;
    }

    private static String getDirection(int direction) {
        String dirString = "";
        boolean comma = false;
        if ((direction & OLE.IDLFLAG_FIN) != 0) {
            dirString += "in";
            comma = true;
        }
        if ((direction & OLE.IDLFLAG_FOUT) != 0) {
            if (comma)
                dirString += ", ";
            dirString += "out";
            comma = true;
        }
        if ((direction & OLE.IDLFLAG_FLCID) != 0) {
            if (comma)
                dirString += ", ";
            dirString += "lcid";
            comma = true;
        }
        if ((direction & OLE.IDLFLAG_FRETVAL) != 0) {
            if (comma)
                dirString += ", ";
            dirString += "retval";
        }

        return dirString;
    }

    private static String getInvokeKind(int invKind) {
        switch (invKind) {
            case OLE.INVOKE_FUNC :
                return "METHOD";
            case OLE.INVOKE_PROPERTYGET :
                return "PROPERTY GET";
            case OLE.INVOKE_PROPERTYPUT :
                return "PROPERTY PUT";
            case OLE.INVOKE_PROPERTYPUTREF :
                return "PROPERTY PUT BY REF";
        }
        return "unknown " + invKind;
    }
}
```

The usage of this class is:

```
java Main ProgramID
```

To find all the properties and methods available for Microsoft Word, you run `java Main Word.Document`. The following code lists snippets of the output:

```
Functions for Word.Document :

...

PROPERTY GET (id = 71) :
    Signature    : boolean SpellingChecked()
    Description : null
    Help File    : F:\Program Files\Microsoft Office\OFFICE11\VBAWD10.CHM

PROPERTY PUT (id = 71) :
    Signature    : void SpellingChecked([in] boolean null)
    Description : null
    Help File    : F:\Program Files\Microsoft Office\OFFICE11\VBAWD10.CHM


METHOD (id = 65535) :
    Signature    : void Select()
    Description : null
    Help File    : F:\Program Files\Microsoft Office\OFFICE11\VBAWD10.CHM

...
```

In the following subsections, you learn how to get/set value for the SpellingChecked property and invoke the Save method.

## Getting and Setting Property Values

Before getting or setting property values, you need to create an OleAutomation object for the OLE document or ActiveX control. You can then use the OleAutomation object to get/set property values and invoke methods.

For example, the following code prints the value of the SpellingChecked property:

```java
OleAutomation automation = new OleAutomation(clientSite);

// looks up the ID for property SpellingChecked.
int[] propertyIDs = automation.getIDsOfNames(new String[]{"SpellingChecked"});
int propertyID = propertyIDs[0];

Variant result = automation.getProperty(propertyID);
System.out.println("SpellingChecked: " + result.getBoolean());

automation.dispose();
```

The OleAutomation object is constructed first. Then you look for the property id for SpellingChecked with the getIDsOfNames method:

```java
public int[] getIDsOfNames(String[] names)
```

To get the property value, you invoke the getProperty method:

```
public Variant getProperty(int dispIdMember)
```

The getProperty method returns the property value. Because the expected variant type is Boolean, you can check the value through the getBoolean method of the Variant class.

Finally, you dispose of the OleAutomation object.

You can set the property value for SpellingChecked in a very similar way:

```
OleAutomation automation = new OleAutomation(clientSite);

// looks up the ID for property SpellingChecked.
int[] propertyIDs = automation.getIDsOfNames(new String[]{"SpellingChecked"});
int propertyID = propertyIDs[0];

boolean result = automation.setProperty(propertyID, new Variant(true));
System.out.println(result ? "Successful" : "Failed");

automation.dispose();
```

This time, you use the setProperty method to set the property value for SpellingChecked:

```
public boolean setProperty(int dispIdMember, Variant rgvarg)
```

The setProperty method takes the property ID and the value object as the arguments. The property value to be set is embedded in a Variant object. This method returns true if the operation is successful, false otherwise.

## Invoking Methods

OLE automation also allows you to invoke methods provided by an OLE document or ActiveX control.

Invoking a method is much like getting the value for a property. The following code invokes the Select method to select all the content objects in the Word document, as shown in Figure 22-3:

```
OleAutomation automation = new OleAutomation(clientSite);

// looks up the ID for method Select.
int[] methodIDs = automation.getIDsOfNames(new String[]{"Select"});
int methodID = methodIDs[0];

Variant result = automation.invoke(methodID);
System.out.println(result == null ? "Successful" : "Failed");

automation.dispose();
```

The invoke method of the OleAutomation class is used to invoke the Select method:

```
public Variant invoke(int dispIdMember)
```

The `invoke` method invokes a method on the OLE object and returns the result of the method. If the OLE method finishes and returns `null`, the invoke method return a dummy `Variant` object to indicate the completion status of the OLE method. If an error occurs while executing an OLE method, the `invoke` method returns `null`.

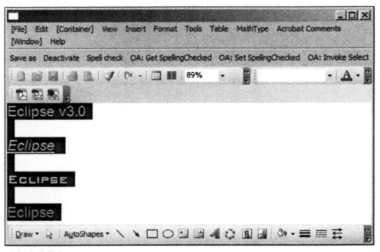

Figure 22-3

# Summary

This chapter showed you how to integrate Windows applications in SWT applications through the OLE mechanism. To embed an OLE document or ActiveX control, you first create an OLE container and then construct a site within the container to manage the life cycle of the OLE object. You can activate an OLE document or ActiveX control to make it visible (in-place activation). With the help of the `save` method of the `OleClientSite` class, you can save the changes made on an OLE document or ActiveX control either to a storage file or a plain file. Simple commands such as `new file` and `save file` can be executed through the `exec` method of the `OleClientSite` class. Advanced commands can be invoked through OLE automation if the OLE document or ActiveX control supports the `IDispatch` interface. Furthermore, you can use OLE automation to get and set property values for the OLE document or ActiveX control. In the next chapter, you learn how to perform advanced drawing with Draw2D.

# Drawing Diagrams with Draw2D

This chapter introduces a simple rendering framework — Draw2D. With Draw2D, you can create complex figures easily. This chapter shows you how to create simple UML diagrams with Draw2D. The sample application displays the selected class in a UML diagram. By combining small figures, you can create manageable complex figures without the tedious code. Draw2D also provides excellent figure connection support. You can easily connect two figures and decorate the connection. You can generate various events with lightweight widgets in Draw2D. You can also register corresponding listeners to listen to events and then react accordingly.

Draw2D is part of the Graphical Editing Framework (GEF). This chapter discusses only Draw2D. For details of GEF, please visit `www.eclipse.org/gef/`.

## Overview

As an Eclipse plug-in, Draw2D provides a lightweight widget system that is hosted on an SWT `Canvas` widget. Draw2D provides powerful rendering and layout capabilities. Figures, borders, and layout managers are the basic elements in Draw2D. You can combine them to create complex figures to suit various applications. In this chapter, you step through the construction of a sample application based on Draw2D. Before going further, let's take a closer look at the architecture of Draw2D.

In Draw2D, the interface `IFigure` represents a lightweight graphical object. A figure can be any visible object — for example, a button, a label, or an ellipse shape. In addition, a figure may contain other figures as its children. You can compose figures to create highly complex renderings. You supply figures to Draw2D and it draws those figures on an SWT `Canvas` widget. The `LightweightSystem` class plays a key role in Draw2D by linking the SWT canvas and figure objects. It draws figures on the SWT canvas and provides an event delegation mechanism. The architecture is illustrated in Figure 23-1.

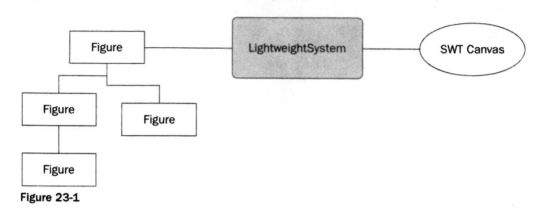

**Figure 23-1**

The following code creates one of the simplest Draw2D applications, as shown in Figure 23-2.

**Figure 23-2**

```
package com.asprise.books.javaui.ch23;

import org.eclipse.draw2d.Button;
import org.eclipse.draw2d.LightweightSystem;
import org.eclipse.jface.window.ApplicationWindow;
import org.eclipse.swt.SWT;
import org.eclipse.swt.graphics.Image;
import org.eclipse.swt.layout.FillLayout;
import org.eclipse.swt.widgets.Canvas;
import org.eclipse.swt.widgets.Composite;
import org.eclipse.swt.widgets.Control;
import org.eclipse.swt.widgets.Shell;

public class Draw2DSample extends ApplicationWindow {

    /**
     * @param parentShell
     */
    public Draw2DSample(Shell parentShell) {
        super(parentShell);
    }

    /* (non-Javadoc)
     * @see org.eclipse.jface.window.Window#createContents(Composite)
     */
    protected Control createContents(Composite parent) {
        Composite composite = new Composite(parent, SWT.NULL);
```

```
        composite.setLayout(new FillLayout());

        Canvas canvas = new Canvas(composite, SWT.NULL);

        LightweightSystem lws = new LightweightSystem(canvas);
        Button button = new Button("Button",
                        new Image(getShell().getDisplay(), "icons/eclipse0.gif"));
        lws.setContents(button);

        return composite;
    }

    public static void main(String[] args) {
        Draw2DSample window = new Draw2DSample(null);
        window.setBlockOnOpen(true);
        window.open();
    }
}
```

In previous chapters, we used the `org.eclipse.swt.widgets.Button` class to represent a button. In Draw2D, the `org.eclipse.draw2d.Button` class is used instead. The main difference between those two classes is that `org.eclipse.swt.widgets.Button` represents a widget that consumes native system resources, while `org.eclipse.draw2d.Button` represents a lightweight button and it does not require native resources. Such lightweight widgets provide graphical information for the `LightweightSystem` class to draw them on the canvas. Many SWT widgets have their own lightweight Draw2D counterparts, such as buttons and labels.

In the `createContents` method, a `Canvas` is created to host Draw2D figures. An instance of `LightweightSystem` is then created with the canvas. Then you create a button with a text label and image label using the `org.eclipse.draw2d.Button` class. The `setContents` method of the `LightweightSystem` class is used to pass the figure object. If you have multiple figure objects, you need to pass only the top-level figure.

Finally, the `main` method brings up the window and displays the button.

To compile and run the preceding code, you need to download and install the GEF plug-in from www .eclipse.org/gef/ and add the `draw2d.jar` file under `$ECLIPSE_HOME/plugins/org.eclipse .draw2d_x.x.x` into your Java class path.

# Creating Simple UML Diagrams with Draw2D

The rest of this chapter describes the features of Draw2D and includes a sample application, as shown in Figure 23-3. The sample application displays a simple UML diagram for a class. The fields and methods of the class are displayed. The superclass of the class (if any) is drawn on the top of the class figure. An arrow is used to show the inheritance relationship between the class and its superclass.

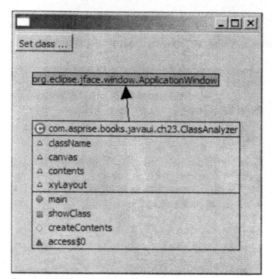

**Figure 23-3**

First, you need to create the figure displaying class members (referred to as a *class figure*). The class figure has a line border and contains three parts. The top part is the class name label. The middle part and the bottom part are two compartments that can contain figures for class fields and methods. For the class name label, you can use the `org.eclipse.draw2d.Label` class. For the two compartments, you need to create a custom figure class that is able to lay out child figures vertically. Here is the code for the implementation of the custom figure, which extends the `Figure` class:

```
class Box extends Figure {
    public Box() {
        setBorder(new BoxBorder());

        ToolbarLayout toolbarLayout = new ToolbarLayout();
        toolbarLayout.setStretchMinorAxis(false);

        setLayoutManager(toolbarLayout);
    }

    private class BoxBorder extends AbstractBorder {

        /*
         * (non-Javadoc)
         *
         * @see org.eclipse.draw2d.Border#getInsets(org.eclipse.draw2d.IFigure)
         */
        public Insets getInsets(IFigure figure) {
            return new Insets(1, 0, 0, 0);
        }

        /*
         * (non-Javadoc)
```

```
     *
     * @see org.eclipse.draw2d.Border#paint(org.eclipse.draw2d.IFigure,
     *        org.eclipse.draw2d.Graphics,
     *        org.eclipse.draw2d.geometry.Insets)
     */
    public void paint(IFigure figure, Graphics graphics, Insets insets) {
        Rectangle rect = getPaintRectangle(figure, insets);
        graphics.drawLine(rect.getTopLeft(), rect.getTopRight());
    }


    }

}
```

There are two important things to note in the preceding code. First, a custom border is created to display a thin line on the top of the box as a compartment separator. Second, the layout manager of this custom figure is set to `ToolbarLayout`. `ToolbarLayout` arranges figures in a single row or column. By default, it arranges the child figures in a column.

Now, you are ready to create the class figure with the following code:

```
class ClassFigure extends Figure {
    ImageRegistry registry = new ImageRegistry();
    // image keys.
    String KEY_CLASS = "class";
    String KEY_METHOD_PUBLIC = "method_public";
    String KEY_METHOD_DEFAULT = "method_default";
    String KEY_METHOD_PROTECTED = "method_protected";
    String KEY_METHOD_PRIVATE = "method_private";
    String KEY_FIELD_PUBLIC = "field_public";
    String KEY_FIELD_DEFAULT = "field_default";
    String KEY_FIELD_PROTECTED = "field_protected";
    String KEY_FIELD_PRIVATE = "field_private";

    String[] keys =
        {
            KEY_CLASS,
            KEY_METHOD_PUBLIC,
            KEY_METHOD_DEFAULT,
            KEY_METHOD_PROTECTED,
            KEY_METHOD_PRIVATE,
            KEY_FIELD_PUBLIC,
            KEY_FIELD_DEFAULT,
            KEY_FIELD_PROTECTED,
            KEY_FIELD_PRIVATE };

    public Box fieldBox = new Box();
    public Box methodBox = new Box();

    public ClassFigure(Class cls) {
        setLayoutManager(new ToolbarLayout());
        setBorder(new LineBorder(ColorConstants.black));
        setBackgroundColor(ColorConstants.yellow);
```

```
        setOpaque(true);

    for (int i = 0; i < keys.length; i++)
        registry.put(
            keys[i],
            ImageDescriptor.createFromFile(
                null,
                "icons/java/" + keys[i] + ".gif"));

    Label title = new Label(cls.getName(), registry.get(KEY_CLASS));
    add(title);
    add(fieldBox);
    add(methodBox);

    // fields.
    Field[] fields = cls.getDeclaredFields();
    for (int i = 0; i < fields.length; i++) {
        Field field = fields[i];
        Image image = null;
        if (Modifier.isPublic(field.getModifiers())) {
            image = registry.get(KEY_FIELD_PUBLIC);
        } else if (Modifier.isProtected(field.getModifiers())) {
            image = registry.get(KEY_FIELD_PROTECTED);
        } else if (Modifier.isPrivate(field.getModifiers())) {
            image = registry.get(KEY_FIELD_PRIVATE);
        } else {
            image = registry.get(KEY_FIELD_DEFAULT);
        }
        fieldBox.add(new Label(fields[i].getName(), image));
    }

    // methods.
    Method[] methods = cls.getDeclaredMethods();
    for (int i = 0; i < methods.length; i++) {
        Method method = methods[i];
        Image image = null;
        if (Modifier.isPublic(method.getModifiers())) {
            image = registry.get(KEY_METHOD_PUBLIC);
        } else if (Modifier.isProtected(method.getModifiers())) {
            image = registry.get(KEY_METHOD_PROTECTED);
        } else if (Modifier.isPrivate(method.getModifiers())) {
            image = registry.get(KEY_METHOD_PRIVATE);
        } else {
            image = registry.get(KEY_METHOD_DEFAULT);
        }
        methodBox.add(new Label(methods[i].getName(), image));
    }

    }
}
```

In the constructor of the ClassFigure class, first set the layout manager for this figure to ToolbarLayout so that child figures are displayed in a column. Then set a line border for the figure.

The background color is configured through the setBackgroundColor method. By default, a figure is transparent. You can use setOpaque to change this behavior. After setting the layout manager and border, add the three parts in order. For each field, a label is created and added to the box containing fields. Similarly, create a label for each method and add it to the box containing methods.

To create a class figure for a class, you can simply invoke the constructor with the class as the argument.

The class details are displayed in a class figure, while the superclass is displayed briefly as a label. You can use an application window to display both items on its content area (see Figure 23-4).

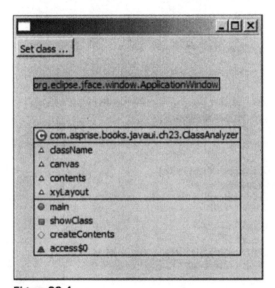

**Figure 23-4**

```
public class ClassAnalyzer extends ApplicationWindow {
    Text className;

    Canvas canvas;
    Figure contents;
    XYLayout xyLayout;

    /**
     * @param parentShell
     */
    public ClassAnalyzer(Shell parentShell) {
        super(parentShell);
        addToolBar(SWT.NULL);
    }

    private void showClass(Class cls) {
        if (cls == null)
            return;

        // removes all existing items.
```

```
            contents.removeAll();

            // draws super class.
            Label sup = null;
            if (cls.getSuperclass() != null) {
                Class superClass = cls.getSuperclass();
                sup = new Label(superClass.getName());
                sup.setBorder(new LineBorder());
                sup.setBackgroundColor(ColorConstants.lightGreen);
                sup.setOpaque(true);
            }

            if (sup != null) {
                contents.add(sup);
                xyLayout.setConstraint(sup, new Rectangle(20, 20, -1, -1));
            }

            ClassFigure classFigure = new ClassFigure(cls);
            contents.add(classFigure);
            if (sup == null)
                xyLayout.setConstraint(classFigure, new Rectangle(20, 20, -1, -1));
            else
                xyLayout.setConstraint(
                    classFigure,
                    new Rectangle(20, sup.getBounds().height + 40, -1, -1));

            // resizes the shell.
            getShell().setSize(
                contents.getPreferredSize().width + 30,
                contents.getPreferredSize().height + 80);

        }


    /*
     * (non-Javadoc)
     *
     * @see org.eclipse.jface.window.Window#createContents(Composite)
     */
    protected Control createContents(Composite parent) {
        Composite composite = new Composite(parent, SWT.NULL);
        composite.setLayout(new FillLayout());

        canvas = new Canvas(composite, SWT.NULL);

        LightweightSystem lws = new LightweightSystem(canvas);
        contents = new Figure();
        xyLayout = new XYLayout();
        contents.setLayoutManager(xyLayout);

        lws.setContents(contents);

        showClass(this.getClass());

        // Creates toolbar items.
```

```
        getToolBarManager().add(new Action("Set class ...") {
            public void run() {
                InputDialog dialog =
                    new InputDialog(
                        getShell(),
                        "",
                        "Please enter the class name",
                        "",
                        null);
                if (dialog.open() != Dialog.OK)
                    return;

                contents.removeAll();
                Class cls = null;
                try {
                    cls = Class.forName(dialog.getValue());
                } catch (ClassNotFoundException e) {
                    e.printStackTrace();
                }
                if (cls != null) {
                    showClass(cls);
                }
            }
        });
        getToolBarManager().update(true);

        return composite;
    }

    public static void main(String[] args) {
        ClassAnalyzer window = new ClassAnalyzer(null);

        window.setBlockOnOpen(true);
        window.open();

        Display.getCurrent().dispose();
    }
}
```

The createContents method creates the canvas and the toolbar item. The contents figure has XYLayout as its layout manager. XYLayout lays out the components using the layout constraints defined by every component. Constraint setting examples appear later in the chapter.

The showClass method is used to create and display both the class figure and the superclass label for a given class. It first removes all the existing items on the contents figure. If the given class has a superclass, a label with green background is shown with the superclass name as its text content, and the label defines the following constraint:

```
xyLayout.setConstraint(sup, new Rectangle(20, 20, -1, -1));
```

**471**

The `setConstraint` method sets the layout constraint for the figure. The constraint object should be of the type `org.eclipse.draw2d.geometry.Rectangle`. The constraint `new Rectangle(20, 20, -1, -1)` specifies that the top-left corner of the figure should be located at position (20, 20) and the figure should be displayed at its preferred size.

Finally, you resize the shell to show all the figures on the screen.

# Adding Connections

A *connection* can be used to connect two figures. Before creating a connection, you need to establish two endpoints for it. These endpoints include the *source anchors* and *target anchors*. An anchor implements the `ConnectionAnchor` interface. If one of the anchors moves, the connection moves with it. In Draw2D, a connection is usually displayed as a polyline. If polylines are not enough, you can decorate connections with endpoint decorations, such as arrow tips.

In the sample application, you need to connect the class figure and superclass figure with the arrow connection, as shown in Figure 23-5.

Figure 23-5

In the `showClass` method, you use the following code to create the connection between the class figure and the superclass figure:

```
private void showClass(Class cls) {
    // Creates the class figure and the superclass figure.
    ...

    // Adds connection.
    if (sup != null) {
        PolylineConnection connection = new PolylineConnection();
        ChopboxAnchor source = new ChopboxAnchor(classFigure);
        ChopboxAnchor target = new ChopboxAnchor(sup);
        connection.setSourceAnchor(source);
        connection.setTargetAnchor(target);

        PolygonDecoration decoration = new PolygonDecoration();
        PointList list = new PointList();
        list.addPoint(-2, -2);
        list.addPoint(0, 0);
        list.addPoint(-2, 2);
```

```
        decoration.setTemplate(list);

        connection.setTargetDecoration(decoration);
        contents.add(connection);

    }

    // resizes the shell.
    getShell().setSize(
        contents.getPreferredSize().width + 30,
        contents.getPreferredSize().height + 80);
}
```

An instance of the `PolylineConnection` class is created first. The source anchor and target anchor are then created as `ChopboxAnchors`. You find the location of a `ChopboxAnchor` by calculating the intersection of a line drawn from the center point of its owner's box to a reference point on that box. As a result, the connection will be oriented such that it points from the center of the class figure to the superclass figure.

You use the `setSourceAnchor` and `setTargetAnchor` methods to set the source anchor and target anchor for a connection, respectively:

```
public void setSourceAnchor(ConnectionAnchor anchor)
public void setTargetAnchor(ConnectionAnchor anchor)
```

After the connection is created, decorate it with an arrow. The arrow is constructed as an instance of `PolygonDecoration`. The shape of this arrow is defined through a point list. The arrow is set as the decoration of the target anchor through the `setTargetDecoration` method of the `PolylineConnection` class.

The connection and its decoration are now ready to be used. The connection is not added to the contents figure automatically. You add the connection as an `IFigure` to the contents figure through the `add` method. Now if you run the sample application, you can see the connection displayed as expected.

# Capturing Events

Chapter 4 covered how to capture events from SWT widgets. Simple widgets in Draw2D can also generate various events. You can register corresponding listeners in order to capture events from `IFigures`. The following are some of the event types that an `IFigure` is capable of generating (the corresponding listener classes appear in parentheses):

❑ **Ancestor change event** (`AncestorListener`): This event is fired for any change in the ancestor hierarchy of the figure.

❑ **Figure event** (`FigureListener`): A figure event occurs when the figure moves.

❑ **Focus event** (`FocusListener`): Focus events are generated when the figure loses or gains focus.

❑ **Key event** (`KeyListener`): A key event occurs when a key is pressed or released.

❑ **Mouse event** (MouseListener): Mouse events are generated when mouse buttons are pressed, released, or double-clicked.

❑ **Mouse motion event** (MouseMotionListener): A mouse motion event occurs when the mouse moves.

You use a mouse listener to add a feature to the sample application: When the user double-clicks the superclass figure, the application analyzes the superclass and then displays it in great detail. The following code does the job:

```
private void showClass(Class cls) {
    ...

    if (cls.getSuperclass() != null) {
        final Class superClass = cls.getSuperclass();
        sup = new Label(superClass.getName());

        ...

        sup.addMouseListener(new MouseListener() {
            public void mousePressed(org.eclipse.draw2d.MouseEvent me) {
            }

            public void mouseReleased(org.eclipse.draw2d.MouseEvent me) {
            }

            public void mouseDoubleClicked(
                org.eclipse.draw2d.MouseEvent me) {
                showClass(superClass);
            }
        });
    }

    ...

}
```

When the user double-clicks the superclass figure, the mouse listener is notified. As a result, the superclass is set as the current class.

# Summary

Draw2D is a simple and easy-to-use widget system that uses an SWT canvas. It provides powerful rendering and layout capabilities. You can combine figures, borders, and layout managers to create complex figures.

This chapter introduced basic Draw2D features through a sample application. You learned how to create complex UML diagrams by combining small figure objects. The chapter also introduced two main layout managers: ToolbarLayout lays out figures in a single row or column, whereas XYLayout allows you to lay out components through layout constraints. With Draw2D's excellent connection support, you can connect two figures easily. Additionally, you can decorate the connection with different types of endpoints, such as arrow tips.

The last part of this chapter introduced event handling in Draw2D. Simple widgets can also generate various events. You can register corresponding listeners to specific events and then watch them react accordingly.

This chapter and previous chapters should provide you with a good foundation for using SWT/JFace. The next chapter draws on the knowledge you've gained in this book as it guides you through the steps of developing a practical application.

# Sample Application

In this chapter, you are guided through the steps to develop a simple FTP client application using SWT/JFace. By drawing on knowledge acquired in previous chapters, you can create full-fledged practical applications. With the FTP client sample application, you learn how to use application windows, actions, menu bars, and toolbars. Furthermore, you learn how to make main UI components resizable by using sash forms properly. You can use drag and drop to improve the user interface and make it more accessible to the user.

## Introduction

The previous chapters cover the SWT/JFace framework extensively. This chapter shows you how to combine all the knowledge acquired to create full-fledged practical applications. You learn step by step how to create an FTP client application such as the one shown in Figure 24-1.

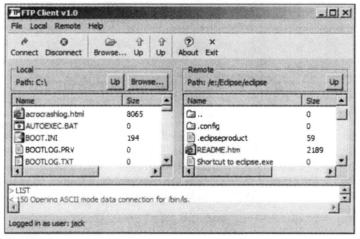

Figure 24-1

The FTP client allows the user to connect to any FTP server and navigate both the local and remote file systems. The user can download a file from the server easily by using the intuitive drag-and-drop feature. Most of the main user interface components can be resized easily by the user to suit his or her needs.

For this application, we focus on the construction of the user interface rather than the FTP protocol details. Apache Commons/Net library is used to communicate with FTP servers and execute FTP commands. You can download the library (`commons-net-x.x.x.jar`) from `http://jakarta.apache.org/commons/net/index.html`. Additionally, you need to add Commons/Net library's dependent package Apache Jakarta ORO library to your Java path, which can be downloaded from `http://jakarta.apache.org/oro/`.

The following sections explain the main steps to create the FTP client. Before you begin, you should have a good understanding of how the UI components are organized. Figure 24-2 dissects the FTP client window.

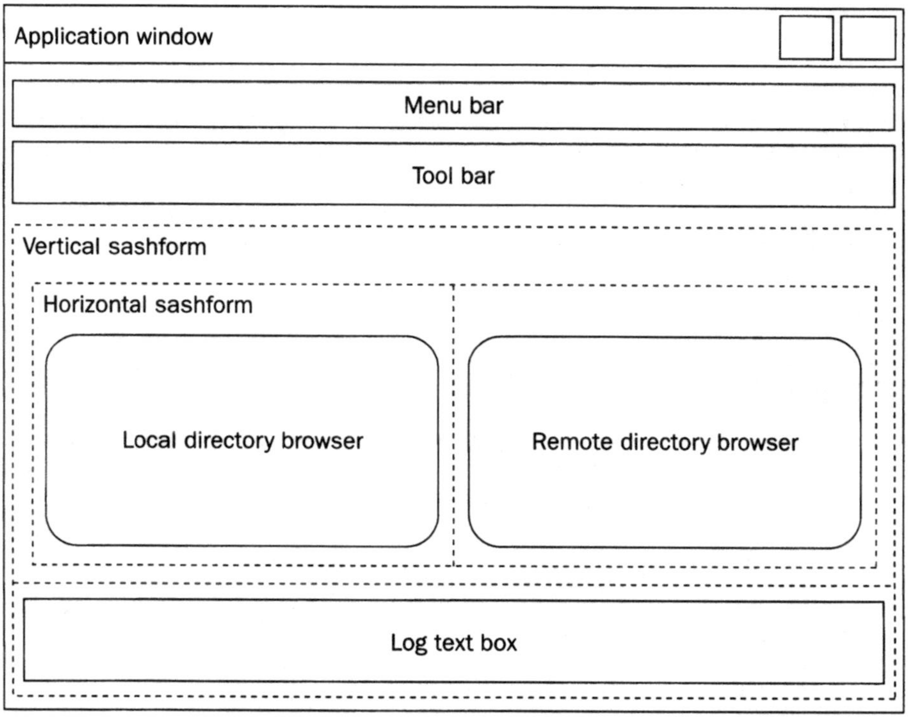

**Figure 24-2**

The FTP client window is an `ApplicationWindow` with its menu bar and toolbar. Below the toolbar is the content area. Sash forms are used to make main UI components resizable. A vertical sash form separates the content area into two portions. The top portion displays local and remote file systems, and the bottom portion prints log information. Additionally, a horizontal sash form is used to separate the local file system navigation components from the remote ones. Next, you learn about each step to complete the whole user interface.

# Building the Skeleton

This section builds the skeleton for the FTP client application window.

## Creating the Application Window

You create the FTP client application window by extending the `ApplicationWindow` class as follows:

```java
public class FTPWindow extends ApplicationWindow {
    TableViewer localDirBrowser;
    TableViewer remoteDirBrowser;
    Label labelPathLocal;
    Label labelPathRemote;
    StyledText textLog;

    ConnectionDialog connectionDialog;

    Action actionUpLocalDir;
    Action actionUpRemoteDir;
    Action actionBrowseLocalDir;
    Action actionConnect;
    Action actionDisconnect;

    Action actionDisplayAbout;
    Action actionExit;

    FTPClient ftp;
    ConnectionInfo connectionInfo;

    /**
     * @param parentShell
     */
    public FTPWindow(Shell parentShell) {
        super(parentShell);

        createActions();

        addStatusLine();
        addToolBar(SWT.FLAT);
        addMenuBar();

        ftp = new FTPClient();
        ftp.addProtocolCommandListener(new ProtocolCommandListener() {
            public void protocolCommandSent(ProtocolCommandEvent e) {
                logMessage("> " + e.getCommand(), false);
            }

            public void protocolReplyReceived(ProtocolCommandEvent e) {
                logMessage("< " + e.getMessage(), false);
            }
        });

    }
    ...
```

All the fields are declared above the constructor. Two table viewers, localDirBrowser and remoteDirBrowser, are used to display local and remote file systems, respectively. You learn how to implement each of them in the next section. A StyledText is used to print log information. ConnectionDialog is a simple JFace dialog that acquires connection setting input from the user (see Figure 24-3).

**Figure 24-3**

The FTPClient class is in the Apache Commons/Net library. We use the FTPClient class to execute FTP commands. For more details, you can consult the Javadoc of Commons/Net library.

The constructor first invokes the createActions method to create all the actions, such as connection and disconnection actions. Then it configures the toolbar and menu bar for the application window. Finally, you create the FTP client object and register a protocol command listener. The protocol command listener logs the command and replies to the styled text control through the logMessage method:

```
private void logMessage(String message, boolean showInStatusBar) {
    StyleRange styleRange1 = new StyleRange();
    styleRange1.start = textLog.getCharCount();
    styleRange1.length = message.length();
    styleRange1.foreground = getShell().getDisplay().
            getSystemColor(SWT.COLOR_DARK_GREEN);
    styleRange1.fontStyle = SWT.NORMAL;

    textLog.append(message + "\r\n");
    textLog.setStyleRange(styleRange1);
    textLog.setSelection(textLog.getCharCount());

    if(showInStatusBar) {
        setStatus(message);
    }
}
```

## Creating Actions

Before you create the menu bar and the toolbar, you must construct action objects. In this application, you use the createActions method to create all the actions:

```java
private void createActions() {
    // Up one level - local dir
    actionUpLocalDir = new Action() {
        public void run() {
            if (localDirBrowser.getInput() == null)
                return;
            File dir = ((File) localDirBrowser.getInput()).getParentFile();
            if (dir != null) {
                localDirBrowser.setInput(dir);
                labelPathLocal.setText("Path: " + dir);
            }
        }
    };
    actionUpLocalDir.setText("Up");
    actionUpLocalDir.setToolTipText("Up one level - local dir");
    actionUpLocalDir.setImageDescriptor(
        ImageDescriptor.createFromFile(null, "icons/ftp/up.gif"));

    // browse for local dir
    actionBrowseLocalDir = new Action() {
        public void run() {
            DirectoryDialog dialog = new DirectoryDialog(getShell());
            String path = dialog.open();
            if (path == null)
                return;
            File file = new File(path);
            localDirBrowser.setInput(file);
            labelPathLocal.setText("Path: " + file);
        }
    };
    actionBrowseLocalDir.setText("Browse...");
    actionBrowseLocalDir.setToolTipText("Browse local directory");
    actionBrowseLocalDir.setImageDescriptor(
        ImageDescriptor.createFromFile(null, "icons/ftp/browse.gif"));

    // connect
    actionConnect = new Action() {
        public void run() {
            if (connectionDialog == null)
                connectionDialog = new ConnectionDialog(FTPWindow.this);
            if (connectionDialog.open() == Dialog.OK) {
                connectionInfo = connectionDialog.getConnectionInfo();
                if (connectionInfo == null) {
                    logError("Failed to get connection information.");
                } else {
                    // connects to remote host.
                    logMessage("Connecting to " + connectionInfo.host, true);
                    try {
                        ftp.connect(connectionInfo.host, connectionInfo.port);
                        if (!FTPReply
                            .isPositiveCompletion(ftp.getReplyCode()))
                            throw new RuntimeException(
                                "FTP server refused connection.");
```

**481**

```
                            logMessage("Connected to " + connectionInfo.host, true);
                        } catch (Exception e) {
                            logError(e.toString());
                            return;
                        }
                        try {
                            // logins in.
                            if (ftp
                                .login(
                                    connectionInfo.username,
                                    connectionInfo.password)) {
                                logMessage(
                                    "Logged in as user: "
                                        + connectionInfo.username, true);
                            }
                            // gets current working directory.
                            labelPathRemote.setText(
                                "Path: " + ftp.printWorkingDirectory());
                            // Lists files.
                            FTPFile[] files = ftp.listFiles();
                            remoteDirBrowser.setInput(files);
                            } catch (IOException e1) {
                            logError(e1.getMessage());
                            try {
                                ftp.disconnect();
                            } catch (IOException e2) {
                                //
                            }
                        }
                    }
                }
            }
        }
    };
    actionConnect.setText("Connect");
    actionConnect.setToolTipText("Connect to remote host");
    actionConnect.setImageDescriptor(
        ImageDescriptor.createFromFile(null, "icons/ftp/connect.gif"));

    // disconnect
    actionDisconnect = new Action() {
        public void run() {
            try {
                ftp.logout();
                ftp.disconnect();
            }catch(Exception e) {
                logError(e.toString());
            }
        }
    };
    actionDisconnect.setText("Disconnect");
    actionDisconnect.setToolTipText("Disconnect from remote host");
    actionDisconnect.setImageDescriptor(
```

```
                ImageDescriptor.createFromFile(null, "icons/ftp/stop.gif"));

        // up one level - remote dir.
        actionUpRemoteDir = new Action() {
            public void run() {
                try {
                    if (ftp.changeToParentDirectory()) {
                        // gets current working directory.
                        labelPathRemote.setText(
                            "Path: " + ftp.printWorkingDirectory());

                        // Lists files.
                        FTPFile[] files = ftp.listFiles();
                        remoteDirBrowser.setInput(files);
                    }
                } catch (Exception e) {
                    logError(e.toString());
                }
            }
        };
        actionUpRemoteDir.setText("Up");
        actionUpRemoteDir.setToolTipText("Up one level - remote dir");
        actionUpRemoteDir.setImageDescriptor(
            ImageDescriptor.createFromFile(null, "icons/ftp/up.gif"));

        actionDisplayAbout = new Action() {
            public void run() {
                MessageDialog.openInformation(getShell(), "About",
                    "FTP Client v1.0\nAll right reserved by Jack Li Guojie.");
            }
        };
        actionDisplayAbout.setText("About");
        actionDisplayAbout.setImageDescriptor(
            ImageDescriptor.createFromFile(null, "icons/ftp/about.gif"));

        actionExit = new Action() {
            public void run() {
                if(! MessageDialog.openConfirm(getShell(), "Confirm",
                    "Are you sure you want to exit?"))
                    return;
                try {
                    ftp.disconnect();
                }catch(Exception e) {
                    // ignore.
                }
                close();
            }
        };
        actionExit.setText("Exit");
        actionExit.setImageDescriptor(
            ImageDescriptor.createFromFile(null, "icons/ftp/close.gif"));

    }
```

The purpose for each action is as follows:

- ☐ actionUpLocalDir: Changes the current local directory to the parent directory
- ☐ actionBrowseLocalDir: Browses for the local directory
- ☐ actionConnect: Prompts the connection dialog and tries to connect to the specified FTP server
- ☐ actionDisconnect: Disconnects from the FTP server
- ☐ actionUpRemoteDir: Changes the current remote directory to the parent directory
- ☐ actionDisplayAbout: Displays information about the application
- ☐ actionExit: Exits the application

## Creating the Menu Bar

After you create all the actions, you can create the menu bar by overwriting the createMenuManager method of the ApplicationWindow class:

```
/*
 * (non-Javadoc)
 *
 * @see org.eclipse.jface.window.ApplicationWindow#createMenuManager()
 */
protected MenuManager createMenuManager() {
    MenuManager bar = new MenuManager();

    MenuManager menuFile = new MenuManager("&File");
    menuFile.add(actionConnect);
    menuFile.add(actionDisconnect);
    menuFile.add(new Separator());
    menuFile.add(actionExit);

    MenuManager menuLocal = new MenuManager("&Local");
    menuLocal.add(actionBrowseLocalDir);
    menuLocal.add(actionUpLocalDir);

    MenuManager menuRemote = new MenuManager("&Remote");
    menuRemote.add(actionUpRemoteDir);

    MenuManager menuHelp = new MenuManager("&Help");
    menuHelp.add(actionDisplayAbout);

    bar.add(menuFile);
    bar.add(menuLocal);
    bar.add(menuRemote);
    bar.add(menuHelp);
    bar.updateAll(true);

    return bar;
}
```

## *Construct the Toolbar*

Similarly, the toolbar is created by overwriting the `createToolBarManager` method:

```java
/* (non-Javadoc)
 * @see org.eclipse.jface.window.ApplicationWindow#createToolBarManager(int)
 */
protected ToolBarManager createToolBarManager(int style) {
    ToolBarManager manager = super.createToolBarManager(style);

    addAction(manager, actionConnect, true);
    addAction(manager, actionDisconnect, true);

    manager.add(new Separator());

    addAction(manager, actionBrowseLocalDir, true);
    addAction(manager, actionUpLocalDir, true);

    manager.add(new Separator());

    addAction(manager, actionUpRemoteDir, true);

    manager.add(new Separator());

    addAction(manager, actionDisplayAbout, true);
    addAction(manager, actionExit, true);


    manager.update(true);

    return manager;
}

public static void addAction(
    ToolBarManager manager,
    Action action,
    boolean displayText) {
    if (!displayText) {
        manager.add(action);
        return;
    } else {
        ActionContributionItem item = new ActionContributionItem(action);
        item.setMode(ActionContributionItem.MODE_FORCE_TEXT);
        manager.add(item);
    }
}
```

By default, the text of an action is not shown if it has an image associated. Instead of adding an action to the toolbar manager directly, you use the `addAction` method to force the text to be displayed even if the action has an image. The `addAction` method does this by creating an `ActionContributionItem` object and configuring its mode to force the text to be displayed.

You've created the menu bar and the toolbar. Now you are ready to create the contents for the application window.

# Creating Application Window Contents

The application window contents are created by overwriting the `createContents` method:

```java
/*
 * (non-Javadoc)
 *
 * @see org.eclipse.jface.window.Window#createContents(Composite)
 */
protected Control createContents(Composite parent) {
    Composite composite = new Composite(parent, SWT.NULL);
    composite.setLayout(new FillLayout());

    // the vertical sashform.
    SashForm verticalForm = new SashForm(composite, SWT.VERTICAL);

    // the horizontal sashform.
    SashForm horizontalForm = new SashForm(verticalForm, SWT.HORIZONTAL);

    // Local dir browser.
    Composite compositeLocalDir = new Composite(horizontalForm, SWT.NULL);
    GridLayout gridLayout = new GridLayout();
    gridLayout.horizontalSpacing = 1;
    gridLayout.verticalSpacing = 1;
    compositeLocalDir.setLayout(gridLayout);

    Group compositeLocalDirTop = new Group(compositeLocalDir, SWT.NULL);
    compositeLocalDirTop.setText("Local");
    GridLayout gridLayout2 = new GridLayout(3, false);
    gridLayout2.marginHeight = 0;
    compositeLocalDirTop.setLayout(gridLayout2);
    compositeLocalDirTop.setLayoutData(
        new GridData(GridData.FILL_HORIZONTAL));

    labelPathLocal = new Label(compositeLocalDirTop, SWT.NULL);
    labelPathLocal.setLayoutData(new GridData(GridData.FILL_HORIZONTAL));
    labelPathLocal.setText("Path: ");

    Button buttonUpLocalDir = new Button(compositeLocalDirTop, SWT.PUSH);
    buttonUpLocalDir.setText(actionUpLocalDir.getText());
    buttonUpLocalDir.addListener(SWT.Selection, new Listener() {
        public void handleEvent(Event event) {
            actionUpLocalDir.run();
        }
    });

    Button buttonBrowseLocalDir =
        new Button(compositeLocalDirTop, SWT.PUSH);
    buttonBrowseLocalDir.setText(actionBrowseLocalDir.getText());
    buttonBrowseLocalDir.addListener(SWT.Selection, new Listener() {
        public void handleEvent(Event event) {
            actionBrowseLocalDir.run();
        }
```

```
});

    Table table = new Table(compositeLocalDir, SWT.BORDER);
    TableColumn tcFile = new TableColumn(table, SWT.LEFT);
    tcFile.setText("Name");

    TableColumn tcSize = new TableColumn(table, SWT.NULL);
    tcSize.setText("Size");

    TableColumn tcDate = new TableColumn(table, SWT.NULL);
    tcDate.setText("Date");

    tcFile.setWidth(200);
    tcSize.setWidth(100);
    tcDate.setWidth(100);
    table.setHeaderVisible(true);

    table.setLayoutData(new GridData(GridData.FILL_BOTH));
    localDirBrowser = new LocalDirectoryBrowser(table);

    table.addListener(SWT.MouseDoubleClick, new Listener() {
        public void handleEvent(Event event) {
            IStructuredSelection selection =
                (IStructuredSelection) localDirBrowser.getSelection();
            File file = (File) selection.getFirstElement();
            if (file != null && file.isDirectory()) {
                localDirBrowser.setInput(file);
                labelPathLocal.setText("Path: " + file);
            }
        }
    });

    // Remote directory browser.

    Composite compositeRemoteDir = new Composite(horizontalForm, SWT.NULL);
    gridLayout = new GridLayout();
    gridLayout.horizontalSpacing = 1;
    gridLayout.verticalSpacing = 1;
    compositeRemoteDir.setLayout(gridLayout);

    Group compositeRemoteDirTop = new Group(compositeRemoteDir, SWT.NULL);
    compositeRemoteDirTop.setText("Remote");
    gridLayout2 = new GridLayout(2, false);
    gridLayout2.marginHeight = 0;
    compositeRemoteDirTop.setLayout(gridLayout2);
    compositeRemoteDirTop.setLayoutData(
        new GridData(GridData.FILL_HORIZONTAL));

    labelPathRemote = new Label(compositeRemoteDirTop, SWT.NULL);
    labelPathRemote.setLayoutData(new GridData(GridData.FILL_HORIZONTAL));
    labelPathRemote.setText("Path: ");

    Button buttonUpRemoteDir = new Button(compositeRemoteDirTop, SWT.PUSH);
    buttonUpRemoteDir.setText(actionUpLocalDir.getText());
```

**487**

```java
buttonUpRemoteDir.addListener(SWT.Selection, new Listener() {
    public void handleEvent(Event event) {
        actionUpRemoteDir.run();
    }
});

Table tableRemote = new Table(compositeRemoteDir, SWT.BORDER);
TableColumn tcFileRemote = new TableColumn(tableRemote, SWT.LEFT);
tcFileRemote.setText("Name");

TableColumn tcSizeRemote = new TableColumn(tableRemote, SWT.NULL);
tcSizeRemote.setText("Size");

TableColumn tcDateRemote = new TableColumn(tableRemote, SWT.NULL);
tcDateRemote.setText("Date");

tcFileRemote.setWidth(200);
tcSizeRemote.setWidth(100);
tcDateRemote.setWidth(100);
tableRemote.setHeaderVisible(true);

tableRemote.setLayoutData(new GridData(GridData.FILL_BOTH));
remoteDirBrowser = new RemoteDirectoryBrowser(tableRemote);

tableRemote.addListener(SWT.MouseDoubleClick, new Listener() {
    public void handleEvent(Event event) {
        IStructuredSelection selection =
            (IStructuredSelection) remoteDirBrowser.getSelection();
        FTPFile file = (FTPFile) selection.getFirstElement();
        if (file != null && file.isDirectory()) {
            try {
                ftp.changeWorkingDirectory(file.getName());
                labelPathRemote.setText(
                    "Path: " + ftp.printWorkingDirectory());
                remoteDirBrowser.setInput(ftp.listFiles());
            } catch (IOException e) {
                logError(e.toString());
            }
        }
    }
});

// the log box.
textLog =
    new StyledText(
        verticalForm,
        SWT.BORDER | SWT.H_SCROLL | SWT.V_SCROLL);

localDirBrowser.setInput(File.listRoots()[0]);
labelPathLocal.setText("Path: " + File.listRoots()[0]);

// resize sashform children.
verticalForm.setWeights(new int[]{4, 1});

// adding drag and drop support.
```

```
    dragNDropSupport();

    getToolBarControl().setBackground(
        new Color(getShell().getDisplay(), 230, 230, 230));

    getShell().setImage(new Image(getShell().getDisplay(), "icons/ftp/ftp.gif"));
    getShell().setText("FTP Client v1.0");

    return composite;
}
```

In the preceding code, we created the complete widget tree. We created two sash forms to make the main user interface components resizable. We constructed two tables for two table viewers. We created a `StyledText` control at the bottom of the window to print log information. We added drag-and-drop support through the `dragNDropSupport` method, which is covered in the last section of this chapter. Finally, you set the image icon and title for the application window.

Until now, only the skeleton of the user interface has been completed. Next, let's see how to implement table viewers for displaying local and remote file systems.

# Implementing Table Viewers

In this application, two table viewers are used to display local and remote file systems. The local file system table viewer takes a file directory as an input and displays all the files contained by it. The implementation for the local file system table viewer is listed here:

```
public class LocalDirectoryBrowser extends TableViewer {

    /**
     * @param table
     */
    public LocalDirectoryBrowser(Table table) {
        super(table);
        init();
    }

    private void init() {
        // the content provider.
        setContentProvider(new IStructuredContentProvider() {
            public Object[] getElements(Object inputElement) {
                File dir = (File)inputElement;
                return dir.listFiles();
            }

            public void dispose() {
            }

            public void inputChanged(
                Viewer viewer,
                Object oldInput,
                Object newInput) {
```

**489**

```
            }
    });

        // the label provider.
        setLabelProvider(new ITableLabelProvider() {
            public Image getColumnImage(Object element, int columnIndex) {
                if(columnIndex == 0)
                    return FileIconUtil.getIcon((File)element);
                return null;
            }

            public String getColumnText(Object element, int columnIndex) {
                switch(columnIndex) {
                    case 0:
                        return ((File)element).getName();
                    case 1:
                        return ((File)element).length() + "";
                    case 2:
                        return new Date(((File)element).lastModified()).toString();
                    default:
                        return "";
                }
            }

            public void addListener(ILabelProviderListener listener) {
            }

            public void dispose() {
            }

            public boolean isLabelProperty(Object element, String property) {
                return false;
            }

            public void removeListener(ILabelProviderListener listener) {
            }
    });
    }

}
```

Similarly, the table viewer for displaying the remote file system can be created.

# Adding Drag-and-Drop Support

When the user drags a file from the remote file browser and drops it to the local file browser, the application tries to download the file from the FTP server to the current local directory. The following code implements this feature:

```
private void dragNDropSupport() {
    // --- Drag source ---

    // Allows text to be copied and moved.
    int operations = DND.DROP_COPY | DND.DROP_MOVE;
    final DragSource dragSource =
        new DragSource(remoteDirBrowser.getControl(), operations);

    // Data should be transferred in plain text format.
    Transfer[] formats = new Transfer[] { TextTransfer.getInstance()};
    dragSource.setTransfer(formats);

    dragSource.addDragListener(new DragSourceListener() {
        public void dragStart(DragSourceEvent event) {
            System.out.println("DND starts");
            // disallows DND if no remote file is selected.
            IStructuredSelection selection =
                (IStructuredSelection) remoteDirBrowser.getSelection();
            FTPFile file = (FTPFile) selection.getFirstElement();
            if (file == null || file.isDirectory()) {
                event.doit = false;
            }
        }

        public void dragSetData(DragSourceEvent event) {
            // Provides the text data.
            if (TextTransfer
                .getInstance()
                .isSupportedType(event.dataType)) {
                IStructuredSelection selection =
                    (IStructuredSelection) remoteDirBrowser.getSelection();
                FTPFile file = (FTPFile) selection.getFirstElement();
                if (file == null || file.isDirectory()) {
                    event.doit = false;
                } else {
                    // the name of the selected file is used as the text data
                    event.data = file.getName();
                }
            }
        }

        public void dragFinished(DragSourceEvent event) {
        }
    });

    remoteDirBrowser
        .getControl()
        .addDisposeListener(new DisposeListener() {
        public void widgetDisposed(DisposeEvent e) {
            dragSource.dispose();
        }
    });

    // --- Drop target ---
```

```
final DropTarget dropTarget =
    new DropTarget(localDirBrowser.getControl(), operations);

dropTarget.setTransfer(formats);

dropTarget.addDropListener(new DropTargetListener() {
    public void dragEnter(DropTargetEvent event) {
    }

    public void dragLeave(DropTargetEvent event) {
    }

    public void dragOperationChanged(DropTargetEvent event) {
    }

    public void dragOver(DropTargetEvent event) {
    }

    public void drop(DropTargetEvent event) {
        if (TextTransfer
            .getInstance()
            .isSupportedType(event.currentDataType)) {
            String text = (String) event.data;
            File target =
                new File((File) localDirBrowser.getInput(), text);
            if (target.exists()) {
                if (!MessageDialog
                    .openConfirm(
                        getShell(),
                        "Overwriting confirmation",
                        "Overwrite file " + target + "?")) {
                    return;
                }
            }

            try {
                FileOutputStream stream = new FileOutputStream(target);
                if(ftp.retrieveFile(text, stream)) {
                    logMessage("File retrieved successfully.", true);
                    // refreshes the file list.
                    localDirBrowser.refresh();
                }else{
                    logError("Failed to retrieve file: " + text);
                }
                stream.close();
            } catch (IOException e) {
                e.printStackTrace();
            }
        }
    }

    public void dropAccept(DropTargetEvent event) {
    }
```

```
    });

    localDirBrowser.getControl().addDisposeListener(new DisposeListener() {
        public void widgetDisposed(DisposeEvent e) {
            dropTarget.dispose();
        }
    });
}
```

The table viewer for the remote file system is set as the drag source and the table viewer for the local file system is set as the drop target. When drag and drop occurs, the FTP file downloading is initiated with the retrieveFile method of the FTPClient class.

The preceding code enables file downloading only from the server to the local machine. As an exercise, you can try to use similar code to equip the application with file uploading.

# Summary

This chapter provided a sample application to show you how to combine various UI components and techniques that were covered in previous chapters in order to create a practical application. First, an application window was created with a menu bar and a toolbar. Then the user interface contents (widget tree) were created in the createContents method. By using sash forms, you made main UI components resizable. You created two table viewers to display local and remote file systems. Finally, you equipped the application with drag and drop to make it much easier to use and more intuitive.

For those who are familiar with Swing, you can spend a lot of time rewriting the sample application in Swing. You will be surprised (or maybe not) by how complicated Swing is to use. SWT/JFace's superior design makes it possible to develop GUI applications with Java quickly and easily.

This book provided comprehensive coverage of the SWT/JFace UI toolkit. You learned how to use SWT widgets. The chapter also covered frameworks that are available in JFace and showed you how to use them to simplify common UI programming tasks. You also learned about topics such as Eclipse Forms and Draw2D. You should now be able to develop practical Java UI applications with SWT/JFace. If you encounter difficulties, you can refer to this book for answers.

# Index

CPSIA information can be obtained at www.ICGtesting.com
Printed in the USA
267300BV00012B/43/P